D1604014

# THE AGE OF
# ATLANTIC REVOLUTION

# THE AGE OF ATLANTIC REVOLUTION

## The Fall and Rise of a Connected World

PATRICK GRIFFIN

Yale
UNIVERSITY PRESS
New Haven and London

Published with assistance from the Annie Burr Lewis Fund and from the Mary Cady Tew Memorial Fund.

Yale University Press books may be purchased in quantity for educational, business, or promotional use. For information, please email sales.press@yale.edu (U.S. office) or sales@yaleup.co.uk (U.K. office).

Set in Janson type by IDS Infotech.
Printed in the United States of America.

Library of Congress Control Number: 2022942833
ISBN 978-0-300-20633-3 (hardcover : alk. paper)

A catalogue record for this book is available from the British Library.

This paper meets the requirements of ANSI/NISO Z39.48-1992 (Permanence of Paper).

10 9 8 7 6 5 4 3 2 1

*For Mary Hope*
*and to the memory of Johanna Griffin*

# Contents

# Prologue

So, IT ALL BEGAN with some rope. In July 1776, just days after the Declaration of Independence had been adopted, a group of New Yorkers assembled on the Commons to celebrate the break from Britain before marching down to the Bowling Green at the southern tip of Manhattan. Here a statue to King George III on horseback, replete with classical garb, had been erected only six years before. Made of lead, the statue was gilded and rested on a marble pedestal, all of which stood fifteen feet high. The General Assembly had commissioned the statue in 1766 because of the "innumerable and singular Benefits" the king had rendered the colony, particularly delivering it "lately from the utmost Confusion and Distress, but Repeal of the Stamp Act." No less a personage than John Adams had admired the statue when he had visited the city earlier. Now the New Yorkers meant to pull it down.

How things had changed in only a few years. When citizens and soldiers of the Continental Army threw ropes around their sovereign and pulled, they decried "the Folly & pretended Goodness of the real George have made upon their Minds, which have effectually poisoned and destroyed their Souls." With the ropes, as one newspaper in Maryland declared, "the Knot is cut." The symbolic act of regicide did not end there. The men and women lopped of the head of the statue, in a move reminiscent of the execution of Charles I a century earlier, and placed it on a pike. One Loyalist was able to get his hands on the desecrated and now uncrowned head of the statue, buried it for safekeeping, and then dug it up to send to Britain to a former lord lieutenant of Ireland named George Townshend, all to demonstrate the intentions of some of

1

Johannes Adam Simon Oertel (1823–1909), *Pulling Down the Statue of King George III, New York City*, 1852–1853, oil on canvas, 32 x 41¼ in. Gift of Samuel V. Hoffman, 1925.6, New-York Historical Society.

the colonists. The savior of the head had ample reason to worry. The despoilers sent the rest of the statue to Connecticut to be melted down into bullets. In all, 42,088 were made from the metal. The numbers 42 and 88 represented totemic symbols for British nationhood, tied as they were to key events that took place in 1642 and 1688, during which the English decided to topple other kings. These bullets would be used in the fight for liberty that ensued. The New Yorkers hoped "the emanations from the leaden George" would make "deep impressions" on the British. Indeed, they would.[1] The toppling of this statue in particular has mythically come to be associated with the loosening of bonds, an untethering from an old order. It would come to be seen as the first scene of the first act of revolution, by those living at the time. And for us today.[2]

What those with the rope could not quite have articulated were transformations on an epic scale beyond their ability to comprehend fully. Beneath the invocation of ideas, seismic changes were remaking the Atlantic world. As much as by new concepts of the person, of governance, and of the economy, the period was defined by broad systemic shifts to which all people had to adapt. The process that was reshaping a system that touched four continents—North and South America, Europe, and Africa—and that reverberated farther still was both troubling and exhilarating, even if it was not quite understood. States would be challenged to keep up with it. Their officials usually tried to do so by reforming the structures or practices in place. And people, like the New Yorkers, responded in kind.

Trite as it sounds, the world was changing profoundly long before the New Yorkers used ropes to announce they would not be tied down. What had been the assumed ways of doing things were now in danger of becoming obsolete. Conventional ideas and ways of organizing politics, the economy, and society could not keep pace with a changing system. Political arrangements tying empires together were ill equipped to address new concerns. What bound the whole together had become a question, and to some people at least older ways of appreciating power could not do justice to the challenge of the new. Old symbols no longer fit.

The experiences of those on the very edges of that system proved a harbinger of what was to come and what would define the period as an age. How the New Yorkers responded also served as an example, writ small, of the stresses and tensions nearly all societies were to deal with, concerns that would ensure new statues would arise after old ones fell— from Paris to Port-au-Prince and from Boston to Buenos Aires. And all the interconnected points in between.

# Introduction

WHAT THESE NEW YORKERS also could not have fathomed is how the tugging of a rope would inaugurate what the Irish radical Dennis Driscoll would call the "age of revolution." He was hardly alone in making such a bold pronouncement. The much more conservative John Adams intoned in 1815 that "ours is the age of revolution and constitutions," yoking the breakdown of authority and its rebuilding in one phrase.[1] In 1762, Jean-Jacques Rousseau had prophesied "un siècle des révolutions," as had Voltaire in 1772. In his first inaugural address in 1801, Thomas Jefferson referred to the period as "an age of revolution and reformation." A generation later, after events in Latin America, Lyman Beecher preached that the period ushered in "an age of revolution and war."[2] Almost canonically, the avatar of the promise of the period, Thomas Paine, enthused: "It is an age of Revolutions in which everything must be looked for."[3]

The age of revolution transformed all. After the New Yorkers tore down the statue, the spirit of liberty, almost like a current of electricity, would course across America. It would then travel to France, throughout the Continent and the Caribbean, back to the British Isles, and eventually find its way to Latin America and Africa. The ensuing conflagration destroyed empires and saw a new understanding of the sovereign power of the state arise from these ashes. It unleashed. It spread. It purified.[4] It would, with time, outlaw slavery, remake reigning ideas of political economy, refashion the status of women, and shake the political landscape. Throughout the Atlantic world from the 1760s through the 1820s, nothing and nobody would be untouched. This earlier age made the modern

5

world.[5] As monuments throughout Brazil, Spanish America, all of Europe, Britain and Ireland, North America, the Caribbean, and West Africa attest, the Atlantic was turned upside down in the late eighteenth and early nineteenth century. What had been unimaginable in 1750, say, the idea that popular sovereignty would be the bedrock of government, proved the rule rather than the exception by 1830.[6]

There is another side. The age begot violence and war. It rode on waves of fear and disorder. It unleashed. It spread. It corrupted. Power was reorganized, as was society, but the tumultuous transition from an old order to a new one did not make for a world of unfettered possibilities. The age ushered in a new era of global empires that would reshape—perhaps decimate—the lives of Indigenous peoples across the globe.[7] The age resulted in the reinvigoration of slavery in places, the use of reason to justify the rule of the few over the many, modern and pernicious conceptions of race and subordination, the empowering of states that could overwhelm the individual, the triumph of unregulated free trade that saw whole portions of the earth marginalized to enrich others—the list could go on.[8] It was one of history's hinges, a moment upon which everything turned, but often for the worse. The age, as Paine's bête noire, Edmund Burke, came to fear, would fetter many more than it would free.[9]

It was, as Charles Dickens said, the best of times and the worst of times. For this reason, and because of the ways this earlier period in the Atlantic marks our world to this day, shelves groan with penetrating interpretations of the age, as you will see from scanning the endnotes below.[10] What sets this book apart? Well, let's return to Paine and Burke for a moment. For a start, consider the bonds between them. They first became personally acquainted over—of all things—a bridge-building scheme Paine was planning. In 1788, Paine wrote Burke a "letter as we begin the world, without knowing it will be long or short." He knew the length of the span he hoped to construct. "The quiet field of science has more amusement to my mind than politics and I had rather erect the largest arch in the world than be the greatest Emperor in it," he told Burke.[11] Burke hosted "the great American Paine" at his home for some time, and they came to know each other reasonably well. What each saw in the other were the possibilities of connections. Burke understood that Paine was tied to a cadre of first-rate thinkers in both the Old World and the New. Few were better networked with the great and the good in the British Isles than Burke.[12]

More significantly, of course, the one responded to the other throughout this tumultuous period. Paine, after all, wrote *Rights of Man* to refute Burke. In fact, Paine opens his preface to the English edition of *Rights of Man* with these words: "From the part Mr. Burke took in the American Revolution, it was natural that I should consider him a friend to mankind." Their "acquaintance," as he observed, "commenced on that ground." As early as 1777, Burke had characterized "the celebrated author" of *Common Sense* as a catalyst that "prepared the minds of the people for independence." How that sense of camaraderie changed.[13] By 1790, Burke came to believe Paine was preparing the world for something quite different from liberation. When Paine decided to take aim at the British establishment, Burke wrote: "I am happy to find . . . that practical Painism has not extended itself that way, and that the Iron Bridge, which I was guilty of introducing . . . has not yet been like the Bridge over Milton's Chaos, an high Road for all the devils of Anarchy to pass."[14]

Such growing animosity between the titans obscures a deeper link. Both participated in networks that spanned the ocean and bound continents together. Both writers saw themselves as part of a broader world of reference points that incorporated places as dispersed as Cartagena and Berlin. All these places, as well as their histories, had been imaginatively amalgamated into a connected whole. And both Burke and Paine relied on a common inheritance to try to make sense of what was happening to their world. A span of iron may not have tied them together, but so much more did.[15]

This book focuses on such connections. The circulation of people, things, and ideas bound the disparate parts of the Atlantic together, a development that deepened once crisis began. Notions of entanglement and connection, what the French call "histoire croisée" or "histoire connectée," are much esteemed by historians today, perhaps too much so.[16] But no other terms capture more fully what made the eighteenth century so enthralling and so vexing. The book argues that the changes that transformed that world and made ours were bound up in the many ways men and women tried to make sense of an intensely networked system changing before their eyes. The knotty challenges of the period also tested the abilities of states to manage the Atlantic. The crises that brought on revolution emerged from attempts to disentangle the world. Only when states came into being that could do so would revolution end. Only a new kind of state could rebind what had been unwound. In the process, people transformed themselves.[17] The period illustrated the creative ability of men and women to adapt to wrenching changes and to reshape the societies in which they lived. Even if they remade the Atlantic in unintended or even unfathomable ways, they always did so in light of the many connections tying their world together.[18]

From conventional perspectives, the study of the age of revolution presents awkward challenges, most especially because the chronologies of the dynamics in so many different places so far from one another do not line up. After all, revolution began in North America in the 1770s and started in Latin America more than a generation later. Moreover, can we characterize what happened far from the Atlantic coast as part of a broader pattern? But if we think of revolution along less conventional and more enmeshed lines, a new chronological and geographic road map of the period comes into focus. The American Revolution did not come to a fitting and simple conclusion in 1787. The French Revolution did not simply begin in 1789. Unrest in Spanish and Portuguese holdings before independence movements also had revolutionary implications. What took place in African societies, in places like Prussia, and in Native American communities far from the ocean bore the stamp of the age. When we think of connection, the terms "center" and "periphery" can often have less purchase. In fact, a place like Haiti stands at the very heart of the period and its fundamental features because of how tied it was to the broader Atlantic. What happened in one place, then, informed what would occur elsewhere.[19] Pulling the thread in one seemingly isolated corner of a network could have dramatic implications for people and places an ocean away.

What follows here is not a conventional history or a study for that matter. It is, for lack of a better word, a synopsis. I mean this term in the way a scholar of the New Testament would use it. The book does not offer a blow-by-blow account of what happened. What single volume could? It proposes, instead, a brief look at the whole to outline the stories of the constituent parts. Synopsis implies viewing the whole and the parts that animate it simultaneously. As such, the book moves between broad systemic changes in many places and the ways men and women in their locales tried to make sense of them, assign meaning to them, and act upon them. Such a synoptic understanding, not so ironically, reached its highpoint during the age itself, when a German theologian named J. J. Griesbach repurposed an age-old way of viewing three of the four gospels side by side to see how they were connected and what such intermingling meant for the larger story the gospels propounded.[20] This book does much the same by offering meditations on the beginning, middle, and end of the revolutionary process as it played out across the broad Atlantic in the one hundred years from 1750 to 1850.[21] It does so by relying on all of the wonderful work done on Atlantic history over the past generation and on the many studies of its constituent parts on this critical period.[22]

To synopsize means looking at representative cases and relating them to one another and a larger narrative. It invites comparison. In fact, it demands comparison. The Atlantic can only be appreciated in specific contexts; nevertheless, the specific only makes sense in light of the Atlantic. Comparing particulars helps us appreciate the big picture and its various aspects in more compelling ways. For the beginning we survey the whole, charting how global patterns of change transformed the Atlantic during the eighteenth century, necessitating imperial reform. The book then centers on the first society to experience revolutionary tumult, British North America. The American case illustrates how an age of empire became an era of revolution because of a crisis of connection. We then travel to the next places to experience the shocks of the period—prominent among them France, Saint-Domingue, and Ireland—to appreciate the central features of revolution during the age: hope, fear, and aggression. Many of the specifics and the stories surveyed here are well known; the book tries to characterize them anew through the prism of the broader picture presented. We wrap up with a study of endings by charting dynamics in the last region to be pulled into the crucible, Latin America, and one place that seemed by the end of the proverbial day to have held at bay the whipsawing effects of the age, Britain. We do so to understand how men and women in these and other places tried to bring the process of revolution to a close. The final chapter takes us once again through the whole Atlantic, but one now transformed, by examining nation building and memorialization, the final steps in binding the whole and its constituent parts together after the unraveling of the old order. Throughout these studies, other places, often left out of conventional treatments, are folded into this story of the Atlantic age. In other words, the book weaves the chronological with the geographic and the thematic, just as the local is interlaced with the broader and the comparative with the sequential. The sum total is an understanding of how an Atlantic-wide process unfolded though time.[23]

No aspect of the process was hermetically sealed. Revolutionary origins for British North America informed events elsewhere. What happened in Latin America reverberated in the United States, challenging the revolutionary settlement there. Events in the Caribbean shook Brazil, West Africa, and the British Isles. And connections between France and the rest of the world shaped beginnings and endings throughout the Atlantic.[24] The book examines this complex interweaving throughout, just as we would study, say, the synoptic gospels. The whole only makes sense when we pull together what are usually seen as discrete dynamics with those occurring far away and when we see how they relate to one another.[25]

Once we see things this way, the age can have apparent and unappreciated beginnings and a number of possible endings. It began when the idea of turning out an old order transfixed people, such as when the New Yorkers grabbed their ropes and beheaded the statue of their king. It also had its start well before people on the ground could even comprehend seismic changes challenging the accepted arrangements of how society was to be structured. A revolutionary era began, therefore, as event and as process, in ways that people could articulate with ideas and in ways they could not. It may have ended that way as well. Similarly, sometimes, men and women were conscious of connections. At other times, not. Ultimately, men and women tried to give meaning to that which lay just over the horizon of comprehension. As they did so, people throughout the Atlantic debated how to impose the power of the state onto a dynamically changing system. Revolution represented the intense competition to accomplish this feat, and people throughout the Atlantic, whether they liked it or not, were caught up in the process and struggle of articulating the fit between sovereignty and system as the world seemed to reel around them.[26]

Along the way, this book parses the phrase "age of revolution." First, what is an "age"? It is, of course, a construct, and men and women in the late eighteenth and early nineteenth century came to believe they were living during an exhilarating and terrifying, but ultimately epochal, moment. They came to such a conclusion by seeing things in places far removed as intrinsically connected. Add to this that the very idea also could have almost talismanic appeal. Such sensibilities captured imaginations at different junctures for different places. When, where, and why matter.[27] Second, the book wonders whether to consider this "age" a moment of *revolution* or of *revolutions*. Think of the difference. The former conjures up a single movement, the second a series of perhaps connected eventualities. The plural implies national or regional disruptions that could appear distinctive. The singular brings to mind the sum total of all these experiences. Perhaps we should ask how the universal and the particular related.[28] Finally, the book tangles with the question of what a revolution is. Here we get to especially vexing terrain. According to a writer who tried his hand at defining the term many years ago, "revolution is one of the looser words." Indeed. The word connotes, of course, some sense of progress and a program for change, the idea that it can be a force unto itself; however, revolution also suggests a process with a beginning, a middle, and an end, when one society after another was remade and through which sovereignty was recrafted. Could revolution be both at once?[29]

The book applies these simple questions to the whole Atlantic. It covers this complicated terrain by taking us through the entangled and connected origins, central features, and conclusions of "this stupendous upheaval."[30] It discusses how people struggled through violence, liberation, and war and in the process came to imagine themselves and the state in new ways. From this imaginative process, all hinging on finding a form of sovereignty that could manage the imperatives of the international system and of the moment, men and women from North and South America, Africa, and Europe—singly and together—would remake the world.[31]

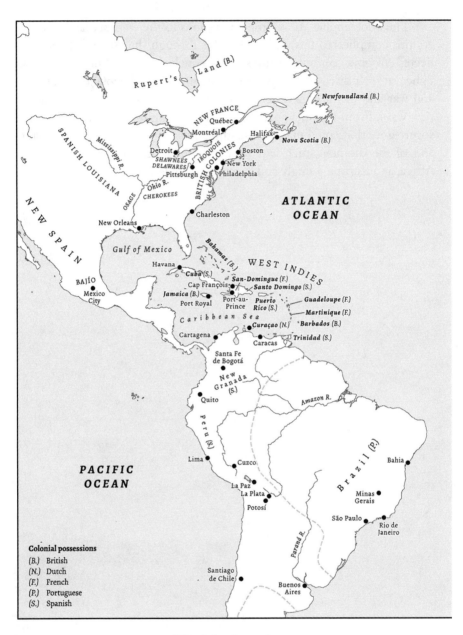

Rupert's Land (B.)

Newfoundland (B.)

NEW FRANCE
Québec
Montréal
Halifax
Nova Scotia (B.)

SPANISH LOUISIANA

Mississippi R.

Detroit
SHAWNEES
DELAWARES
IROQUOIS
BRITISH COLONIES
Boston
New York
Pittsburgh
Philadelphia
Ohio R.
OSAGE
CHEROKEES

NEW SPAIN

New Orleans

Charleston

ATLANTIC
OCEAN

Gulf of Mexico

Bahamas (B.)

WEST INDIES

Havana
Cuba (S.)
Cap François
Jamaica (B.)
Port Royal
Port-au-Prince
San-Domingue (F.)
Santo Domingo (S.)
Puerto Rico (S.)
Guadeloupe (F.)
Martinique (F.)

BAJÍO
Mexico City

Caribbean Sea

Curaçao (N.)
Barbados (B.)

Cartagena
Caracas
Trinidad (S.)

Santa Fe de Bogotá

New Granada (S.)

Quito

Amazon R.

PACIFIC
OCEAN

P e r u (S.)

Lima
Cuzco

La Paz
La Plata
Potosí

B r a z i l (P.)

Bahia

Minas Gerais

São Paulo
Rio de Janeiro

Paraná R.

Colonial possessions
(B.)   British
(N.)   Dutch
(F.)   French
(P.)   Portuguese
(S.)   Spanish

Santiago de Chile

Buenos Aires

The Atlantic, 1763.

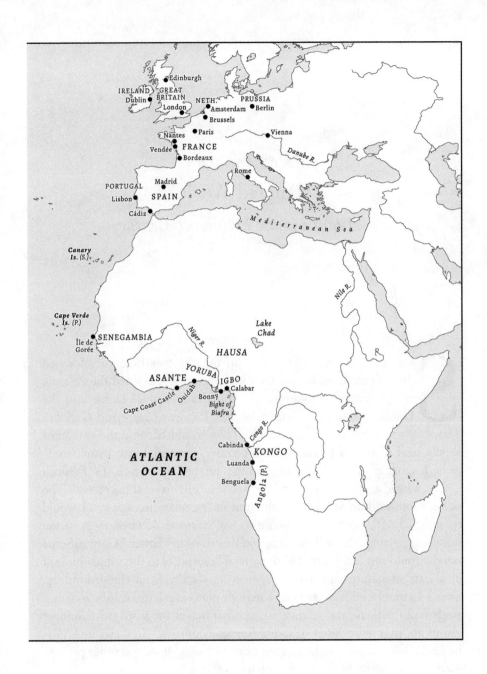

Edinburgh

IRELAND  GREAT  
Dublin  BRITAIN  
London

NETH.  PRUSSIA  
Amsterdam  Berlin  
Brussels

Nantes  Paris  
Vendée  FRANCE  Vienna  
Bordeaux  Danube R.

PORTUGAL  Madrid  Rome  
Lisbon  SPAIN  
Cádiz

Mediterranean Sea

Canary  
Is. (S.)

Nile R.

Cape Verde  
Is. (P.)

SENEGAMBIA  Niger R.  Lake  
Île de  Chad  
Gorée  HAUSA

YORUBA  
ASANTE  IGBO  
Cape Coast Castle  Ouidah  Calabar  
Bonny  
Bight of  Congo R.  
Biafra  Cabinda  KONGO

ATLANTIC  Luanda  
OCEAN  Benguela  Angola (P.)

# CHAPTER ONE

# A Tangled World

## *The Atlantic in the Eighteenth Century*

OME OF THE GREATEST writers in the eighteenth century focused
their finest work on an age-old paradox that defined the Atlantic
on the eve of revolution. The Londoner Daniel Defoe and the
Dubliner Jonathan Swift published *Robinson Crusoe* and *Gulliver's
Travels* in 1719 and 1726, respectively. They would become the two most
widely read stories of the eighteenth century, translated into many European languages. They both suggest the lure of adventure. In *Robinson
Crusoe*, a headstrong young man heads to sea, only to be shipwrecked. The
ocean captured him and his imagination in the most literal way. "I would
be satisfied with nothing but going to sea," Crusoe declares, even to the
point of ignoring "the will, nay, the commands of my father." Conventional
bonds would not hold him. He dreams of "escape." He then finds himself
in a state of nature and has to reconstruct society from the ground up.
Swift's Lemuel Gulliver starts as a mature man, eager to explore and, as a
student of medicine and science, to see what makes the word tick. Gulliver
claims an "insatiable desire of seeing foreign countries." To do so, he knows
he has to head to sea. So, he teaches himself "navigation, and other parts of
mathematics useful to those who intend to travel."[1]

The darker aspects of venturing are evident in both accounts as well.
At one point, Gulliver is tied down, forced to do the work of a mean and
little people, even as he is ordered by his new tiny masters to overawe

their foes and do what he cannot in conscience do: bring "a free and brave People into Slavery." "I found," he recounts, "my Arms and Legs were strongly fastened on each Side of the Ground." The little men— petty in stature and in demeanor—then put him to use through coercion, offering sustenance as they do so.[2] Shipwrecked after he himself has been held captive, Crusoe makes his way to Brazil and subsequently agrees to venture to Africa to find men and women to enslave. He then, most famously, enslaves Friday when he tries to build his world.[3]

If we want to understand the paradoxical nature of the Atlantic world in the eighteenth century, we should consider an even more representative writer, one who traveled and experienced the world that Defoe and Swift only described in prose. He did so bound like both Gulliver and Friday. Here's how his tale begins. Olaudah Equiano was born in modern-day Nigeria in what was known as Igboland. In 1756, just as all European powers were engaged in a new conflict, he was kidnapped along with his sister and then sold to other Africans engaged in slaving. He was one of more than 53,000 Africans captured for the Atlantic slave market in that year. In the years that followed, the annual numbers would continue to grow. Equiano recounted how he was sold from master to master and eventually was moved near the coast, where he first encountered Europeans. Here he saw his new world. "The first object which saluted my eyes when I arrived on the coast," he wrote, "was the sea, and slave ship, which was then riding at anchor, and waiting for its cargo." In a slaving factory, a site where European avarice met African Indigenous practices, he was uprooted from all he knew dear. He was placed on a ship set to sail to the New World. Now he endured the trauma of the Middle Passage, sale in the New World, and cruelties at the hands of a number of masters in the Caribbean and in Virginia.[4]

Every bit as much as Swift and Defoe, Equiano wrote a gripping adventure story that suggests how the Atlantic captured imaginations.[5] He composed, if you will, an eighteenth-century *Odyssey* that, like the tales of Gulliver and Crusoe, centered on the ocean. Though he was enslaved, shipboard life defined his world. He toiled for a while on a plantation and eventually was sold to a master who traded with French, British, and Dutch merchants in numerous ports. Over the course of his time as an enslaved person, he traveled to Cadiz, Oporto, Nice and Belle Isle, Falmouth and London, New York, Savannah, Port-au-Prince, Havana, Kingston, and Cartagena. In other words, as his memoir attests, he crisscrossed the Atlantic throughout his life, making his way to all the chief ports of all the imperial powers of the day. Along the way, he witnessed shocking cruelties, as, for instance, when he saw an African tortured in Montserrat. With time, Equiano would find his way to England, where he purchased his own freedom. He wrote of how he was baptized in London, embraced the vital piety coursing throughout the Atlantic at the time, and then joined a society dedicated to ending the slave trade. Eventually, he would become an important symbol for abolitionists. Like Defoe and Swift, he would write to try to understand the essential characteristics of his time-in-place and to make his way in society.[6]

Equiano's story revealed the barbarity of the institution of slavery and its central significance to the eighteenth century. This, of course, we know. What it also underscores is how the institution of slavery drove the creation of an Atlantic system that so beguiled Swift, Defoe, and Equiano himself. The movement that was part of Equiano's life was shared by hundreds of thousands of others, free and unfree. The ships he worked on, along with thousands of others, brought the goods that drew the Old World closer to the New. What had been places divided by an ocean were now imaginatively bound together as one. This rebinding of Old and New, too, underscored the appeal of writing about travel. Most critically, these worlds were tied together through the work and suffering of so many others like Equiano. "Surely this traffic cannot be good," he reckoned, "which spreads like a pestilence, and taints what it touches! which violates that first natural right of mankind, equality and independence, and gives one man a dominion over his fellows which God could never intend!" From London to Paris, the liberating notions he gave voice to arose along with the trade that was the period's most manifest debasement.[7]

The Atlantic-wide crisis that would define a generation and be termed an "age" began with the experiences and assumptions of people such as Equiano, Swift, and Defoe and the terrors and hopes about which they wrote. Through the work of the enslaved and the ships that brought them to the New World, networks emerged that turned the Atlantic from a geographic space into a system, one that entranced writers and readers. This transformation would have dramatic effects for how people understood themselves and the world around them. The process laid out new possibilities for many, just as it structured new limits for so many more. It suggested freedom and exploitation. Most critically, the manner in which the Atlantic was integrated challenged older ways of conceiving of space, time, and change itself. This is indeed what Swift,

Equiano, and Defoe were up to. The Atlantic became a place of inter-twining allegiances, exploitation, and opportunity. Its entanglements led to adventure. They also occasioned war, amplified the power of the state, and led to all sorts of new competition between world powers. Transformations also presaged the advent of new ways of conceiving of trade, mobility, and labor.

The changes were global in scope. Lines of commerce and authority bound the whole world together by tying together subsystems of exchange, in the same way Gulliver was tethered to the beach. Yet, changes played out most poignantly in the Atlantic. Here networks grew most dense and tan-gled. Here thousands sailed—some free, many more unfree. Here goods in ships created channels of communication, and new media emerged to ani-mate the new system. Here people like Defoe would question the very basis of culture and society.[8] The Atlantic became the focus of seismic change be-cause here states competed with one another and tried to assert themselves through war making. Eventually, the vast transformations associated with consolidation of the system would create tensions that would lead to an At-lantic-wide crisis. Revolution would begin because of that crisis. This was the world Equiano, Swift, and Defoe created in life and on paper and the one all people of the period had to navigate.

That the Atlantic captured the imagination of all people living along its coastlines was not new. From the moment Europeans began imagining the Americas less as a "new world" and more as an extension of the old to be exploited and competed over, the ocean became less of a mysterious barrier and more of a saltwater road. Settlers from European regions in-fluenced by the Columbian exchange and the emerging imperial econo-mies peopled new and far-off lands. While Native Americans struggled with disease in their own New World, Africans were drawn into the maelstrom of encounters in the most pernicious way. Demonized by Eu-ropeans as inferior, some were captured by traders and pirates to be sold into chattel slavery in the Americas. States vied with one another for the spoils of the Americas, and some regions, such as the Caribbean, became competitive crucibles of conflict. All the while the goods from the Amer-icas transformed European patterns of consumption, and soon whole so-cieties were addicted to tobacco and sugar.

Although it is anachronistic to use the term, we call the economic arrangements that bound center to colony mercantilist. Though the term "mercantilism" was, in fact, coined in the nineteenth century, the idea has some utility. The premise was simple. Colonies would provide raw materials that would be shipped to the center. Those at the center, given the predominant ways of conceiving of trade, wanted to bring in more specie than would leave. Colonies, many created by companies and some planned by the state, existed to benefit the mother country economically. English colonies were yoked like spokes on a wheel to London, French settlements to Paris, and others in similar fashion. There were any number of Atlantic worlds, however tenuously each was held together. "System" is really too strong a word. What they shared in common, albeit along parallel lines, was the exploitation of land and the victimization of Indigenous peoples to gain access to that land. If colonizers had the wherewithal to ignore Native Americans, which defined the experience of the Spanish and the English, they did. If they did not have the numbers, such as was the case with the French, they cooperated, but with an eye to eventual dominance.[9]

All sorts of political arrangements bound these Atlantic empires together. We use the word "empire" to describe how the space was managed; however, the term is a bit of a misnomer. In fact, these composite states may have been held together by vaunting ideologies but little else. Some were ruled as if they were centralized. The French Empire that reached to the interior of North America offers an ideal type of this sort. Yet even if the Crown claimed to rule this empire, on the ground it was a ramshackle affair, managed by relationships forged between traders, Natives, and priests. If fish, furs, and faith created this empire, precious little else sustained it. Other empires, like the English, had little rhyme or reason. England ruled dependencies in any number of ways: through company charters, by way of powerful proprietary clients, with direct royal government, as kingdoms, as factories, or through archaic medieval contrivances. A great deal of governance was bound into patronage networks. The Spanish fell somewhere between the two. They claimed to have a bureaucracy created for their "ultramarine" holdings, but powerful local creoles—that is, people born and raised in the colonies—saw to their own affairs. The empire was divided into rational administrative units—viceroyalties and provinces and audiencias—but it really functioned as a "mosaic."[10] Sovereignty in the period was of a porous quality. Metropolitan officials were generally happy to have creoles rule their worlds as they saw fit, so long as they could sustain a limited set of political and economic goals while maintaining some semblance of order and not complicating imperial rivalries.[11]

The state existed with a limited sense of what it was and what it could accomplish. The myths of sovereign rule had a powerful appeal and often were rooted in medieval institutions, such as the Crown or, in Britain's case, the "Crown-in" another medieval institution, Parliament. The state maintained the orderliness of society, and this arrangement had more or less held together since the time of the Reformation. Yet, for all the official bluster about sovereignty, the state did not have the capacity to make good on its claims of control. In fact, even regions close to the center enjoyed autonomy. Those living on imperial margins paid deference to the rhetoric of control, or imperial grandeur, but in fact the state could not exercise authority, except close to home and not in a sustained manner. This happened for different reasons. The French, for instance, had created a Bureau of Colonies to manage empire in a centralized fashion. But the navy did not have the ability to make good on articulated aims.[12] Everyone tended to wink and nod and get on with their lives. Only episodically did state power impinge.

The Atlantic represented only one part of a broader global dynamic.[13] Nonetheless, the Atlantic became the chief site of ambition and of European hopes and dreams, however modest they were at this time. By the end of the seventeenth century, it had become a space defined by metropolitan pretensions of control, the development of creole cultures far away from the center with a great deal of autonomy, and whole groups exploited for land and for labor. The Spanish offer perhaps the most idealized type of the Atlantic kaleidoscope. They controlled the wealth-producing regions of Peru and Mexico. They had holdings from the Caribbean to Cape Horn and north of the Rio Grande. Officials believed they had created a highly bureaucratized colonial structure, centralized in design, and they worked to create a "closed" network. With mining as the central feature of the imperial economy, and with locals able to control Indigenous peoples in their midst, officials could keep an eye on rivals. The conceit of control was based on a world in which competition could be managed.[14]

The ties that bound the centers to the peripheries proved tenuous at best. The comings and goings of ships were not regularized. The governments in London, Paris, Madrid, and Lisbon only intervened in colonial affairs intermittently, usually during times of crisis. Questions still abounded of how peripheries would be governed, regardless of metropolitan pretensions of sovereign status, but few saw the need to address such questions. In this era of "arrangements," if we could call it that, such ways of doing things functioned as well as could be expected, and usually no one asked for much more.

As William Butler Yeats would say, all was about to change utterly and quickly. We tend to think of our age as the first era of globalization. Nothing could be further from the truth. The eighteenth century witnessed dramatic change, challenging older ways and precedents. But in this earlier period of global transformation ambitions centered on one part of the world, the place that was most intensely networked: the Atlantic. Between 1713 and the mid-1740s, the Atlantic, the Americas, and Europe in general experienced what could be called a "Long Peace." The term does not refer only to North America, when the Iroquois and Algonquian-speaking peoples in the Great Lakes region ended endemic warfare and hammered out an accommodation. It refers to the period when hostilities over global domination between European powers ceased—for the time being at least. In this moment, what could be called "the Pax Atlantica," the Atlantic was transformed, as networking intensified.[15] With peace, the lives of all in this period began to revolve around global patterns of movement, centered on the Atlantic, involving people, goods, and ideas.[16]

The eighteenth century differed profoundly from the period preceding it. The scope and scale of movement and trade grew immensely in the eighteenth century. The Spanish, in fact, would be the first to see the contours of this new world. Its truck and feeder lines became much more complex as peripheral societies developed and diversified.[17] This story of change and adaptation, though, is anything but straightforward. It is complex and variegated. Atlantic transformation depended on migration and commerce. It also rested on coercion. To understand it fully, we should start with this dynamic.

As settlers in the New World began to gain a greater hold of interior regions wrested from Indigenous peoples, they looked to the Old World for the labor necessary to make land more productive. A greater reliance on the enslaved from Africa became the answer. In the process, the Atlantic was remade. All told, eleven million men and women from Africa were sent to the New World before the complete abolition of the slave trade, both licit and illicit, in the 1870s. The vast majority were enslaved in the eighteenth century. "Societies with slaves" soon became "slave societies," that is, places dominated by the institution of slavery.[18] Slavery proved the catalyst to the transformation of the Atlantic. With the direct exportation of men and women from Africa, ship crossings became more predictable.

Networks became denser. The products that the enslaved provided with their labor, such as tobacco, sugar, rice, and coffee, were sent to Europe. Think of Glasgow and its ties to the tobacco trade in the British American colonies. Slave labor transformed the city. Through the trade, the "tobacco lords" refashioned the cultural and economic life of a city that became an important hub for the import and export of the leaf. Meanwhile, trade within and among colonies grew apace. With slave labor, the eighteenth century became the Atlantic century, and there could be no denying its exploitative nature. To cite just one example, French cities were to rise or fall with the ups and downs of the slave market and the slave economy. Bordeaux, Nantes, Marseille, and Le Havre competed with one another for the spoils of the slave-based plantation economy in the Caribbean. A large proportion of the shipping of each place went to Saint-Domingue in the eighteenth century, by and large because nearly half of the world's sugar was processed there, as well as most of its coffee, and merchants from these cities in France came to own plantations in the slave colony. Sugar played an outsized role in the Atlantic and in Saint-Domingue, the place most closely associated with it. It lagged behind only Brazil in the number of the enslaved it consumed. In fact, with the sale and oppression of Africans in Saint-Domingue, these French cities entered a "golden age."[19]

It is difficult to underestimate the significance of Saint-Domingue to the changing Atlantic economy in and cultural contours of the eighteenth century. Saint-Domingue emerged as the richest capital-producing site in the Americas. Coercion could keep production going.[20] Not only did the colony bind the French Old World to the New, it also served as the center of the greater French Caribbean. French New Orleans, for instance, depended on Saint-Domingue, both as a site of connection and as a model. The port city, which tied the Mississippi to farms in the Illinois country and this region to the Great Lakes and the center of New France in Quebec, was first and foremost a Caribbean society. It was to be another Saint-Domingue, both commercially and in terms of how planters would treat the enslaved. It, too, quickly adopted the *code noir*, and its linkages to the more important slave society in the French Caribbean mimicked and paralleled the British relationship between coastal South Carolina and Barbados. Saint-Domingue, then, stood as one of the age's great Caribbean nexuses, and for the French the preeminent.[21]

The Atlantic served as midwife to a global shift of integrated markets that we associate with capitalism. Again, slavery explains a great deal of

how this happened.[22] Take the case of Brazil. Brazil had been a slave society from its origins as a Portuguese colony. In the seventeenth century,
sugar began to dominate some regions, and Portuguese mariners who
had been selling men and women from Africa to all comers focused their
efforts on Brazil. Astutely, sugar was called the "engenho" of society.
Soon, Brazil would have other drivers. With the opening of gold mines,
slave importation reached new heights. Bahia took in five thousand to
eight thousand of the enslaved a year, and it is estimated that 40 percent
of all those imported from Africa arrived in Brazil to feed its insatiable
demand of labor. The gold-mining industry secured the link between Africa and Brazil, turning the ocean in between into a coherently organized
economic space.[23] The upshot for the Portuguese Atlantic was that parts
of Africa and Brazil became as one. Slavery connected them.[24]

The story of Olaudah Equiano demonstrates the ways that Atlantic
ties now bound people and connected far-flung regions. The sort of factories where he was bought and sold had become the chief nodes of Atlantic consolidation, and they served as entrepôts reaching deep into the
African interior and thence to ports in the New World.[25] His story was
not unique. The integration of whole regions in Africa into an exploitative Atlantic transformed them in fundamental ways. Whether the people were considered Ibo or were Catholics from the Kingdom of the
Kongo, and whether the slave traders sailed under British, Spanish, or
Portuguese flags, European demand for New World labor encouraged
the capture and sale of men and women to fuel further development of
the Atlantic economy, yoking together places like Guyana and Liverpool
in the bargain.[26]

Of course, the immense growth of the slave trade from 1680 to the
end of the eighteenth century had dramatic implications for culture and
society in West Africa. The leap in demand changed the tenor of African
slavery and of slave raiding. Warfare also grew in intensity in some regions, as the price of persons increased. The growth of the trade in humans encouraged other forms of trade as well. Africans wanted more
European goods. People in Senegal, for instance, hoped to procure everything from basins to iron bars. Rulers were able to collect customs
duties on the enslaved. They also needed more weapons and European
goods as the slave trade fomented regional conflict, all of which encouraged further slave raiding. Others were overwhelmed by new demands
on the state, and in some places disorder was becoming the order of the
day. This in turn created yet more uncertainty and a further weakening

of states, which contributed to more raiding and fighting. And so it went. The Igbo, or Ibo, country, where Equiano was captured, is a perfect example. It became one of the largest suppliers of men and women for the Atlantic market because of its fragmented sovereignty and the concomitant failure of order. This is how West Africa was connected to the whole. The end result? The state could not handle the new demands of the Atlantic, and war was becoming endemic.[27]

As more lands were opened up to productive use, free migration also increased. Men and women from the very margins of Europe now sought their destinies in a land-rich and labor-starved new world. Countrysides were commodified in much the same way labor was, as all were drawn into the Atlantic maw.[28] Irish and German men and women headed to North America, creating tensions with the descendants of Englishmen and women already there, while settlers from Cantabria in Spain left for New Spain (Mexico). New migrants also came from the Canary Islands, Galicia, Asturia, and the Basque Country. These mobile men and women opened up new areas to settlement and to productive use, increasing the size of hinterlands tied to provincial trading centers. Basques soon enmeshed themselves in the creole elite of Santiago de Chile. Philadelphia grew into the predominant city in British North America as migrants came in and claimed new land for mixed farming, then sent their crop surpluses to the city and out into the Atlantic, enriching merchants— both those trading in people and those trading in goods—as they did so. The same went for the humble and ambitious men and women who headed to places like Mexico City. They came, as one put it, to "make America."[29]

In a remarkably short period of time economic links tied English, French, Spanish, and Portuguese societies in the Americas to their respective metropoles more tightly than before. These links occurred in parallel fashion. Silk woven in Spitalfields in London embellished bodies in Philadelphia. Sugar grown in the French Caribbean sweetened the chocolate of consumers in Paris. Silver mined in New Spain adorned jewelry in Cadiz.[30] Throughout discrete Atlantics, a consumer revolution gripped the imagination of everyone tied to the Atlantic. The ocean exploded in goods. And the supply affected the demands of courtiers and journeymen in places as varied as Paris, London, Philadelphia, and Buenos Aires.[31] With increased flows, the reach of the Atlantic grew. The catchment area for Philadelphia stretched into the backcountry of the Carolinas. Scope and scale increased dramatically with integration, pulling more people into the webs of an increasingly networked world as they did so. The Atlantic depended upon such symbiotic relationships, now essentially made possible by the growing wealth of a merchant elite. The changes depended on goods, a rising middle class, the growth of the commercial power of a number of trading nations, and unprecedented demographic shifts. All imperial centers and their provinces an ocean away experienced as much. The saltwater space became a set of imperial systems running in parallel with one another.[32]

More critical for the story of the revolutionary age than the parallel development of the Atlantic was the interconnected nature of imperial/colonial systems. Interconnection occurred in licit and illicit ways. Here is just one small but telling example. Images of the Prussian monarch appeared on enameled snuffboxes filled with tobacco from America traded by other nations. Think of the sorts of complex connections this one object reveals.[33] Or take a more conventional story. We now know that French trade with the rest of the world increased by more than four times, and tenfold with its colonial holdings, over the course of the century, mostly underwritten by the trade to and from the sugar islands. In the French case, smuggling accounted for a great share of that flow, which was outstripping political controls put in place in the previous century to ensure colonies served metropoles. Nantes and Bordeaux grew through such tangled trade. Soon networks became denser, and France passed more trade through Spanish Cadiz than any other power. Meanwhile, as the demand for the enslaved became voracious in the French Caribbean, Dutch traders filled in when French shipping could not supply requisite numbers.[34] So normal was smuggling in some French port towns, such as New Orleans, that officials did not bother to comment on trade with Spain. Doing so did not even entail a wink or a nod; in fact, officials condoned it. Meanwhile the men and women of the port town referred to the on-paper illicit commerce with the British and Dutch by the sanitized term "foreign trade."[35]

Precious metals drove entangled consolidation, as they could be swapped legally and illegally for all sorts of European goods. Even runaway slaves participated in these economies.[36] The Atlantic ebbed and flowed with silver. Treasuries depended on it, and regions vied with one another to produce and sell it. In fact, with the density of networks emerging in the Atlantic, silver production began to shift in Spanish America from Potosi to Bajio in New Spain. Soon Mexico City would grow wealthy through the exportation of silver, and mines in New Spain became engine rooms of further Atlantic systematization. That silver, most of which crossed imperial lines, could be found throughout Europe.[37] Gold also sustained line-crossing networks. Brazil imported most of what it needed from countries other than Portugal, and gold from mines in Brazil allowed it to do so. Gold, traded through convoluted networks, proved critical to Britain's ability to wage war in the eighteenth century.[38]

For the Spanish and the Portuguese, so close to each other in South America, smuggling became the chief economic activity for some regions. The porousness of the vast Spanish Empire, spanning two continents, made it difficult to police, and in some regions—such as the Spanish Main and the east coast of Central America—crossing imperial lines became a way of life. Piracy, not surprisingly, flourished as well. In places like the coast of Venezuela, so close to the port towns of the Caribbean where the traders of so many countries vied, smuggling was the norm.[39]

Even the British employed Spanish traders as go-betweens with the even more hated French. For their part, the French relied on Anglo-Americans, who provided a great deal of the timber products that went into creating sugar mills in Saint-Domingue.[40] Entanglements encompassed regions far removed from one another. The merchants of the "city-state" of Boston had created a connected world tying together such far-off regions as Peru and the Netherlands and Germany. Their trade relied on the links between West Africa and the West Indies. These ties even involved ships fitted out for the scavenging of Spanish wrecks. In fact, Daniel Defoe commented on one of these episodes at great length.[41]

Even if "entanglement" has become an all too trendy concept, the term captures what was emerging as the defining characteristic of the eighteenth-century Atlantic. In the eighteenth century, connections and entanglements drove processes, events, and peoples.[42] They enriched, oppressed, infuriated, excited, and complicated. In the provinces, they created a cadre of wealthy merchants and planters, who made fortunes from the exploitation of labor and the trading of goods, both of which depended on the crisscrossed nature of the Atlantic. British officials believed that up to one-third of all American trade was illicit. Most infuriating was that an alarming amount of trade involved colonists with Britain's traditional enemies. Tangles could be convoluted. Ships from New York and Boston engaged in complex series of deals with Dutch traders in French ports and with planters from Saint-Domingue after crossing Spanish lines.[43] Portugal grew dependent on grains from Virginia and the Carolinas, which came by northern Europe. Traders from South Carolina lobbied Britain's Parliament because so much indigo traveled to Britain from the French Caribbean. And Spanish silver mined in South America was the currency of choice for merchants who shipped tea to warehouses in England, whence middlemen sent it to America, where it was sweetened with sugar produced by the enslaved from Africa in the Caribbean, especially the French colony of Saint-Domingue. If they could get their hands on cheaper tea, North American colonists would trade with the French and the Dutch, who used their permeable networks, which stretched from Denmark, Germany, and Poland to the Danish Caribbean, Long Island, and Rhode Island. Perhaps as much as a quarter of tea consumed in Britain's North American colonies was of the "Dutch" or smuggled variety.[44] Throughout the Atlantic, actors transgressed theoretically sovereign boundaries with abandon, and much of the economic vitality and cultural energy of the Atlantic was sustained through such crossings. Entrepôts in both the Old World and the New depended on the autonomy to cross boundaries.

Unsurprisingly, nowhere were these growing entanglements more prevalent than in the slave trade. The first few decades of the eighteenth century witnessed all sort of traders, acting almost as independent free agents, vying with one another to bring humans across the ocean. The image of a free-for-all comes to mind. The British would soon play a prominent role in this burgeoning arena of free and often unregulated trade. With the end of the Royal African Company's monopoly on the slave trade, all sorts of people now attempted to enrich themselves. Those who could ship the enslaved in the most cost-effective way could supply all empires, whether licitly or illicitly.[45] After the War of Spanish Succession, when the British were granted what was called the "asiento," or the monopoly in shipping persons from West Africa to Spanish South America, international tensions only increased. Spanish bullion spilled into British ports, most into Jamaica, just as the contraband trade in the enslaved grew by leaps and bounds.[46] Ironically, it also hastened the development of the plantation economy of Cuba when the island, too, began producing sugar with a reliance on African labor.[47] Here the contraband trade dominated, overshadowing licit commerce. Much of that intercourse bound Cuba to Jamaica, and it encompassed slave traders and the enslaved, smugglers and merchants.[48] The French, too, were becoming reliant on such crossings. Needing access to credit, they relied on Spanish silver to keep their treasuries solvent, and to that end merchants and officials ensconced themselves in Cadiz, the most important port in the Iberian Peninsula. They also became expert at slave buying, usually from other powers.[49]

As these examples suggest, slavery heightened the intensely networked nature of an already complex world, and all throughout the Atlantic were bound to its convoluted imperatives. In slaving factories in West Africa, British merchants and pilots, and the Dutch as well, supplied the plantations of all imperial powers in the New World. Consider just one town: Ouidah, in what is modern-day Benin. French, British, Portuguese, and even Danish traders operated there. Most of the people traded went to Bahia in Brazil. A great many headed to Saint-Domingue. Later, it would be Cuba.[50] In the New World, the mixing of people could make for some surprising results. In South Carolina, enslaved men and women taken from the Kongo—a place shaped by the Portuguese—had military experience, which would be put to good use in rebellion against planter elites, and were Catholic, which would add to the distinctive character of African American spirituality.[51] Or take the case of the French. French merchant houses, which had tentacles in Cadiz and South America, came to dominate the trade in sugar, leading to the growth of port cities. Fully one-half of the sugar consumed in Europe was produced in the French West Indies by the 1770s.[52] This activity had an unwelcome knock-on effect for the British. The rise of French production in particular alarmed the British; yet, their colonists traded with the hated French, especially merchants from New York, many of whom were Irish and "displayed a vigorous contempt for British navigation laws."[53]

Ships connected, but people on them entangled. They, especially those who toiled or ventured on ships that crisscrossed the space, created the new imaginative parameters of the Atlantic.[54] Just think of two peoples to appreciate the ways all were complicit in creating such an imbricated world. The Irish, mainly Catholics, loaned themselves out as merchants, priests, and soldiers to European sovereigns, and increasingly this work saw them move throughout empires. Some earned fortunes in licit and illicit trade with other nations. The wealth they accrued, and the connections to the Spanish and the French they fostered, allowed family members to enter the Atlantic net and so help extend networks farther still. Priests looked out after Irish soldiers serving foreign powers. Merchants tried to further the interests of the other two groups, reinforcing connections between places and among occupational groups. These same merchants also worked closely with contacts in London, which was becoming a center of finance for an increasing number of Atlantic ventures.

One of the great untold stories of Ireland in this period is how these developments spurred the growth of Irish cities, which made confessional boundaries more permeable.[55]

Catholics were not the only ones to adapt to a connected world. Most migrants from Ireland to the British North American colonies were Protestant. Though they left as rents were rising and as land in America seemed available, they simply did not connect the Old World and the New in simple push-and-pull fashion. They produced linen, for which merchants, many of whom in both Ireland and America were involved in trade with sugar islands, imported flax seed from the Middle Colonies. Their mass movement alarmed British officials, who now worried, because of increased friction with France, about the loyalty of the Irish should war arise. Ireland, after all, was a depot for manpower. Migrants settled on areas that had just been cleared of Native Americans, and they soon made pushes to the west, where they would encounter Indigenous peoples allied with the French. The produce the migrants raised on these lands enriched merchants in Philadelphia who sent what the Irish raised in America to many ports throughout Europe and to slave colonies in the Caribbean. The simple movement of peoples from one place, then, bound the whole system together in multiple ways, sending out threads to the farthest verges of that system.[56]

Saint-Domingue fostered an even more complicated web of connections.[57] The capture of men and women in West Africa transformed the economies there, creating unending conflicts. They traveled to the French colony on the ships of many nations, enriching some but creating envy among others. In places like Saint-Domingue, they produced an addictive substance that proved a cheap energy source and that created new wants and needs in Europe. The most vibrant sector of France's economy was dependent on sugar. The labor of the enslaved of Saint-Domingue created employment for large numbers of French workers and built the ships and fed the armies that France used to contest British pretensions in the Atlantic.[58] Sugar would spur greater activity elsewhere throughout the world, as the substance was put into coffee grown in Brazil, chocolate harvested from cocoa beans in places like Martinique, and tea imported from halfway around the world. Not surprisingly, merchants from many countries would vie with one another to get it at the cheapest price, usually resorting to smuggling to do so. Sugar underscored whole industries in regions far from the slave islands, in New England, for instance, where it was used to sustain rum production. This

employed thousands, in distilling and in building the ships to keep supply up with demand, and many more worked to provide wood products
and foodstuffs for the clandestine trade to the French islands on ships
often outfitted by Irishmen out of places like New York or Spanish ports.
Some of these workers in New England would be the same migrants
from Ireland, who harbored ambivalent ideas about their relationship to
Britain. And so it goes . . .

   This was a century of what one scholar rightly calls "border crossers."[59] In this world, English merchants traded the enslaved to Spanish
holdings in the New World. New Englanders shipped their fish to Catholic Europe. Those in the eastern Caribbean traded counterfeit coins with
Jamaicans and Rhode Islanders. Indeed, coins from all countries functioned as currency in the Caribbean.[60] Elites in Buenos Aires enriched
themselves with the trade of silver from the mines of Peru and contraband
from Brazil, much of which was sent to the British. Traders from Buenos
Aires vied with those in Montevideo who specialized as intermediaries in a
number of smuggling networks.[61] Those on the margins could exploit the
nature of the system better than most. Natives living on the Caribbean
coast of South America, known as Tierra Firme, confounded officials by
striking trading deals with French, British, and Dutch sailors.[62] Irish merchants used their ties to the Caribbean, to Catholic France, and to Britain
to enrich themselves by exploiting the system's interstices. Rather unsurprisingly, inhabitants in the west of Ireland, even in remote Connemara,
made smuggling a way of life because of their connections to Cadiz and
Nantes, and the scale of it alarmed British authorities. Montrose in Scotland, a town near Aberdeen with ties to the Baltic and to the tobacco trade,
became a smuggling center. The layout of Montrose and even the design
of homes reflected the fact that here even commerce with the enemy,
France, was welcome.[63] England itself was not immune. A collection of
smugglers called the Hawkhurst Gang plied their craft in the 1740s with
impunity. Smuggling, after all, had become central to the economy of
Kent, where they worked. Similarly, a French gang led by a folk hero
named Louis Mandrin used violence and a rough sense of justice to trade
in contraband tobacco and to stick it, proverbially, to the Farmers General,
which was supposed to collect duties for the state in exchange for the right
to trade tobacco.[64]

   Most of the trade that occurred, even across imperial lines, was
sanctioned, even if in some cases imperial officials gave their blessing to
the clandestine to make it legal. Nonetheless, we can be forgiven for

thinking that what occurred outside the law defined the Atlantic. Arguably it did.[65] As the system developed, the formally illicit took on a pronounced prominence and appeared to become representative of what the Atlantic had become, especially because the law created complications of its own. The rate of change outpaced the ability of the state and its administrative apparatus to manage flows. Moreover, laws had been established earlier on to stop what we could call rogue entanglements, but officials had a stake in boundary crossing. London's wealth depended on the Atlantic. The same went for provincial cities, some of which were wholly dependent on the entangled system. The cases of Bordeaux and Cadiz are telling examples. Both places grew and developed as Atlantic cities, and they were transformed just as much as, if not more than, New World entrepôts such as Philadelphia. These two places represented almost perfect manifestations of what made the Atlantic a system. Both tied slave societies in the Caribbean and along the Spanish Main to the metropoles. Both became nexuses for the development of wealth. Both yoked creole elites culturally and economically to their mercantile confreres in the metropole. Both served as hinges between the Atlantic and the capitals Paris and Madrid. Finally, Cadiz and Bordeaux were sites where what would have been discrete networks converged. Inhabitants here, too, thrived on the sort of illicit trade that by definition crossed imperial realms, just as they needed elites conversant with the trade and culture of other empires.

If any one nation epitomized the new Atlantic, it would be the Netherlands.[66] The Dutch acted as go-betweens between different powers on a sizable scale and traded the enslaved with whoever would pay the best price, from Brazil and Portugal to the British Caribbean. The islands the Dutch held in the Caribbean such as Saint Eustatius and Curaçao became way stations for ships of all nations, as Dutch merchants disregarded laws and conventions. In these polyglot places, inhabitants created an almost "free trade zone," mixing legal and illegal commerce between the Spanish Main, North America, and the rest of the Caribbean. Dutch Guiana, straddling Venezuela, had become by mid-century a "borderless" society. The central state did not even try to regulate, nor could the conglomerate, the Dutch West India Company, which was responsible for the plantations there. Empire here, if we could call it that, was improvised and created on the ground by people tied to all sorts of trading partners. What developed was what was called the "Dutch trade," the illicit movement of goods between the Dutch and Danish ports in the Caribbean, Cap Français and Port-au-Prince in Saint-Domingue, and places in British North America, such as the city that specialized in such traffic: New York.[67] The Dutch trade, which thrived on entanglements, contributed mightily to the consolidation of the Atlantic.[68]

Before this time, in the late seventeenth and early eighteenth centuries, networks tended to be monoglot and bound within discrete imperial worlds. So men and women from the British world as a rule corresponded with others within their national circle, even if the connections they created spanned the ocean. Benjamin Franklin serves as a prime example. However worldly he became, in the early years of his professional life his networks incorporated mainly English-speaking regions within a world circumscribed by British sovereignty. With time, this changed. Franklin's correspondence came to include those from a broader sweep of the Atlantic, and his lines of connection intersected with those of others who also had been writing within monoglot cultural worlds. Through such crisscrossing, what we could call a republic of letters was born, one that drew from any number of Atlantic cultures and could not be tied down to sovereign claims.[69] Franklin was only one rather well-connected node in a complex and growing "epistolary network," which itself was the sum total of other overlapping webs, each developing along with the Atlantic.[70]

Franklin epitomized another key change. Print culture developed to allow a necessary flow of information, both the sort that strengthened distinctive imperial lines and the sort that allowed crossing. The newspaper could be likened to the internet of the age. It offered people fingertip knowledge of the latest happenings in the world beyond their purview, facilitating further integration. Franklin's preoccupation with issues such as provincial agricultural improvement and the circulation of "currency" throughout the Atlantic system stemmed from his access to print in his brother's newspaper shop and eventually to the newspaper he owned, the *Pennsylvania Gazette*. Print made this world go round every bit as much as trade. Not coincidentally, he published essays arguing that paper currency would entice even more migrants to Philadelphia. He suggested, in other words, that Americans needed to embrace the burgeoning system's imperatives. These views were shaped by the work of others throughout the crisscrossed Atlantic. Not coincidentally, French theorists would turn to Franklin to argue that France had to follow suit. Because he worked in the newspaper business, he had his fingers on the pulse of a world of information that was becoming as interlaced and as sophisticated as the very changes he tried to digest.[71]

System and ideas intersected to sustain the "globalization of imagination." Atlantic print networks stretched from Boston to Halle, where J. J. Griesbach was educated and where he published his most important works on the synoptic gospels.[72] Atlantic consolidation produced the ideas that animated peoples on both sides of the ocean. For the French, nearly three thousand titles on the subject of political economy appeared over the course of the century, with the lion's share published after French Atlantic commerce took off in the 1750s. These works came out at a faster pace than the very form we associate with modernity, the novel, and their appearance encouraged French readers to go further afield and read the works of notables in other places struggling with the same issues. A 1754 advertisement, for instance, noted that a translation of one of David Hume's treatises on political economy was "snapped up as fast as the most agreeably frivolous book." The French, like others throughout the Atlantic, were becoming anxious about their ability to compete in a changing system. In a similar vein, consider Hume's Scotland. Thinkers from Scotland fretted over luxury and what it entailed, just as they wanted to be part of a burgeoning world of consumption. They looked to those from other countries to devise their ideas. They were hardly alone, and the sum total of the struggles to make sense of new concerns and possibilities drove men and women to look to others grappling with the same issues. In the process, the consolidation of the system only became more pronounced.[73]

Intellectual networks reflected the reach of Atlantic-wide transformation. All sorts of theories and classification schemes emerged to explain differences occasioned by so much extensive human interaction. Explaining human difference became all that more urgent when economy and power depended on doing so. French theorists, for instance, believed that the Old World, by its very nature, was superior to the New World, and that climate and geography could shape cultural difference. Its people were more intelligent; its animals larger; its plants more varied. Or so they argued. Benjamin Franklin and Thomas Jefferson, themselves amateur racial theorists, disagreed.[74] The Spanish devised ideas of race that argued that those born in the Old World enjoyed advantages over those in the New. In places like Venezuela, people were parsed into a dizzying variety of categories. These categories, in turn, informed a series of debates about the differences and similarities between *peninsulares* and creoles in America.[75] In Britain, moral philosophers in Scotland were developing ideas that all peoples moved through discrete stages of experience and development, even as they borrowed from Spanish and Portuguese racial classifications. As people became more civilized, they believed, their manners became more refined. Even the Spanish, long thought of as a people who rejected the burgeoning new world of thought, rooted their understandings of the diversity of humanity in the same sorts of ideas that led the Scots David Hume and Adam Smith to devise the models they did to account for human difference. Similarly, understanding history's patterns became more urgent still with the new challenges and opportunities presented by a changing system. This project transfixed thinkers like Kant, Hume, Montesquieu, Rousseau, Voltaire, and Gibbon. The new world that all were enmeshed in had to be explained. All of them, not surprisingly given the era in which they were living, posited that history moved in a progressive direction.[76]

We usually refer to the ideas ascendant in the period as those of the Enlightenment, an enlightenment, or perhaps even Enlightenments. Scholars have spilled gallons of ink trying to define the effervescence of thought that crossed boundaries as easily as people and goods during the period and that similarly defined the period of Atlantic consolidation. Whichever term we choose, many throughout the Atlantic reckoned that reason could interpret the world, that human nature was knowable and perhaps fungible, that societies and polities should reflect that nature, that happiness and comfort could exist in this world with progress, and that people should enjoy certain rights as individuals. Each nation employed a different term for what could be regarded as a process, sensibility, movement, or transnational spirit. French *lumières*, the German *Aufklärung*, and British Enlightenment figures championed "un esprit philosophique presque tout nouveau." These worlds of ideas, shared and growing in parallel fashion, stretched from universities down to coffeehouses, Masonic lodges, and salons. In its many guises, it was, however we would label it, premised on understanding, advancement, and happiness.[77]

Each country developed its own distinctive Enlightenment ethos. Prussians, for instance, focused on the state and the person of the king. An avid reader, an accomplished historian, and great friend of Voltaire, Frederick the Great proved the model of the enlightened ruler, albeit an autocratic one.[78] Catholic nations, too, subscribed to the new visions of the person, the world, society, and politics that were beginning to fascinate all sorts of people in both the Old World and the New.[79] Church hierarchies, older assumptions about politics, and what made a person a person now came under scrutiny as a vibrant press allowed for the dissemination of new ideas. The growth and appeal of the press and of Enlightenment sensibilities in France, Rome, Portugal, and Spain encouraged the pope to suppress the Jesuits.[80] Enlightenment represented an Atlantic-wide phenomenon.

This is the now conventional view of what the Enlightenment meant and entailed. Yet such ideas spoke to the ways in which contexts were shifting. New vistas were open for untold numbers of persons, and new possibilities were emerging, just as new inhuman institutions were taking shape to provide labor and claim land. In a world of free agents, often exploiting one another, the idea of the individual had great purchase. The same held for the autonomy of travel, which freed people from older obligations to the land and to institutions like the church. The economy, politics, and society became, trite as it sounds, questions to be addressed, and the answers to them could no longer be assumed. Enlightenment was the movement or sensibility perfectly suited to the Atlantic. It revealed how a changing world that privileged autonomy and movement implicitly and explicitly challenged older ways of social organization.[81] We could even say that the Enlightenment helped create the integrated Atlantic as much as it was created by it. New ideas justified, rationalized, and allowed what was happening, just as they aimed to release energies and ambitions and to use the fruits of integration to better European society.

Not all, of course, were heirs to such ideas. Thinkers wrote off the enslaved from Africa, even if they used new justifications of race for doing so. Enlightenment begot unenlightened ideas about subjugation and about the rank ordering of races.[82] Women, too, did not enjoy equality in the eyes of theorists. Writers throughout western Europe grappled with the great questions of what made a person a person and what made societies function and evolve. But rarely did they include women; in fact, they only did so to strengthen patriarchal understandings that virtually all subscribed to. While writers questioned anything and everything, they refrained from discussing the equality of the sexes.[83]

All this being said, if we are looking for a universal rule for women and the Enlightenment, we shall not find it. In Catholic Spain, women participated in an artistic and cultural public sphere, just as men did. They wrote, they painted, they debated. In fact, women played an important role in advancing the ideal of progress in Spain. But doing so did not imply, at this juncture in any event, an undermining of patriarchy. In Scotland, women took part in the kingdom's intellectual culture as well, even if the level of immersion was bound by reigning assumptions of the feminine. Women in places like Edinburgh remained less visible than in, say, Paris or London, and they tended to construe who they were within custom and tradition. Even those who could be deemed assertive, such as the market women in the streets of Paris, did not fight norms or conventions, however much they pushed against their boundaries. Enlightenment was riddled with contradiction, and this was especially evident when it came to women.[84]

While so much was changing with the Atlantic, some things remained the same. The Enlightenment began to raise concerns, however. If societies could progress, could people as well? Were women bound to the roles they inherited? Could the "improvement" of women be tied to the progress of a society? Ultimately, Enlightenment thinkers, a number of them women, composed questions where none existed before. Women, as much as nearly everything else, could now be considered the subject of history.[85]

The many changes engulfing the whole Atlantic forced all to adapt. The Spanish and Portuguese, in fact, were the first to do so. Rulers of a giant empire yet relatively weaker than their rivals, the Spanish had little choice but to recognize the trading rights of other nations and that they would have to share the spoils of their empire. Interpenetration became state policy. As we know, the Spanish allowed the British to trade slaves to Spanish holdings. They ended up extending such courtesies to all. French, Dutch, and British merchants would enjoy the right to trade silver, and, perhaps most important of all, the Spanish would lose their hold on the Caribbean. The closed system they had envisioned became "porous."[86] At the other extreme, the Portuguese seemed well seasoned to this new world of Atlantic border crossing from the get-go. By the time the system was integrating, they had already begun creating a connected empire that though on paper was centralized, in practice afforded locals a great deal of autonomy. Officials focused their energies on strengthening ties between Brazil and Africa, particularly with Angola. With wealth focused on slavery and plantation agriculture, they did not discourage interpenetration. Brazil loomed larger than ever as the eighteenth century progressed in the imaginations of the Portuguese. And more and more skilled migrants sailed there to build new lives.[87] Brazil loomed just as large, if not larger, in the life of Angola. Brazilian merchants created direct links between the two colonies. The ocean did not divide the two places but connected a vibrant, if brutalizing, South Atlantic world.[88]

The Portuguese case raises one of the enduring motifs of the Atlantic century: people demonstrated an amazing adaptive capacity. The Irish of the eighteenth century offer a great example. As increased and entangled trade remade their worlds, and as they found themselves marginalized by change in Ireland, they took to ships to head to America. Here, too, they

shaped themselves to a more cosmopolitan world, as they encountered Indigenous peoples, newly arriving Germans, and entrenched English settlers.
Africans, too, remade themselves as the Atlantic remade their cultures.
Whole peoples transformed Indigenous ways of doing things to account for
change. Slavery itself serves as the clearest expression of such adaptation.
Groups began to adapt the African understandings of slavery once European avarice entered the equation. As they engrafted an older system onto a
newer one, they transformed traditional ways, and soon instead of trading
prisoners of war, some groups hunted people to sell to Europeans. Other
groups adopted new means of economic production. Iron manufacture,
even in areas dominated by stateless groups, became the chief activity of the
period in places like Guinea Bissau, all on account of Atlantic trade. Those
same connections between Brazil and Angola that powered the slave trade
also reshaped slavery and cultural and economic relations in Africa, especially once growing demand for gold throughout the Atlantic led to an
increased demand for slave labor to supply it.[89]

The same dynamic gripped the New World, from cities and villages to
plantations and frontiers. In both the Caribbean and the rice-producing
plantations in North America, those men and women who toiled on the
land as enslaved persons, those uprooted by Atlantic integration, faced existences of suffering and exploitation. Nonetheless, they discovered novel
ways not only to deal with debasement but also to create community in
the most dire and constrained circumstances. Melding African and European cultural forms, they devised new ways of imagining family belonging,
religious ritual, language, and work. These acts of adaptation further entangled the Atlantic. To cite just one example, a man called Francisco or
Francisque had moved between Iberian, British, and French Atlantic
worlds. He was captured, masquerading as a gentleman, as "a creol de fi-
ladefi," in New Orleans in 1766. Other enslaved persons knew him as an
"Englishman," though he professed to be Catholic. A character much like
Equiano, his peripatetic life took him at the very least from Philadelphia
to Havana and the French Caribbean. This Atlantic shape-shifter, moving
between worlds that in theory should have been discrete, was the norm.
Even those most heavily exploited—the enslaved—took advantage of entanglements to reknit lives and cultures. This process represented the
means through which all people became "creolized." They took what all
corners of the Atlantic had to offer to remake themselves.[90]

If these people, who faced the most daunting challenges of early
modern globalization, could adapt, everyone could. To appreciate adapta-

tive capacities, consider the sensibility we would normally think of as almost prototypically "American." During the eighteenth century, in the
wake and the midst of the great changes of the period, men and women
up and down the British Atlantic coast embraced a form of vital piety, a
movement we call the Great Awakening. They did so, it could be argued,
to make sense of wrenching change. Consider how they understood the
new birth less as a communal experience, as it had been a century earlier,
than an individual expression, akin to the way Enlightenment thinkers
conceived of the person. Moreover, even though New Lights, as they
were called, rejected the implications of conspicuous consumption of the
age, they used the chief vehicle of consumption, the newspaper, to relate
the comings and goings of revivalists. Multilayered networks made re-
vival possible; indeed, they strengthened ties between colonies and the
metropole in the process. Revivals and preachers helped produce—just as
they reacted to—a changing world. Accordingly, they proved the colonial
American variation on the British Atlantic theme. The Scots focused their
energies on universities; the Irish grew fascinated with improvement as
an ideal. Each strategy allowed those with different histories to deal with
their status as peripheral peoples within an integrating system.[91]

Natives in America, too, adapted in creative ways with the changing
fortunes of their world, creating cultural syncretisms and even religious
sensibilities that paralleled those of white societies around them. They
learned how "to dress for success on the frontier" by adopting the fashion of settlers, even as prophets encouraged Natives to reject white ways
and resurrect older avenues for finding meaning. At an even more elemental level, those people shattered by the settlement of Europeans and
the intensification of Old World demands for the products of the New
World, as well as by the resulting violence with other Indigenous groups,
remade themselves and created new bases of identity almost whole cloth.
The Catawbas of the Carolinas offer perhaps the best example. They had
not even existed as a people until the shocks of integration hit the pied-
mont of the Carolinas. Different peoples, all compromised by integration, banded together to create a new group.[92]

Such dramatic ways of finding meaning in a more globalized system
had implications for aspirations as well. It is too simplistic to say that deferential relations between the lower sort and those higher up on the social
ladder defined the Atlantic world before 1750. Nonetheless, what we could
call ascendancies were becoming more prevalent. These took a political,
economic, social, religious, and cultural cast. The taste of one group of

men and women dominated nearly each Atlantic society. The Irish Ascendancy serves as an ideal example of this type. Members of the established church ruled Irish society, and though Ireland represented a province of Britain, these churchmen, as they were known, enjoyed privileges others did not. All ascendancies assumed command of any given society by certain markers, and these markers laid out the divide between those in power and those out of power, just as they represented the most salient dividing line in any society. Ireland's Ascendancy assumed control of the country because of religious confession. Other ascendancies, such as those in France, relied on nobility, and those in Spain on bloodlines. Crossing boundaries was more possible than ever in the Atlantic, but its consolidation also strengthened the hands of dominant groups within each society.[93]

Up to a point, that is. A new mercantile elite also hoped to secure political privileges commensurate with its economic power. Its members also sought status. In doing so they tried to ape their betters, strategically contest their standing, and wriggle their way up the established ladder. Think here again of Benjamin Franklin. He hoped to be accepted in Britain as an equal to its elites. He bridled at the thought that some considered him a backward provincial. He realized that even though he owed his wealth to changes in the Atlantic system, he had to play by the older rules if he hoped to achieve a new station. He had to court the right patrons if he had any chance of securing a position as a gentleman.[94] At the same time, the system and its shifting hierarchies created the strangest sorts of hybrid persons. Peter Williamson, for instance, was born in Scotland, moved to America as an indentured servant, and returned to Scotland to open a coffeehouse. Here he regaled the citizens of Edinburgh, presumably even those writing the theories of how humans and societies developed over time, with stories of the Indigenous inhabitants of North America. Though he styled himself a gentleman, he was labelled an upstart by his betters. Fittingly, he knew and admired Franklin. This should not be surprising. Both embodied a vibrant and multifaceted enlightenment sensibility. Both crossed boundaries with abandon. Both were suited for the unregulated and exploitative Atlantic. Both bumped up against its glass ceilings.[95]

Status still mattered in this world, even if its bases were shifting. Visual culture suggested how rising creole elites now hoped to become masters of the entangled Atlantic and over the societies they inhabited. Artists like John Singleton Copley painted portraits of subjects such as John Hancock, a Boston merchant who had grown wealthy from smuggling. He was not alone. Isaac Royall also sat for Copley. A planter from the Ca-

ribbean, he fled the region after a slave insurrection and moved his family
to New England. Here he continued to trade in the enslaved, with whoever could offer the best price. He also traded in the stuff they produced.
His ability to navigate the tangled Atlantic allowed him to enrich himself
and also to raise children who would inherit the creole world he was creating. Royal's wife posed for Copley, as did his daughters, all to announce
their status. What are called *casta* paintings in Latin America did the same
work. They announced to everyone the lineage and standing of those who
sat, so that all could appreciate where the sitter stood in a racialized peck-
ing order. These images enabled a creole elite to put down a marker of
status for metropolitans and also for those who lived in the periphery. If
integration of the space was one defining characteristic of the period, creoles flaunting wealth and status like peacocks would be another.[96]

Adaptation had its limits. The new Atlantic economy enriched some
but marginalized others, both in the Old and the New World. New
needs and new symbols of status enthralled everyone, even if some were
falling behind economically. Men and women employed old notions to
make sense of change, but the change itself did not map comfortably
onto older arrangements. The poor could still argue that economic relations should represent more than the sum total of supply and demand,
that they implied obligation; but in a world transformed, such ideas had
less and less purchase. The risks but the potential implicit in working for
wages meant more to many than the safety nets and limited mobility
within an older moral economy. So long as the economy roared, working
men and women would thrive and enjoy the freedom with new arrangements. But what if the Atlantic economy stalled?[97]

These dilemmas gripped all regions touching this world, but they
played out in distinctive ways and tended to be tied to the histories and
social fissures within each society. In England, for instance, new up-and-
comers, who had made their money in a mercantile economy, challenged
their betters by pressing for admission to older privileges, by trying to
marry sons and daughters into a landed elite, and by clamoring for political rights that reflected their newfound wealth. The nouveaux riches of
France did much the same. In places farther afield from these centers,
the same dynamics took hold.[98]

In the peripheries, things played out a bit differently. Crisscrossing and
systemic integration complicated relationships within empires. Through
Atlantic-wide changes, what had been colonies were now clearly provinces
of the metropole, even if the centers did not exert a great deal of authority

over these provinces. In such places, a group of self-confident merchants and traders came of age, and they began to embrace what we could call a "creole nationalism." As they grew closer to metropolitan culture through trade, they also began taking pride in their place of birth. We see this in places as far afield as New England, Ireland, and Latin America.[99] Relying on the political autonomy and the economic possibilities of the emerging system, these people were soon importing the goods that allowed them to flaunt their status as the natural rulers of their societies. American historians call this process for the colonies "Anglicization," suggesting that the colonies and colonists were becoming more consciously English in culture over the course of the eighteenth century. Scholars have now expanded this idea to show how "British" the provincials in America were becoming. At the same time, these same Americans also sensed that they were somehow distinctive. They experienced what we could liken to a simultaneous push to and pull from the metropole.[100] Peoples, goods, and ideas streaming across the ocean made this possible. Yet, the same was happening for those in places controlled by the French, the Spanish, and the Portuguese.

Consolidation was making creoles "amphibious animals." They wanted metropolitans to accept them as cultural equals but also needed to style themselves leaders of their own societies. These societies still enjoyed autonomy, but integration bound them more securely to the center. So, creoles could claim loyalty to the Crown, as they did throughout Spanish America, and still try to demonstrate their links to the "Indian" past, even as their status depended on the servile status of Natives. The Irish Ascendancy made exactly the same sort of move in the eighteenth century.[101] Creole elites also found themselves trapped in the middle between metropolitans, on the one hand, and, on the other, Indigenous and/or enslaved peoples in their midst. This bind made for a paradoxical relationship to the center even as it created an energy that pushed against established constraints and bounds. Such dilemmas explained a great deal of cultural ferment in Mexico, North America, the Caribbean, Brazil, and Ireland.[102]

The changes that defined the period were as dizzying as the various ways men and women gave voice to change. Just think of one of the greatest pieces of prose in the eighteenth century: Voltaire's *Candide*. Just as Robinson Crusoe plies the Atlantic, where he hopes to realize his heady ambitions, only to be shipwrecked, Candide goes journeying. The Atlantic network creates the civilized world he ventures from. It also gives him the vocabulary, the categories of understanding, to appreciate his plight. In this story of discovery, the protagonist Candide reflects the many incongruities that the new world coming into being had created. He deals with the militant capitalism of the period, exotic goods and people from America, slavery, the promise of the new world and new wealth, conflicting ideas, and the republic of letters. In this upside-down world, he weighs the French Enlightenment against the British Enlightenment. He, too, points out the contradiction of how exploitation went hand in hand with civility. Like Swift's Gulliver and Defoe's Crusoe, Voltaire's Candide served as a lens to a world that was transforming in fundamental ways.[103] And as a product of the system, Candide's tale became through print culture a catalyst to further integration.

The system proved as unstable as it was dynamic. In some ways, the Atlantic of the mid-eighteenth century looked like the Caribbean of the late seventeenth century, a place beyond the line. In the earlier period, states would not necessarily go to war over disputes in a region in which the ambitions and claims of so many European states overlapped. The term "place beyond the line" had also suggested that what happened in the Caribbean stayed in the Caribbean, that here the normal rules of behavior or of law did not apply.[104] Such had the eighteenth-century Atlantic become. States entertained visions of regulating their own imperial claims, to make straight the tangles of integration and so rationalize the great levels of development that defined the space. But the scope and scale of that development, as well as the ways so many claims intersected and clashed, made such pretensions impossible to act upon. States did not have the power or the reach to remake the Atlantic as they saw fit, even if they were increasingly drawn into conflict over it.

The system, to use a scientific metaphor, had reached an unstable stasis. And because the future of all the Atlantic empires now rested in this space, the tangles were sure to ensnare. Certainly two of the greatest figures of the Enlightenment saw things this way. Both Adam Smith and Immanuel Kant foresaw an Atlantic in which states would try to control persons and markets to increase the power they needed for the struggles they faced in Europe. The "jealousy of trade," as Smith put it, would lead to more frequent and more intensive conflicts. Kant thought that, once unleashed, inevitable wars over trade would reshape Europe and decimate Indigenous peoples. They were not far off.[105]

The changing nature of warfare in the eighteenth century reflected these dramatic transformations. Throughout much of the early part of the century, all European powers and their respective colonies fought a succession of wars over dynastic rivalries, conflicts that centered on Europe. The state could, of course, always raise taxes and levy war. But before mid-century, the bark of the state proved worse than its bite. State authorities sometimes struggled to manage those on the margins within their own boundaries. Scotland offers a good example. Try as they might, officials in London could not dictate for the kingdom to the north, even after suppressing a rebellion in 1745–46.[106] Moreover, war was expensive. The British and French, though rivals and each intent on obtaining power at the expense of the other, imagined fostering freer, less protectionist trade to keep the peace. Peace made for good business. War did not.[107] But as the century wore on, and as the Atlantic grew into an integrated system, warfare increasingly began to center on the Americas. For what transpired across the Atlantic now had dramatic implications for what happened in Europe. The acceleration of capital investment in land, goods, and labor provided officials with the means to build what we could call "the fiscal-military state."[108] Such a state was made for war.

The conflicts that embroiled states grew in number over the eighteenth century. They became longer in duration. They involved more people. Their intensity increased. And they extended beyond Europe. Survival in an anarchic and increasingly competitive world driven by the rise of a "global capitalism" dictated as much. By mid-century, the Atlantic was primed for explosion.[109] The War of Spanish Succession may have started over dynastic rivalries, but increasingly states leveraged the power conferred by the Atlantic to wage war. After the hiatus of the Pax Atlantica, warfare became enmeshed with dynamics propelled by Atlantic change. The War of Austrian Succession followed close on the heels of a few decades of systematization. The outcome of this war, too, despite its name and though it began as a European power struggle, would hinge on which nation could dominate the watery space and the spoils it promised.[110]

All played out in the epic conflict of the period, the Seven Years' War. Fittingly, the war began on the farthest verge of the changing Atlantic, the Ohio Country.[111] It would soon engulf the whole world. Names are telling. Americans named it, of course, the French and Indian War. In other words, they saw it through the prism of immediate threats to their lives, liberty, and property. They used the name even if they appreciated this conflict also centered on Austro-Prussian rivalries on the Continent.[112] Europeans used the more sanitized phrase "Seven Years' War," referring to the formal declaration of war in 1756 and its end with a treaty in 1763, which dates, of course, reflected the timeline of Continental warfare. Cleverer minds have called it the Great War for the Empire, for it set newly empowered empires against one another. Others still refer to it as history's first world war.

Each of the names works—all depends on what is stressed—but perhaps another term captures what made this war distinctive. This was the War for the Atlantic World. Though fought on every known continent, though involving men and women from as far off as India, it stemmed in large part from the changes wrought on an Atlantic scale that defined the eighteenth century and the competition that went hand in hand with them. Moreover, its scope and significance developed as they did because of the need and the ability of states to leverage the tangles of the Atlantic and translate these into power on the battlefields and the oceans. Or to stand up to those states that could do so. The War for the Atlantic, too, just like the ideas and the bodies and the goods moving across the ocean, would act as midwife to further systemic development. It arose from the world it had a hand in creating and sustaining. It would serve as a first catalyst for the revolutionary-age cataclysm that was to come.

French attempts to claim the Ohio Country in the late 1740s set the conflict in motion. The region represented a border area between a British empire clinging to the Atlantic coast and a French one bound to rivers in the interior and the Great Lakes. The fortunes of France's New World enterprise hinged on controlling this space peopled by Natives who had grown in power because they inhabited a "middle ground" between Europeans.[113] With the competitive stakes heightened, even those farthest away from the center—indeed, especially those—found themselves in the center of disputes about the shape of the whole. Here lay the future of the system. As the size of armies increased, as economies grew more dependent on their colonies, as slave-based plantations became engine rooms of capital development, as more and more men and women ventured overseas because of new systemic imperatives, places like Ohio took on greater importance. Here those on the move would find a reservoir of available land for settlement and for speculation, so long as they could displace Natives. Here the Indigenous hold on the continent confronted European control of the coast. As these new encounters loomed, buffer regions between imperial regimes, such as Ohio, became flash points of conflict. The so-called militarized capitalism that was driving and defining the Atlantic dictated that here an epic story of eighteenth-century development would play out.[114]

The stakes were clear for the two principal protagonists of this Atlantic drama, the British and the French. The British metropole was growing dependent on its colonists both as producers and, most especially, as consumers. Britain had willy-nilly encouraged its people to compete relentlessly in the world, all the while looking the other way as colonists flouted mercantilist trading rules. As more and more men and women from the peripheries of Europe streamed into Middle Colony ports, and as more and more elites in their colonies saw Ohio as a money-making venture, British officials realized they had to act to channel these forces and forestall others from stopping them. Stakes seemed just as high for the French, not merely because of trade, but because of international struggles over power. The French had, up to this point in the eighteenth century, focused their energies on the European continent, where France's base of power and influence lay. With the growth of the importance of America to European power relations, they reoriented strategy toward regions beyond Europe.[115] The French recognized the importance of the Caribbean to its economic ambitions. Saint-Domingue mattered more than ever. Moreover, New France had to be defended and the Ohio Country had to be won to maintain the integrity of the whole. The French were banking on their historic connection with Natives there to help them retain what they were claiming. Ohio proved the key for France and Britain's Atlantic empires. This is where they crisscrossed.[116]

The War for the Atlantic World involved all the major powers of Europe now vying for dominance of the European continent and the places entangled with it far away. The age's changes had touched all the nations of the Continent, even Austria and Prussia, and they, too, now had to compete with Atlantic-focused powers. The new calculus of global power enmeshed them as much as those directly engaged with the Atlantic, reshuffling alliances in the process. Spain, too, even if its economy lagged behind that of the others, had an opportunity to resurrect its fortunes if it could reanimate the connections to its increasingly wealthy, though decentralized, American empire. Portugal, a second-tier power on the Continent but owner of critical slaving factories in Africa as well as one of the most profitable colonies in the New World, also could not escape the furies of the war once it began. The watery space had become the focal point of European power relations and economies; no one could ignore the logic of the system.

The war would dwarf any that came before, and for the first time in history, the western edges of the Atlantic would become a central theater of conflict. This required states to do things and to finance movements that officials could never have dreamt of before. So leaders dispatched armies from the heart of Europe to the American frontier. Troops fought on the European continent as they always had, but they did so with

greater urgency and on an unprecedented scale, as states wielded amplified power on the battlefield. And in their own societies. Prussia's successes, for instance, stemmed from its ability to yoke state power to
popular patriotism. Prussians were not alone in this regard.[117]

We do not need to recount the war in great detail, but early in it
France had used its competitive advantage with Natives to win some key
victories in the Hudson River Valley. The experience of the French in
crafting an empire with Indians as partners now served them well.[118] The
British had not done so—in fact, they had more or less turned a blind eye
as their colonial subjects mistreated Natives. Now the French reaped the
fruits of their policy. Though the British initially suffered setbacks because
of their stubborn refusal to cooperate with Indigenous peoples, they soon
were able to turn the tide of war because of the state's ability to take advantage of systemic change in ways the French could not. Under the leadership of William Pitt, the British designed a strategy that would allow
them to strangle the French by bottling up French ports in North America. With no goods entering the Saint Lawrence seaway, allies deserted the
French. Soon the British seized the capital of New France, Quebec, in an
epic battle that saw James Wolfe fall but defeat the Marquis de Montcalm.
The British had also secured the very center of French ambitions in Ohio,
Fort Duquesne. Soon the war in Europe and other places in the world
came to a conclusion. The British stood as the winners.

If the War for the Atlantic World began in Ohio on the very verges of
the system, it would end in one its centers, Paris. In 1763 near the square
where Parisians had erected a statue of Louis XV very much like the statue
of George III in New York, statesmen from the belligerent powers met to fi-
nalize the settlement. The war would serve as a touchstone for men and
women throughout the Atlantic. By the terms of the settlement, officials and
common people alike, metropolitans and provincials of all stripes, sensed
that they had lived through something notable and momentous. All believed
that the period represented what we could call a "moment." And whether
the moment would generate hope or fear depended on perspective.
The French surrendered the lion's share of their New World empire. Fortunately, as Voltaire quipped, though they had lost millions of acres of snow in
an inhospitable land, they still controlled Saint-Domingue. This violent
place would continue to drive the French economy. Still, France had suffered a humiliating defeat and now worried that it had lost the race for Atlantic empire and that new struggles to remain relevant would commence.
Men and women throughout the British Atlantic, by way of contrast, reacted

to the end of the war with jubilation, particularly over what they had won. And it was estimable. The British, with what the French handed over to them and what they won from Spain, now controlled a massive territorial empire, one stretching from the Arctic Circle to the Gulf of Mexico and from the Atlantic to the Mississippi. They also gained some islands in the Caribbean.[119]

All had to reckon with costs, even the winners. Most prosaically, concerns for both France and Britain centered on money. The war nearly broke both powers, however much state capacity had increased with war making. The British had proven nimbler in funding the machine of war, particularly with the fine-tuning of its fiscal military state. The French had not been able to reform their financing to pay for war on a new scale. Officials of both nations would have to figure out how to manage the moment while managing debt, which would lead states to rethink relations between center and periphery and between metropolitans and subject peoples in the colonies. They knew if they did not act, they would fail to meet the moment and all it offered.

Along with the French, the war humbled the Spanish and the Portuguese. Spain lost Manila and Havana in fighting, which it won back in treaty negotiations, and the Floridas, which it did not. Even though Portugal had been allied with Britain, it too found itself holding a losing hand. Ironically, the Iberian powers had savaged each other in the New World, as the war occasioned conflict and competition along their borders in South America. Spain and Portugal licked their wounds by shoring up their defenses against each other in South America. Portuguese officials moved the Brazilian capital to Rio de Janeiro, largely because of the violence that had engulfed regions closer to Spanish holdings. To defend their more exposed frontiers, the Spanish followed suit by creating a new viceroyalty with its capital in Buenos Aires, all to ensure it could withstand attacks by Portugal. Both measures were defensive in scope, designed to ensure they would lose no more in the aftermath of the war.[120]

For all the headiness of the moment, signs were emerging that things were amiss, that somehow a way of doing things was out of equilibrium with the ways the world had been shifting. The signs first revealed themselves in remote regions of empire. A few examples will suffice. In the Spanish New World empire, unrest began to grip regions far from the administrative centers of empire. Officials in Peru near the Andes reported in the 1760s and early 1770s a series of sobering disturbances.

Those on the very margins of society, Native peasants in this case, were engaging in protests against established rulers. The problem was quite simple: local elites were squeezing them for more revenue, as the state needed greater resources in the years after the war. These sorts of disturbances, of course, were not new. Peasants recoiled at innovations that impinged upon their ability to keep body and soul together; indeed, they expected, as a rule, that the state would appreciate the legitimacy of airing grievances. But in this case, action was taking a more political turn and betokened a concerted level of mobilization. The elites certainly saw things this way. They interpreted the threat as political.[121]

Similar dynamics were at work on Britain's peripheries. In Ireland, rural insurgents did what they normally did when their betters disregarded traditional understandings of economic relations. They houghed cattle, mutilating them by cutting tendons or hamstrings. They threatened landlords who evicted them. In some cases, they murdered. But after the war something was changing. Peasants in Ireland, like those in Peru, began to act in more overtly political ways, or at least Ascendancy elites interpreted things this way. Disturbances at the hands of disaffected Catholics, in part, stemmed from the insistence of the British state to view Ireland as a vast reservoir of manpower to fill the ranks of its armies. In this instance, the British could act vigorously to suppress insurgency. Ireland, after all, was a close periphery.[122]

Bigger problems loomed farther away. Indians in the Ohio Country, many of whom had fought side by side with the French, were resisting the new regime the British were foisting on them. To control the vast area ceded by the French, the British instituted garrison government and the sorts of policies that left Natives with little autonomy. Natives in the west, under the leadership of an Ottawa war chief named Pontiac, rose up to contest British authority. Some preached a message of the rejection of European ways and customs, encouraging Natives throughout the western edges of the Atlantic system to reembrace older traditions to address the new challenges of the day.[123] The British struggled to put down the rising. But officials realized that they could never hold the frontier without the cooperation of the Indigenous peoples. They regrouped and instituted more flexible policies, of the sort the French had employed before the War for the Atlantic.

Other tensions were evident in other places far from the center but central to the new system. In the eyes of metropolitan officials, far more worrisome than a revolt among Natives on the land reserved for future settlement, or Catholics bristling against their exclusion from the political nation in Ireland, or unrest among peasants in Peru, was slave rebellion. Tacky's Revolt in Jamaica, which took place in 1760, laid bare the oppressive and exploitative nature of Atlantic integration, as planters recoiled from a violent uprising among their enslaved labor force. The revolt was shaped by Atlantic dynamics. Many of the rebels had experienced war in Africa, which in and of itself had been exacerbated by the growth of slave raiding with the rise of the Atlantic system. The level of bloodshed in Tacky's Revolt dwarfed that of the Battle of Quebec, and suppressing it required a coordinated response from metropolitan and colonial authorities. In its wake, taxes went up, as did barracks, all to protect the vital interests associated with the British sugar trade. Meanwhile, planters in Saint-Domingue dealt with a strange series of poisonings that killed thousands. The so-called Macandal affair elevated white fears about the restiveness of the Africans in their midst. Both events called on creoles to consider how confident and how anxious they were as masters of these places that stood at the very crossroads of the Atlantic.[124]

It was not only the world's powers that struggled with enslaved and subject populations in the wake of the war. The Dutch, who had flourished with systematization, had to manage a revolt in one of their peripheral holdings. In 1763, enslaved rebels took over the small and isolated Dutch colony on the Berbice River in what is known as Guyana today but what was then called the Wild Coast. Here, where coffee and sugar were produced for export, the rebels created a government and kept Dutch forces at bay for the better part of a year. Authorities had to enlist Natives and other enslaved persons to put down the rebellion, at a terrible cost to the enslaved. The colony never recovered.[125]

A crisis of integration would begin in the North American colonies for the British and in places like Peru for the Spanish. The first stirrings of provincial discontent did not demonstrate a newfound attachment to ideas of autonomy and rights or even that creole communities were coming of age. They pointed to a sobering reality: just at the moment those in Europe's centers were beginning to revisit imperial governance, they could not project their power to the very margins of their empires, even if the urgency to do so was growing. The stresses and strains that went into creating a system in a geographic space would produce tensions that would first grip the edges and that creoles would struggle to define and articulate in the coming years. These tensions had their roots in the dynamics that defined the eighteenth century, including how colonies became provinces, how slavery and the expulsion of Indigenous inhabitants shaped the memory and tenor of social relations in these provinces, how provincial elites had developed a culture attracted to and suspicious of metropoles. Tensions would become the stuff of crisis when states had to work out how to manage the integrated Atlantic that had just emerged from a costly war. All who lived on the Atlantic littoral would be drawn into this drama. The tangled ways Europeans, Africans, and Natives and creoles in America would do so would become the defining characteristics of their lives from this point forward.

CHAPTER TWO

# Disentangling the Atlantic

## *A Primer for Imperial Reform*

A LL STRUGGLED WITH THE idea of empire after the War for the Atlantic. Even William Pitt, the great architect of British victory, was confounded, and perhaps even driven to madness, by the daunting prospect of using the power of the state to manage the Atlantic system. Every official in Britain tussled with the problem. Parliament, Pitt was convinced, had to be supreme, and it had to govern the empire in much the way it ruled over the kingdoms of the British archipelago. Parliament, he came to believe, could legislate and could regulate the trade of the Atlantic, but in his mind consent of the governed represented a fundamental notion of what Britishness entailed. The right to consent to laws made also extended to Americans, however that right would be defined. They were not, Pitt famously put it, the "bastards" of England. Others thought this perspective foolish. Order could only be sustained if Parliament extended its authority over the provinces, and no hand-wringing was necessary. Americans could be taxed, a group of officials believed, though they were not represented in Parliament. Ultimately, these conflicting points of view led to an extraordinary series of debates in Parliament. They centered on the idea of how empire should be reformed.[1]

The idea of reform transfixed those on the margins in much the same way it did for those at the center like Pitt. Americans, Scots, and the Irish all addressed the direction reform should take. For it became

almost axiomatic that the empire, given the new world heralded by Atlantic integration in the wake of an epic war, had to have a more definitive shape. Provincials applied their aspirations to the moment. With the
war's end, perhaps the empire could be imagined in new ways, all hoped.
The moment seemed both momentous and plastic. It demanded change.

Particularly in the heady and anxious years after their victory over
France, many British writers, officials, and even artists, whether in London or in the provinces, tried to devise a formula that would work for
Britain as it tried to come to terms with Atlantic empire. All agreed that
the riches of Atlantic consolidation had to be harnessed, and they all knew
that empire would have to be reimagined, along with power. The question
was how. The moment strained treasuries, to be sure. But it also taxed
imaginations. For Britons, imagining empire, and how it would function,
became the most intoxicating problem to be solved. It dominated elite
and popular culture, in America, the British Caribbean, Ireland, Scotland,
and England. It also consumed the lives, and in some cases the careers, of
statesmen.

The British were not unique in this regard. All Europeans tried to
comprehend the moment with general Enlightenment principles mediated by their own distinctive histories. For the Spanish, the enlightened
Crown would bind the whole together, and only proper authority could
bring prosperity and order to the chaos of the Atlantic.[2] The French, too,
devised an imperial vision, even though they had lost the war. They tried
to reinvigorate national spirit and create a new basis for collective belief
after defeat. From ashes, French leaders suggested, France would have to
discover how to rise again. That meant reforming.[3]

Before this period was to be known as an age of revolution, it was the
age of reform. The War for the Atlantic led to far-reaching discussions of
how to rationalize the Atlantic system, to make it comprehensible and
manageable. Reformers hoped that the tangled nature of a system they
saw as inherently anarchic could be made straight along national lines.
In so doing, all peoples were using the concepts they had at hand to try
to order and rationalize a world which they saw as unregulated, but in
which the stakes had grown. The task could not be ignored, and they
used the only tool they had—sovereignty—however ill or well adapted it
was for the job. Eighteenth-century understandings of state power came
with rigid and inelegant apparatuses—bureaucracies, decrees, laws, and
assumptions—that had to be fitted on a complicated space defined by
fluid movement.[4]

The task of imagining empire depended on complex negotiations. To be sure, those at the center, as Pitt's story suggests, argued over the best course to take. Those on the very edges of empire were bedeviled by reform as well. The provincial process, however, was more complicated still, as it was mediated by distinctive considerations and ideas, including the will or the ability of creole elites to control men and women in their own societies. Provincial leaders born and raised in the colonies had to consider their positions in empire and within their own societies. These multilayered tugs-of-war would entrance all and became the very stuff of empire making. In the process, some imperial officials would be emboldened to design centralized and comprehensive visions of empire, and some would end up with empires that willy-nilly had flexible structures.

These negotiations would also lead to the initial stirrings of an age of revolution. If the crisis that would engulf the Atlantic had its first tremors in the Ohio Valley and in places like Peru and Munster just after the war, it would emerge full blown on the periphery when more thoroughgoing and systematic reform was implemented. In the places farthest away from the centers of authority, where sovereignty would prove most difficult to extend, men and women would contest how officials imposed empire onto the dynamic Atlantic. Doing so magnified for many the significance of the moment. It also led to violence that imperiled the very empires reform was designed to sustain.

What follows is a primer on reform. Far from a straightforward affair, reform proved vexing. The empires that on paper needed reform most comprehensively shied away from it. The empire that seemed on paper the strongest passed the most exhaustive measures only to fall apart in the process. Reform did not only involve imperial governance. It revealed disequilibrium between imperial political structures and economic and social realities. It also placed people even on the very edges of empire, especially elites, in perplexing binds, and in some cases it precipitated destabilizing violence. A process designed to untangle the Atlantic led to its own complexities.[5]

Reform followed certain rules. The first was simple enough. Rule Number 1: In the wake of the War for the Atlantic, reform became the order of the day for all.[6] For victors and for vanquished, the winners and the losers in the struggles over systemization, those who fell somewhere between the two, and even those who did not participate in the war but who were affected by Atlantic consolidation, the nature of a more competitive world dictated thorough reform. Perhaps West Africa offers the purest example of reform in this regard. We are apt to see Africa as an outlier in the story of the broader age. That would be short-sighted. The ramping up of the slave trade, which was the way integration was experienced in much of Africa, also pressed leaders to create "fiscal military states." States had to adapt to new realities and more rigorous competition. Much of this competition had to do with securing bodies for—or protecting them from—the slave trade. With more demand, and more rulers apt to supply, conflict was becoming more prevalent. Together, these pressures encouraged leaders to centralize to make for more efficient taxing measures, to figure out how to put more men under arms, and to secure more weapons. The state had to remake itself to accomplish these goals. Leaders, then, refitted their states and their societies for war. The end result was that power was centralized and institutions remade. The states of the Upper Senegal River and Asante along the Gold Coast proved especially successful at reforming; in the process, they proved the best at weathering future storms and managing the Atlantic. Those that did not provided a steadier flow of captives for the Atlantic and continued to suffer from instability.[7]

Africa provides a template for us to appreciate Rule Number 1. And with good reason. For all, ordering things anew took on an urgency because of the dog-eat-dog nature of the Atlantic world. Throughout the Atlantic, states began to reconsider ruling structures, accountability, and efficiency by tweaking institutions, recasting governance, and overhauling antiquated ways. And this gets us to Rule Number 2: Reform programs also differed. Officials in each country tried to reimagine institutions, approaches, and structures in the light of their distinctive histories and the particular tensions they faced because of how consolidation affected them, just as officials in West Africa were doing.[8] In this way, specific reform measures spoke to the ways each society functioned.

Let's look at a few examples with the first two rules in mind, and let's start in the place we would not expect the entangled Atlantic to exert much influence: the European continent. Russians initiated reforms by adapting German models of governance, themselves based on Enlightenment principles, to Russian ways and institutions. They created a police state that could manage society's many tensions and make a large space governable by recourse to an enlightened despotism. Prussians also engaged in reform in similar ways. They had more urgent reasons than most, as they were almost creating a sense of the people and the state of

Prussia ex nihilo. Amalgamating new territories won in war with diverse populations meant that they had to devise governing practices that could sustain a national system of institutions, all to allow Prussia to compete on the world stage. Keeping with Prussian traditions, the person of the ruler came to epitomize the state. To vie with other European nations meant that bureaucracies geared for localized concerns were retrofitted for expansion. As a result, a peripheral Prussia became an important player through war and enlightened state making. Austria did much the same. Maria Theresa and then Joseph II remade state, army, and society to thrive in a more competitive world. Maria Theresa went so far as to ban tracts supporting emigration to America. She did not want population siphoned off or to lose potential soldiers that would fill the ranks. Joseph II would put the state at the center of the social good. Both these Austrian reformers, pointing to the distinctive glories of the Austrian past, were turning their back on the Atlantic to sustain their Continental aspirations.[9] Indeed, Prussia, Russia, and Austria focused on strengthening the appeal and the apparatuses of the state to compete with those rivals that could leverage Atlantic empires.

The need to reform may have stemmed from the outcomes of the War for the Atlantic World, but all players in the European state system had to follow the same path, even if they did so in distinctive ways. And now Rule Number 3: All states would experience tremors far from centers of power for doing so. For instance, Austrian attempts at reforming its Continental empire led to early resistance at the margins. In this case, it was not a colony but the region around Brussels. Joseph II's ideas included controlling the church, revising the curriculum at universities, and dispensing with older ways of managing local regions. In the early 1780s, he would initiate such change in Belgium, a place that held its liberties and its autonomy dearly, infuriating locals and instigating a rebellion among those who would fight to maintain ancient privileges. Reform, therefore, revealed cracks where it was applied, exacerbating tensions between center and periphery in the process. Those places farthest from metropolitan control pushed back more quickly than others, and often most insistently.

Rule Number 4: Meaningful reform had to be backed by the power of the state if it was to be implemented. No power, no reform. The Prussian state was able to enforce its will upon its peripheries, and it rarely strayed beyond what it could do. Hence, the state tended to wield power efficaciously. To return to Austria, although resistance to Joseph II began along the margins, he had the capacity to put it down. He knew he had to. In this more competitive world, the ruler who could use new means of statecraft to make his or her rule more effective stood to have a competitive advantage over rivals. The resort to force, then, represented another tool in the reformer's tool kit, but one that had to be used with care and only as local needs and systemic imperatives dictated.[10]

Sometimes locals could push back, making things difficult for reformers. This certainly happened in Africa; in fact, reform occasioned a great deal of tense negotiation, and the same could be seen in Europe. Throughout Europe after the Seven Years' War, as states large and small struggled through reform to adapt to new imperatives of a changing system, those on the margins resisted. Resistance did not represent some grand orchestrated and coordinated movement. Each of these movements sprang from attempts at more closely reining in or incorporating peripheries into administrative centers. Corsicans, led by Pascal Paoli, rose up first against the government in Genoa intent on curtailing provincial rights and then against the French, who acquired the island and tried to rule it. The French put down resistance. Poles resisted those powers around them and their own ineffectual government. Greeks pushed back against Ottoman reform measures. In Scandinavia, people did much as Belgians were doing against central authority. For each action of reform, there was, in other words, an equal and opposite reaction in the farthest verges of state authority. Sometimes pushback led to suppression, sometimes negotiation, sometimes acquiescence.[11]

Measures pursued on the African and European continents offer a helpful glimpse of the rules of reform. But only up to a point. The most ambitious reforms, and the most creative, involved European states with "ultramarine" empires. These had to reckon most fully with the costs of victory and defeat in the Atlantic war. The years after the war were universally marked by attempts to untie the tangled knots of the Atlantic and to map discrete models of sovereignty more effectively onto a chaotic space. Needless to say, the task usually generated heated debate. Let's take a look at the losers in the struggle first, for they were as invested in reform as the winners, if not more so.

When it became clear near the end of the War for the Atlantic that France would suffer a humiliating defeat, a number of French officials advocated following a more British model of economic development that promised to favor industry and free trade. The task was urgent. By 1764, servicing the debt incurred by the war, and the wars preceding it, took up

60 percent of the state's revenue. Because of smuggling, or so the thinking went, the state had not been able to reap the benefits of the system.
But did the state have the resources to act and to project force across an
ocean? Any reform, some officials reckoned, had to begin with an admission that the state could not control the economy in such a dynamic
space. Others countered that the state had no choice; it had to direct affairs. Loss in the war served as a catalyst for such a debate.[12]

The struggle in France between the two positions opened the door to
a probing critique of "despotic" institutions, as some argued that only a
root-and-branch overhaul of the state and its approach to political economy could allow the nation to take advantage of a changed Atlantic. Reform, however, would not take shape along these lines.[13] It would have to
cohere to prevailing French understandings of power. Reform would follow an absolutist model of governance that had defined France since the
time of Louis XIV, one based on the sovereignty of the Crown. After 1763,
ministers initiated sweeping changes of the army and the navy, all with
an eye to readying it for the next fight against the British. They enlarged
the bureaucracy and tried to use their influence to buttress those elements
of the economy that would enrich the merchant class but that could also
serve the state and the military. This was fine, as these moves worked
within conventional understandings of sovereignty in France. In this way,
the state apparatus could grow, and officials would not have to tinker with
that most vexing of problems, taxation.[14]

Though the French had lost nearly all of their Atlantic empire, they
had some confidence in their ability to reshape empire. They emerged
from the war believing in the essential nobility of the people and of the
nation they owed allegiance to. Theirs was still the "Great Nation." This
sensibility allowed the French to enter the postwar world with a firm belief in the superiority of the nation and their future as well. It would
allow them to reform with some hope of reviving Atlantic fortunes.[15]
Moreover, though they had lost all of snowy Canada and some islands,
including Grenada, they still had the jewel of their empire: Saint-
Domingue. This trade had taken off in recent decades.[16] So when it came
to making empire more competitive, all eyes turned to this slave society.
Officials hoped to develop new lines of authority to rule Saint-
Domingue and to regulate trade to and from the island colony. The ink
had not even dried on the Treaty of Paris when the French government
foisted unprecedented taxes on Saint-Domingue. The state promised to
make concessions in other areas—like militia service—to make the tax

more palatable.[17] Whatever French officials did, it still beat trying to enact taxes for the metropole.

Reform, though, did not go according to metropolitan plan. Planters in Saint-Domingue took on the task of reordering their society with great enthusiasm; however, they aimed to strengthen their hands as they "improved" their society. Though on the hook for taxes, planters used the reforming moment to introduce new methods of controlling the enslaved. With support from merchants growing wealthier in places like Bordeaux, they tightened racial hierarchies to maintain control of the labor force on the island. Free people of color had enjoyed many of the privileges of whites as the economy of the island was developing. Now they found themselves hemmed in by new exclusionary laws.[18] Using the old tried-and-true trick of playing the race card, planters encouraged poorer white French settlers to see that they had more in common with planters. Doing so allowed creole elites to hold a firm line when it came to determining how far reform could and should go and whom it should benefit. They suggested that what was good for whites in Saint-Domingue was good for France.[19]

Even if the French would have preferred a centralized version of imperial authority, they realized that they had to adapt in the face of realties. Undoing the entangled nature of the Caribbean proved impossible, and so they amended what they hoped to accomplish. Some ports, they conceded, could be open to foreign trade. At the same time, the state still insisted that all sugar had to come to France. Officials would not compromise metropolitan monopolies that had flourished with systemization. The new hybrid arrangement still proved profitable. As planters seized more autonomy, as merchants enjoyed the best of all worlds, more and more of the enslaved were brought to the French Caribbean, many—not so ironically—from a reforming West Africa. These measures, which spurred the further debasement of Africans and free people of color and which would enshrine "whiteness" as the ultimate marker of status and mastery, would lead to a golden age for the island. The French process of reform further encouraged the French Atlantic economy to grow. In this instance, reform impulses from the center strengthened the creoles' hand. Nonetheless, through such initiatives, the French had, much to the chagrin of some British officials, enhanced the profitability of the bit of empire that remained, though they had not solved their debt issue. This empire that had become smaller was primed for prosperity, even if on balance the metropole was not.[20]

Even if planners invariably began with great ambitions for change, they had to play the hand they were dealt. The Portuguese case offers an instructive look at this theme. The Portuguese were fighting an almost rearguard action to reacquire the imperial initiative that they had lost before and during the war. They struggled under the shadow of the British and under a consequent trade deficit. Now, they wanted to reassert their independence. They faced challenges. Gold remittances from Brazil were falling, and the tremendous earthquake of 1755 destroyed not only much of the city of Lisbon but also the cargo of the Brazilian fleet, which had been stored in warehouses in the city. Under the leadership of Sebastião José de Carvalho e Melo, later to be named Marques de Pombal, the state tried to carve out a niche for the Portuguese Empire to thrive amid these trying circumstances and constraints. Pombal nationalized commerce as much as he could, tried to bring an end to the contraband trade in gold and silver to and from Spanish Buenos Aires, and he sought to curtail the economic might of Jesuit trading companies.[21]

The Portuguese also had to confront a structural anomaly created by Atlantic integration. Almost all Portuguese officials recognized that the balance of power within the empire had tilted to the west. Brazil had been flourishing, and Portuguese administration had not kept pace. The Crown, Pombal believed, needed more firm control over the whole. With this in mind, he sought to overhaul the colonial system, to regulate the economy, and to ensure that lines of imperial authority were clear and unambiguous. Foreign interference was to be curtailed. Up to this point, all comers traded enslaved persons with Brazil. This would have to end. Reformers also wanted to regulate the massive migration from Portugal to Brazil, one that dwarfed even the movement of men and women from Ireland and Britain to the North American colonies, all to try to restore imperial balance. And so decrees went out, and officials were dispatched.[22]

The key rested with untethering the Portuguese empire from the entangled mess of the Atlantic without abandoning the ocean and what it represented. Pombal did all he could to reclaim ports in Africa from British and French interlopers. Traders from these two nations had run Portuguese merchants out of slaving factories by offering better terms for captives. Now Pombal aimed to reestablish Portuguese supremacy in regions along the African coast. He wanted nothing less than to thread the ties between Africa and Brazil exclusively through Portugal. He also used the chaos of the period to double down on a mercantilist approach. He created the Company of Grão Para and Maranhão to establish a monopoly over the trade in humans between Guinea and Amazonia. Here the institution would thrive, and soon Amazonia became an important rice-producing region. Reform in this case led to unexpected Portuguese success and untold African suffering. Slave imports to what had been a marginal region of Brazil jumped through reform measures.[23]

Reform, though, did not restore imperial balance or undo tangles. For all of the changes proposed, the Portuguese had to follow the rules dictated by the reform primer. They may have wanted to centralize, but with time they realized they could not. Pombal, for instance, had grand plans of stemming the tide of contraband. He issued orders to police ports to ensure Portuguese shipping was given pride of place. Yet, he came to realize he could not stop the flow. He bowed to constraints, especially as the Portuguese did not have the power to extend meaningful authority across the ocean. He also initiated a tariff policy that was flexible, all to stimulate certain industries in which the Portuguese enjoyed a competitive advantage. Brazil was organized into captaincies, which were overseen in differentiated ways depending on local needs and ambitions. Local elites were brought into ruling arrangements and gained a voice on fiscal matters as well. When all was said and done, to make this empire function meant seeing Brazil as the centerpiece of empire and allowing creoles to enjoy a share of power.[24] Through all of this innovation, one thing was clear: creole elites could not be alienated. Brazil, like its sugar, remained the engine of the Portuguese Empire. Rather unsurprisingly, reforms, if anything, strengthened the hand of Brazil's exploitative class. Perhaps these creoles, now working directly with merchants from Angola to import their labor supply, did not need the mediating hand of Portugal to navigate the Atlantic.[25]

The Spanish learned the same basic lesson as the Portuguese, that reform followed scripts. They also discovered that reform usually delivered a mixed bag of results because it depended on a multilayered process of negotiation, of bid and counterbid. The Spanish case presents a story as complex as the empire itself. Reform revealed how different regions fared differently and how some places fractured in unpredictable ways because of it. Reform exposed as many tangles as it rectified.[26]

The Spanish, like the Portuguese and the French, recognized the need to modernize finances, to crack down on contraband and smuggling, to right the treasury, and to establish more meaningful control over porous political structures. In particular, the humiliating loss of Havana during the war refocused energies on imperial change. Officials of Bourbon Spain wanted to treat the provinces as colonies in a centralized and efficient empire. Ossified ways, they hoped, had to become a thing of the past. Imperial bureaucrats, for instance, wanted to create a cadre of trained men who earned their positions by merit to take up important administrative posts.[27] Reformers adapted old practices for new purposes. Schools for orphans, to cite another example, where unfortunate young men had been prepared for going to sea, became elite training centers for the Spanish Navy. Reforming officials proved as ambitious as they were adaptable. They hoped to levy new taxes, to reorganize the army, expand the navy, and shore up defense at key points, particularly the Caribbean.[28]

Looking to their past, the Spanish believed that centralized sovereignty, the sort that held sway in the metropole, represented the best way to manage the system. For them, more control was necessary. Before the war, different regions were considered almost equal partners in empire, even if the Crown was supreme. Now officials sought to make all the colonies unambiguously subservient. Spanish reformers sent new administrators from the metropole and created new viceroyalties, all with the idea of rationalizing empire.[29] It was hoped that all this restructuring would help clamp down on all the entanglements.

What is striking is how similar these plans were to all the others, even if the basis of authority was conceived distinctively in each place. Convergence among reformers was not coincidental. All the powers were addressing the very same issues in the very same historical moment. They all sensed how heightened imperial rivalry necessitated basic change. They also emulated one another. Spanish planners, in fact, followed closely what the French and especially the British were doing. They read the same Enlightenment theorists. But they effected reform in a way that held to Spanish conceptions of sovereignty. The cult of regalism became the new imperial glue and the stuff of reform. Regalism was more than a rhetorical rallying cry. Officials used the person of the monarch as both carrot and stick, encouraging even the most recalcitrant of provincials to embrace reform measures. Therefore, just as the French did, the Spanish worked with what they knew. Centralization under the Crown would point their way forward.[30]

In theory, that is. On the very verges of Spanish imperial authority, plans met with resistance on the ground. After the war, when the British took over the eastern half of the North American continent and won the Floridas in the treaty negotiations, Spain was given control of the region west of the Mississippi. Many French remained, and they were not happy with the new state of affairs. Just as the British had done in the Ohio River Valley, the Spanish wanted to shore up rule in the regions ceded by the French. They expected to bring an end to "French laxity." In the meantime, they had to figure out how to manage a place at their very colonial periphery bordering British holdings to the east. Carlos III dispatched an Irishman, Alejandro O'Reilly, to bring consistent Spanish rule to Louisiana. He was the right man for the job. Anti-British to the core, he became a strong proponent of centralizing reform. But the Natives there, especially the Osage, demanded the autonomy they had enjoyed under the French. Given the distance of places like the Arkansas River Valley from New Spain, officials had to recognize that centralization would prove impossible. O'Reilly had to concede that plans could only be realized by courting Native allies. Willy-nilly, Osage power grew, as the Spanish recognized the limits of reform in a place so distant from other settlements.[31]

Like the French, then, the Spanish would have to improvise. The experience of Spain's principal reformer offers a case in point. José de Gálvez insisted that a free trade system—or *commercio libre*—had to be constructed to rerationalize Spanish holdings. This was not an approach Adam Smith would have understood; it did not call for free trade between different imperial systems. Rather, it established a boundless world of trade between and among Spain and its many holdings that could, in theory, undo the system's entanglements. At its heart, the new system was to function like an "imperial machine."[32] Gálvez hoped to draw more port towns beyond Cadiz into the Atlantic system and to bring more traders into the imperial orbit. Soon ships from more ports were heading to and from Cuba, Santo Domingo, and Puerto Rico. In this, Gálvez enjoyed some success, especially with Havana. Planters and Crown officials there agreed with Madrid that freer trade between the constituent parts of the empire and less reliance on merchants from competing powers would bring stability and prosperity to Cuba and safeguard it from neighbors. Ultimately, reformers reckoned Spain's reengagement with the slave trade would box out competitors and yoke Cuban planters more effectively to the metropole. Liberalization of this sort, Gálvez wagered, would encourage a bit more ambition. All would enhance the authority of Madrid, or so he told himself.[33]

Such was not to be the case. In fact, Gálvez, like Pombal, had little power to follow through on sweeping reform. The reforms, and commercio libre in general, enriched those creole merchants with ties to metropolitan

ports and to places throughout the Americas. Those, however, who relied on
trade with other Europeans, the people who profited from entanglement,
faced an uncertain future. The same for those who produced goods in Spanish America. Cheap goods from Spain now flooded the market, imperiling
some futures. Divisions, therefore, loomed. A growing cadre of elites in the
peripheries enjoyed a greater sense of autonomy and a more heightened
sense of participation in the empire. Others, hampered by reform, were
growing disaffected.[34]

Because the state did not have the power to police the whole continent of South America, and because Spain could never supply all the
wants and needs of consumers in the Spanish New World, smuggling and
transshipping continued apace. Through the institution of the new "machine," and the flouting of it, some peripheries would flourish; however, in
the balance, some would struggle.[35] Buenos Aires, for instance, experienced nothing short of a boom, as free migrants and the enslaved
streamed into the city. Reform allowed those in the viceroyalty of La Plata
to trade silver directly within the empire. Buenos Aires prospered at the
expense of those living in the Andes.[36]

Even if silver allowed some to profit more than others, it also helped
to integrate the provinces of empire. It was, in fact, with silver that Spain
enjoyed its greatest successes. Part of the reform impetus stemmed of
course from increased competition in the Atlantic. For the Spanish, to
compete meant protecting Cuba, their jewel in the Caribbean. That entailed money for beefing up the navy, supplying colonial militias, and rebuilding colonial forts. Remittances of silver mined in New Spain and in
Peru paid for defense of the empire, in particular the Caribbean. With
time, New Spain would take on the lion's share of the imperial burden,
and it would be considered "a silver metropolis." Because competition
continued apace, the demand for silver from New Spain grew dramatically,
tightening the bonds between it and Cuba in the meantime.[37]

Reform could create a zero-sum dynamic between regions. Some
places thrived, while others languished. The Spanish case illustrates how
this also happened within regions. Reform usually revealed deep-seated
provincial divisions. The Spanish first learned this lesson in Quito, where
textile producers suffered because of reform measures. Here, tax increases
led to violence. More concerted resistance took place in New Spain,
where tobacco farmers also revolted over being squeezed by their provincial betters, once those at the center demanded more revenue. In this
case, authorities were able to negotiate a compromise. And those same

Natives on the Caribbean coast of South America who traded with all comers burned and looted settlements and missions when Spanish authorities tried to crack down on illicit trade.[38]

In the late 1770s and early 1780s, more ominous rebellions continued to grow in intensity in the Andes. Here locals were beginning to rise up in more coordinated fashion against tax collectors and merchants. Both were now exacting more than ever. This was the region that had lost out to Buenos Aires. Reform in this instance became a "detonator," and protests reported earlier began to coalesce.[39] A number of larger rebellions engulfed whole regions. Those who acted as go-betweens between Natives and local elites styled themselves rebel leaders, even taking their names from Indigenous legends. Some, such as insurgents who besieged La Paz, tried to recover a mythic peasant Indigenous past. For some that meant reimagining a future of self-determination. As a rule, local insurgencies did not aim for independence, even if they led to mass politicization.[40]

What was most worrying for creole elites was that the Andean rebel leader, Túpac Amaru II, suggested that Blacks, Natives, and mestizos should band together. Moreover, those in the rebel movement began to embrace, like those confederated with Pontiac in North America, a common Native past. The parallels between the two movements a continent away are striking. They both were stirred by reform, and those on the receiving end of reform programs reverted to imagined pasts to bind groups together. In the process people were mobilized.[41] Only the scale differed dramatically. The Túpac Amaru rebellion involved many more people. Ultimately, insurgents believed that their marginalization stemmed from rapacious Spaniards. Beginning in Cuzco, rebels attacked the estates of leading creoles, though they took issue with Bourbon reforms. For all their mixed motives, this much was clear: the rebellion was set off by reform and the ways the tax loads on Natives increased.[42]

Officials tried to contain much of the violence, but there is no doubt that people in Peru had been politicized by reform. Soon, the south fell under rebel control. Disturbingly, from the Spanish perspective, the hub of the rebellion was Potosi, the empire's great source of silver. Interestingly, though, rebels did not seek to create republics or to claim the rights that stirred those figures transfixed with the Enlightenment. They rebelled in the name of the king against innovators and to restore an old order. This unrest created turmoil and large-scale violence in two large regions. It necessitated the dispatch of thousands of troops. But it did not imperil the state. In some places, a creole elite would not let that happen. In others, especially the lower Andes beset by an Indigenous insurrection, elites tried to but could not crush a resistance. So, wisely, they relented. This episode would not spell the end of resistance movements in the Andes, even if more than a hundred thousand insurgents lost their lives.[43]

Although reform measures did not achieve all that the Spanish authorities hoped for and dreamt of, they revealed two sets of tensions: those that spanned the ocean and those within creole societies. The first tension was evident throughout Spanish America. Subjects in New Granada, for instance, who relied on smuggling to find a fit in the Atlantic economy and whose sense of community depended on it, took up arms and resisted Bourbon attempts to quash illicit trade. In the short-lived uprising that took place at the same time as the Túpac Amaru rebellion, rebels claimed to protect what they regarded as traditional privileges, and they saw reform as a refutation of an older understanding that had obtained between center and periphery. Led by creole elites, insurgents marched on Bogotá demanding officials undo the most vexing reforms that impinged on their liberties and their ability to exploit the Atlantic. They did not seek independence. They did not march for revolution. They believed old systems of accommodation had broken down and hoped to remake what had been lost or forgotten. The so-called Comunero Rebellion was squashed as soon as troops could be raised to put it down. But there is no doubt that reform set it off.[44]

The second tension demonstrates how reform created tangles of its own. Reforms and changes sometimes threatened the rights creoles held dear; nonetheless, these same creoles always had to weigh potential threats from below, particularly if the masses became politicized.[45] Quito offers an example of the balance that creoles had to strike. In 1765—as we shall see, an important year for the fortunes of British imperial reform and for Britain's American subjects—wealthy property owners and clergy fought to suppress an anti-tax demonstration that was taking the form of a popular insurrection. They did so, but only local authority had saved the colonial administration from grave difficulties.[46]

These varied episodes point out how creoles with a stake in society often opted for order over autonomy. There was nothing unusual about provincials pushing back once metropolitan officials reformed. Nor was there anything out of the ordinary as provincials redefined themselves vis-à-vis the center. In South America in the wake of reform measures, creoles were apt to consider themselves "American" and opposed to

"Spanish." They protested and rioted for established ways of doing things and for the freedom to benefit from what the Atlantic had to offer. Better conceived of as a process, the give-and-take between the periphery and the center constituted parts of a broader calculus of what the state could or could not do and would or would not do.[47] Yet, elites in imperial peripheries always weighed pushback against other, more elemental concerns. They had good reason to fear race war or ethnic conflict. Creoles knew that their status depended on historical oppressions or the exclusion of peoples from the political nation. This applied for Ireland's Ascendancy, elites in Peru and Mexico, and even wealthy merchants in Belgium.

All in all, through complex negotiations and trade-offs, the Spanish had managed to contain any potential broader imperial crisis, not by design but by doing what the variegated tensions of empire allowed. The complex back-and-forth that defined the reform process for them would set the table for a Spanish resurgence of sorts in the Atlantic. Silver from Peru and increasingly from Mexico shored up the treasury. The autonomy of creoles and remittances from the "imperial tax state," both key features of Bourbon reform measures, far from imperiling empire, allowed Spain to remain a power on the world stage. To the loser belonged these spoils, even as growing unrest from below suggested choppy sailing ahead.[48]

For a complete appreciation of the pitfalls of ignoring the rules of reform, we have to look to the British. The winners of the War for the Atlantic World, in fact, initiated the most thorough set of reforms of all imperial powers. They had good reason to. The costs of victory were high. Though they had won the war, managing space and debt presented dramatic challenges. Beginning in 1763, officials debated how they should approach both issues. These discussions would confront creole elites an ocean away with unpalatable choices. The British case, as the Spanish and Portuguese examples also suggest, reveals another important lesson about reform: it affected all but always centered on the fears and hopes of elites.

Those at the center seemed certain of one thing, and in this regard William Pitt was part of a chorus: sovereignty for an oceanic empire had to reside in Parliament. This institution, more than, say, the Crown, had become legitimate enough at home and efficacious enough throughout the British Isles to lead officials to believe that its authority could be extended across an ocean. This assertion was sure to cause a stir. Though Parliament had legislated for the colonies before, it did not have clear jurisdiction to govern far-off plantations. Most settlements, after all, had been established under the authority of the Crown. Precedent to the contrary, with victory over the French in the war, Parliament, all in the center assumed, was the only institution up to the task. Many provincials would have other ideas.[49]

The questions those at the center faced were urgent. Because of the need to raise money to service the debt and to control far-flung territories in the face of increased competition, should reformers centralize empire? Should they have it garrisoned? Should Parliament tax the colonists to address the debt issue? Should a broad structure be created that could answer the concerns of all? Should colonists, now considering themselves provincials, claim the rights of those at the center? Should Parliament federate power? In other words, the British faced the same sorts of questions that all expanding powers did, and the specific answers Pitt proposed proved just one of a number. One thing was certain for all: they had to be answered. This process, too, was sure to cause a stir.

In the British case, reform packages merged distinctively British traditions with newer Enlightenment ideas. Britons believed, as did all Europeans, that empire posed all sorts of difficult problems, especially in light of the economic and social changes wrought by consolidation. British officials wondered how *imperium* could or should be balanced with *libertas*. Liberty, the watchword of British identity, had much greater purchase now that so many people were empowered though mobility, both geographic and upward, generated by Atlantic consolidation. Creoles in the provinces, especially, valued liberty. They had benefited most tangibly through freedom from state interference to pursue the happiness that entanglements conferred. Now Britons suggested that Parliament could protect liberty, so long as it did so with an eye toward progress. On this theme, many eyes turned to Scotland. Through the work of well-networked scholars, the Scots advocated a notion that societies could march through successive developmental stages, eventuating in the creation of polite and commercial societies. The state, then, could play a role in fostering such development for the whole, so long as the balance between libertas and imperium held and so long as everyone accepted Parliament as the seat of sovereignty. Or so officials convinced themselves.[50]

The merger of older and newer ideas mediated by Parliament, all glued together by wishful thinking, sustained the first tangible and the most comprehensive attempts to map sovereignty onto the Atlantic. The program was first clearly manifest with the Stamp Act. Parliament passed the act in 1765 to raise money to keep troops on North American soil.

Most assumed, quite reasonably, that it would just be a matter of time until France sought to win back what it had lost. The measure mandated that official documents and everyday items like newspapers be printed on stamped paper for which a duty would be paid. In passing it, Parliament assumed that sovereignty quite naturally had to extend from itself, that it was the only institution capable of reforming empire. Other measures passed from this point forward pointed to the same set of assumptions: Parliament had to integrate the Atlantic politically; and the provinces in North America had to effectively be made part of the state.[51] To those officials who promoted measures like the Stamp Act and later the Townshend Duties, which placed duties on certain goods imported from the metropole, it appeared self-evident that Parliament had to treat the colonies like Roman provinces. The so-called Declaratory Act, though passed by a group that considered taxing the colonists anathema and that included Burke, nevertheless established the notion that Parliament could pass laws for the colonists "in all cases whatsoever."[52]

These acts are best construed as moves designed to rationalize power in the Atlantic. Parliament passed laws in these years designed to regulate entanglements as well. Some measures like the Sugar Act enforced old laws on the books. This law would crack down on that chief manifestation of Atlantic entanglement: illicit trade.[53] Ministers designed others, like the Townshend Duties, to shore up those offices that oversaw trade and regulated it. Yet other measures spoke directly to the issue of control of watery space. As early as 1758, one British official argued that the state could no longer tolerate "usurpations." America had become too important to the British economy, and entanglements could bring further war, but if managed properly, prosperity to the center.[54] Indeed, the first postwar act Parliament passed for the colonies—the Customs Enforcement Act—targeted trading abuses and empowered naval officers to act as customs officials. The measure recognized the severity of the problem, one that had grown through wartime smuggling.[55]

Officials intended to engage the process of integration and aimed to have the state profit from it. Legislation and plans by the Board of Trade addressed the unregulated movement of goods, the entanglements, and the unfettered movements of people from one place to the other. A little-known measure highlights how British officials were viewing things differently from before. The Board of Trade hoped to encourage the development of Nova Scotia because, it was hoped, the place—and the trade from it—could be integrated into the prevailing system of political economy. Yet when promoters proposed settling Irish Protestants there, the board vetoed the move, worrying that their leaving would increase tensions in Ireland. The empire, officials began to see, had to be a system as well, and it needed to operate that way to match the changes of the Atlantic. All was meant to bring method to the madness of integration, to help the state balance the budget, to use central authority to keep Britain clear of the entanglements that could lead to war, and—last but not least—to govern America. Officials set their sights especially on those creole elites—merchants and speculators—who used entanglements to enrich themselves.[56]

This does not mean that the British wanted to revert to what we could call simple mercantilist models of political economy. Officials expected to harness and regulate the Atlantic's potential, not stem it. They recognized that though they officially embraced mercantilist ideals about trade, they could not halt interimperial trade. In fact, they did not want to halt it. So while the urgency of the moment impelled officials to design acts to curtail provincial wealth generation, it also pushed them to come up with newer ways of addressing the possibilities of the moment. The Free Port Act of 1766, for instance, created a number of free trading centers in the Caribbean that could skirt the rules imposed by the Navigation Acts, allowing, for instance, the exportation of enslaved persons to other European powers. While state authorities would police North America to ensure that the center benefited from foreign trade, they freed up some merchants in the Caribbean to work across imperial lines. Smuggling, once transformed into licit trade, could benefit the state.[57] Critically, Parliament and the Board of Trade would direct, manage, and exploit—all from the center—even ongoing entanglements. The free port idea was geared for profit and for competition. It was designed to tie up the slave economies of rivals to British traders and to break the Dutch in the Caribbean.[58]

In other words, British Atlantic reform would impose a clear sense of sovereignty and authority on the whole. The sovereign power of the center, Parliament, nearly all these acts announced, would now run the show. Reformers also believed that subordinating colonies would prove the only means to ensuring that virtue flourished for empire. The vision incorporated all regions. At the same moment that officials hoped to use the tool of parliamentary sovereignty to bind the colonies more closely to the metropole, they also saw that the near margins of Scotland and Ireland could provide the necessary manpower to garrison the empire.

Not surprisingly, more than half of British troops came from these places.[59]

Of all the European powers, therefore, the victors of the war devised and, more important, were able to implement serially the most far-reaching and invasive reform measures. They did so because the stakes had become so high and the need to raise revenue so pressing. And because victory in what was regarded as a pivotal moment was intoxicating. They also had a few advantages and a distinctive impetus. Their colonial holdings in the New World were not as complex, extensive, and well developed as, say, Spain's. Spanish holdings far outstripped those of Britain.[60] Moreover, the costs of victory and the reach of the state separated the British from the rest. Through war making on a global scale, the state had the capacity to act, to make good on what was promulgated. That capacity did not allow the state to do whatever it wanted. It still encountered limits. But even these could be addressed by reform. To cite just one example, the American west proved a difficult space to manage, especially in the wake of earlier rebellions against centralized authority, like Pontiac's War. Officials realized they could not project power to these far peripheries effectively without incurring greater debt. They therefore decided in 1763 to hive off the west from the east by running a line through the wilderness over which they would not allow settlers and speculators to venture, what they called the Proclamation Line. Beyond it, the army would keep a low profile and so allow Natives some level of autonomy. The measure would stop the untrammeled movement of men and women that had become one of the troubling features of the Atlantic. To the east of the line, the site of established colonial governments, they would pull their subjects into the nation, and for these people they would pass laws, enact taxing measures, try to create structures and institutions that would allow for centralized control, and dispatch troops if need be to ensure that subjects acquiesced.[61]

Why the British achieved what they did illustrates the reasons other Atlantic empires had to rein in their ambitions. For the French, Portuguese, and Spanish, reform, of course, took more modest forms, for the very same reasons the British had to apply more robust measures. The French case was really not surprising. France held the most profitable plot of land in the world, and reforms that increased the autonomy and wealth of planters there and merchants at home served everyone's purposes, except perhaps those of the state's treasuries. Loss, however, had shrunken empire, or at least grand pretensions of a vast Atlantic empire.

The Spanish case presents greater complexity. On paper, the administrative divisions into audiencias and viceroyalties suggested both an understanding of the importance of centralized authority and the wherewithal to see it through. In fact, the extent of their holdings and the sophistication of creole societies in America, and the resulting tensions, would make centralization a far more challenging task for the Spanish than it did for the British. The Portuguese, by default, had to recognize the growing asymmetry of their empire, that a Brazilian tail was beginning to wag the imperial dog. Reform, therefore, could go only so far in these cases.

The Portuguese, French, and Spanish enjoyed one advantage the British did not. They did not become entangled in the reform script. They heeded it, even if they did so with difficulty and reluctantly. But not the British. With the state acting as never before, a great debate both within and outside British governing circles was taking place on the implications of reform and of empire. Reform measures encouraged all to ask in this new age how the center should govern the whole. In Portugal, France, and Spain, because of more modestly proportioned measures, questions centered on the sovereignty of the whole did not arise, at least at this time. Most critically, while modest reform in these empires ensured that provincial elites bought into empire, in the British case centralizing reform threatened to alienate creoles. The French, Portuguese, and Spanish, therefore, avoided the ideological thickets that would ensnare the British.

And ensnare, of course, they did. Britain's American subjects reacted with determination once Parliament passed the Stamp Act and the Townshend Duties, letting their thoughts be known through rioting and principled argumentation. Nothing unusual here. In fact, we could liken such resistance to the Comunero Revolt in New Granada. America's rebels did not want revolution or independence. Benjamin Franklin argued that Americans felt aggrieved because a "thread" of both affection and commerce had bound them to Britain.[62] Nonetheless, reform packages spurred them to consider their status within empire. With the Stamp Act and Townshend Duties protests, colonists argued that they, too, should enjoy the rights of those in the metropole and refused to think of themselves as second-class subjects. They wanted to enjoy the Atlantic as it was when it was becoming a system. They resisted. Parliament pressed further.

Pushing back was not necessarily novel. In fact, the ways American creoles gave voice to their concerns, through riots and resolutions, did not differ from the way other provincials in the British Isles had acted when

Parliament had tried to claim authority over them. Irish and Scottish subjects had a long history of principled resistance to English incursions on their rights. What Americans were engaged in amounted to the negotiation phase of reform, albeit a robust version, over how power would be articulated in the new Atlantic. They pressed for their autonomy. They had grown accustomed to it, and the freedom it conferred ensured that they could continue to take advantage of the spoils of the Atlantic without having to bear the burdens of imperial sovereignty. The Scots and the Irish in the past had also weighed such considerations. So, too, did French subjects in Saint-Domingue and Spanish subjects in Peru.[63]

One writer in particular was able to crystalize the bind Americans found themselves in. Styling himself "Farmer from Pennsylvania," John Dickinson laid out the stakes of what the colonies were addressing as one act after another was passed. Parliament was making Americans second-class subjects in the empire, and it was acting in ways it should and could not: marginalizing Americans in a society they had created. Parliament had no rights over them. American colonies had been created under the Crown. Parliamentary interference in provincial affairs represented an unprecedented innovation. Yes, Parliament, he conceded, could regulate for empire; it could not legislate for colonies. As the press from colony to colony published his letters, Dickinson proved a catalyst for appreciating the nature of what was happening. All attention now centered on the state.[64] Because it did, this reform process threatened to open the lid of a Pandora's box, a lid the French, Portuguese, and Spanish creoles had managed to keep shut.

Opening the box began as American creoles dealt with their transatlantic predicaments. As each metropolitan move led to provincial counter-move, which brought on a counter-countermove from the center, it was clear that reform brought men and women in the colonies back to first principles, principles most would rather have forgotten about. How was power distributed? Why did some groups enjoy privileged status? How had settlers acquired land, and who would labor on it? In other words, the longer and more insistently provincials pushed back, the more fully they confronted the tensions that lay beneath the surface and the power relations that animated them. All societies have such demons lurking, and these relate to the distribution of power and the historical injustices that had determined that distribution; but in most instances, men and women take these issues for granted, ignore them, and fail to grapple with them. With thorough reform, and the dance of move and countermove that the

British initiated in the late 1760s and early 1770s, no one could deny or dodge such questions. They had to be addressed.[65]

The questions were locally inflected if universally shared by American creoles. Virginia planters wanted to ease the burden of debt to British merchants. They resisted tax measures because debt imperiled their status in the empire and their control at home. These men valued their independence, and entanglements had seen them become indebted to British merchants. However ambivalent they may have been about the ways Atlantic trade immiserated them, they did not want it to stop. They certainly did not want to be taxed. Their status at home and control over their slave labor depended on the Atlantic. Philadelphia merchants wanted to expand their trade. They became vigorous supporters of an unregulated Atlantic, even if they had to admit that many in the city were languishing in the postwar economy. They could discern tensions within the city on the horizon. The same went for well-connected Bostonians. They wanted to halt the stagnation of their port town. Integration had helped some of the wealthy become wealthier, just as it had driven others to the poorhouse. Popular protests against the Stamp Act and the Townshend Duties in the city revealed how divided the city had become. South Carolinians wanted to maintain the slave trade and control over their captive workforce on their own terms. New Yorkers wanted to keep trading with all comers, just as they had before and during the war, allowing many to maintain wealth and status in an increasingly stratified city. As Parliament passed new laws, all these groups experienced what we could call a provincial dilemma that was both Atlantic-wide and local in nature. The dilemma took on a political cast once reform measures were on the table. The particulars of the binds each group of creoles faced informed the limits of resistance.[66]

Reform had created a provincial confluence to resist reform. Yet each of the debates necessitated discussions of the basis of power in each society, between haves and have-nots in some places, and between the enslaved and the free in others. In the past, in the days before reform, provincial status did not chafe or bind. Ambiguity, the uncertainty over who or what really ruled, had allowed the colonists to have the conceit of enjoying "the best of all possible worlds," as Voltaire's character Pangloss would say. They could have their autonomy and the fruits of Atlantic entanglements, too. Clarity promised an end or an attenuation of both. It did so by thrusting the colonists onto the horns of the provincial dilemma.[67]

Under normal circumstances—and let's return to the primer—provincial anxiety and resistance led either to coercion or to acquiescence on the part of the state. In this instance, it led to neither. The reason is simple. Americans had one important advantage the other British provincials did not: distance. Projecting authority to North America and across much of a continent an ocean away, enough to police cities and ensure subjects respected parliamentary measures, meant more men and more money. Sending troops to Ireland and Scotland cost little; in fact, barrack systems existed in both, and troops regularly rotated through the kingdoms. Such was the case to keep any sort of mischief or rebellion at bay. British officials did send troops in 1768 to Boston, but just enough to enflame tensions rather than resolve them. The ministry soon reversed course and withdrew the troops in the wake of the Boston Massacre, when occupying troops opened fire and killed civilians. Distance made the task of maintaining order in America that much more difficult, even as it was becoming more urgent.[68]

What, then, made Americans tip? What made them cast caution to the wind and gamble that they could manage the many tensions now erupting through reform? Part of the answer is "design." To Americans, British reform initiatives took on the cast of a troubling pattern, as one reform measure followed another. They believed, and in this they were right, that Parliament meant to subordinate them. They convinced themselves that they would not come into the empire as equals with those in the Old World. The patterning of events as measure followed measure convinced them that they and the British could find no middle ground. Distance allowed Americans—in fact, gave them the imaginative space—to articulate this pattern and to resist. If the British would have been able to send sufficient troops, encouraging most to realize that resistance was futile, things may well have calmed down.[69]

The other reason is just as simple. Americans were relatively free of existential fears. This encouraged them to push back. Just compare Americans to others in the British orbit. For Americans, the hated and dreaded French, those bogeys to the north, had left. In Ireland, such was not the case, nor would it be. Members of the Ascendancy worried about Catholics in their midst, who made up three-quarters of the population. Though churchmen controlled the levers of power, the connection to Britain, and the fact that troops could be barracked in Ireland, guaranteed not only their supremacy in the kingdom but also their basic security. To be sure, Protestant patriots used the moment, too, to press British officials for greater autonomy for the kingdom in much the same way Americans were doing. Yet, for all the sound and fury, they had no doubt that the British connection guaranteed their enjoyment of life, liberty, and property. For all their gesturing over provincial autonomy, they dared not sever the link with Britain.[70] The Scots found themselves in similar straits. Though Highlanders had attached themselves more securely to the state, especially through military service, their rebellions against established authority remained fixed in the memory of Lowlanders and the English to their south. The army kept a presence in the Highlands, but the potential of rebellion determined that most Scots understood that union with England had more benefits than costs. The Caribbean colonists also experienced a similar dilemma—whites, that is. Planters needed authority to keep their "other" under control: the enslaved in their midst. Understandably, they tended to acquiesce to measures such as the Stamp Act.[71]

Britain's North American subjects, the white ones, did not harbor such fears. Even planters in South Carolina argued from a position of confidence. Such was not the case for creole elites in the Andes, overwhelmed by revolt from those below, or of planters in Saint-Domingue, who, like whites in the British Caribbean, feared slave rebellion. Americans walked a fine line few would or could at this juncture. Still devoted to the Crown, they leveled arguments rooted in their rights as free-born subjects to contest what Parliament hoped to do. People from places like Boston that had at first grown through the process of integration and then stagnated became the most ardent opponents of parliamentary reform measures. Not surprisingly, those who had to weigh the costs and benefits of integration and reform more carefully, such as South Carolina planters, proved more cautious. But eventually they too would see the virtues of greater autonomy, once they became convinced of their ability to control their captive workforce.[72]

As in the Spanish case, British reform occasioned complex responses even in areas far removed from the provincial centers of power, with the same destabilizing results. For instance, reform posed complex threats to Native communities. With France gone, Native groups did the best they could to stave off domination by the British. And the British relented in the wake of Pontiac's War. But as pressures mounted from the east because of the fallout from reform there, officials waffled with the west. Soon British officials in America proposed bending the Proclamation Line in ways that compromised the Cherokees and the Shawnees. More to the point, the British buckled because of unrelenting pressure from speculators, both the well connected in the colonies and some in Britain. Natives, then, faced difficult choices over how they would respond when it became clear that the British would or could do little in fact to protect their homelands.[73]

The pressures led to fractures within groups. They also generated new possibilities for bonding together. For some, generational struggle within Indigenous communities would define the day. Cherokees, for instance, began breaking apart over approaches to reform measures. Older leaders argued for accommodation. Others countered that resistance amounted to the only viable option. As was the case with the Osage farther to the west, those espousing this view tended to be younger. The same was happening to the Shawnees, but the results differed. Once their dilemma became clear, they began to seek out other nations to create their own confederations. Shawnees looked to Cherokees to revive the sort of confederacy that had been forged in the time of Pontiac. Calls for unity were some of the fruits of reform in the Ohio Country. Shawnees and those they lived among, such as the Delaware, made it clear that they would resist further incursions on their land and that they deemed agreements made without their consent invalid, such as those hammered out by Crown officials with the Iroquois. This should all sound familiar. The same home-rule/rule-at-home tug-of-war that ensnared white colonists in the east, began to define the lives of Natives in the west.[74]

Reform, just as we could expect, revealed and exacerbated fault lines, but once metropolitans refused to relent, it placed local elites in existential binds very much like those creoles experienced in Peru and in New Granada. In Boston, for instance, those who had been left behind by integration and those struggling with a postwar recession resented the merchants who had enriched themselves through smuggling. In fact, when unrest gripped the city with the reform measures of the mid-1760s, the poorer sort vented their anger on their betters. But they did so in a way that played into the growing crisis over home rule. Ultimately, they allied themselves with merchants such as John Hancock to confront home-grown officials like Thomas Hutchinson. Boston was not an outlier. All places had their tensions that could erupt if order broke down. In other areas, race represented the most salient fault line, and planters were highly conscious of the potential combustibility of the category. In still other places, ethnicity created concerns. What kept tensions in check, in the absence of effective governmental control, was the fact that so many people channeled energies against the state. This may have threatened the central authority of empire; nonetheless, it also ensured that tensions did not explode.[75]

In a response to reform we would see throughout the Atlantic with time, American colonists articulated their fears, and even their hopes, by arguing about what made them British and what made them American. As sovereignty was cracking, some writers created an imagined past in which settlers had, without help of those in the metropole, fought Natives, or "savages" as they called them, to turn a state of nature into a state of society. What Parliament was threatening to do was turn back the settlers' developmental clock. Colonists could claim that they were acting now to protect their self-interests in resisting the destabilizing reform measures of Parliament, measures that disrupted what had been won by their ancestors.[76] The use of such arguments suggests that Americans were engaged in what we could call creole rebellion against established authority.

On the edges, therefore, the first cracks in imperial sovereignty became evident.[77] The cracks had always existed, but Atlantic consolidation widened and deepened them. The reform measures that followed brought them to the surface. Perhaps the British could have left well enough alone and heeded the advice of the statesman Edmund Burke to undo any designs on America and embrace the status quo ante, what he famously called the era of "salutary neglect." Given the imperatives of the age, tinged with a sense of urgency and the heightened competition around the world, such proved impossible. The British could not let America go.

What happened after the failure of reform is the stuff of history books. Repeated attempts to integrate the empire through reform followed by refusal to give in to provincials resulted in secession and concomitant civil war within the empire. We normally call this state of affairs the American Revolution.[78] The litany of events that led to American independence is well known. The crisis took on the cast of inevitability as event followed event, falling into a seemingly inexorable pattern. The year 1774 marked the moment of ultimate break. Events in that long year, lasting from the last months of 1773 to the first of 1775, sorted men and women into diametrically opposed groups and pushed many past the brink. In that stretch of time, Parliament passed the Tea Act to save the East India Company from bankruptcy. In the process, Parliament targeted those provincials who made their money from selling the tea of all nations to consumers. The act began a train of events that led to the so-called Tea Party, when Boston's self-styled Sons of Liberty threw the tea shipped to Boston into the harbor. They dressed as Natives, suggesting that they were now beginning to embrace an American identity. This move then set off a series of British countermoves, one more provocative than the next, to drive the Americans back into the imperial fold. Parliament passed a number of measures called the Coercive Acts, which American referred to as the Intolerable Acts. These, among other things, closed the port of Boston pending payment for all the tea cast overboard. Bostonians lost the right to govern themselves as well. To add insult to injury, Parliament also decided to address the growing chaos out west, and unseemly land grabs in the offing, by placing much of the Ohio River Valley under the jurisdiction of Quebec. Americans, these acts announced, would not be able to take advantage of what the Atlantic or the Continent had to offer. But it was all too late. Britain's sovereignty had effectively ended, witnessed by the way Americans throughout the colonies were banding together to help the beleaguered Bostonians. Americans through their local and now intercolonial assembly, the Continental Congress, were beginning to do the stuff of government. Then, of course, shots rang out in Lexington and Concord. . . .[79]

Rather than reciting in detail how the Stamp Act/Townshend crisis led to the Boston Massacre, and then the Tea Act, to the Tea Party, to the Intolerable or Coercive Acts, and finally armed engagements—the list that led seemingly inexorably to revolution—we should consider what these episodes meant. They represented the first instance of faltering sovereignty in an Atlantic age, when it was becoming clear that metropolitan plans could not effectively manage the many tensions that had emerged through consolidation. Other Atlantic powers left well enough alone when they experienced provincial pushback. On balance, they recognized the limits of their power, a sensibility driven home by loss in the War for the Atlantic. The British did not. Only then did things fall apart.[80]

They did so in two ways. First, the empire began to collapse. Second, this one part of the British Empire that was breaking off was also tearing apart at its seams. Reform set off both crises. By 1776, recognition of this twinned dynamic had become "common sense" to many, to cite Thomas Paine's famous catalyzing pamphlet published in that year. As much as Burke's invocation of "salutary neglect," Paine's simple observation about the plight of Americans within empire at this moment pointed out in the starkest terms what reform had wrought and what it had revealed. Given the transatlantic and local pressures evident to all, independence at this juncture indeed appeared to be commonsensical to enough men and women for creole elites to declare it a goal. For growing numbers, remaining in the empire would not quell disorder or address the larger concerns about America's relationship to a changing Atlantic.

The Declaration of Independence illustrates how the crises over home rule and rule at home, both initiated by imperial reform, intertwined. The Declaration, at its core, represented a realization in print form of how Britain's sovereignty was failing on the margins of its empire and how America had descended into an uncertain state. To be sure, the Declaration lists grievance after grievance justifying why Americans could and should break away, but it does more than this. It tells the world of the state of affairs in these newly formed united states once British sovereignty teetered. The Crown in Parliament could no longer protect its subjects, and this failure had plunged Americans into a state of nature necessitating a new social contract. Into the vacuum of power now stepped citizens conscious of the need to restore order lest the tensions that were emerging through the sovereignty crisis lead to further strain. The crisis set off by reform forced all Americans—Native and settler, white and Black, male and female—to confront pasts as they reckoned with power in the present and how it would be articulated in the future.[81]

The complex and entangled series of breakdowns that reform precipitated, a drama that would be played out across the rest of the Atlantic world with time, would fracture American societies along their fault lines. Revolution followed independence. As British authority faltered, men and women, many for the first time, were playing the role of actors. Common men served in local administrations, on committees of correspondence, and in conventions, those provincial institutions set up to fill the void left by the loss of sovereign authority. Whites were not the only ones who played a role. The enslaved used the opportunities afforded by unrest to run away or to join British lines and fight. Natives, especially young men, saw an opportunity for rolling back white settlement in frontier regions. Ultimately, as sovereignty cracked, some stepped in to create institutions for maintaining some semblance of order in a society breaking apart along fault lines. Yet some also saw the chaos of a society adrift as a singular opportunity for freedom. The ideas they heard and articulated encouraged them to grasp it. Quite understandably, *Robinson Crusoe* became one of the best sellers in the colonies at the time, but not because of how it spoke to entanglements. By 1776, the novel's plot, which saw a man struggling in a state of nature, alone in the world, while trying to figure out his relationship with an enslaved man, Friday, spoke powerfully to the plight the colonists found themselves in in the gray space between sovereignty and anarchy.[82]

This does not mean that liberation was in the offing. The impulse for independence did not effectuate revolutionary change, even if one served as precursor to the other. The role of women in the colonies is a case in point. As the crisis unfolded, women stood on the front lines, asserting themselves at the very edge of prescribed bounds. They led subscription drives for nonimportation agreements. They preached the nonconsumption of British goods, especially tea. As authority was faltering, they policed patriotic sentiment and demonstrated the classical republican notion of virtue by what they did and did not do. To put their money where their mouths were, they wove homespun and brewed substitutes for tea. They had become as enmeshed as any persons in the process, both of independence and later of revolution. They did so by engaging both through the work they did, whether they supported home rule or contested it, whether wealthy or poor. All participated.[83]

Though they would play critical roles in society while their husbands went away to fight, women did not seek to overturn gender norms or patriarchal conventions. Nevertheless, in the process of becoming actors they were changing their prescribed roles, especially as the crisis over home rule dragged on and touched on questions of who was to rule at home. They were moving political activity from the home to the outside world. This process would only be heightened once America was thrown into revolutionary tumult.[84] The result would be both subtle and profound. Challenges to the imperial status quo and to patriarchy, part of a broader story that would be played out throughout the Atlantic, revealed the beginnings of a shift from arbitrary rule.[85] This change started with the complex response to reform.

We see with the failure to heed the reform primer another theme that would be replayed throughout the Atlantic in the following years. With war and revolution came traumatizing and enlivening uncertainty that reform unwittingly unleashed. Some experienced euphoria at the possibilities of change. Others wrestled with fear. The area around New York City, more or less equally divided between patriots and Loyalists, experienced years of appalling violence and unrest. The same goes for much of the south. Neighbor killed neighbor, settling old scores and using the war as a pretext to fight for control of local communities. The enslaved used the chaos of the moment to declare their independence. Even those places that were not divided between the two competing programs for sovereignty, like much of New England, endured a coercive occupation by patriot forces. The bark of some of the communities that policed New England could be worse than their bite; nonetheless, the group that could claim the mantle of sovereignty determined the standards of any community. Although Americans after 1775 would be engaged in a long war lasting until 1781, they were also caught up in an uncertain process that hinged on who could reestablish sovereignty after it had effectively collapsed. The faltering of sovereignty could and did initiate extraordinary violence, just as it occasioned hope and fear. Without certain sovereignty, all became cacophony.[86]

Throughout the 1770s and 1780s, after the collapse of British power in the American part of its empire, men and women were playing roles they were not accustomed to. This applied to white colonists, men and women, to Natives, and to the enslaved. Caging the furies would prove vexing. As people became actors, older established ways were brought into further disrepute. Deference as a strategy had less salience. The world of British North America, once the process of revolution began, was being turned upside down. Ironically, the state that had seemed poised to reform its Atlantic the most comprehensively found itself bound up in such confounding conundrums.[87]

Not all throughout the Atlantic fell apart. Ironically, it was those empires that seemed the weakest and had been the most retrograde, the Spanish and the Portuguese, that withstood the tensions from imperial crisis. Reform was tried, but because state capacity was not as developed, reforms were not expansive, and metropolitan authorities could not comprehensively foist programs on the peripheries. Creole elites could live with what they and those in the metropole negotiated together, and they were wise to do so. In fact, as the British struggled, many Spanish and Portuguese creole elites enjoyed autonomy, the support of the metropole, and in most cases control of their own societies. We could almost call their experience, playing on Burke's famous phrase, one of "salutary engagement." At this moment, in any event, they had solved the dilemma that had pushed those creoles living in North America toward rebellion. Or, better, they had averted it.[88]

Though all construed this as a moment that required urgent action if empires were to be able to compete in this new Atlantic world, the one nation that was able to realize this possibility, to meet the moment, saw its empire fall apart. The crisis, after all, did not stem from the difficulty of imposing a set of political structures on a geographic space that had been woven together through trade and culture but came from the hubristic belief that such a difficult task could be managed. Revolution started with British officials and their belief that they could regulate the world's tensions and harness them for the state. At the first instance of the revolutionary era, Britain found itself confronting provincials who contested this conceit. France, Spain, and Portugal muddled through, in the process turning the necessity of provincial autonomy into the virtue of sovereign flexibility. They would survive, and even thrive, at this moment.

The collapse of sovereignty in the wake of failed reform revealed one last rule of reform. Creoles in British North America and throughout the rest of the Atlantic, as a provincial people, were necessarily a people of paradox: anti-imperial when it came to the metropole and imperial when it came to dominance at home. This paradox, the manifestation of Atlantic systematization, structured choices and determined action.[89] And because of metropolitan strength or weakness, both actual and perceived, different creoles negotiated this paradox in different ways. For North Americans, independence now became the answer. In South America, not yet.

The "yet" matters. The British experienced a more accelerated version of what all would experience in the coming years because they went to the end of the reforming script when and where all became tangled. Others stopped acting at some earlier point, just before the climax or, depending on perspective, the precipice. Nonetheless, the British present would become the Atlantic world's prologue. Because of the very nature of that deeply networked system, shock waves could not be contained. The Atlantic world was so imbricated that it was folly to believe that one crisis over sovereignty that had turned into revolution would remain isolated. The logic of the system would not allow it. What followed would with time demonstrate just how knotted the world had become.

# CHAPTER THREE

# The French Connection

## *The Hope of Revolution*

DID THOMAS JEFFERSON PERSONIFY the age of revolution? The evidence would suggest he did, but in anything but straightforward ways. Jefferson built his great estate Monticello in Virginia as an homage to enlightened thought and, of course, he wrote the Declaration of Independence. Yet, he was a slave owner and would father children with an enslaved woman, Sally Hemings. He idealized the yeoman farmer, whose virtue, he believed, stood as the only sure means of guaranteeing that the Revolution's spirit would continue to liberate America. "Life, liberty, and the pursuit of happiness" could belong to Americans, so long as they maintained their independence. Yet, Jefferson also served as architect of American expansion westward and the displacement of Natives. For Americans, he remains a puzzle.[1]

Really, there is nothing surprising or remarkable about what this man represented. Most acknowledge that the age of revolution turned on what we would consider contradictions—remember Dickens—and even people living during the age saw things this way. Yet, focusing exclusively on the period's many paradoxes and disjunctions obscures another feature of the age that Jefferson epitomized: how connectedness defined this world and this period. We must understand, first and foremost, that those caught up in the drama of revolution were trying to give meaning to what they saw happening around them—integration, reform, then dis-integration. And making meaning revolved around making connections. Meaning became imperative because of the ways people tied together events in their minds. We have seen how American colonists did so with the train of acts that Parliament put in place to try to reform the Atlantic. They became revolutionaries once they turned a series of events into what seemed an inexorable pattern. Patterns, though, did not only have to be chronological. Some of these, indeed the most powerful ones, would be geographic. They stemmed from connections across space.

In the period when Americans were fighting for home rule and struggling with the contest to see who would rule at home, they were looking more to connections and continuities than to contradictions and disjunctions. They needed to win a war, and they turned to Britain's great enemy France for aid. Americans had a bit of a love-hate relationship with the "Great Nation." Americans had fought side by side with the British during the War for the Atlantic World against the Catholic French.[2] Now they needed recognition and help, and so diplomatic teams, led by Benjamin Franklin, worked to secure a treaty between the rebels and France. Americans were of two minds in these years of revolutionary intrigue. So was Jefferson, but for more complex reasons. He admired the intellectual culture of France, its rich history, and the vitality of the place. But, ever contradictory, Jefferson also saw another France, a vice-ridden place, a country still in thrall to Catholicism, a nation that ever stood on the edge of despotism. Here were the two aspects of classical political theory— virtue and vice—existing in the same place at the same time.[3] He embraced the cosmopolitan sensibilities of the enlightened, but he always wondered what tolls national inheritances exerted on a people and their ability to change.[4]

His dilemma seemed to resolve itself when France was gripped with revolutionary euphoria. Just as Americans seemed to be bringing some semblance of order to their own society after the war against Britain had been won, Jefferson was in Paris. Here, he witnessed the first stirrings of revolutionary tumult. He was beguiled. When men and women besieged the Bastille, Jefferson saw the possibilities of a new world being born before his eyes, one that included America. The American Revolution and what was happening in France, he thought, represented one single moment of liberation. As he put it, French liberty was critical "to stay up our own" liberty. Perhaps the limitations he saw in America could be rectified through the French example.[5]

So powerful were the connections Jefferson made in his mind that he could even forgive what some thought to be the violent excesses of what was happening in France. Sometimes, he suggested, the ends of a broader revolutionary moment could justify the means employed in France.[6] Even if some innocents died to free France, "the liberty of the whole earth depended on the issue of the contest." He would rather see "half the earth desolated" than revolution in France founder, because what occurred in one place could determine the fate of others. His world was tied together. "I look with great anxiety for the firm establishment of the new government in France," he argued in 1791, "being perfectly convinced that if it takes place there, it will spread sooner or later all over Europe." The United States and France, bound together, could create a new world order. Or so Jefferson hoped.[7]

He was not the only one to fasten on such a connection. The man who would be a great revolutionary leader and radical visionary, the Marquis de Condorcet, became one of his closest associates in Paris. Condorcet published a series of essays in which he claimed to be an American from Philadelphia witnessing France's struggles. He could discern "the Influence of the American Revolution on Europe" and hoped to make France a republican state. He thought it imperative to chart "the influence that the independence of America will have on humanity, on Europe, and particularly on France." As he put it, "The spectacle of the equality which reigns in the United States and which assures their peace and prosperity can be equally useful to Europe." America, he believed, offered an example that France had to follow.[8] The circulation of liberty through Atlantic networks, he and Jefferson believed, lay at the heart of what was happening throughout the Western world.[9]

Dreams of liberation sprang from connection. A writer from England and a member of radical circles, Mary Wollstonecraft, had been invested in the French Revolution from its earliest days. She had written a scathing rebuttal to Burke early on. She saw him almost as women were stereotyped in her day: "the weather-cock of unrestrained feelings." More famously, she wrote *A Vindication of the Rights of Woman*. In pressing for women to leave the condition of "convenient slaves," she was allying herself with Condorcet, who also published a famous tract on that theme. What happened in France entranced her. Progress, Wollstonecraft and others hoped, could finally begin. Humanity had, she figured, "a glorious chance" to obtain "more virtue and happiness than has hitherto blessed our globe." Tellingly, the arguments she made tying virtue to character echoed what

Jefferson had written in the Declaration of Independence. Only with the end of oppression and dependency could character flourish, which could then become the basis of the virtue necessary for a just society. In fact, Wollstonecraft's ability to link the cause of women to that of the enslaved, as Condorcet also did, pointed out the seemingly paradoxical position Jefferson found himself in. In 1792, she finally fulfilled her dream and visited the very city that inspired people far off to imagine new possibilities.[10]

Connections made the world go round for these three; however, what they missed, understandably so, were deeper ties. Revolution in one place led to attenuations of authority in others because of the ways the process of integration bound together regions and societies. In part, the French Revolution, like the American Revolution, had its origins in such entanglements. Those same Atlantic tensions that contributed to the crisis of sovereignty for the British, and that were first felt on its peripheries, also gripped France. France erupted because the political upheavals stirred by the stresses of integration coalesced with social tensions that were emerging for the very same reasons. Britain's colonies broke apart along their fault lines when the systemic crisis hit; so would France. Failed reform would work as a catalyst of crisis there as well.

The tremors from that seismic event would be far more long-lasting and far more far-reaching because of the size and history and importance of France. France was one of the world's great powers and perhaps the most networked imperial center in all of the Atlantic. France was tied to colonies, and shock waves would travel there. Through competition for power, it was bound to all the great states of Europe. Repercussions would be felt in these places. France arguably served as the nexus of the Enlightenment and the broader republic of letters. So events in France, especially when they touched on issues of sovereignty, would reverberate throughout the network. What would occur in France, therefore, would confront men and women from places as far removed as the Caribbean and the European continent with similar dilemmas about sovereignty. More important, connections did not have a simply straightforward effect. They could work like a feedback loop. What happened in the United States could inform debates about political inclusion and colonial status in Saint-Domingue, which in turn could shape evolving conceptions of what it was to be a citizen in an increasingly tumultuous France, all of which reechoed in Saint-Domingue and the United States. Indeed, France's slip into the sovereign abyss complicated the search for order in America. All remained entwined.[11]

Connections created a kaleidoscopic landscape, reflecting how the Atlantic had become a crisscrossed space over the previous decades. The idea of connection offered unprecedented promise, just as it offered compelling ways of seeing the world and its problems.[12] Much of the period's complexity, therefore, hinged on how men and women gave meaning to dramatic change in one place and, in so doing, inspired others. Some saw opportunity and possibilities for liberation from older structures. Some championed what we could call radical ideas to fill vacuums of authority. That others far off were entertaining such thoughts encouraged such thinking all the more.[13] The period was one of exhilaration because of how places, through revolution, seemed more bound together than ever before. Throughout the Atlantic, people created and recreated visions on a continual basis situationally and fluidly, judging shifting contexts and remaking meaning. This process, in conjunction with deeper changes beyond the comprehension horizon, further heightened a sense of connectedness. This era, one increasingly marked by institutional meltdown, in fact turned on connection, transforming an age of reform into an age of revolution and—for a moment, at least—firing imaginations.[14]

First, the simplest of connections: America seemed to set off a chain reaction of sorts in the 1780s and encouraged men and women to imagine what "revolution" meant.[15] As Thomas Paine had said in 1776, in an almost prophetic way, "the cause of America is the cause of mankind." In the fluid Atlantic, particularly in the years between 1776 and 1789, the world was filled with new possibilities. America opened up the prospect of driving out despotism. This sensibility proved especially alluring to those on the margins of the Atlantic, those far from the centers of power.[16] Places as far away as the Italian city-states reeled from the news in America. The Florentine Filippo Mazzei, who lauded the Pennsylvania state constitution and befriended Jefferson, hoped his home could live up to what he took to be the American example. Peter Leopold, the Hapsburg grand duke of Tuscany, planned ambitious reform measures, including the drafting of a new constitution for Tuscany that would be based on American models.[17] The American Revolution reverberated all the way to Vienna. In 1778, to cite just one example, Johann and Maria Schuster brought their baby boy to Saint Stephen's Cathedral to be baptized. They named him after American representatives in Paris. Benjamin Silas Arthur Schuster bore the first names of Franklin, Deane, and Lee, and the proud parents invoked the Americans as godfathers in absentia.

The "public clamor for America," as one person called it in Vienna at the time, was pronounced, so much so that the monarchy banned the writings of Samuel Adams.[18]

Even the least likely place on paper to experience revolutionary intrigue in the wake of happenings in North America, Portuguese Brazil, stirred with revolt. Of course, here reform tied creole elites more securely to the center because it secured greater autonomy for them. Yet, local tensions erupted after even modest reforms when people looked to the North American revolutionary example. In 1789, in Minas Gerais, a rebel named Joaquim José da Silva Xavier, nicknamed Tiradentes, hatched a plan to kill the governor and declare independence for the region. He was upset with new tax collection policies and the sweetheart deals many connected merchants enjoyed with imperial and provincial reforms. He pointed to North America as his inspiration. Rumors flew that he was contemplating freeing enslaved persons, worrying officials that Brazil could be turned upside down.[19]

Brazilian elites need not have worried. The rebellion failed. No one rallied to the cause, not even the enslaved. Creole elites saw to it that such a dream for a new order would not be realized. Wisely, after easily putting down the rebellion, they relented a bit by repealing the tax that had led to unrest.[20] Though divisions existed between those who benefited from reform and those who did not, the fault lines within this society were not threatening to split open, even with inspiration from the new United States. Clearly in some regions older ways of handling pressures could still work or at least maintain order.

Brazil did not appear to be a candidate to follow North America down the revolutionary path. Ireland did. America and Ireland were tethered together in all sorts of direct and indirect ways. They made up important parts of the nascent British Atlantic empire. Trade and shipping bound the two places together, as did the steady flow of migrants over the course of the eighteenth century. The spinning and weaving of linen made Ireland one of the most important cogs in the Atlantic machine, and soon this fabric was being consumed up and down the Atlantic seaboard in America and even as far west as the frontier, where many Irish migrants settled. Moreover, Ireland had become an important node of Enlightenment thought, especially the sort that questioned reigning political arrangements within the empire. Ireland, like America, was a province of the British world. Its status as such became all the clearer after the Seven Years' War when successive British ministries thought that Ireland's surplus of manpower could stock the armies needed to defend the new empire. In this thinking, American revenue could complement Irish troops to manage the empire, and reform measures aimed at Ireland in the years after the Treaty of Paris reflected this hope.[21]

Officials in Britain, and their minions in Dublin, had good reason to fear an Irish conflagration in the wake of what had taken place in America, and they were keenly aware of the ties between one place to the other. No sooner had hostilities broken out than dissenters in the north threw their support behind the American patriots. So, too, did some members of the Irish Ascendancy, those in particular who bristled at Ireland's subordination to a British Parliament. Even some Catholics, including Irish speakers, voiced support for George Washington and the rebels. Ultimately, a reinvigorated patriot party in the Irish Parliament in Dublin would push for, and win, trade concessions within the empire for Irish producers and their ultimate prize: Irish legislative independence. Modeled on what the Americans had achieved, this seemingly revolutionary achievement demonstrated that Ireland was a nation and that it, too, could benefit from a changing world it had a great hand in shaping. Though still under the Crown, Ireland's Parliament would enjoy supremacy in the kingdom.[22]

What did not happen in Ireland, though, proves as instructive as what did happen. Ireland did not revolt. Catholics remained relatively quiescent, and parliamentary independence did little, if anything, to address their plight. In fact, most Catholics embraced loyalty to the Crown as a means of achieving a greater share of rights. Ultimately, the bid for independence represented an attempt to stem the tide of potential radicalism. Parliamentary independence kept Ireland tied quite closely to Britain during a moment of political instability throughout the Atlantic. Britain still controlled the purse strings and the legislative agenda. Britain more or less already ruled Ireland directly through the office of the lord lieutenant, part of a reform measure in the late 1760s. For all the excitement about independence and its evident bonds to America, Ireland was still dependent.[23]

The reason is twofold, and instructive if we are to understand why some places overturned anciens régimes and some did not. For a start, the Irish Ascendancy needed British might, and the threat of British troops, to keep Catholics in their place. The fear of Catholic insurgency ensured that the British and the Ascendancy in Ireland would maintain troops at the ready should Catholics clamor too insistently for their

rights. Political violence would be beyond the pale. So true independence, akin to that of the Americans, could not be countenanced by Irish
rulers or even contemplated by the British. Second, these years did not
allow the most salient divisions in Ireland to crack open. Although political disputes and intrigues kept things on the boil, no great contingencies
gripped the imaginations of the Irish to turn divisions into unbridgeable
and politicizing cleavages. Social tensions, then, were not channeled into
political programs or political insurrection. Ireland would remain quiet.
For now. For our purposes, the Irish case reveals how teasing out the
ways one revolution does or does not touch off others is more complex
than even the Brazilian-American case suggests.[24]

In Europe, Genevans and the Dutch seemed to be other likely candi-
dates for yoking local discontent to the American example. The ideas of
Americans especially resonated with those living in regions between
great powers in Europe. Genevans would be the first to embrace the possibilities of the moment, and in 1782, inspired by America and by their
own long history, men and women took to the streets to lay claim to
their rights. Alas, their neighbors would not allow this to happen. Eventually French forces would put an end to the radical experiment on their
border. Ironically, some of those involved would find their way to Ireland
to establish a settlement called New Geneva.[25]

The Dutch had a similar experience. In the early 1780s, a pro-
American movement called the *Patrottenbeweging* took shape to press for
democratic change. This case looked the most promising for extending
revolution beyond America.[26] It is tempting to imagine that the ideas some
of the Dutch espoused would lead to the same outcomes as in America,
that this movement would become "Europe's first major democratic revolution." The contexts differed profoundly, though. Would-be rebels who
supported the Americans were ultimately constrained by the ways they
had profited from the Atlantic. They happened to be leading capitalists,
and they owned a great deal of the debt of both Americans and Britons.
The ruling house of Orange backed the British, even if the state officially
tried to take a neutral stance. War, after all, complicated business. Once
merchants from Amsterdam began supplying Americans, the British declared war; and when the French threw their support behind the Americans, the Dutch found themselves caught in the pincer of power politics.
Moreover, the United Provinces were divided by region and by class.
Though the country experienced some rioting and the takeover of local
governments by patriots, the Dutch failed to rebel. Intrigues collapsed

once Prussians sent a force to help Dutch authorities regain control to maintain European stability. This was what could be called "an abortive revolution," but only because order could be restored by authority.[27]

Finally, Spanish America would seem another potential site for rebellion once revolution gripped North America. After all, South America was bound to North America by all sorts of ties, and it paralleled the north, both in the ways systematization of the Atlantic changed its societies and in how reform transformed its relationship to the center. In Spanish America, as had been the case in the north, creoles were beginning to think of themselves as "American." What happened to the north enthralled many in Latin America, and they devoured the works of Paine and Franklin and the writings and speeches of Washington, Jefferson, and Adams. North America spoke powerfully to many frustrations in many places, particularly for that stratum of society that had, like the Samuel Adamses and John Hancocks of North America, been hamstrung by reformist measures. North America would prove an inspiration for rebels in Venezuela who wanted to unseat what they regarded to be a flawed colonial government. Spanish America, however, did not rebel. Property owners as a rule did not support radical measures that could politicize the many groups below them. While creoles from Mexico to Chile were transfixed with political power, they also thought of social order, and so considered their provincial dilemma quite soberly. The history of popular revolts chastened any would-be creole nationalists. Separated by viceroyalty, economy, and daunting geography, creating a common cause for Spanish America would prove difficult. Even if creoles detested what the central administration was doing, they still saw themselves bound to the Crown and afraid of politicizing their societies. In fact, they viewed the connection to the Crown as one of the sources of their rule and of stability. This, more than anything else, tied them together and tethered them still to empire.[28] The American Revolution did not inspire, at this moment in any event.[29]

Then there is France. With good reason, one scholar has suggested that "France's first turbulent 'American colony' was Paris itself!" Parisians, we know, would soon be fighting their own war of independence, in their case one against a Versailles monarchy. They may have drawn inspiration from America, but they were addressing their own complex set of issues.[30] This provocative observation underscores a crucial point we should consider when we look for Atlantic revolutionary ties. Undoubtedly, America served as a catalyst to events in France, a story we know well. America's success inspired ideological commitments.[31] But charting connections, as we see from the other cases, can be a complex affair. Sometimes inspiration is not enough. Revolution, after all, does not only start through ideas. It stems from deep-seated grievances, structural imbalances and injustices, politicization, and government action or inaction. Revolution turns on power and who wields it. We could place these variables under the category of process. Revolution also hinges on events or contingencies. Finally, it involves how men and women perceive what is happening around them and to them. In the French case, ideology, process, contingency, and perception intersected in complex ways. These intersections centered on the Atlantic. Their story is anything but straightforward. It has many layers and was shaped by France's many complicated ties to the Atlantic and to America.

Take, for instance, the views of officials. When they thought of tying America to France, they thought in terms of the connections implicit in power politics. To say the French viewed the American cause with ambivalence would be about right. On the one hand, they saw the Americans as potential proxies weakening their most bitter rival. On the other hand, the idea of a rebellion against monarchical authority worried them. So even as Franklin and the diplomatic team tried to receive a hearing to persuade the French to join their cause, the French government proved standoffish, waiting to see how events unfolded before they would decide one way or the other what to do. To them, what would happen hardly seemed inevitable. After an American army defeated the British at Saratoga in 1777, Franklin finally received an audience with the king, and ultimately the French lent their support to the Americans in their fight against Britain.

The decision of France to support the American patriotic cause in the service of power politics would prove critical for the fate of America in all sorts of complex ways. The war, after the alliance with France, pitted Britain and its chief rival in another global war. The decision also bound France into the tangled world of alliances, something that would indirectly help the American cause against the British. France entering the conflict also mattered because its participation ensured that the Netherlands joined as well and, more important, Spain too. As early as 1775, Spaniards were supplying the rebels with money and matériel. In June 1779, Spain allied with France to declare war on Britain. They did not sign an alliance with the rebels. Spain joined not to liberate anyone but to gain as much of the British Empire as it could. This was a fight like all others that had come before it, they reckoned, one that would once again shift colonial boundaries. Of the places for the taking, the Spanish eyed Britain's Caribbean sugar islands, those engines of Atlantic integration, in particular Jamaica. By controlling the Gulf of Mexico and Central America, and that toehold onto the North American continent, West Florida, the Spanish could maintain a tighter hold of their colonies and shipping routes on which the empire depended. They were in it for reasons similar to France's: to hold on to what they had and to extend their power if possible.[32]

For whatever reasons these two powers joined, their entry determined American rebel success. The pressure France and Spain exerted in a global war helped Washington keep his army fighting.[33] The slave-dominated sugar islands were now at stake, and befitting their significance in a still tangled system, the British dispatched troops from the northern colonies to protect their interests in the Caribbean. With a whole Atlantic enterprise in the balance, the British were now stretched beyond capacity. Once a French fleet and troops helped a Franco-American force, led by Washington, to surround a British army at Yorktown, they had to sue for peace. The American rebels only won, in other words, because Britain was trapped in the tangles of the Atlantic with France's entry. Connection helped France avenge the earlier loss.[34]

It's at this point that things get interesting when we survey connections. The French decision to help the Americans deepened an internal crisis that had begun before the War for the Atlantic. France struggled with "oceans of debt" run up during the war. Much of this stemmed from the shipments of goods and arms across the ocean and in naval operations in the Atlantic. The navy had sunk the treasury. The new war only exacerbated the situation. By the time the Americans were claiming victory, the French were, in fact, wondering how to address the issue. That debt accrued from France's failed attempts to navigate the tensions of the Atlantic.[35]

Officials knew, following the primer, that reform had to happen at the center and that only it promised a way out of their financial mess. A succession of minsters had tried to initiate critical reforms after the first War for the Atlantic with the aim of freeing up the Crown to govern more efficiently and to raise money more effectively.[36] They, too, relied on new ideas of statecraft and a new belief in the efficacy of improvement to justify such attempts. These came to naught at the center. Again and

again, either resistance proved too much, as interests remained entrenched, or inertia proved too difficult to overcome, so daunting were
the many tasks because of the breadth and depth of the problems to be
addressed. The French, then, kicked the proverbial can down the road.
The task became more urgent after the second war, during which they
sided with the Americans. The debt that grew to unmanageable heights
threatened to become greater still. The new level of global conflict that
both wars unleashed, with successively heightened stakes and greater
scope and scale, meant that states had to operate on year-round wartime
footings. This new reality pushed finances to the breaking point. For the
French, the debt was not the issue per se; rather, it was the debt's coupling with antiquated taxing structures and procedures that could not do
justice to the new threats the state had to face that proved so perplexing.[37]

   With fiscal issues paralyzing all, officials would have liked to look
to France's wealthiest colony for help. They dared not do so. Saint-
Domingue had become even more important to the metropolitan economy
with the two wars, and some hoped the slave society would underwrite a
new golden mercantilist age. They had some reason to be optimistic. Trade
in the French Atlantic more than doubled over the course of the eighteenth
century; in fact, this sector grew more quickly than any other. Whole sec-
tions of France were animated by Atlantic-oriented commerce. Bordeaux,
for instance, long tethered to the Atlantic, became the home of fabulously
wealthy merchants by mid-century. Nantes, the main slave-trade port, grew
in prominence as well.[38] Slave owners and the merchants who specialized in
the trade of goods that the enslaved produced had grown so powerful
through integration that they could manipulate the levers of government to
their satisfaction.[39] The French, then, would have to manage their burdens
without the benefit of the empire.

   On this score, compare France to Spain after the war that gave
Americans their independence. Spain still had vast colonies. More significantly, it had through reform developed mechanisms to extract wealth
from New Spain so as not to imperil the metropole. Silver, of course, increasingly sustained the whole. This difference, in fact, helps explain why
the Spanish were able to avert an imperial crisis at this juncture. Spain
still maintained an empire, and though it had run up debt as well and had
to raise taxes, it confronted both concerns by exploiting that empire.[40]

   Not so the French. Extricating themselves from the tangles of debt
made for unpalatable choices. The French would have to raise taxes,
though they had to address Byzantine restrictions to do so. They would

have to figure out what spending could be cut, though administrative
hurdles awaited in doing so. But most pressingly they had to solve the
rabbit warren of competing sovereignties within France if they were to
manage the new age. Provinces struggled against the center. The Crown
tussled with courts and with local assemblies of notables. Even provincial
rule was accomplished along a number of competing lines. Such diversity
in and of itself did not create a problem. The French from time to time
encountered fiscal problems; but the eighteenth-century crisis dwarfed
earlier ones. Bankruptcy seemed a very real possibility.[41]

Only once the French reckoned with the fact that they were facing a
fiscal crisis because of the implications of Atlantic consolidation did they
look to America. They devoured everything they could about the American war and about the revolutionary changes engulfing America. It
would not be too much of an overstatement to say that France experienced a mania for all things American. Reports carried daily events of
what was happening, in terms not only of the war but also of how Americans were reconstituting a society and a government from a state of nature. Here what Rousseau had written about only decades earlier was
happening before their eyes. This explains why Benjamin Franklin so
fascinated the French. They revered him not only as an Enlightenment
figure, and a charming one at that, but also as the living example of a
simple American, a natural man, who had reached the pinnacles of salon
culture from the edge of the known world. He epitomized the shift some
French were prophesying they would have to make as they were struggling with their own reform crisis. Americans had created liberty out of
their lot. Could the French?[42]

The American ideological connection makes sense only in this tangled context. At the very moment the French were on the verge of declaring bankruptcy, a people on the other side of the ocean suggested a
way forward. This did not mean that the French expected to embrace the
cause of revolution. Even those who wanted to do all they could to prop
up royal authority saw the virtues of learning from the American example and could discern the benefits of beginning things from scratch.
From afar, the American tale looked uncomplicated. Or so it seemed, as
the French confronted their many knotty challenges, and as events in
America suggested the best of all possible worlds. Perhaps they could
evade the snares that reform would entail if they started the world anew.

With time, the French would lose interest in America. Commentators also understood that America, an exotic place, was not the same as

France and was much less complex. But at this moment, despite differences, men and women drew exciting connections and parallels where and when they could. America offered a comparative case study that allowed all to see France more clearly, even if what tied these two places below the surface of the readily apparent was anything but simple.[43] So began a moment of wishful thinking.

If Atlantic history has any virtues at all, it should offer possibilities for comparing one place to another within a broad system. Its transnational focus should also allow us to discover how processes of change, though essentially the same, differ in their incidentals. France is not exempt from these observations. They apply even to that revolution often seen as definitive and as exceptional. France's crisis after the global war set off by rebellion in America was akin to Britain's after the War for the Atlantic. Both crises were bound by the implications of Atlantic integration.[44] French reform measures stemmed from the same impulses. The French Revolution, then, should be framed as an Atlantic story.[45] What follows is a story we know. But it is here told in the light of comparisons to other places and connections to broader trends. France's experience in these years just after America had gained its independence resembled what had just happened an ocean away. More significantly, France's lot at this juncture had a dramatic effect in so many other places. Hope abounded throughout the Atlantic, largely because of what was going on there. Finally, France in the late 1780s offers a compelling case study of some of the central features of the age and helps us see how people came to see this period as an "age." France served as both model and template.

The Atlantic chickens came home to roost in 1786, when the king learned the state was teetering on the brink of bankruptcy. What followed almost took on the cast of farce, but it demonstrated that the state was not up to the complex task of the day. As was the case with Britain, well-connected and well-read grandees who thought they had the measure of history's patterns proposed reform measures at what was generally believed to be a critical moment. Reform stemmed from the belief that society and government could be remade once officials understood how to harness the patterns of the past to address the problems of the present and produce a map for the future. France's chief reformer after the American war, Charles-Alexandre de Calonne, believed that France had arrived at a crossroads and had to be remade to take advantage of the changes that had gripped the world. He and others would try to bring France up to speed to the economic and social trends of the day.[46] Most notably, he advocated what could be called a free trade approach to address the integration of the Atlantic, leading him to push for a commercial treaty with France's bitter rival, Britain.

Calonne hoped to turn smuggling into revenue-producing trade and eschewed corrupting competition, which would inevitably lead to costly war. He advocated an intensive internal works program, as well as an overhaul of the system of collecting taxes and of administration, including reining in and rerationalizing the rule of local parlements. Taking a page from the game plan of reformers in other empires, especially the British, he believed he had a small window of time. As soon as it became clear that new measures would have to be enacted to save the state from financial collapse, Calonne invited a group of Notables to discuss a new plan for financial and bureaucratic reform. The meetings collapsed.[47]

This is where the comparisons with the British case break down, at least in part. The British did not call sovereignty into question at home even if empire fell apart along the edges. For the French, sovereignty became the question of the moment. The calling of the Notables was mismanaged, but, more to the point, it demonstrated that the Crown was not acting the part of a sovereign. Events and eventualities had eclipsed the ability of the government to act. Calonne was trying to reform a regime that was effectively abdicating authority, and given the nature of the changes that had swept through France with globalization, the attempt emboldened those who thought they should have a voice in governance. The Notables incited other bodies, such as the parlements, to stand for their rights and to resist any new measures they did not subscribe to. In fact, the plan heightened confusion, the sort that central authority could not quell. The eighteenth century had hollowed out the Crown's authority, even if the king claimed to rule with divine favor.[48] The regime could not handle the task of modern governance and the relentless demands of the Atlantic system.[49]

Once the early meetings to find a workable plan broke down, and as soon as popular opinion reawakened as a result, the king had no choice but to convene a group known as the Estates-General to figure a way out of the mess. The body, representing the three great estates of the kingdom—the nobles, the clergy, and the commoners—had met in the past during moments of crisis. In theory, the Estates-General could counsel the Crown and add legitimacy to what was expected to be undertaken. In this instance, they were being convened when it became clear the Crown could not address the problems of the moment.

This dramatic convocation underscored that the old regime was now dead, as dead as King George's rule had been in America once his authority had effectively collapsed in 1774. At that moment, Americans filled the vacuum of power and began to style themselves as self-sovereign. What followed in France was strikingly similar, but it played out more spectacularly. For the French, the authority that collapsed was not relegated to the colonial structure; rather, the central state fell apart. It did not do so with the bang of the Bastille. The storming of the old prison represented more symptom than catalyst. Deeper issues beyond the ability of contemporaries to see were at work.[50]

To understand how and why, let's get back to connections and parallels. France, no doubt, was experiencing a political crisis that Britain had been able to avert. The Crown had more or less given all the initiative of reform, its content and direction, to other parties. In so doing, it suggested that sovereignty was negotiable, and many groups were happy to step into the breach, to grasp power, and to formulate their own plans for reform and for French government. Nonetheless, if not for a few critical factors, this story would have appeared much like Ireland's— caught up in a great imperial and revolutionary moment, France would have opted for reforms to governing arrangements and structures. The critical factors were contingent events, the accidents of history, that along with political disputes and intrigues transformed the tensions that defined French society into the explosive material that brought it crashing down.

As had been the case with America, sovereignty collapsed because of the flow of events and how people interpreted and ultimately connected them. Once the king had called for a convocation of the Estates-General, his chief minister did not give delegates directions on how they were to constitute themselves. He also did not give them any plan for reform. The convocation was to be open ended. In such a fluid context, indecision proved decisive. Soon enough members of the Third Estate realized that they had an opening to determine how the Estates-General would function and potentially how governance could be reorganized. Compounding the problem was the sense that the convocation represented a watershed moment. In just the same ways Americans had seen the period after 1763 as critical for the future of empire, Frenchmen of all stripes sensed a similar window of opportunity in 1789. All men with property were empowered to vote for representatives of the Estates-General, and they imbued the convocation with great possibilities of redressing all sorts of wrongs, most especially the privileges of the other orders. It would be wrong to say that the divisions between the three estates represented the most salient ones in France. The kingdom was riven with all sorts of fault lines; but the crisis exacerbated differences within and between the estates.[51]

With some justification, Jefferson saw the whole pageant of the Estates-General as an opera.[52] He meant the pomp, but he was also spot-on when it came to genre. Twists and turns, not inevitability, determined the libretto. And here we come again to contingency, for it played a leading role in this critical moment during which process, context, and meaning intersected. The decisions that potential delegates had to make to reform the kingdom played out against the backdrop of catastrophic social conditions. In the year before the Estates-General convened, France suffered from harvest failures and terrible storms, creating hardship for the poor. This did not represent an aberrational event. Nor did the rioting that followed. Normally, in such circumstances the powers-that-be respond by placating and lowering prices or by sending troops and halting disorder. Instead, officials let the problems fester. They seemed worried that troops would not do what they were asked. So, popular discontent spread. Paris, in this hyper-politicized context, became "a boiling pot of agitation," in which intrigue reigned.[53] Boston all over again but on a massive scale, in other words. Indecision again had dire consequences for the government.

Once the Crown failed to send in troops to quash popular tumult, liberating ideas had new powerful purchase. Men and women worried over "despotism," that the government would crack down or dictate what the Estates-General would do. All, including the poor, had imbued the moment with such import that any rumor could set them off. Uncertainty defined this critical period, and hope and fear commingled. When pronouncements from the Third Estate delegates seemed to suggest that meaningful change was on the horizon, people's hopes were raised to unreasonable levels. In other words, the French in this context saw eventualities much as Americans had twenty years earlier. They created patterns of events to make sense of any new event, and soon such patterning took on inexorable shape. They interpreted each new eventuality through the lens of the pattern, and soon all became almost trapped in a logic of events.

The intersections with and parallels with the American case are evident. Each crisis started with Atlantic integration, and the process of revolution, for each, turned on sovereignty. Both crises began with reformist agendas, to remake the state in light of changes it was not designed to handle. And in those places in which the central authorities did not act with decision, they found themselves addressing much graver concerns. The failure of government to act accelerated events.[54]

In each place, voices emerged as sovereignty collapsed, offering a vision of the crisis that captured the imagination of those around them. The Abbé Sieyès and John Dickinson served these crystalizing roles. Both characterized the problem in ways that resonated deeply and broadly. Sieyès, perhaps, was the moment's greatest thinker. Sieyès's genius lay in tapping into an idea that the French had found so alluring just after the catastrophe of the first War for the Atlantic: that they were a distinctive people because they already formed a "nation." As he stated, "The nation is prior to everything. It is the source of everything." When Sieyès argued that the Third Estate should be and was in fact the "nation," his words seemed prophetic and presented a compelling way of thinking about past, present, and future. Just as was the case with Dickinson, his sentiments helped to reorder a troubling reality and give it meaning.[55] Sieyès's words resonated because of the belief that all were living in a moment. More people began to see events in new ways and to imagine new narratives as they knit together contingencies. As this occurred, the old fractured; societies, which were not up the challenges of a changing world, reached tipping points. Revolution began from this dynamic.[56]

In both instances—in America a few decades earlier and in France in the late 1780s—an increasingly politicized people were taking on unaccustomed roles, and with the vacuum of power, they began to sense that they had an opportunity to reanimate sovereignty. These included, of course, France's arrivistes, those who had grown in status through Atlantic integration but who still were cut out of political life. To cite just one example, business leaders argued that they deserved to rule because of how much Atlantic trade had transformed French society. They made the claim that now the old way of thinking about society and governance should be a thing of the past. They also deserved a ruling voice. The American story, once again, provided a template.[57]

Others found voices as well. Food shortages in the countryside and old hatreds in cities took on a new valance because the crack in sovereignty gave all an opportunity to participate in political life. All, including the poorest in society, began to interpret the day-to-day struggle through the political.[58] The same had happened in the British North American colonies. The French entered this exhilarating and challenging crucible once the Third Estate wrested control of the Estates-General from the clergy and the nobility. Refusing to be directed on how to constitute themselves or to think of their roles as bound by the older categories of the three estates, members of the Third Estate conceived of themselves as the nation. They invited the other two estates to join them in a unified assembly. People like Sieyès suggested the combined body represented more reasonably what the kingdom had, in fact, become over the course of the eighteenth century: a society that was diverse, whose wealth was no longer tied to older notions of status. This sentiment was fully realized when members of the Third Estate collected a number of representatives from the other two estates to declare themselves the National Assembly. Far from aspiration, this move, like the drafting of the Declaration of Independence in 1776, recognized reality for what it was. The Crown's sovereignty was little more than a fiction. All lived in a malleable state of nature. A new social contract, which cohered more faithfully to a new social reality, was necessary for order to be restored.

At first glance, such an agenda would seem radical. In fact, it could be construed as conservative. Politicization, after all, knew no bounds. These representatives of the Third Estate found themselves confronting the dilemma that reform visited on all creole elites throughout the Atlantic. They were as concerned as the government was with the growing unrest in cities and in the countryside. A whole new way of organizing society did not serve the interests of anyone in the nation. The lid, they hoped, could be placed back on society once arrivistes took their rightful place as rulers alongside the Crown and the nobility. So-called radicals, such as Samuel Adams of Boston, had tried to do exactly the same thing.

At this point, the French in the National Assembly confronted the same questions he had. Could they manage social tumult? And if so, how? Could they put the genie back in the bottle? Some prophesied that once the National Assembly did its job of reform and designed a new constitution, the "revolution" would be over. Certainly Jefferson, a witness to these proceedings, thought as much.[59] Reformers in the National Assembly hoped, in other words, that France's revolution would be conceived much as America's. Perhaps it would be defined by something as irenic as the signing of a document, such as the Declaration of the

Rights of Man, which enunciated hopeful principles of rights and of civic responsibilities and that captured the euphoria of 1789. Would that the defining image of revolution be an oath in a tennis court or a vote for an assembly. But as unrest continued to grow in Paris, as common people were pressing for their issues to be addressed, some grew concerned that soon other images would define France.

Revolutions start for complex reasons.[60] What is clear is that fiscal, social, and economic concerns—some fundamentally shaped by changes in the Atlantic—converged on the question of sovereignty. In the process, the people of France became both politicized and mobilized. For years, the nation fixated on the state of the state. Discord, then, led to vacuum. And, as one historian contends, "the French Revolution was the process by which this vacuum was filled."[61] In France, as happened in America, all tried to give meaning to events and to place contingencies into narratives, and as they did so, competition to inscribe meaning on the moment heated up. This act of connection grew only more compelling as people looked to other places, like America, for inspiration.[62]

A new world was aborning. On July 14, 1789, of course, common men and women stormed the Bastille in Paris. More than anything else, posterity would remember this event as the beginning of the Revolution, even if at the time it suggested an ending. The men and women of Paris besieged the medieval fortress in the name of the new order emerging before their eyes. They did so to collect arms and, more significantly, to ratify the sovereignty of the National Assembly. The Bastille symbolized all that appeared antiquated and authoritarian. At the same time, it was clear that the assembly did not only confront the sort of dilemma that defined the whole era but was poised right on its horns. The crowd, after all, paraded severed heads as trophies—these did not come from statues—and many now connected this event with others in France to create a potentially more troubling narrative of what revolution could entail. The National Assembly stood as the only body that could stand between the politicized and chaos, even if at this juncture the body seemed to channel the anger of the people.[63]

We should not lose sight of this fact: though blood flowed, hope abounded. The teetering of sovereignty, just as had been the case in Britain's American colonies, opened possibilities for many. But, again as in the American example, not in expected ways. In America, women had played critical political roles in the heated home-rule/rule-at-home debate. The same would happen in France. Look no further than the women who worked in some of the market stalls in Paris, the *Dames des Halles*. They, too, were considered critical players in the French urban economy. They, too, had a history of standing up for their traditional rights. With the "October days," that moment when France tipped into hyper-politicization, the Dames took the lead, just as American women had done in places like Boston in the late 1760s and early 1770s. With fears of bread shortages and of rumors flying about those close to the king continuing to live lives of excess while insulting the symbols of the day, these women marched on Versailles. These were the people who famously escorted the king back from Versailles to Paris, when it appeared to them that he was waffling on supporting the Revolution and failing in his duties to protect them and their families. In general, they argued that as mothers and as economic agents they could contest any measures that compromised the vital roles they had to play in French society.[64] In the revolutionary vortex, women were redefining who they were as context allowed and as contingencies suggested. They did not seek to make a statement. But in this context of uncertain sovereignty they did, and so were transformed.[65]

They were not the only ones. Mary Wollstonecraft had entered the city at a time when more and more women were stepping outside the traditional bounds of patriarchy. Just as the Dames would famously "spank" nuns who had disciplined their children over political offenses, other women were rising to the moment as well and sensing the possibilities for liberation. Other writers produced works aimed at questioning the patriarchal basis of society, as institutions like the church and the Crown came under greater scrutiny. Condorcet, of course, wrote one. So, too, did the playwright Olympe de Gouges, who also supported the emancipation of the enslaved. Like Wollstonecraft, she pressed for women to enjoy political rights. She suggested that the issue of exclusion could not be premised on innate capacity but was based on socialization. With sovereignty hanging in the balance, then, people found their voices, and some began to imagine new possibilities for how society should be structured. The idea of connections, in a networked Atlantic where sovereignty remained a question, only heightened such imaginings.

Connections could make for a boomerang effect. Just consider a complementary story emerging on the other side of the ocean in the very same year—1789—that Parisians stormed the Bastille. In that year Americans ratified a new constitution, a process that suggested they had withstood the

tumult of the period. Indeed, at this very moment, when the hope and uncertainty of revolution seemed to be gripping France, the new United
States appeared to be succeeding. Americans, too, faced, estimable hurdles,
even if they had won their war for independence. Dealing with a politicized people, America's new leaders fretted over how to end revolution.
Men and women, Black and white and Native, had for years been struggling with the uncertainty of war and the exhilaration of freedom. In the
process, many had become as self-sovereign as those who were storming
the Bastille. The ideal of "we the people" was not a pious fiction but an ani-
mating fact of American society. The new United States reeled from a host
of concerns, some understandable but all challenges to reconstituting
order. These included economic and financial uncertainties, the memories
of civil wars that had been defined by appalling violence, unrest on the
frontiers, and the specter of returning veterans to cities and towns. At the
very moment in 1786 that Paris was stirring with popular intrigue, farmers
in western Massachusetts rose up to contest the limited nature of change in
the wake of war. Though they had fought for the patriot cause, they were
not seeing the benefits they had expected. Instead, the wealthy around
them and those in the east were prospering. Shays' Rebellion, like the risings in and around Paris, elicited the same fears from America's equivalent
of the Third Estate. America's leaders after independence were elite creoles
or arrivistes no more. With the British now gone, they grasped the reins of
power, holding positions commensurate with a socioeconomic status
achieved through Atlantic integration. They had a stake in a return to
order. But the visions they had of the future were potentially compromised
by those of lower status.[66]

The press for a constitution stemmed from the same dilemma the
National Assembly grappled with at exactly the same time: how to come
up with a new program of sovereignty that also could sustain order in a
politicized context. The constitution helped achieve just this. It was designed to fix a set of vexing problems.[67] It muted popular participation in
the cause of creating an efficacious regime that could stand among the
nations of the earth. It also brought some semblance of stability back to a
society ripped open by revolution.

The outcome was far from certain. That said, Americans had some advantages. The most significant one stemmed from the ways that war had
simplified the process of revolution. Because the war pitted two distinctive
programs of sovereignty, the revolution had "sides." One side clearly won.
As for those on the losing end, some of the most articulate—the elite—left.

By and large, wealthy Loyalists, who had done the most for the British cause, sailed from the United States. Their departure made any potential revolution settlement a bit simpler. These could have been what the French would call "counterrevolutionaries." Many more Loyalists worked to reintegrate themselves into society, such as more rank-and-file men and women in South Carolina. They asked for and received forgiveness in exchange for allegiance to the new regime.[68] Those pressing for an end to upheaval also had race at their disposal. And they used it unapologetically. Slavery would stay as it was. Despite being peopled by Natives, the frontier would be open as a safety valve for those who were on the economic margins but who also had to be politically recognized for their service to the state. Some tensions could be projected onto both Natives and African Americans.

Therefore, the ends of America's revolution were bound up in the beginnings of the Atlantic system and reflected the ways America had been integrated into the whole. Not so ironically, it was the movement of Africans across the ocean and what they produced that changed the Atlantic from a space to a system. The removal of the Indigenous peoples, all to encourage European settlers arriving from the other side and to raise crops for Atlantic commerce, served a complementary purpose. The fruits of integration now belonged to all whites, not only connected elites. This, too, is what the American Revolution accomplished. Liberation occurred for whom it could, given the constraints the so-called founders encountered after a prolonged period of politicization.[69]

All of this may have been the case, but by 1789 the whole Atlantic had one narrative of revolution, and a thrilling one at that. Americans by this year seemed to offer a story of uncomplicated endings and a blueprint or model for revolutionary success. The ratification of the Constitution suggested that revolution could end well. In the same year of 1789, France seemed to offer a similar story, even if one tinged with troubling signs of violence. Even this place that stood as the apogee of ancien régime Europe could change. To be sure, elites wrestled with dilemmas as those below them had become politicized in the exhilarating atmosphere of the late 1780s, but with the National Assembly acting as a sovereign power in partnership with the Crown, and the pronouncement of a new Declaration of the Rights of Man that would serve as a set of guiding principles, the bumpiest parts of revolution seemed in the past.[70]

With this comforting tale of origins and of seeming endings, euphoria swept much of the Atlantic. The tale suggested regeneration, all borne along the networks established by Atlantic integration.[71] France became an inspiration for all sorts of people who had grievances or those who were discovering as much. From this moment, the idea of an "age" commenced. People imaginatively linked the movements together. They perceived issues in their own home contexts through the lens of the French and American examples. The idea bespoke singularity, even if people experienced the period and its challenges through the prism of local tensions and pasts. Through the concept of an age, men and women throughout the Atlantic began to turn a revolution from a process into a promise. They created an idea of an age to explain, to give meaning, and to justify what was happening to their world. From the vantage point of 1789, as the National Assembly took control of a constitutional monarchy and as American republicans ratified their Constitution, revolution appeared liberating and manageable.[72]

Events in 1789 heightened a sense of connection. The early innings of the French Revolution captured the imagination of many Americans in the very same way the American Revolution so enthralled the French. It spoke of new possibilities in a world dramatically and sometimes troublingly changing. Events in France encouraged many in the United States to believe that the marginalization of some in the wake of revolution could be undone. In fact, what was taking place in France sustained the idea that the American Revolution was not yet finished. Most simply, some seeing the example of France and the more radical pleas for liberation called the institution of slavery for what it was: a contradiction to the liberating languages that had justified rebellion against established authority. Even poorer whites saw they would remain on the margins economically and socially in the new republic. The French Revolution showed another possibility of revolution, one not fully achieved in the United States. Such a turn of sensibilities exhilarated some.[73]

So Americans, some at least, lionized what was happening in France in the days after their states ratified the Constitution. Hoping to effect a more radical agenda, a number created Democratic-Republican societies, going back to the early days of revolution in America and emulating the French, who were doing the very same thing at that very same moment. These societies in America were designed to press for a more fulsome understanding of rights. For their members, the order now championed by elites that seemed to be taking hold in the wake of the Constitution represented a new form of oppression, one that necessitated an emulation of what French insurgents were doing. Perhaps the most radical of

these to spring to life in America could be found in the west. Here settlers were complaining that the state was failing to look after their lives,
liberties, and property. As the French were beginning to appreciate and
as Americans were learning, ending a revolution is not an easy affair.
This basic fact offered exciting possibilities for some, while it worried
others, especially those with a stake in the new status quo.[74]

Ongoing ties to France, now invigorated by newspapers and publish-
ers on both sides of the ocean, created this dichotomous effect. Paine
makes sense only within this transatlantic context, one forged in America
and then reforged in France. He used the ties the Atlantic public sphere
offered to connect dots in the most hopeful way. He and others would experience nothing less than the "Happiness of seeing the New World re-
generate the Old." The new age would free all, and its effects would
spread. Such was the case because of how enmeshed places far removed
remained. The assumptions underscoring "ignition" or "currency," whichever metaphor employed, suggested how hopes could travel, and how
they could destabilize structures and government, how each movement
was, in Paine's phrasing, "another link in the great chain." Continuing
struggles over sovereignty far away encouraged men and women to reconsider who they were and their own societies in a new light, one enliv-
ened with possibilities. The independence of South America, Paine even
prophesied in *Rights of Man*, would be next.[75]

Americans were not exceptional. The hope of a new age of connection
enthralled many, including the Irish. Although Ireland had gained legislative independence in the wake of America's break with empire, what happened seemed cosmetic. Ruling arrangements within the kingdom had
not changed, and Britain still controlled Ireland. By 1789, however, Ireland had two models of inspiration. Fervor for France entranced all sorts
of people in Ireland just as America did for France; the American example
of a successful break from Britain gave hope to those in Ireland exasper-
ated with the status quo. The conjoined examples resonated differently in
the 1790s because of changes in social and political context. Catholics in
particular now saw that the earlier reforms did nothing substantive for
them; in fact, reform measures seemed to strengthen the hand of the
British state in Ireland. Britain, after all, was now employing Irish manpower as never before to protect empire. Liberalization through reform
had been promised, but it proved so limited as to be galling. No matter
the rhetoric, religion still represented a badge of inferiority. Events else-

where led the lower sort to see their plight in political ways and to target the political system as the reason for their marginalization. In other words, tensions grew for the very same reasons they had in France and earlier in America, even if the particulars of Irish life differed from life in both of these places.

The story of Ireland after the French Revolution revolves around a group called the United Irishmen. They fitted the Atlantic mold. These were middle-class radicals who were benefiting from the changes in the global economy. They were as attracted as many Americans to the French cause. They, too, saw possibilities for overturning old ways and gaining a status commensurate with their aspirations. In particular, they hoped the liberating rhetoric coming from France would purge the great cleavage in Irish life and the chief obstacle to any meaningful change, the religious divide. Some Catholics now composed part of the merchant class; but the masses seemed trapped by the strictures of an old order. If the French could consign their past to oblivion, so too could the Irish. Or so the thinking went. At issue was the link to Britain. If it could be broken, Ireland could enjoy the promise of the new age and succeed in the very same way America had. Irish radicals, again largely Protestant urbanites, held fast to this ideal, though in fact they dreamed of a world in which what they regarded as the worst excesses of Irish Catholic belief would dissolve before the force of reason. Perhaps Catholics could leave the most superstitious aspects of their worldview behind. Then Ireland could stand as a nation.[76]

Ireland's history, though, could not be wished away. Here we come to an aspect of an "age" that is often forgotten. A great deal of revolutionary intrigue stemmed from "men of no property." In the 1780s, Ireland was beset by rural and urban insurgencies. These activities were taking on a political edge at the very same time the people in Paris were standing up to an oppressive ancien régime. Most of these insurgents did not fit the picture of the sort of revolutionary the United Irish intelligentsia favored. Nonetheless, these "Defenders," as one major secret society came to call itself, were attracted to the United Irishmen because they saw how political tensions were coalescing with a struggle for economic rights and social status. And they, too, looked to France as a model. Soon Catholics, who viewed Protestantism as a problem, were also supporting the idea of a republic and figuring a future in which Britain would not be a part. The same kinds of merger of political crisis and socioeconomic grievance that fueled and channeled insurgency in America and France now gripped Ireland. By the early 1790s, Ireland lay on the brink of a very different sort of age.[77]

Because of its long connections to the Atlantic, Ireland added to the complexity and excitement of the moment. Many Irish radicals made their way to America, intensifying debates there and stimulating more revolutionary intrigue. Radical emigrés from all parts of Europe, but especially Ireland, saw America as a critical experiment. Here revolution had to succeed. They joined American Democratic-Republican societies. In them, they encouraged the lower sort especially to state their grievances, continue their struggle, and fight to ensure that the Revolution would not end. Some, such as the publisher Mathew Carey, used the press to link what they saw as three related movements: the American Revolution, the French Revolution, and the bid for an Irish republic. They hoped to use networks they were forming in America and their ties to France to press for Irish freedom. They, of course, spoke in terms of connections, and they sought to foster these. In fact, what made the idea of connection compelling was the fact that all three places had been or were caught in the same sets of Atlantic dilemmas.[78]

Nonetheless, regardless of how or why ideas spread, men and women were becoming enthralled with the possibilities revolution seemed to offer. It seemed throughout the Atlantic that a new spring lay on the horizon, that perhaps the worst vestiges of an older system could painlessly and liberatingly be done away with. Only if older strictures were removed would a new day dawn. As one revolution informed events in another place, this sort of promising ideal captured the imagination of those addressing change and reform. Who could not be moved by such a hopeful belief, that freedom could come through struggle but without heavy cost? Of course, the dissemination of ideas made for selective interpretation. The French did not dwell, for instance, on the violence of the Carolinas in the American Revolution or the atrocities in New Jersey. Irish radicals hailed those ideas that promised liberation, without pausing to consider the potential dark sides of human nature or the state of nature. At this heady moment, United Irish leaders did not fully appreciate that any potential alliance with Defenders perched them on the same horns of the politicization dilemma on which the National Assembly sat. All were caught up in a new patterning of events that emphasized certain aspects of the age but occluded others. This gave radicalism its mobilizing and organizing power; it also made for its glaring blind spots.

In some places, then, this age became an "age" without calculation of potential costs. All throughout the Atlantic, the young especially hailed the new possibilities events in France portended. In Germany, for instance, Immanuel Kant wrote that this moment "in the history of the world will never be forgotten, because it has revealed at the base of human nature a possibility for moral progress which no political figure had previously suspected." Other figures of the German Enlightenment believed that finally history had shifted to the track of progress, that the endless cycles that had led to human misery had now been overcome by electrifying events. France, they all knew, was the greatest nation of the world. If it could experience such a change, their smaller states could as well. In universities, students and faculty boned up on their Rousseau and Voltaire, all with a sense of heady optimism.[79] Even some Prussian officials, of all people, hailed the events in France at first—less so from ideological attachment, it should be noted. Revolution threatened France's alliance with Prussia's chief rival, Austria. The enthusiasm—it should also be noted—did not last.[80] Nevertheless, with America, with Ireland, and most especially with France, it was becoming easy to connect geographic and historical dots.

Connections, of course, could foster other emotions. An age, after all, could portend something troubling as well. Indeed, in some places, even if people voiced hope for change, the state acted against any sort of radical intrigue. Take Britain, for instance. The ideas of France certainly made their way there, carried by the same networks that sustained trade and migration. Paine's *Rights of Man* caused a great stir and led some to believe that liberation for all in Britain lay just around the corner. The great Whig leader Charles James Fox declared the French Revolution "the greatest event . . . that ever happened in the world."[81] Early on, in the wake of the fall of the Bastille, reforming schemes in Britain had mushroomed. The belief in progress and that the human condition could be improved, seemingly demonstrated by events in France, was now vindicated. Men and women then turned their attention to all sorts of practices and institutions in need of a makeover. Mary Wollstonecraft discovered her vocation in this way at this time. Parliament, slavery, rural life, the church, prisons, urban crime—all could be addressed in this moment. In fact, officials almost competed with one another to lead reforming ventures. Moreover, with the loss of the colonies in America, many Britons thought that changing established ways would be critical for making the empire function. Britain seemed in the midst of, if not an age of revolution, then "an age of reform."[82]

But reform could only extend so far. In Scotland and in England, groups of radicals hailed events in France as presaging a true change in Britain. Yet the state could and did act to curtail such hopes. Even though it struggled in Ireland because of the convoluted political arrangements binding that kingdom to Britain, the government faced few obstacles at home and suppressed domestic radical intrigue. Burke, of course, worried about ideas and their implications.[83] His alarm had extraordinary purchase. Radical networks were ferreted out. The state most certainly did not initiate a reform campaign for homegrown problems. Officials seemed to sense that reform, at this moment and in this context, meant opening a Pandora's box. Controlling the press allowed the British state to control the message of the moment. In no way would the British state surrender its sovereignty. It went on the offensive to preempt any sort of crisis that was gripping other Atlantic societies. The state did not allow ideas to find arable ground.[84]

Other areas seemed relatively untouched. Such was the case for Latin America. The case here parallels Britain's. To be sure, creoles throughout Spanish America read with great interest about what was happening in France. They had a greater hunger to learn of what had occurred to create the United States, and the politically charged texts of the day circulated in every society in South America, even if they were not accepted whole cloth. Creoles discussed the latest events and publications in cafes and *tertulias*, salons that began springing up throughout the Hispanic world around the time of the French Revolution. The lower sort was meeting in taverns to hear about and discuss what was happening across the Atlantic.[85]

Nonetheless, creoles had a stake in stability. And the state did all it could to keep such ideas out. Ideas alone could not ignite revolution here. With no substantive attempts at political reform, various sorts of tensions never politicized and never led to a crisis affecting the state. The question of sovereignty never arose, because officials did not make it a question. There were, to be sure, some occasions of violence, and events in France mobilized the disaffected, as happened in Peru. But such instances of insurgency never had broader purchase, because they remained localized and did not animate broader tensions that could be directed toward political ends. Local elites remained vested in order, and so they did all they could to do what the British were doing in Britain. Connections, then, animated revolutionary unrest and mobilized hope only under certain conditions.[86]

One final place merits attention when we consider connections and their complex relationship to revolution. For it represented the place that a great many did not want to consider part of this age. If there was any one place that terrified nearly all, most especially whites, it was Saint-Domingue. Any disturbances in this hyper-connected slave colony, especially the specter of slave insurrection, were sure to send shock waves through the wider world. More specifically, the France of 1789 remained as tightly bound to Saint-Domingue as ever before. Each would fuel and feed off the other, as had been the case in the past.[87] Just as it seemed that Americans might be getting a handle on the disorder of the period by maintaining slavery on a legal basis in the Constitution, the island was wrestling with the new order taking shape in France and with uncertainty. Rumors flew. Some enslaved persons had certainly heard of the calling of the Estates-General, and on learning the news some refused to work, hoping the king would free them.[88]

Surprisingly, and no doubt to the relief of creole elites, these issues did not involve many of the enslaved directly. In fact, unrest in Saint-Domingue began as an attempt by planters there to gain greater autonomy within the French imperial system. Concerned over calls in the National Assembly for freedom to enslaved persons and an extension of the Rights of Man to all colonists, including poorer whites, or, as they were known, "petits blancs," planters fretted about how ties to France could imperil them. They then used the very ideas of the Third Estate—particularly a fear of "despotism"—to justify a bid for greater local control. What they did resembled what members of the Ascendancy had done in Ireland in 1782. Though they maintained their allegiance to the French state, they pushed out royal officials and established their own assemblies, which they dominated, to manage their own affairs. As in the Irish case, they did so as a preemptive measure to ensure that those in their midst, a majority, were not politicized by Atlantic currents.[89]

What was happening here appears as a variation on so many predominant themes of the period. White planters in Saint-Domingue faced a dilemma akin to Irish churchmen. In their midst were not only petits blancs but also persons who did and did not enjoy all the rights of whites: free people of color. Like Irish dissenters, who were separated by religious confession from a full enjoyment of their rights, free people of color could not claim a full measure of their rights because of the salient dividing line in the Caribbean colony: race. Not Black but not white, they inhabited a political gray space. Needed to serve in militias to protect the colony in a competitive Atlantic world, they nonetheless did not have a political voice. The National Assembly allowed this seemingly anomalous state of affairs to continue, much as the British Crown had allowed the Ascendancy to rule Ireland.[90]

Free people of color took their case to France. They declared that if they remained in a proverbial purgatory of status, slave rebellion was sure to break out. In this regard, they had a vested interest, as many owned Africans themselves. What they resented was race being used as a badge to keep them in a subservient position. While planters lobbied to be part of the Estates-General, so too did free people of color, and both groups were accorded representation. Though some in the National Assembly were sympathetic, the planters also had powerful friends in the assembly. Merchants, especially those from rich Atlantic seaports, did not want to see the status quo in the colonies affected by what was happening in France. They encouraged the National Assembly to turn a blind eye to lobbying by free people of color.[91]

Like American colonists, planters in Saint-Domingue who had bene-fited the most from entangled integration pushed for a greater share of home rule in the face of more troubling dynamics among those below them. Saint-Domingue also contained men and women with deeply held grievances that were heightened by a recent crisis. Events in France set the whole mechanism in motion. This should not surprise us. The island colony was a place that had perhaps the widest-ranging connections of any Atlantic society. It was bound to multiple centers and peripheries throughout the system, even if planters tried their best to ensure no news made it to the island. Given the networks of the enslaved and free people of color, this proved impossible. News and rumors moved to, from, and through Saint-Domingue. The "common winds" of revolutionary intrigue moved along networks with sailors and the enslaved, from places like Cuba, Jamaica, the south in the United States, and the Spanish Main. These winds—and the ships that were propelled by them—brought pub-lications from France. Even a condemned enslaved rebel had on his per-son pamphlets printed in France championing "the Rights of Man and the Sacred Revolution."[92]

In other words, the connection between Saint-Domingue and France threatened to become a mirror image of the tainted tie between Britain and its American colonies in the early 1770s. In Saint-Domingue, though, planters had taken control of their society before government in their midst effectively collapsed. They had seen the patterns before, and in no way did they want to invite a power vacuum if unrest were to grow in France. They most certainly did not want royal authority to fall apart as it had done in North America. They acted more or less like elites in Latin America to ensure local control was propped up, just as creoles in Latin America did all they could to keep the contagion from their shores.[93]

What happened next in Saint-Domingue spoke to the promise and peril of the age and the peculiar ways they intersected. Vincent Ogé, a leader of the free people of color, at first hoped to win rights for his people through the National Assembly in France. He proposed ideas to maintain order in a slave society. He, too, worried over the threat that "menaces us," as he put it, and hoped to protect his property and that of other planters. He wanted free people of color to be recognized as "Americans," a new people who should enjoy the same rights as whites, a group he and others called "French colonists." This formulation, which downplayed race as the most salient category of difference, recognized an economic reality: Ogé and others like him contributed mightily to the island's economy and to its stability. They, he suggested, kept the lid on a volatile society. When he was outmaneuvered, he decided to try to win rights by threatening violence.[94] Collecting arms, he headed to Saint-Domingue to let white planters know that in this new enlightened age the old ways and the new racialized hierarchies that had been devised to maximize profits from Atlantic integration could no longer stand. Ogé led a failed rebellion against authority, and when he was caught, he and his conspirators were hanged. Peace came once more to autonomous Saint-Domingue. The planters had their freedom. Few others did.[95]

It seemed that there were limits to freedom in this new age. If we survey it, what we find is that many throughout the Atlantic were redefining who they were in the period. They were becoming citizens, and theirs was a story of entangled hopes. Such was the case for the Third Estate in France, churchmen in Ireland, and white provincials in America. In the postcolonial societies of the United States and in Saint-Domingue—in 1789 at any rate—the enslaved would not have their freedom. In a newly autonomous Ireland, Catholics would not be deemed part of the political nation. Though the status of slaves and Catholics differed profoundly, the parallels at this moment are striking. In each of these places at this time, creole elites seemed to have things well in hand, just as they seemed poised to reap the benefits of the integrated Atlantic without the complications of older accreted ways. For this chapter of the age of revolution, liberation came for whom it could, given the historical and geographical constraints of the Atlantic in this period. But this pattern did not obtain everywhere. Where the state acted with vigor, as Britain did, such was not the case. The same held true for Latin America. In both instances, older ways could be preserved, largely because sovereignty had not teetered and contingent events did not encourage people to see things in new ways.

One could have said right at this moment, and some did, that revolution appeared over, that stability had come once more, and though blood had been shed, the liberty won had been worth it. Springtime, however, had come to an end. The first whiffs of a new season were coming from the burning sugarcane on the island of Saint-Domingue.[96] George Washington, for one, sensed something beyond euphoria as he scanned the Atlantic. Washington paid homage to what he called the "wonderful" revolution in France. But he issued a warning: "The revolution is of too great a magnitude to be effected in so short a space and with the loss of so little blood."[97] He knew that bloodshed and liberty, alas, went hand in hand. Maybe the Jefferson of paradox is the right one to focus on after all.

CHAPTER FOUR

# The Gordian Knot of Fear

## *Violence in the Sovereign Abyss*

THEN, THE OTHER SHOE dropped. If we fast-forward a few years from the events that electrified the Atlantic in 1789 and betokened new possibilities for liberation, we find that France was now struggling with fear, uncertainty, and violence. The heady dreams of creating a stable constitutional monarchy had passed. No sovereign body ruled save a regime running things at the pleasure of what some called "the mob." Disorder was spreading. France's most profitable colony, Saint-Domingue, was rocked by violence, but the sort that terrified nearly everyone: slave insurrection. Fears were amplified as deference crumbled and as news swept through planter societies because of events elsewhere.[1] Fear, it seemed, sustained hysteria in just the same way hope sustained motivation.

One French revolutionary leader, one who believed violence was necessary to purge society of all its old debilitating and oppressive trappings, drew a direct line from hopes in France to events in Saint-Domingue. Jean-Paul Marat argued that if Frenchmen at home were throwing off their chains, the enslaved could and should also. "If the laws of nature precede those of society and if the rights of man are inalienable," he declared, "then whatever complaints the white colonists have against the French nation, the mulattos and the blacks have against the white colonists." Subjugation, Marat believed, was subjugation. "To bring

115

down the cruel and shameful yoke that oppresses them, they have the right to use all possible means, even death, should they be forced to massacre their oppressors to the last man," he argued. The rights that whites claimed also pertained to Blacks. All could be free. Violence would make it so. Horror, Marat believed, served as just deserts for planters.[2]

Things were not so simple on the ground in Saint-Domingue. A former enslaved person, and now leader of free people of color, Toussaint Louverture, had chosen his last name because he saw a new "opening" for him and others like him in the fluid disorder that was gripping the Atlantic. He led groups of insurgents attacking plantations in the north of the island. Soon the region was rocked with violence, and news of the bloodshed transfixed all in the Atlantic. Yet, the opening that this unrest seemed to betoken would not unlock doors for everyone. Saint-Domingue was a complicated place. Lines of status crisscrossed in confounding ways, all made more complex by ties to a France torn apart and to other imperial powers in the Atlantic. In the maelstrom of revolution, Louverture decided that he could not style himself a freedom fighter for all; he had to try to sign on to deals that compromised the rights of some. The trade-offs, he recognized, stemmed from Saint-Domingue's now cruelly tangled relationship to the French metropole and the confusing ways race and status intersected in Saint-Domingue. He had to tussle with all these conundrums as he saw fields on fire. It seemed no one or nothing could deliver the island from the chaos engulfing it.[3]

For Louverture, violence had deep roots. He saw twisted connections that animated the Atlantic and that twisted people. "It would be easy for me to prove, if I had more time," he wrote, "that it was the Europeans themselves who first put torches in the hands of my unfortunate brothers and who played the leading roles in the murders and fires that were committed." The French had plunged all into a state of war. Only Blacks worked to ameliorate the condition: "It was the blacks who, when France was threatened with losing the colony, used their arms and their weapons to conserve it." The French, therefore, bore the blame. They had not only offered hope of liberation, they also offered a model of fear. "We can certainly reproach the people of Saint-Domingue, including the blacks, for many mistakes and even horrible crimes," Louverture conceded. "But," he asked, "in the battle between despotism and liberty, have we not seen the inhabitants of France itself, where society's rules are well-established, give themselves over to all the excesses that the enemies of the blacks reproach them for?" In a stinging rebuff to those at the center, he concluded: "If, because some blacks have committed cruelties, one could argue on that basis that all blacks are cruel, we would have the right to accuse the French in Europe and all the world's nations of barbarism."[4]

Violence became that which transfixed and that which terrified throughout the Atlantic. Some used terms like "contagion" to appreciate what was happening. And there is little doubt that what transpired in one place created a response in others. Violence energized and fascinated. It also repelled. The same networks that made revolutionary ideas seem so promising also brought stories of atrocities and of uncertainty. These tales reverberated through the networks established earlier on. They crossed imperial lines with ease, especially the most lurid examples or rumors. Every bit as much as the heady springtime stories, these revolutionary narratives too could propel people and events.

The connections between Marat and Louverture gesture to one last point. Saint-Domingue and France experienced violence that could appear strikingly similar. In both places, violence was tied to the breakdown of sovereignty. They were both caught in the same process, one that North Americans had struggled with only years before. The French colonial and metropolitan stories, however, differed from the American case because of the depth of violence. It could not be channeled or domesticated so easily. In Saint-Domingue, it could never be placed in categories of patriot and Loyalist as neatly as it did for those Americans breaking away from Britain. In fact, violence contorted allegiances and complicated the fault lines that defined status in the place.[5] As Marat understood but accepted, violence and liberation were parts of the same twisted knot.

In the troubling gap between sovereignty and anarchy, fear and violence prevailed, and they animated the network. We are apt to believe that only the state can wield the sort of violence that can inspire mass fear; in fact, in these years, more horrifying was the failure of state authority or, more precisely, those moments when sovereignty was up for grabs.[6] The terrors that for many came to define the excesses of the age, then, were not incidental to the process. They were woven into its fabric, just as Washington had prophesied. Terror could not be disentangled from the collapse of authority in contexts wrought with uncertainty.[7]

This troubling pattern obtained not only in Saint-Domingue and France but in all those places experiencing revolution. It could be seen everywhere revolution touched. Usually it was explained away as aberrational. But it was deeply rooted in the process of revolution as it played

on the distinctive characteristics and contradictions of each society. Revolution moved individuals along an emotional register bounded by unbridled hope and unendurable panic. Close to the fear side of that
register, men and women necessarily wrestled with its near cousins,
anger and rage. The quick shift from one end of the emotional spectrum
to the other made for a deep sense of betrayal. Vengeance usually became
the chief motivation.[8] Vengeance could be easily politicized. And it
spread. In these critical years throughout the Atlantic—1790 to 1793—
the world turned, just as the tide of revolution did, doing so along these
axes of hope, fear, anger, violence, and vengeance.

France served as the hub of fear in much the same way it did for hope.
Just at the very moment it seemed that the French Revolution was coming to an end, with a settlement rooted in the rights of man, a new constitution, and a weakened monarchy, France disintegrated. How did it
happen? And so suddenly? The violence of the Revolution and the resulting Terror have loomed large in imagination, even if many more died in
battle than on the scaffold. We have tended to conceive of it as something
extraordinary, something wholly unexpected, given the vaunted language
that gave birth to what is often considered a progressive revolution.
Emotion and unpredictability reigned. "It seemed," one historian writes,
"that each participant was part of an invisible, intricately linked chain
leading hectically who knew where." Such an observation has left us ask-
ing again and again a simple question: Why revolution in 1789, and why
terror in 1793–94?[9]
    Even before the Terror devoured the radical Condorcet, conserva-
tives had answers at the ready. Those who worried about the fabric of society once its institutions began tumbling down and old taboos were
swept away had prophesied that bloodshed would follow. Burke is only
the most famous of them. Though he had passed away before the Terror,
he had assured his readers that what the Paines of the world hoped to accomplish would necessitate great upheaval and violence. The descent
into a world of terror, when no one could control society, would inevitably lead to the Terror, to the state appropriating fear and violence. At the
time, of course, he seemed a crank and a reactionary. In light of the high-
sounding rhetoric about all people gaining the rights that nature intended them to have, conservative voices seemed like eighteenth-century
Chicken Littles. They connected the dots of what was happening around
them, and with their dim view of human nature they came to believe that

a person freed of old obligations could be a person unconstrained by anything. Then—as the old phrase went—terror could become the order of the day.[10]

For those embracing a more hopeful view of human nature, it could be argued that France seemed to get the revolution it deserved. The potential for violence reflected the levels of accreted rot to be purged. Then events took over. As Paine suggested, the people had been "corrupted" by the ancien régime that was itself propped up by oppression and violence. How could people thus formed have acted otherwise once goaded? Mary Wollstonecraft cast violence in a similar light. She suggested that, perhaps, France's history of exclusion was so great and affected so many for so long that necessarily reform would take time and the process of change was bound to be challenging.

Events suggest both camps got some things right. And some things wrong. Let's return to them. So excited were men and women in France after the National Assembly declared an end to the ancien régime that it was easy to believe that a new age was dawning. With exuberant celebration came more joy when tithes were done away with, when church property was confiscated in the name of the nation, and when old feudal obligations were abandoned in law. At first the common sort, who were now flexing their muscles in the streets of Paris, applauded everything that the Revolution was accomplishing. Of course, the landed gentry found themselves vilified for their association with an older discredited way. The king, too, sensed that he was living at the pleasure of the many. Unable to move or to voice his opinion about events in France, he continually surrendered his authority in the hope that each instance would placate those around him. Instead, it empowered them, and justifiably so. Common people were reclaiming what should have been a birthright. Freed from age-old shackles and from rituals meant to keep them in their place, men and women for the first time could step outside history and its many accretions of subservience to stand as the equals of others. As reform followed reform, many sensed new opportunities for themselves and for their children in a society that had been defined by status and by the rituals designed to inculcate inequality. Many found the possibilities of the new age intoxicating, especially as one layer of tradition fell after another. Burke could not quite bring himself to appreciate these realities.

Fear represented a flip side of this coin, something Paine struggled to comprehend. The French nation was on collective tenterhooks, as each new event, or even an interpretation or misinterpretation of an event, could cause panics. With the panics came violence. When word spread of plots by Catholic priests who would not abide by the new order, or of Prussians planning to invade to save the king and the ancien régime, or of peasants withholding precious food, common Parisians indulged in collective violence. Violence conferred power, and it soon became apparent that they ruled the capital city. When the king tried to flee the country after yet another bout of violence, he was captured and put under house arrest. This for a monarch who had lost his sovereign power but who was monarch nonetheless. Who ruled France?[11]

The answer lies in the question itself. In the immediate years after the heady days, no one could be certain who ruled. In these years, with no stable authority, the revolutionary moment energized and radicalized. It also pitted one group's interests against another's, but often in complex ways. Take the case of the Dames des Halles, the working merchant women of Paris's streets. They fed the metropolis and, though poor, were important players within the economy. They became even more important when disorder beset Paris. Early measures to stabilize France in the years of tumult included price controls. Well-to-do women applauded these measures. The Dames opposed them, in some cases violently and always vocally. Though supporting the liberating logic of revolution, they resisted laws and measures that threatened their ability to support their families. These active citizens became even more so with the uncertainty of revolution—these were, after all, the very women who escorted the king back to Paris in the early days of the Revolution. The moment of uncertainty in France encouraged them to amplify their older ties to class, occupation, and historic roles, just as they embraced the new revolution. They, and presumably others, proved as fluid as the contexts they were trying to navigate. After 1789, context became liquid-like because of the failure of authority, empowering common people in the process.[12]

Though common women were swept up in the vacuum of power, and amplifying their voices through it, some struggled. Just consider Wollstonecraft. Viewing the first chapter of the Revolution with hope and expectation, she strained to make sense of what followed. The people unfettered did not seem to be freed of cruelty. France had not progressed as she had expected; in fact, she came to see that Jacobin excesses curtailed the possibilities of liberation for women. What seemed so promising early on began to fall apart before too long. Wollstonecraft's hope that human nature could improve began to slip as events in France took a disturbing turn, and with it earlier radical visions that connections portended.[13]

The absence, not the presence, of power divided groups. Absence corrupted, it energized, and it shattered illusions. These represented just a few of the dynamics people encoutered in the sovereign vacuum. As had become evident in other places in which government had failed, the violence that went hand in hand with the process of revolution acted as a solvent, parsing groups into all sorts of categories, undoing some bonds while tying people to others. Most confounding of all, these categories were shifting like the wind with each event and each attempt by some group to claim the mantle of authority. Such shifts compounded the questions swirling around sovereignty. They only amplified uncertainty, which exacerbated violence, which then further heightened uncertainty.[14]

French men and women found themselves struggling to give meaning to what was happening around them and what they were doing. Just as they used metaphors to understand what revolution meant, they also adopted certain ideas from nature to make sense of and legitimate violence. Doing so naturalized what seemed on the face of it so aberrant, so unnatural. Equilibrium, they hoped, could return once violence had been expiated and had run its natural course. Violence stemmed from vengeance—that much people recognized. They also hoped that such energy would be spent, almost like a volcano after an eruption. Or that was the expectation. Of course, in making meaning of violence, people were also legitimating more violence.[15]

Perhaps, after all is said and done, the answer to our question of how this could have happened will remain an "enduring mystery."[16] Nonetheless, this much is clear. With the sovereign void, France fell apart along its seams. Some set their eyes on the Catholic Church and used this moment to undo its status in the kingdom root and branch. The ideas now ascendant certainly justified dismantling the institutional church and also its rituals and theology. As shouts of liberty filled the street, a church based on the now discredited idea that men and women were inherently fallen creatures had little purchase. Some areas, however, clung to the older ways. In deeply Catholic rural regions, people hated the new order, and they held onto older notions of sovereignty. We usually couch these sensibilities as counterrevolutionary. They were anything but. These voices represented another aspect of French society collapsing because no legitimate authority had emerged to reconstitute order. Just as France split over religion, therefore, it also fractured because of region. Finally, it collapsed as those invested in the ancien régime fled the country to plot a counterstrike against the new order. These émigrés, again usually characterized as counterrevolutionaries, were competitors for the soul of the country in the sovereign vacuum. Religion, monarchy, and region represented the most salient divides in a country reeling, and as these became points of conflict, fear escalated.[17] The upshot was this: for all the hope inspired by 1789, France had fallen into an abyss, as different voices clamored for distinctive and contradictory visions in a plastic time.

A concatenation of events, both domestic and international, moving along networks, drove the "second revolution." This revolution, better conceived of as part of a broader process, inspired not exhilaration but anxiety. It rode on rumor. Somehow murky forces from abroad, usually tied to the king, were intent on slaying revolutionaries and returning France once more to the state of the ancien régime. Even though the new National Assembly was more inclusive than any other in the world, and some were declaring that a history of the French Revolution should be written, lurid tales of violence in the provinces and of threats from royalist émigrés and invading armies sustained a level of uncertainty that would not allow France to leave the crucible. Sometimes these tales focused on what was happening in Saint-Domingue, leading some to fear they would lose the most profitable colony in the world to chaos. They should have been more concerned for themselves. The deeper France descended into revolution, the more fearful everyone became. Rumor after rumor now swept through the country.[18]

As the people turned a process of change, a revolution, into a program of action, the Revolution, the targets for fear and fury became clear.[19] Just as Americans had been able to channel discontent against the British or against a patriot program, French men and women could exercise the same sort of Manichean thinking against themselves. Fear drove people to the extremes of the spectrum, where they sought security and where they hoped, vainly, that a pure vision would cast out the demons that threatened all. In this way, radical royalists were the exact mirror images of Jacobins. Those who supported a return to the ancien régime and its certainties viewed things this way. Common people, those threatened by uncertainty and by violence, embraced this way of seeing the world. In the process all became actors in an almost set-piece drama. Meanwhile, those in the National Assembly perceived themselves struggling with the dilemma of a politicized people. Certainly, they dared not articulate it. With precious little middle ground left, this "obsessive mentality" took hold. In Paris some of these voices, particularly of the Jacobin variety, stood ascendant, claiming legitimacy and the mantle of progressive and enlightened values.[20]

The distinction between revolution—a process—and Revolution—denoting unity and inexorable logic—represents a moment upon which the process of redefining sovereignty turned. It did so for America, and it would do so with vivid effect in France. In France, it centered on the person and body of the king. Louis XVI found himself part of the Manichean narrative playing out around him. As soon as he had been discredited for resisting the idea and logic of the Revolution, people in Paris started to imagine a republican regime free of monarchy. The unimaginable then become conceivable. If he plotted against "the Revolution," as it was now termed, he could not stand above the law.[21]

When we focus on the competition to remake sovereignty as the stuff of revolution, not just hopeful ideas, these events loom as large as those of 1789, but for reasons other than those trotted out by the Burkes and Paines of this world. By 1791, the people of Paris had become the chief actors who controlled the city. They embraced the most radical vision of the Revolution. Though the rest of the country reeled with uncertainty, in this one city at this time a vision of certainty had arisen. The voices of the people also represented that chief constraint that limited what could be done and said.[22] The state, or what there was of it, tried to pry away the monopoly of violence from the hands of the many. But the many unencumbered from the old represented the closest thing to a state. So, unsurprisingly, in early 1792, the king—the very symbol of a state now discredited as another was trying to claim legitimacy—was executed. As Maximilien Robespierre aptly put it, there could be no "revolution without a revolution." With the king's death, the most insistent vision of what Revolution meant stood as the basis of what passed for the state. No other voices would be countenanced. Some radicals appreciated what the moment allowed and tried to bring the only order they could from it. Terror would order all. In theory, that is. This attempt to wring stability from chaos, by using fear as a tool, caused sixty of France's eighty-three departments to spiral out of control. France faced the possibility of "disintegration" through the attempt to integrate by terror.[23]

To be clear, many people died in France during the Terror. The number guillotined in Paris stood at 2,639, with a further fourteen thousand sentenced to death elsewhere in France after some sort of trial. These numbers are substantial but not that large when we consider what people suffered throughout the age. More critical were the emotions the Terror occasioned, the images it conjured, the unknowing, and how its form seemed to contradict so many of the stated principles of those who used it as a weapon. Coupling this with the fact that people killed in the name of political rebirth explains why the episode puzzled and troubled people.[24] A retreat from enlightened thought? The apotheosis of that thought? A tarnishing of what should have been liberating? The lamentable but necessary diminishment of liberty to promote equality? Who knows.[25] But we think we know this much. Scholars have of late encouraged us to look beyond the logic of the ideas themselves, positing that perhaps terror was not epiphenomenal but in fact lay at the heart of the revolutionary experience and process. Somehow it did not represent an aberration but the defining feature of the revolutionary moment. When the state collapses, with violence as a cause and an effect, the furies emerge.[26]

The Revolution, in one scholar's words, then became "a rollercoaster that brooked no counter-argument."[27] In France, power now belonged to the shrillest. As Georges Danton intoned, "Let us become terrible so as to prevent the people from becoming so." What was left of the state, in a stressed society, resorted to terror to pursue revolutionary purity and to avoid anarchy. The Revolution would now create a "new man," without reference to the past, requiring a new calendar, new gods, new revolutionary saints, and an amnesia about what had come before. It wiped the slate clean, and many would find such revolutionary iconoclasm appealing. The competition to remake sovereignty dictated as much.[28] What could be regarded as an exceptional approach to harnessing France's distinctive revolutionary energies took on a universalized cast.[29]

Descent into fear, uncertainty, and almost unrestrained violence did not happen by design. It arose from the fracturing of sovereignty and the failure of any new order to emerge that would or could restore order to a society cracking along its many deep fault lines, and from the ways in which frightened and exhilarated people tried to manage this process. What was design was the appropriation of the process of revolution by the state in the name of Revolution. In other words, what happened in France after 1790 mirrored what had happened in America after 1775, even if it outpaced the American case. Though separated by fifteen years, both dynamics followed the same pattern. As soon as an old sovereign order collapsed, competition ensued to fill the void, and violence was the result. Until, that is, some group had the wherewithal to bring some control by some means to society, even if provisionally.

This drama would be played out all across the Atlantic, just as had happened earlier in America, though not to such startling effect. Here we come again to the parallels of process. Anywhere sovereignty cracked, violence resulted and fear spread, as societies broke down along their historical tension points. We would be wise not to forget the logic of connection. The city in which debate over sovereignty took place, the place from which rumor spread and to which innuendo from places far and near arrived—Paris—at this moment lay at the center of a networked world. What happened in Paris would not stay in Paris.

The tug-of-war between sovereignty and violence defined the experience of men and women in Saint-Domingue, which brings us back to Louverture's world. In 1791, reports flew of the enslaved rising up in the northern plains of the island, killing whites and burning plantations. Soon disturbances spread. It seemed clear at once what was responsible. Events in France had energized enslaved persons. The way things played out paralleled what had happened in France only two years before. A drought had made things hard for planters, and they pressed their labor force to work harder to make the harvest profitable. This contingency then combined with stories of what was happening in France, mobilizing men and women to rebel. In fact, tales circulated of enslaved persons holding copies of Paine's *Rights of Man*. The enslaved knew of events in France, and if some of their knowledge was scanty and incomplete, they understood the essence. Common people had found power through resisting. Those who toiled on plantations had discovered it through the Atlantic lines of communication that had brought hope to so many others.[30]

This is certainly how those who owned plantations and who had a stake in the old colonial order saw things. Events in France indeed had a catalyzing effect. But what the owners perceived less clearly was how the debates over sovereignty in France had also led to similar struggles within Saint-Domingue. The creation of a National Assembly in France had given groups with some status in Saint-Domingue, such as free people of color, the opportunity to press for their rights and to break the color line. They did not necessarily want to end slavery, but they did want political power. What was happening in France dictated that they could take such a course. Most white planters preferred to keep the color line, to ensure that political power was tied to race even if it was not necessarily bound to servile status. As these debates became heated, and as those lobbying in the metropole tried to win over each faction to its own way of thinking, Saint-Domingue found itself in the same sovereign never-never land as France. Unsurprisingly, the enslaved rose up when planter control teetered.[31]

With sovereignty compromised, the level of violence and its frightening aspects were predictable given the coercive nature of the slave regime in Saint-Domingue. Men and women declaring their freedom repaid former masters with the sort of abuse that had been visited upon them. In other words, as was the case in North America and to a lesser extent in Ireland after the years of imperial reform, this society cracked along its defining dividing line. These lines were deep, indeed almost chasm-like, and unbridgeable, made more so by years of racialized exploitation. While many throughout the Atlantic struggled with exclusion, most in Saint-Domingue confronted something categorically different: domination. Violence reflected this condition.[32] Blacks from Africa who had been enslaved in the north of the island had no chance of climbing a status ladder. They had no opportunity to have a stake in the system. So they burned it down. They would do so effectively, as many who would emerge as leaders had military experience from war in the Kongo. These ties of experience meant as much as connections to France.[33] Ultimately, this revolution was inspired and instigated by those "from below," every bit as much as the French Revolution.[34]

Free people of color in Saint-Domingue found themselves in similar straits, though their plight was more complicated and rooted in exclusion. The island's grandees still sidelined them from political power. When they grew frustrated because French revolutionary authority could not enforce a new hoped-for order in the colony, they too resorted to violence. Free people of color did so with more hope than the enslaved. They aimed to create a society in which they could have a voice. Some allied themselves with the enslaved against whites. Others made pacts with whites against the enslaved. A large number of petits blancs argued that unrest was gripping the island because the color line had been broached. They, too, armed themselves.[35] But no single group could gain the upper hand. So violence festered, threatening to become a war of all against all. No party could claim a monopoly on violence or atrocity.[36]

French authorities could not manage the situation. For a start, the French were preoccupied with their own revolutionary crisis in the metropole. Though the example of France stirred hope among the enslaved in Saint-Domingue, the Terror strained the ties of sovereign French authority.[37] Moreover and relatedly, the French themselves were divided. Royalist and revolutionary—and those somewhere in between—each tried to use various groups to strengthen their hand at home, only contributing to the uncertainty in Saint-Domingue. In other words, the French interpreted events in Saint-Domingue through the distorting lenses of their own Manichean struggle between republicanism and royalism, lenses that could not quite make out the complex dividing lines of the island that were growing blurrier by the day because of the flow of events in France. In Saint-Domingue royalist and republican tangled with free and unfree, white and Black, wealthy and poor in confounding ways. The collapse of sovereignty muddled any sort of clear choice.[38]

More to the point, with France reeling from violence of its own and with enemies at its gates, the thought of sending a force to end the bloodshed in Saint-Domingue proved an impossibility. All parties in Saint-Domingue looked to France for deliverance. None could come. The only motivating factor that offered any hope was the fact that the island, potentially, was an economic engine of empire. With insurrection and the resulting disorder, sugarcane fields lay in ashes and coffee was not being exported. The French slave trade had fallen apart, and the trade of Bordeaux—that Atlantic node—had shriveled. Ending the chaos on the island, all in France wagered, could bring profits to the metropole. But no one had ability or vision enough to make good on this connection.[39]

Events in France and in Saint-Domingue were tethered in the minds of everyone across the spectrum. For those who opposed the Revolution, it was becoming clear that happenings in one place exacerbated problems in the other. To defeat the enslaved meant reinstituting some stability in France. Ending insurrection in the colony would also mute the shrillest voices in the National Assembly. The same held true for those who saw this as a moment of liberation for both places, especially the few who saw violence as a midwife to substantive change. What was happening in Saint-Domingue served as proof positive for their vision of the difficult path from an old oppressive world to a new enlightened one. If France could free itself through such means, the thinking went, so could even one of the most oppressive colonies in the world. Others on both sides of the aisle saw the more practical aspects of interdependence. Whoever could control the situation in Saint-Domingue could use its riches to defend France from external threats and from internal enemies. Whoever controlled Saint-Domingue possessed a powerful piece in the struggle for authority at home. But given the circumstances on both sides of the French Atlantic, this hope amounted to wishful thinking.[40]

In April 1792, belligerents called a truce of sorts in Saint-Domingue, but only after exhaustion had set in. Louverture and others in his same position brokered it. Most parties in France agreed to the bargain that would be struck. Whites and free people of color decided slavery would still exist and free people of color would have political rights. Now two groups, both recognizing in some sense the sovereignty of the French republic, worked to suppress the insurrections that were gripping the island. Unsurprisingly, it would not hold. Given the nature of revolution, as the French were learning at the very same moment, it could not hold. And another event, or contingency, was sure to set off violence and the tangled cycle of hope, fear, and panic once again. Too many people had tasted freedom. Too many had seen possibilities, and too many with substantive military experience still struggled with oppression.[41]

What happened in Saint-Domingue would not stay in Saint-Domingue. Events there inspired a mixture of emotions elsewhere, perhaps more so than from any other place. This is not hyperbole. Historians tend to view the colony's experience as both the most extreme version of what would happen in the Atlantic and the one that epitomizes in its starkness the central features of revolution. So did those who lived throughout the Atlantic. When much of the Atlantic, most certainly creoles and metropolitan officials, gazed at Saint-Domingue, the overriding emotion was one of "genuine alarm." To a great extent, race and racism explain why the place was demonized. Lurid tales of Blacks and violence, the two interchangeably linked in the minds of many already addled by racism, evoked and invoked horror. Racialized fears encouraged many throughout the Atlantic to draw a direct line between France and Saint-Domingue. The connection epitomized everything that some people worried revolution really presented but were fain to admit. Maybe optimistic visions of the human condition were not entirely well founded. Perhaps Hobbes was right.[42]

Like no other place, Saint-Domingue reminded those with any stake at all in the Atlantic system of the zero-sum nature of the revolutionary process: one group's greatest hopes corresponded to another's deepest fears. When some caught in the maelstrom of competition looked to Saint-Domingue, it occasioned hope. These would include figures as varied as the enslaved throughout the Atlantic and even some creole elites. Simón Bolívar twice visited Saint-Domingue and was aided by insurgents there. What the enslaved were doing on the island inspired those on the intensely networked island of Curaçao. In 1795, on hearing news of events in Saint-Domingue, the enslaved there launched a major rebellion.[43] In

Brazil, soldiers who had been enslaved wore medallions inspired by Saint-Domingue. The same went for rebels in Cuba and eventually those who led slave uprisings in the United States.[44]

The stories of Saint-Domingue, carried over the many networks of the still animated Atlantic, elicited the same range of responses as events in France had. For most, though, panic became the operative emotion. Violence in Saint-Domingue encouraged planters in places far removed to police their enslaved and those below them on the socioeconomic ladder with a renewed vigor and vigilance. Even though Bolívar relied on the help of the formerly enslaved from Saint-Domingue, he did not want to import its revolution to South America. Race war he dreaded above all things. Jamaica, where planters cracked down on any hint of insurrection, offers a prime example of such concerns.[45] The planters had no doubt that what had transpired in Saint-Domingue, as one of the most connected places in the Caribbean if not the world, could occur in Jamaica, a place just as bound to all places in the Atlantic. They worked to ensure it would not.[46]

With the fears occasioned by events in Saint-Domingue, we also see a precursor to what would happen throughout the broader Atlantic in the years to come. Revolution and the fear of it led to war, a phenomenon also tied to the entanglements of the period. The Spanish dreaded what was happening in Saint-Domingue, and they especially grew concerned about the eastern end of the island of Hispaniola, their colony of Santo Domingo. As violence escalated, they sent troops from Puerto Rico to the border that Santo Domingo shared with Saint-Domingue. At this point, they weighed these reasonable concerns against what they might gain. The Spanish realized that if they supported the enslaved in the French colony, and if the enslaved prevailed, Saint-Domingue might be Spain's for the taking. They, therefore, cast the die and began arming enslaved rebels as "auxiliary troops." They would promise their auxiliaries freedom if they helped such a cause. Things did not work out as the Spanish hoped. Though the auxiliaries would occupy a chunk of northern Saint-Domingue in the name of Spain, the new army proved "maddeningly independent." The Spanish proved just as inept at managing the situation as the French had. And the uncertainty of Saint-Domingue was now bound up in the even more complex tangles of international war. War seemed to tie hopes and fears damnably together.[47]

What would happen in Ireland paralleled the Saint-Domingue experience. This is not surprising. Both, after all, were colonies of Atlantic-oriented empires. Both had a history steeped in exploitation. Both had a mix of people enjoying varied statuses, all the products of colonization and of history. In much the same way the tangled relationship between France and Saint-Domingue explains the vector of colonial violence, the Irish story is bound to the nature of its ties to Britain. As in Saint-Domingue, perceptions in Ireland would change over time as events in France and across the ocean presented new possibilities and challenges.

Ireland, of course, was not Saint-Domingue. Most Irish in the eighteenth century struggled with exclusion, not race-based domination; nevertheless, the broad outlines of the two experiences an ocean away appear so similar because they were caught in the same process. Because of the French connection, Ireland, of course, had become a tinderbox of twisted tensions and old hatreds, again much like Saint-Domingue. Ireland, many came to believe at the time, would revisit its past unless the ties to Britain were cut. The United Irishmen, in the wake of events in France and its descent into violence, understood that the Irish past would be prologue if Britain could divide and conquer the kingdom once more. The fault lines in Ireland seemed as deep and as potentially violent as those in Saint-Domingue. Again, breaking the connection to Britain offered the only means of escaping the furies of Ireland's past and those of the Atlantic's present.[48]

The United Irish believed they could make Ireland anew. They thought as much because they were a hyper-connected people, as tied to movements in other places as any group of self-styled revolutionaries. France served as a shining example, even as revolution had become increasingly violent. There, after all, a deeply Catholic nation was being re-made in the revolutionary crucible. The example of American revolutionaries tossing off British rule inspired the Irish. The United Irish declared, as part of their catechism, that the tree of liberty first grew in America, bloomed in France, and was destined to flower in Ireland. They hailed the enslaved rebels in Saint-Domingue as part of this story. They celebrated Olaudah Equiano when he visited Ireland, and they devoured his *Narrative* when it arrived in Ireland.[49] One of their leaders, Theobald Wolfe Tone, looked at the broader Atlantic and envisioned the creation of "a free republic in South America," as he made plans to do just the same for Ireland. He knew violence was necessary. Through it, he hoped to help remake the world.[50]

It did not turn out to be that simple. What happened in France, especially the violence, crystalized lines of divisions in Ireland. Intending to bring more allies into the fold, the United Irish leaders now actively sought an alliance with disaffected Catholics. They would add power and threat. Even though Defenders knew of and praised Paine's *Rights of Man*, they interpreted liberation through confessional competition. The mobilization of the Defenders caused many Protestants to retreat from ecumenical enlightenment to the old bastions of sectarian hatred. Out of the maelstrom of growing disorder, the Orange Order was born. Created by the wealthy to protect their status in a politicized world, the order enlisted poorer Protestants and reaffirmed that their place in Ireland ultimately depended on the subjection of Catholics. The British state also stepped in, infiltrating the United Irishmen and trying to crush the movement. Suppression radicalized some elements. The United Irish now aimed at nothing less than creating a republic through violence, just as the kingdom was militarizing for what appeared to be civil war.[51]

Officials knew that United Irish leaders were looking to the example of republican America and now communicating with republican France to mobilize the Irish nation to fight for its freedom. With the political arrangement of 1782 now completely discredited, and by extension the reigning relationship between Britain and Ireland teetering, the sort of uncertainty over sovereignty that had unleashed revolution in America, France, and Saint-Domingue now reared its head in Ireland. Ireland, too, was poised to enter the crucible. With the Terror, with the sugarcane fields ablaze in Saint-Domingue, with America fresh in the minds of all, it seemed the Atlantic revolution had arrived on Britain's doorstep.[52] Fear was weaponized. Reports of violence and mass mobilization began to appear.

Ireland sitting on the revolutionary edge set off a frenzy in Britain. Sensing a pattern in France, in Saint-Domingue, and most troublingly in Ireland, those running Britain reassessed the age. Events seemed to vindicate Burke. As the government cracked down on any group sympathetic to France, it scuttled any reforming initiatives. Fearing the connections within a radicalizing world growing increasingly violent, most Britons now hailed the timelessness of their institutions and the wisdom of tradition. Those who still held to the now discredited enlightened vision were hounded by the state.[53] Indeed, some charged that harsh measures represented Britain's version of "a Reign of Terror." The government suspended habeas corpus, outlawed organizations, and imprisoned radicals. It did what it did to keep certain ideas out of bounds.[54] The British, in effect, erected ideological borders to keep revolution out.

Hopes mobilized people, and fear moved states. And this held for places far from the Atlantic. As France was tied to all European nations, through diplomatic channels and through print, people on the Continent, too, would have to contend with the conundrum of revolutionary connections. Many places on the Continent witnessed minor episodes of unrest break out. These disturbances never threatened the status quo; they did not grow very violent; and they remained local in inflection and scope. In Germany, for instance, the age transfixed men and women. Some discussed and debated events in places as far away as Saint-Domingue.[55] Others in Germany moved to action. In these years of growing violence, small groups of insurgents took to the streets in Rhenish areas and, in larger demonstrations, in Saxony. Authorities easily suppressed them. As a rule, authorities had only to contend with local eruptions of discontent, even if the language couching discontent was new. So officials did not have to act with the same vigor that the British did. That said, if a larger conflagration were to engulf the German states, authorities would be gravely challenged.[56]

This is generally the story on the Continent beyond France. France proved an inspiration to some and a dread fear to others. But the state had the wherewithal to maintain control. Take the case of Brussels. Events in France offered the occasion to question the grip Austria had on Belgium. For years, more and more men and women began to question Austrian sovereignty, just as they saw more Austrian troops in their midst, now necessary to maintain order in the far-flung province. Violence broke out as men and women tied what was happening at the moment to earlier attempts to press for Belgian autonomy. What happened in France did indeed touch off a rebellion. In early 1790, under the banner of the Catholic Church, the Belgians, now calling themselves such, rose up, ousted Austrian troops, and claimed the new republic as theirs. No sooner had the republic been declared that it began to disintegrate along its fault lines, something that had not happened in the earlier episodes. Soon people from different ethnic regions and from different classes and occupational groups were threatening each other, as everyone tried to reconfigure sovereignty in an increasingly anarchic situation. Many feared that Belgium would become like France. This did not come to pass. The Austrian state had the power, and was willing to deploy it, to safeguard its authority. By the end of 1790, the short-lived Belgian republic had been swallowed up once more by Austria.[57]

The Belgian case points to a few observations about how violence spread. Ideas in and of themselves could be intoxicating to some and terrifying to others. But they worked in two ways. First, they could be likened to seeds, as the United Irish argued. They sprouted into something more if they fell on the right ground, where older ways could not keep up with newer pressures and possibilities. In other places, such was not the case. Second, they acted as solvents, revealing the tensions and dividing lines in each society, as their invocation required men and women to revisit the basis of status and rule in each society. Both grievances and social tensions, of course, were conditioned by distinctive historical factors. In those states with older structures, which could not manage the tide of mass politicization that reforming agendas unleashed, and if debate centered on sovereignty, all sorts of voices and violence filled the vacuum of sovereignty.

Unless, that is, the state could be mobilized to coerce. Violence emerged from old hatreds voiced in new ways in contexts men and women regarded as fungible and electrified, and only if the state could not respond to channel or stem it. In these fluid contexts of hardening hatreds and unrealized hopes, the state had few options. If it did not act expeditiously, all could fall apart, and unbridled competition along lines sure to foment violence would ensue. If officials did so with a sense of urgency, as they had in Britain, the lid could be kept on. For all of our talk about hopes, fears, and networks, revolutionary ferment began and ended with sovereignty.

Ironically, revisiting the place where revolution had apparently come to an end tells us a great deal about its essential characteristics. So, let's return to America. As we have already seen, when it comes to revolutionary dynamics, we have to trace both connections and parallels. This applies also to terror. First, connections. The Terror in France entranced Americans, in much the same way it had the rest of the broader Atlantic. In the case of the United States, though, citizens read of events in the wake of their own revolutionary experience. A few still held the French Revolution to be a sister event to the one in America. They followed the line of Jacobins in France, hoping that true liberation, the sort that had been forestalled in America by its revolutionary settlement, could be realized by linking America to broader and continuing revolutionary ferment. Radicals employed categories imported from France to champion their vision and lambaste their enemies. But these people did not represent the norm, particularly with the turn to terror. Most people of nearly all political stripes recoiled at the Terror in France, even those who had joined

Democratic-Republican societies. The unstated assumption in the United States was this: the uncertainty of revolution had been done away with; not all may have agreed on every aspect of the settlement; but nearly all hoped to consign the violence of the past to the past. A fairly straightforward story.[58]

Just as straightforward was that what was happening in Saint-Domingue proved even more troubling. It hit, in every conceivable way, closer to home. Slave insurrection was something few aside from the enslaved at this stage welcomed. It represented for white southerners the sum of all fears. The enslaved, by definition, did not have agency. If they were taking things into their own hands, the world was turning upside down in ways most Americans could barely comprehend.[59] But the issue was this: they did have agency. Planters from Saint-Domingue fled the island with their enslaved persons amid the violence gripping it. Many left the colony for other slave societies, with different imperial histories but with similar colonial structures, including the United States. The "French Negroes" among the refugees alarmed and challenged all. They also inspired those who were enslaved.[60]

For whites, the challenges were more unambiguous and the choices starker. The presence of radical Black voices threatened the status quo in cities like Savannah and Charleston. For those to the north, slave revolt would threaten to undo the union of the states. The union amounted to a fragile accommodation brokered between southerners and northerners that had been accomplished to address revolutionary uncertainty in the first place. For both groups, Saint-Domingue loomed large. All Americans could see the refugees in their streets. The whites among them came with lurid tales that terrified Americans, ones that suggested the world was reeling from the excesses of republican thought. White Americans in no way wanted a Black Jacobin presence in their midst. They worried that the enslaved arriving from Saint-Domingue could have been radicalized and so could politicize the enslaved on American plantations. These exiles also confronted everyone with the most glaring contradiction of the age: independence and its relationship to slavery. How could the United States be a "slaveholding republic"?[61]

America, therefore, potentially reeled from continuing Atlantic connections. These issues of enmeshment proved even more bedeviling than before. Those from Saint-Domingue, especially, were attuned to events in a connected world. Refugees further destabilized already volatile political contexts, revealing that even presumed endings could not be hermetically sealed from continuing connections. Ongoing porousness could at best be managed. Fears were amplified by the arrival of even more radicals and reactionaries to the shores of America as the Terror was engulfing France. United Irishmen began arriving in larger numbers than before as the British state began to crack down on what was becoming a revolutionary movement. They continued to see the United States as a republican asylum; but now few Americans were willing to extend them a hearty welcome.[62] The context had changed to such an extent that they now seemed agents of disorder.

The new United States did what Britain was doing to navigate the newly repoliticized Atlantic. The state did all it could to ensure that revolutionary networks remained inert. In fact, state actors worked hard to sunder troubling connections. The Alien and Sedition Acts were designed to do just that: to keep radical voices and persons at bay; and to ensure that revolution in other areas of the Atlantic would not reanimate American tensions that had not been rectified by the American Revolution. The acts were designed to establish a cordon sanitaire and to ensure that the United States did not once again enter the abyss.[63]

Nonetheless, not all threats came from without. Here we come to the complex story of parallels. At this juncture, just as they fretted over the Terror in France and events in Saint-Domingue, Americans confronted fears on the very edges of the new nation. The one place stability was failing was in the west. Officials could not address the search for order there, and as a result the people's attachment to the state was becoming undone. Much like Ireland or Saint-Domingue, the place was breaking down along its fault lines. On the one hand, common white settlers vied with speculators and the wealthy for land in the west. On the other hand, both had to contest Indigenous peoples for it. Natives, especially in the Ohio Valley, where thousands of Euro-Americans were settling, also remained mobilized after revolutionary tumult. Younger men had overthrown older ways and alliances, as they resisted the onslaught of settlers. These same settlers expected that the newly formed state to the east would support them in removing or killing Natives, freeing up land for them to settle. Speculators expected the state to remove barriers to trade and to development.[64]

Natives used a number of different strategies to contest expansion. Some, such as the Iroquois, brokered alliances and attempted diplomacy with officials from the east. They had good reason to do so. The Iroquois League, which was composed of six nations before the Revolution, had been shattered by war and by American scorched-earth policies. The Iroquois used all their creativity to navigate the age, including trying to ally themselves with the British. Others, especially where settlement was focused, created alliances for war making. Under Shawnee leadership, Natives confronted successive armies sent west by the new United States. They would not allow settlers to establish beachheads in the region. They rightly saw the troops sent as storm troopers of settlement and expansion. The Natives outfought them.[65]

Things became even more tangled in regions along the Gulf Coast where the Spanish had been. The decision of the Spanish to attack places like Pensacola and Mobile during the War for Independence mobilized the whole region. What had been a connected world defined by interdependency now confronted the zero-sum reality of hard choices. Chickasaws, Creeks, and Choctaws wondered if this new claimant to their homelands, the United States, would act as yet another nation in the region or if it was intent on subjugation. In the recent war, these Natives had fought for their own reasons within an imperial global struggle. They had held onto their autonomy. What inhabitants of that world could not handle were lines made hard and fast between territories and between peoples. The Spanish had bowed to the realities imposed by the region. The question these people faced was whether the new republic would also be thus constrained. Given the pressures the United States faced from a politicized white citizenry and the belief that the war against Britain had won land for the taking, both in Ohio and along the Gulf, many began to dread what the future held.[66]

Therefore, even in regions far from the ocean, Atlantic patterns played out and tangles reached. The two largest barriers to peace for the new republic besides squatters and Natives were the British, who remained in frontier forts after the war, and the Spanish, who threatened further expansion onto the continent. The British would remain, until Americans made good on prewar debts owed to British merchants and until Loyalist claims were realized. The Spanish, who feared the spread of radical ideas to their New World holdings, hemmed in the new republic, claiming the Mississippi River as theirs. Spanish intransigence over the issue stymied producers in the Ohio Valley, who wanted an outlet for their trade. These competitors would not permit the state to establish meaningful sovereignty in the west.[67] All the while, the Natives who inhabited lands on the edge of the new republic were placed in all sorts of binds between Spanish and American claims, between British and American aims, and between settlers and the government that hoped for some semblance of peace along its frontiers. The uncertainty further convinced Natives to form confederacies in the both the north and the south.[68]

Finally, events in France may also have been encouraging Indians in the Ohio Country and the Gulf region to reimagine possibilities for a broader community. We have long known how the American Revolution, and its resulting fallout, led to the dissolution of Native polities, like the Six Nations, the restructuring of nations, like the Catawba, and the creation of new amalgamations, like the multi-nation Nativist confederacy in Ohio. Yet, many of these may well have become possible because of flows of communication to and from revolutionary France. Natives fastened on news of events that electrified and terrified whites living in the east. News reached them through established networks. Of course, many hoped that France would somehow return, not as a colonizer but as a counterweight; however, we cannot underestimate the possibility that adopting revolutionary ideas of republicanism from France, particularly the universalism that so alarmed many citizens of the United States, helped meld peoples together, fostered renewal after a period of suffering, and set the Natives apart from those who would take their land. In the process, many reinvented themselves to confront the new colonialism. Needless to say, this eventuality did not lend itself to the reconstitution of order for the white polity trying to emerge from revolution.[69]

The west had become a combustible knot. The American Revolution settlement depended on trade-offs, as we know. Some won, and some lost. Nearly all Natives had surrendered a great deal. They were not the only ones. Common whites had won only the proverbial half a loaf. What if common whites mobilized to contest the settlement? What if they tied the American revolutionary experience to new eventualities in the broader Atlantic? Grievances would stir such connections. The west played a vital role in cutting such connections. It served as a safety valve for white discontent. It gave those potentially disaffected a stake in the revolutionary settlement. But how would the state address Natives in the west? These men and women, just as politicized, wanted to protect what they had. In the west, grievances were bound to collide.

In this instance, the hatreds between and among groups produced a dynamic very much like that of other places struggling with violence at this very moment. By the mid-1790s, Indigenous peoples had rejected the state; speculators began to look to other sovereign powers that could help them realize their vision for a western political economy; and poorer whites flirted with western independence or alliances with Britain or Spain, threatening to establish a state that could protect them and their interests. In such a sovereign vacuum, violence increased. It did so following the prevailing revolutionary patterns, through contingency. In this case, it was the decision of the new government to enact an excise on distilled spirits. The new tax hamstrung the poorer sort especially, who had few economic outlets save potable whiskey. First incensed by the excise, they tied this eventuality to a broader set of concerns. They reacted by threatening and enacting the sort of violence seen during the War of Independence.[70]

Ominously, these "whiskey rebels" saw events in Ireland and in France as inspirational. The intensity of the violence there encouraged the use of anti-statist rhetoric, symbols, and rituals—many from the American revolutionary past and the revolutionary Atlantic present—all of which made the situation graver still for the United States. The end result was the American west was threatening to come undone, and it did not appear that the fledgling republican state had the resources or capacity to ease tensions, manage or blunt them, or to coerce. Indeed, so pronounced was violence becoming that America was threatening to break apart.

There is more to the American story, much more, most of which only comes to light as we think of the United States within an Atlantic context. We have, for instance, long asked, "Why no Terror in America?" Maybe we have not looked closely enough. If terror is state-sponsored violence, then much of the newly independent American South would seem to fit the bill. The disruptions of war turned southern slave societies upside down. The enslaved had fled, others had died from disease. In the wake of war, planters in South Carolina and Georgia sought to remake the world they feared losing. Plantations were reorganized, and the enslaved were put to work once more. In this context, the example of Saint-Domingue made planters and officials that much more vigilant when it came to sniffing out any sort of intrigue, real or imagined. To say planters and officials were terrified of events there would be an understatement. They saw "slave conspiracies" where none existed. Or they construed isolated incidents as linked to others. Connection, real and imagined, haunted them. They no doubt had some grounds for these fears. The enslaved did indeed catch wind of Saint-Domingue, encouraging planters to use the many levers provided by a federal system to forestall revolutionary intrigue. The state, too, was complicit in sustaining this order.[71]

Perhaps the new United States had not dodged the Furies brought on by Atlantic ties after all. In fact, the ways violence was targeted at those on the margins cohere to the broader revolutionary pattern. In the American context, Blacks suffered from an American Terror, especially those on plantations. In the years after independence, the plantation system was reenergized, and new men and women were brought over in chains from Africa to feed it.[72] Natives, especially, suffered for the vindication of the American republic. We are now just beginning to appreciate how much anti-Indian fury fueled the American Revolution. Washington harbored intense anti-Indian prejudices. More to the point, he had dispatched the armies under John Sullivan that had destroyed Iroquois communities. Commanders had also led what can only be regarded as genocidal raids against Indians, such as the infamous killing of ninety-six peaceful Indians at Gnadenhutten. Even though officials did not yet have the ability to wage effective war against Indians in the Ohio Valley, at least not yet, they knew that if they failed to do so, their vision of the republic could be lost.[73] White settlers, after all, needed places to settle.

This dynamic was as central to America's revolution as the sentiment of anti-aristocracy was to France's Terror. Of course, the slaughter or expulsion of Natives in Ohio, egged on by settlers, was more terrifying than sansculottes intimidating officials to send men to the guillotine in Paris. But in terms of the revolutionary process, they are worth comparing. Just as officials in the newly sovereign United States turned their attention to Natives to bolster a new regime, those in the ascendancy in France at the time of the king's execution resorted to the Terror to prop up their legitimacy. In a context of contestation, and in the crucible of revolutionary competition, fear could create rule.[74] The greatest trick Americans played was to make all of this vanish.

Once we transnationalize things, then, terror would seem inextricably bound up in the revolutionary process. Because in each of these places in the revolutionary abyss stakes were so high and competition to remake sovereignty so fierce, the line separating those inside from those outside the newly imagined community could be drawn in blood and fear. The French used the word "terror" because it conjured all sorts of associations with older conceptions of church and state. It could be readily employed.[75] But the impetus to use violence to distinguish between peoples and groups was not particularly French. It tempted all. Both universally shared and intensely local in inflection, it was bound up in the entangled nature of the eighteenth-century Atlantic, just as it demonstrated how each society affected by revolution was haunted by the ghosts of its past.

Perhaps the best place to understand how fear worked in the Atlantic was where it did not reign. Latin America was the dog that did not bark, an exception that proved the rule of the complex connections between the universal, the local, the tangles of the Atlantic, and the role of the state. At issue here, as elsewhere, was sovereignty. But not its exercise. Spain and Portugal, of course, faced potentially immense challenges as the new and troubling chapter of the Atlantic revolutionary age unfolded. Controlling peoples and ideas an ocean away over vast expanses, ensuring that hopes and inspiration did not travel through networks, proved more daunting for them than for nearly every other state. Yet, for ultramarine empires the best imperial strategy to avoid the snares in the network of fear meant doing as little as possible. For Spanish and Portuguese officialdom, the key to surviving the tumults of the age involved strengthening, not attenuating in any way, the power of local ascendancies. If locals had free rein, they could check the sort of violence generated in France and in Saint-Domingue. But, of course, the cost of sovereign inaction was more oppression.

This did not happen through some sort of grand strategy. In Latin America, the modesty of what reform achieved in the past shielded the Spanish and Portuguese Empires from falling to pieces. They had a few things in their favor. Tensions between groups, for a start, were not as complex as they were in places like Saint-Domingue. To be sure, the empires that were emerging in the era of Atlantic reform relied for labor on slavery. Creole elites fretted about Saint-Domingue, certainly in places like Venezuela and Brazil, where enslaved and free Blacks outnumbered whites. But some planters in Spanish America had developed a more sophisticated and hybrid model of slavery that rewarded industry.[76] More important, the ability of creoles to control and manage the labor force strengthened their case for greater autonomy. As they prospered, officials at the center reckoned that so long as illicit commerce and the trade in precious metals were policed, they should leave well enough alone. In other words, the sovereignty of the whole remained secure, and with no vacuum of authority, the crisis that played on both hopes and fears could be averted. Not by design but by a lack of power, coordinated effort, and overarching vision, these empires proved resilient and impervious to the

destructive tensions of the day. The crippling dividing lines were managed at the margins by those with a stake in the system.[77]

Intent on avoiding the crisis gripping the whole, both Spanish officials at the center and elites in the provinces worked to bind the whole
together more securely. Leaders in the metropole and in the colonies
viewed the ideas inspiring French revolutionaries as "toxic"; they just enjoyed more success in sealing them off. As opposed to what was happening elsewhere, the empire experienced a moment of great economic,
cultural, and intellectual vitality. Such was the lot of creole elites, in any
event. The reason is simple: whereas tensions had led most others to
question regimes, these self-same sorts of tensions encouraged those in
the Latin American world with a stake in the system to support the regime. Empire, for more and more, had its benefits.[78]

Such arrangements could not keep all fires at bay. Venezuela offers a
case study of how the mingling of fears and hopes could politicize even a
remote region. Far removed from the centers of prosperity and power in
Spanish America, the Captaincy General of Venezuela had no printing
press and little of what we could call a public sphere. Yet, communications networks that relied on word of mouth and on growing literacy
drew its peoples into the world of revolutionary intrigue. The Franco-
Caribbean connection may have terrified officials, but it enthralled those
on the margins of a marginal place. Rumors, news from visitors, and stories and ideas spreading through an oral and text-driven web of communication inspired rebellions against authority and conspiracies against
officialdom, local hierarchies, and even the Crown. Intrigue persisted,
culminating in the development of a small mixed-race republican movement.[79] But this did not prove the norm.

As a rule, local rulers prevailed. Empowered by what the central state
did not do, creoles never saw the need for independence. They were
freed to play the role of an old ascendancy and served as proxies for the
sovereign, policing both ideas and peoples. In Venezuela, those creole
elites who found themselves dealing with the potential of slave violence
did what planters in Jamaica were doing. They cracked down on any intrigue among the enslaved. Or they opted for conciliation. All government strategies were premised on control and rooted in fear of
connection. Similarly, taking a page from the book of North Americans,
Mexican liberals, who had been heartened by the early years of revolution in France, saw that revolution in their own lands could portend social anarchy. So they policed themselves. Ties in this Atlantic could

indeed spread radical ideas; they also could encourage others to do what they could to avoid destabilization.[80]

Ultimately, with no imperial crisis, violence over the competition to see who would rule at home never materialized. Creoles did not have to face the dilemma that had vexed so many throughout the Atlantic. In fact, even in a world of intense connections, a place riven with dramatic fault lines could become more stable, even more prosperous, because of what metropolitan officials did not do. Take Cuba as an example. To be sure, Cuban planters dreaded what had happened in Saint-Domingue, and they did everything in their power to keep radicalism at bay. They tried to ensure, as well, that ships from the island did not carry the enslaved from Saint-Domingue, "infected," as they said, with revolutionary ideas. They policed their plantations with vigilance. They also had the autonomy to take advantage of the Atlantic-wide crisis of fear. From this moment, Cuba—as a sugar-producing slave-based economy—took off. As fields filled with sugarcane burned in Saint-Domingue, planters here took up the slack. The world still needed sugar, and Cubans were happy to supply it. The institution of slavery thrived with slave rebellion next door, and the numbers of enslaved people imported to the island from Africa soared as production reached new heights. By the 1820s, more sugar would leave Cuba than from Saint-Domingue and Jamaica. While freedom was in the air in Saint-Domingue, oppression increased in Cuba. The autonomous and empowered planters spoke of the "happiness" of the period. Entanglements did not prove their undoing but made them wealthy. What had been a backwater and smuggler's nest now became the new Saint-Domingue of the Caribbean—or what it had been.[81]

The Portuguese followed another model still, though they did so in response to growing threats from the Atlantic crisis. Exports from Brazil boomed, largely because of events in Saint-Domingue, and Lisbon's balance sheets, finally, were in the black.[82] Yet, elites in Portugal and Brazil retained a healthy fear of tumult. The rising in Minas Gerais, which had been inspired by the American Revolution, remained fresh in their minds. Though the rebels had hatched their plans before events in France were coursing around communications networks, officials reacted to the news of the abortive plan in the wake of what had happened in France. Local elites and metropolitan officials, therefore, saw the event through the kaleidoscopic lens of the connected revolutionary Atlantic. Both feared it presaged a new spirit of rebellion in light of what had happened in France and in Saint-Domingue. Metropolitan authorities responded at first in ham-fisted ways. But soon they came up with a plan of compromise—again willy-nilly, out of necessity, and through weakness—that would grant even more autonomy to elites in peripheries. The Brazilian ascendancy would control its own society.

This sensibility would soon define economic relations as well. During another regional crisis, this one in the sugar-growing area of Bahia, some who resented Portuguese imperial trade policies were rallying others up and down the socioeconomic ladder to their cause. They were playing with fire. Soon mulattoes were clamoring for greater liberties. In other words, a potential replay of Boston and of Paris. The Bahia agitation came to naught, but it alarmed metropolitan officials sufficiently to liberalize trade in just the way they were liberalizing political relations within the empire. They did not surrender authority to forces beneath them; rather, they gave greater power to creoles in the provinces, with the hopes, much as had happened for the Spanish Empire, that autonomy would ironically bind the provinces more closely to the center.

Compromise represented the only viable way forward and ensured that revolutionary disorder did not visit Brazil. The binds almost became gossamer-like, just like the ones Edmund Burke had argued Britons should revert to in order to avoid an all-out crisis with North America's creole population. The Portuguese had taken just such an approach at this moment, realizing that tightening screws would alienate elites and lead them to question imperial authority. Creoles in Brazil were happy with the new state of affairs, most especially because they consciously feared what rebellion and disorder portended in sugar-growing regions dominated by the enslaved. They knew that if they resisted the government, they would have a Saint-Domingue on their hands.[83] They had learned how fear in the networked Atlantic traveled and functioned, and how imperial crisis could lead inexorably to vacuums of authority and so politicize cleavages. The Luso-Atlantic experienced neither, through local action and metropolitan inaction.

Let's fast-forward a few years. As some places struggled for the first time with the sorts of tensions many had wrestled with for years, glimmers of the endgame would become apparent in United States in 1801. In that year, Thomas Jefferson would win the presidency. With his inaugural address, he famously argued that Americans could no longer be seen as partisans drawn into the dizzying currents of the age. They needed to emerge from it if the republic was to survive. "We are all Republicans, we are all Federalists," Jefferson declared. By 1801, when he was entering the president's mansion in the newly rising city of Washington, D.C., Americans had done a great deal to bring their Revolution to a close. They had found political stability. They had come to terms with the new political economy, yoking American plantations and farms to a system increasingly premised on free trade. The men who had fought and sacrificed in these years were recognized politically, even if the Constitution muted their voices. The revolution settlement recognized that popular sovereignty could not be wished away, even if elites still controlled the political levers of the system and would gain the most economically. And they had created a state that could stand among the nations of the earth. Just as significantly, they were creating a vision of a nation, of themselves as a distinctive people—a people *of* the age but not in it.[84]

What was happening elsewhere, in no small part, informed the American search for order. Jefferson himself, who had embraced the possibilities of revolution in France as something that could further extend liberty for some in America, recoiled at the Terror. It moved him and many others away from the radical fringe and toward the center.[85] He was also terrified by what was taking place in Saint-Domingue. He was right to worry. The enslaved from the island were arriving in New Orleans, right on his doorstep, as refugees.[86] The American South still relied on slave labor to remain competitive in the Atlantic economy. Saint-Domingue represented, for him, a troubling contingency that could undo the newly formed settlement unless it were contained. Of course, as the Brazilian example suggests, he was not alone. Americans had good reason, given the tensions swirling in the broader Atlantic, to get their house in order. The Atlantic still remained a tangled place.

In this way, the outlines of endings lay on the horizon even as some in the Atlantic world were just being plunged into uncertainty. And even Americans continued to fret that unless they managed their connected world with vigor, they would be tossed once more into what Jefferson referred to as a "storm" from which they were just finding a "happy port."[87] He knew one issue more than any other, that which arguably made America and the Atlantic, could plunge all into that sea once more. And Saint-Domingue pointed it out. All struggled with different sorts of pasts and the tensions they occasioned. For Americans, as for those in Saint-Domingue or Brazil, tensions and pasts intersected with race. With good reason, Jefferson called slavery in the era of revolution a "deplorable entanglement."[88]

The seeming contradictions and entanglements that Jefferson is remembered for to this very day—that freedom and slavery went hand in hand—were at this point issues most would rather ignore. Saint-Domingue served as a vivid reminder of the truly incommensurate relationship between the two. Even if America's emerging settlement tried to reconcile the irreconcilable and to keep the peace in doing so, the fact of their incompatibility in the emerging world could not be wished away. As long as violence continued in the Atlantic, as long as connections to places still reeling endured, these contradictions had to be confronted, and because of continuing connections, any provisional settlement would always be imperiled. So even though America seemed to moving toward endings, fault lines still remained, the type that the Atlantic world reminded everyone of. The age had not ended.

# CHAPTER FIVE

# The Web of War

## *Making States and Unmaking Empire*

BECAUSE ITS HOPEFUL AND dreadful aspects were bound together, revolution caused all sorts of disruption. For most, though, revolution came because of disruption.[1] As the age progressed, the main solvent that broke down society was war. War affected most places touched by it in the same way. When and where it raged, sovereignty collapsed, as a rule. With war, we also encounter one of the period's most conspicuous ironies. War did not necessarily do this by design; on the contrary, it was often employed to bring an end to the entanglements of hope and fear.

The age was defined as much by aggression as it was by revolution.[2] Like hope and fear, aggression spread. Because of how enmeshed European power politics had become with Atlantic-wide dynamics, war in one place would touch off conflict in others. Through connectedness, even places on the very margins of the Atlantic would be transformed by aggression and the fears and hopes it generated. Aggression could not be disentangled from revolution. One chapter of warfare could be called the French Revolutionary Wars, and the next the Napoleonic Wars. Whichever term we use, whether we see war as a series of struggles between France and different coalitions or as part of a continuum going back into the eighteenth century, it was all bound up in the tangles of older European rivalries and Atlantic competition.[3]

Three of the men more responsible than most for prosecuting warfare at this moment appreciated the connection between revolution and war and tried to exploit it. Napoleon Bonaparte believed in his own glory. As he put it after he claimed political power in France, a republican leader "is not like kings . . . who see their states as an inheritance; he needs brilliant deeds, and, therefore, war." He also believed that war abroad could bring to an end revolution at home. In this regard, he reckoned war would chain the furies for France. Although he agreed with France's Jacobins that freedom could be in the offing for humankind at this time, Napoleon did not regard himself as a revolutionary missionary. For him, warring with the world served strategic purposes. It kept the men and women of the nation focused on things beyond themselves and their fellow citizens. "Without an army, without force, without discipline, there is no political independence or civil liberty," he believed. War also ensured that fearful and aggressive neighbors did not try to put an end to revolutionary France. Aggression did more. The revolution, through the Terror, had consumed its own. Having armies in the field occupied the most politicized in campaigns. Securing glory for France could ensure that the nation did not tear itself apart. Napoleon and his generals were fighting to achieve these linked goals. "It is the soldier," he claimed, "who founds republics; it is the soldier who maintains them." With good reason he has been called revolutionary France's "blacksmith," beating guillotines into swords.[4]

The same went for two of his great nemeses, Admiral Horatio Nelson and Arthur Wellesley, the Duke of Wellington. Convinced—and even terrified—that the revolutionary "contagion" could spread because of how it inspired people, these men fought in part to kill the virus by slaying its host. Nelson and Wellington led British forces in what turned out to be the great struggle for the revolutionary period that lasted almost unabated from 1793 to 1815. They oversaw a massive popular mobilization, when one in five men of age bore arms for Britain. Officials recruited men from the Scottish and Irish peripheries, and they came to rely on English militias to meet growing demand for numbers.[5] They had good reason to clamor for men. France had created a mobilized juggernaut. Nelson complained he needed more ships and sailors if he was to do his job. Wellington continually asked for more troops from Britain and Ireland, and at times he felt he had to "beg" for them. To fight France "on tolerably equal terms," as he put it, required unprecedented numbers over a long period of time, and no one could say for how long men would be needed. The uncertainty of the age, and the certainty of France's ability to mobilize, demanded that Britain, too, be "an armed nation."[6]

Such arming brought benefits. British leaders also dealt with an increasingly politicized people. Having them labor aboard ships and fight on battlefields far from Britain promised, just as was the case with the French, to tame or to domesticate the forces that threatened to overwhelm the country. It did something more. Fighting for the state yoked people to that state. In other words, politicization, far from threatening, could be harnessed for a new age of warfare. War, in both the French and the British cases, buttressed the state and the search for order, even if Napoleon and Wellington did so for two very different regimes.[7]

Admittedly, these nations were the exception. In other places, war initiated revolution, as more than anything else, it quickly de-stated regimes. Aggression fractured societies up to this point immune from violence on the Continent. Of course, this was not a new story, and the eighteenth century was chock-full of tales of rampaging armies moving across borders. But with modern warfare, with whole populations mobilized to contest new threats—made all the more ominous because of the increased capacity of the state—the effects were more traumatic. To meet fire with fire, those touched by war would have to revisit sovereignty. In doing so they risked politicization. War also overturned those empires that had thus far escaped the dislocations of the age. The men and women of the Spanish and Portuguese Atlantic world had survived the sovereign crisis that had bedeviled empires in the wake of reform. Now, aggression compromised the empires of negotiation they had created. War in Europe confronted people throughout Latin America with all the difficult dilemmas that had visited so many places during the age. With warfare, even those places more or less inoculated from revolutionary intrigue fell to pieces.

The sum total of the period's aggression, the third operative emotion along with hope and fear, was what we could call the War of the Revolutionary Age. It trapped nearly everybody in its web. Some pulled on the threads to ensnare others and save their nations. Others did so to defend themselves. Still others hoped to foster war to achieve liberation. Many people found themselves forced to fight to keep body and soul together. Eighteenth-century ways of knowing were not so much challenged as shattered by the duration of warfare waged as never before. All were thus caught because of the threads that had been spun during the age of Atlantic consolidation. Like hope and panic, aggression thrived on networks. War created, just as it destroyed, and it became the chief means, again through connections, that hopes of liberation mingled with fears of violence.[8] Entanglements only made it massive in scope and scale.[9]

The place farthest removed from the Atlantic—in fact, the interior of a continent—offers an instructive tale about war and the age. The story starts with George Washington a few years before Jefferson's election. With the so-called Whiskey Rebellion, western insurgents were questioning the sovereign power of the new postrevolutionary government. Their actions presented the state once more with the threat of revolutionary violence. As Natives killed whites and whites savaged Natives, settlers were pleading with the new government for protection. With only hollow promises and a few expeditions sent out, which were easily repulsed by the Natives, speculators and common settlers found common cause, and together they began clamoring for greater autonomy in order to press for their own vision of the west.[10]

Washington's government finally responded. Afraid that the sort of violence gripping France could raise its head in the United States, the new regime dispatched not one but two armies to the west. In so doing, Washington was putting a lid on any sort of settler insurgency, while paving the way for long-term grievances of westerners to be addressed. The first army was sent to crush the westerners' rebellion; in fact, it scattered it. The new state would claim sovereignty over its territory. At the same time, a special force was training to do battle with Natives. Prepared to fight a guerrilla war, these troops were to address what the government regarded as the Indian menace in the Ohio Valley. Doing so could serve a number of purposes. First, it could assuage white fears, even as the other army was suppressing the settler insurgency.[11] Second, it could clear groups like the Shawnees off a great deal of land that would enrich speculators and could provide land for the poorer sort. The second army, the Legion of the United States, led by Anthony Wayne, prevailed. The force was not that considerable, but it proved credible enough to pacify much of the west. In 1795, the new order was christened at a place called Greenville with a treaty between the United States government and formerly hostile Natives. A line would separate Natives from whites, one designed to move.

Ironically, Washington was at pains to declare the United States neutral in the warfare overtaking the Atlantic in the 1790s. Nonaggression in the international realm would allow the fledgling state to remain independent and allow its institutions to grow.[12] Aggression, however, won the west for the settler state. However small these armies may have been that marched west, and however tiny garrisons in the west would be, both allowed for expansion. The arrangement was precarious but effective.[13] Moreover, at this same time the Spaniards ceded their exclusive rights to the Mississippi, and the British agreed to leave their western forts. The whole west up to the Mississippi lay open, free of international tangles. With this new arrangement, the new nation had created a massive land reserve. Settlers could stream west instead of clamoring for rights and destabilizing things in the east. Under these circumstances, Natives had little choice but to move.[14] Thus the fledgling state figured out how to solve the knotty settler-Native dilemma in the west.

Jefferson designed the system that emerged from war and that canonized this dynamic. He envisioned a west of self-replicating microrepublics that would be yoked together in a federal union. Initially, he gave these regions classically sounding names that hid their actual purpose. His genius was to suggest that new states created in the west could join the union on exactly the same terms as older ones. This federal arrangement would encourage a democratic people to settle in such places and to clamor for statehood. Once territories earned statehood, they could join the union, and the men and women living there had the coercive power of the new state to defend them and their interests. The new system curtailed the forces that would have torn the new nation apart, giving those politicized in the east a vested interest in expansion. They could become colonizers. The west would serve as safety valve.[15] The western arrangement—forged through war—displaced tensions inherent in a democracy across the continent. The key was that the state now managed this arrangement. At times, the new state would go to war reluctantly to clear Natives off land. It worried about ongoing entanglements with other powers in a world of war and how hostility with Natives complicated these. It would have to depend on state militias for manpower because of its relative impotence. It would be beholden to the racist attitudes and land greed of western settlers. But if the state did not respond by going to war, its integrity was threatened.[16]

Jefferson laid out the vision for the new state of affairs with his lovely sounding, evocative phrase "the empire of liberty." He meant empire could serve liberty in two ways. American empire could be a place where liberty thrived. It could also be a place where liberty could be recreated. This empire would do so as empires had always done. It operated through coercion and displacement of other peoples. Jefferson saw

Natives as the equals of whites in terms of innate capacity. But he also regarded them as culturally backward. They would, he hoped, develop with time and so embrace the ways of Euro-Americans. But time was not on their side. Jefferson's empire of liberty could not wait. If the revolutionary settlement was to be secure for the new nation, if revolutionary intrigue and uncertainty were not to define the political culture of the new nation, the state would have to expand. The postcolonial state could and would act in neocolonial fashion, even if it proved unwilling at times.[17]

Conquest in some regions, or the collapse of a "middle ground" of accommodation, allowed officials to believe they controlled much of the continent. Of course, a great deal of this was self-serving myth. In areas farther south of the Ohio Country, such as the Arkansas River Valley, any pretense of control was just that. Native groups, such as the Quapaws and the Chickasaws, determined their own destiny. In fact, they could use tensions and the threat of war to their advantage, strengthening their hand vis-à-vis Europeans and settlers in creating a "native ground." They also invited those who had been demoralized in the east, such as groups of Delawares and Shawnees, to move west of the Mississippi. The movement would only continue as war and disruption continued to the east. Aggression weakened some and strengthened others. In fact, it encouraged the Quapaws to confront their greatest rival in the region—not a European power but a Native one: the Osage.[18]

Yet, there is no denying that the new state system of central government willing to expand and states able to coerce was primed to grow at the expense of Indigenous peoples. This sort of aggression was not necessarily hardwired into a settlement process that began with the first encounter between Europeans and Indians; rather, it emerged from the age and the logic of revolution. The state was empowered by popular mobilization but intent on keeping it within bounds. This conundrum necessarily tethered the United States to expansion. The United States, and especially its constituent parts, would sponsor programs premised on expulsion, deportation, and even extermination. The conventional term "Indian removal" does not capture the active role the state would take in gobbling up territory that had been set aside in previous eras for Natives. Even if Indigenous groups were resurrecting old ways to create native grounds, the writing was on the wall.[19]

Many of Jefferson's contemporaries believed that aggression could serve the purpose of ending conflict. In fact, a belief in human progress, and the inevitability of peace coming with enlightenment, silenced older moral scruples about war. History would bring war to an end. Until it did, even wars of extermination could be countenanced. Armies, then, could justify engaging in "total war." States could and did mobilize their cultures and societies in prosecuting war. Soldiers would fight with ideological fervor. They would do so with a hatred of their enemies and a faith in the justness of their causes in ways not seen since the Reformation. Once one nation indulged, all would have to follow suit.[20]

The proximate causes of the age of perpetual warfare began with the French. French aristocrats were inveigling other states to invade France in order to topple the new order and put the old one back in place. In so doing, they gave governments, such as that of Prussia, a strategic opening to secure their western borders at the expense of what they believed to be a compromised French nation. Prussia, therefore, went to war against the republican government, even allying with its traditional rival, Austria. Austrians were particularly vexed by how events in France threatened Belgium. They saw in the new French regime a grave challenge to their holdings on the very borders of France. Together the Austrians and the Prussians couched themselves as counterrevolutionaries.[21] Others responded to the threat France represented, either defensively or with an eye to a golden opportunity. Russia, for instance, saw Prussia and Austria focused on the west and Poland lying in a vulnerable position. It then acted.

It's as if revolutionary France had pulled a loose thread from the fabric of power relations in Europe. Soon, the threads lay in a heap. The only nation that initially remained on the sidelines was Britain. The government of William Pitt the Younger, the son of the reformer, was transfixed with events in France, but officials realized that plunging the nation into war at this moment could prove risky, especially as those on the kingdom's margins were championing revolutionary ideas themselves. Wisely, he sensed that war could destabilize an already fragile set of arrangements. The execution of Louis XVI changed such a calculus. This step amounted to an act of war against a worldview and the assumptions that underscored all good government. Thus, Britain too was pulled into the maelstrom. In February 1792, France declared war on Britain and Holland. It would do the same on Spain five weeks later.[22]

As the world around them reeled with hope and fear, the French invited this state of affairs. The revolutionary government of 1791, under the Constituent Assembly, claimed it was renouncing the fighting of dynastic wars. Nevertheless, the same government that instituted the Terror believed that war clarified things. It allowed the government to ferret out those who still secretly contested the Revolution. If they could be purged, then the true work of revolutionary reformation for French society could begin. Moreover, the French government believed that neighbors were being pushed toward war by thousands of French royalist refugees, who did all in their power to convince other nations that a republican France represented an existential threat. These became for the French regime the ultimate bogeys. If revolutionary leaders could secure the borders and convince the other powers not to meddle in French affairs, stability would come to France. France, though fearful at first, welcomed foreign adventures for domestic reasons.[23]

The French justified their aggression by invoking the "will of the people." Quickly after 1789, the French occupied Corsica and Avignon and renounced treaties that bound the people in Alsace through feudal obligations to German princes. The government used the idea of popular sovereignty to rationalize the grabs. This new regime, created by the will of the people, announced that it was now responding to others in similar straits. This rationale would be employed from this point forward. For those peoples deemed backward and not yet properly enlightened—how Jefferson viewed Indians in America—the French regime would remake institutions through an insistence on "pouvoir révolutionnaire." Through the power of revolution people would learn to find their will. Beginning in 1794, just as the Terror ended and French armies were marching across Europe, the process accelerated. The new justifications for conquest would eventually underscore the creation of new states in the Netherlands, Switzerland, and Italy.[24]

In these so-called sister republics, what we could call the national and the transnational were bound together. The transnational is easy enough to discern. In a breathtakingly quick time, French armies, or the threat of French armies, encouraged Swiss, Dutch, German, and Italian men and women to declare republics of their own. For all these places, war challenged the sovereign status quo. In place of older forms of association and governance, republicans in each place insisted on democratic participation. Popular sovereignty, in a moment of sovereign uncertainty, filled a void. These "sisters," it should be pointed out, did not see each other as brothers-in-arms: the French republic acted much more like a "dominant mother" than a "caring sister."[25]

That said, French intervention did not amount to simple conquest. Some national realities had to be respected, even by the French, and the exigencies of war made for give-and-take. The Dutch experience offers an apt example. In 1795, France invaded the Netherlands. The Batavian Revolution witnessed the dissolution of an old regime and the creation of a Dutch Republic with the help of French intervention. It also saw this society fracture along old tension points. Same story that we have seen before, in other words. The most radical among the Dutch welcomed the French because of their belief in the power of revolutionary ideas to usher in a new society. They pushed for a centralized state, one very much like the one that had emerged in France. Others resisted. The poorer sort had now become politicized as well, and they used the moment to try to win back local autonomy that they feared would be swept away by radicals. The conflict created political stalemate.[26] Ultimately, the Dutch did not want to go down the path of Jacobin terror. They realized that civil war was the worst kind of conflict. So they meshed French ideals with their own and initiated republican reforms in ways that would afford people time to appreciate new democratic ideas. The French had to bow to these constraints, even as their presence provided the new Batavian regime with enough stability to avoid fracturing.[27]

Newly occupied territories became veritable land banks. With the old engine of the eighteenth-century French economy—the Caribbean-centered empire—gone, France at war had little choice.[28] Territory taken worked just like the American west for the new United States. The new government, most terrifyingly to its neighbors, mandated that the army would reeducate any place it occupied. Old states were toppled. In their place, the occupier installed new puppet regimes on its borders. Tribute would then flow into the center. To sanitize the move, officials even dreamt up classical-sounding names for the new republics, just as Jefferson had done for the Northwest Territory. The parallels are striking, so much so that one wonders if they devised the strategy by imitating one another. For the record, they did not. Revolution and war intersected in just this way for two nations with intersecting histories.

With this rationale, the French expanded the nation to annex Belgium. Leaders believed that the nation should inhabit its "natural" boundaries. Instead of taxes going to Austria, money would flow to France. Through threats, conquest, and conciliation—and some combination thereof—new republics emerged that created a loyal and lucrative phalanx between France and its many enemies to the east, including one even in Rome itself. Though billed as liberation, these initiatives in fact witnessed the "birth of the modern client state."[29]

With the buffer provided by conquest, France enjoyed early successes against the Prussians and the Austrians. The reason stems from the fact that the French people were extraordinarily motivated. French generals could get men out into the field when others balked. They could also throw troops at enemy positions. France had the largest population in Europe. Many of these people were now deeply motivated to fight against the revolutionary government's enemies. Mobilization had already been accomplished by revolutionary ferment. The army tapped into this sensibility. During the Terror, the government passed the famous *levée en masse*, through which officials conscripted all able-bodied men into the army. With this move, revolutionary energies were channeled into the war effort. This new politicized society had created a new way of aggression, one attuned to a hyper-democratized society. As men in the field now turned their anger and resentment to foreign enemies, the state was wielding a formidable tool.[30] The French did so most spectacularly through the generalship of a young commander named Napoleon Bonaparte, the figure who had figured out how to harness the new promethean power of a mobilized citizenry.

War could be dynamically, or paralyzingly, destabilizing. It could generate the sort of uncertainty and chaos that destroyed regimes. It could also produce adaptations to new sorts of struggles.[31] Take the case of the German states. Suffering defeat after defeat at the hands of the French, the two great Central European powers, Prussia and Austria, stood by helplessly as France dismantled the old Holy Roman Empire, or German Reich, bit by bit. Some of it, France absorbed. Other parts were reorganized. Some states, such as the Kingdom of Westphalia, it created whole cloth. Without a past, the new state relied on French ideas to create a bureaucracy. In some cases, as with the new Confederation of the Rhine, the dissolution of older ways led at first, as we would expect, to increased tensions between different groups. These places, as had been the case in other revolutionary settings, threatened to come apart along their fault lines. Protestants and Catholics, older guilds and merchants, vied with each other in an increasingly unstable environment. Nonetheless, French occupation offered great stability. The Confederation of the Rhine became a French vassal state defined by order. The French would use it as a bank that could be dipped into for occupation, administration, and the European war effort. In exchange, the region received a modern state system. In German lands, reform came without the sort of crisis that had befallen regions bordering the Atlantic.

The French would not allow the lid to come off; they needed the resources.[32]

For the interior of the European continent, war confronted everyone with unprecedented challenges—but not the sort that wreaked havoc in Atlantic empires. War brought losses that humiliated Prussia and Austria. War also occasioned reform. As was clear from very early on, both states would have to remake themselves if they were to compete with France in this new age. They, too, had to mobilize à la France, and Prussians proved adept at adopting the model of their enemy, even as they worked to ensure that the politicization genie could be put back into the bottle. Prussian reformers did not want to create Jacobins. They motivated their peoples to fight by playing on the theme of revenge in what some saw as almost a holy war. In doing so, they rallied people to the state, in the process creating a sense of Germanness. What had been "subjects" were remade into "citizens of the state." Prussia and Austria could maintain old hierarchies, as their capitals were not occupied for long lengths of time. Their churches remained untouched. No group threatened the regime. Some clamored for revolutionary transformation, but in both cases the state had the wherewithal to stifle such voices. Prussia and Austria, therefore, emerged relatively unscathed from a period during which coalition after coalition fought the French amid humiliation after humiliation.[33]

One way of thinking of the experience of these states in these years of warfare is how we usually conceive of Native American polities. War split Native groups, such as the Cherokees, into feuding factions. War led others to reimagine themselves as a people, to rally to a renewed idea of nation. Think of the Shawnees. It created the impetus to seek new allies and look far afield for those who shared the same concerns. It also encouraged groups, like the Shawnees and the Delawares, to embrace old ways anew in the face of new threats. The Shawnee brothers Tecumseh and Tenskwatawa, the former a unifying warrior and the latter the prophet of resistance, come readily to mind. War strengthened the hands of some, such as the Osages and Quapaws, and set them against one another. War in Europe, as it did for Native Americans, acted as both solvent and catalyst, challenging old ways and creating the possibilities for new ones. Of course, war did this culturally; it also did it politically. Prussia, in this regard, serves as the European model for all these dynamics. It started the age as a landlocked polity and transformed itself from a marginal player into a Continental power through war.[34]

A famous American scholar named Charles Tilly once observed that "war makes the state, and the state makes war." That simple and well-known aphorism finds its clearest expression on the European continent in these years. By necessity, war made for adaptability and creativity, especially in its new, more all-encompassing form.[35] Many on the European continent, either by vying with the French or by being reorganized by them, were able to achieve the sort of reform that all had found elusive. It came, of course, with a terrible toll. This new form of war, one relying on mass mobilization as never before and ensnaring people far and wide, would cost the lives of four million.[36] But we could say the same of the American continent, though the body count was less, for the revolutionary age in any event. The same dynamics were at work that transformed polities of middling power, like Prussia, into imperial states that demanded the respect of enemy and ally alike.

Britain faced a more challenging time, largely because of Ireland. Warfare on the Continent brought Ireland back into the revolutionary picture in two contradictory ways. First, more and more Irish troops were serving in British units, and now most of these happened to be Catholics. With increased competition between states to mobilize more and more men, it was critical for the British state to look to Ireland for manpower even more insistently than in the past. Now even Catholics could apply.[37] Many Irish were thus becoming wedded to a British state that historically defined itself against Catholicism. Yet, many Catholics, of course, remained disaffected by the British connection, and the example of France suggested that old orders could be toppled. Anti-state sentiment in Ireland combined, if you will, American and French aims: independence from what many regarded as the oppressive and debilitating relationship to Britain, and a radical blueprint for changing society. Some Protestants, particularly some Presbyterians in the north, subscribed to this vision, even if their neighbors were fleeing into the Orange Order. Others held to older resentments and interests, such as many Defenders, though now they yoked their interests to the United Irish movement. Warfare against France crystalized these positions.[38]

Second, as was the case on the Continent, war destabilized Ireland. This story brings us back to French ties. Even as any form of political radicalism was quashed in the British center, on the Irish periphery radical insurgency thrived. For this reason, French commanders fastened on Ireland as the ideal site for invasion. They reckoned that the people would rise up, now led by a republican movement allied with France. United Irishmen traveled to France to coordinate plans, and a landing of a substantial French force was planned for Bantry. Napoleon also hoped the Irish would eventually serve as interpreters when he invaded England. Alas for the United Irishmen, the landing never came off. Storms would not allow it. Meanwhile, the British state had compromised the United Irish organization. With suppression, what was left of the movement began to splinter confessionally. Ultimately, a modest number or rebels, largely Presbyterian led but also peopled by Catholics, rose up in Ulster. The rising was brutally put down. In 1798, as all of the Atlantic reeled with uncertainty and word was spreading of French intrigue and of Irish insurrection, the British government sent troops to smash what remained of the revolutionary organization.[39]

The move set off a period of civil unrest, in which Ireland fractured. In some areas of the southeast troops massacred Catholics. Most of the perpetrators came from North Cork and were Protestant. The murders and the whisperings of revolutionary intrigue touched off a *grande peur* in the kingdom, of the kind that had gripped France at the start of the Revolution. The atrocities prompted a rising, but one that was uncoordinated and soon descended into a sectarian bloodletting, as Defender rage took aim at Protestants. In Wexford, rebels had some stunning successes until they were outmanned and outnumbered and overwhelmed. The aftermath was horrific. Government forces slaughtered rebels at a place called Vinegar Hill. Catholics killed innocent Protestants, just as the government and Protestant bands murdered Catholics. The rebellion was put down with "universal rape, plunder and murder."[40]

Warfare, therefore, set off both revolutionary ferment and civil war in Ireland, combining the other central features of the period, beguiling promise and terror. The ideal of a United Ireland, one of churchmen, Catholics, and Dissenters fighting arm in arm for an Irish republic ran into the reality of an Ireland that had been historically ordered by sectarian difference. Old hatreds and fears overwhelmed any revolutionary plans and hopes once rebel leaders flailed and the government tried to reassert control. As long as Irishmen killed each other, the state would be able to step in and reassert its sovereignty. Ultimately, the French sent a small force that landed in a village in County Mayo. To it, a number of Irishmen rallied, some hoping that France would help the beleaguered Catholics of the kingdom. The troops were on no such mission. They hoped that Ireland would rise up. It did not. Though they scored a few early victories, the rebels and the French were overwhelmed by British forces, who were now streaming into the kingdom to reinstitute order.

Ireland, then, proved another telling casualty of the Atlantic revolutionary moment. The rhetoric of the day bespoke liberation; the reality was a bit more sordid, as the past was unearthed. For places like Saint-Domingue, tensions revolved around race and status. In America, race and class represented the lines that determined access to power. In Ireland, religious confession trumped all. War revealed and exacerbated such cleavages. Any sort of organization, regardless of the ideas that animated it, would have to struggle against them. As the British tried to clean up the wreckage of yet another rising and sectarian bloodletting, they began to sense that Ireland needed a new sovereign arrangement, especially since the rest of the Atlantic was still aflame.[41]

For Britain itself, the story was more straightforward. War offered terrible clarity and focused energies in a world of uncertainty. Britain embraced a patriotism that mirrored France's. Leaders played upon traditional fears of radicalism and Catholicism to make the case that France once again stood as the antithesis to all that the British prized. This sensibility was not conjured ex nihilo. As the American Revolution had come to a close, loyal Britons retreated into a more insular sense of what it meant to be British. The earlier war, especially as France entered it, made them suspicious both of republicanism and of Catholicism, just as they hailed the Crown-in-Parliament as a font of stability. The French Revolution and the wars that followed against France only heightened those beliefs. It is important to stress that this appeal did not stem only from the experience of well-to-do Loyalists. It also emerged from below. Lower-class Britons also championed the ideas of their distinctiveness and the liberties they enjoyed. They reveled in the belief, however much reality dictated otherwise, that they alone stood against the tyrant, and that they were almost, to use an anachronistic phrase, a thin red line separating barbarism and civility. The realities of a world at war, in which states faced existential challenges, only encouraged such thinking.[42]

In fact, the crisis in Britain occasioned by warfare with France strengthened the bases of order. Just as in France, it did so in large part because of the unquenchable demand for manpower. Britain's army and navy needed men to fight the French on the Continent and much of the rest of the world on the high seas and to defend Britain from possible invasion. As in France, the growing army and navy proved the salve to potential fracture points at home. The army became the place for those from the margins of Britain to serve. Of course, a large proportion of the army that fought Napoleon came from Catholic Ireland and from Scotland. Scots remained the foot soldiers of empire and mainstays of the British war machine. But their inclusion in the army gave them a stake in the state, and as it did so, their ethnic distinctiveness could supplement, rather than detract from, the British nation. This is not to say that Englishmen did not serve; they did so in droves. This was a truly "British" effort, one that drew on all the nations of the British Isles.[43]

War made revolution, and revolution made war. States powered by a politicized citizenry and by empires that stretched across oceans had almost limitless resources to hammer each other, and the motives to do so. France, more quickly than most, had seen the possibilities of the age for harnessing revolutionary forces. Britain followed suit, channeling its people into service for the state against France. The British knew they were playing with fire. Politicization, which they had witnessed in the Irish case, could prove just as combustible to the state as it could constitutive.

The French were learning of these many challenges in their own Ireland, a place called the Vendée.[44] As France confronted armies on the battlefield, provincial unrest sprung up in regions far from Paris. Provincials were protesting the conceit of Paris to control the nation's politics and to speak for the country as a whole. Some of the protest movements threatened to spawn civil wars. The most serious was taking shape in western France, in the Vendée, where mass conscription set off perhaps the most daunting challenge to the republic in the first few months of its existence. The crisis centered on the monarchy and on religion. So long as France remained a constitutional monarchy, some elements that resisted the Revolution could be assuaged. The king as person and as symbol betokened an older order that many still embraced. The Catholic Church too was an important marker of the old order. In the Vendée, the people defined themselves by both. As the government turned against the church and with mass conscription now in the offing, the Vendée rose up. People here refused to fight for a cause that contradicted all they believed in. Calling themselves the Catholic and Royal Army, they turned on their internal enemies.[45]

The government dispatched troops to the region, and soon battles were fought between opposing forces in what was quickly becoming a vicious civil war. Estimates of the dead vary, but most would reckon that between two hundred and fifty thousand and three hundred thousand perished, perhaps as many as four hundred thousand.[46] Of these at least a hundred thousand were republicans, though that number might have been as high as two hundred thousand. The scale of death and suffering dwarfed Ireland's, of course, but comparisons can be made. The "blues," as republican forces were called, employed the most pernicious means of putting down what they regarded as rebellion. Of course, it was anything but. The struggle to construct efficacious and legitimate sovereignty had not ended.[47] The "hell columns" could justify terrifying violence because of how those in the Vendée threatened the very essence of the new form of sovereignty emerging in France. A reversion to the old order was now unthinkable.

Tellingly, this represented the most violent episode of the French Revolution. It demonstrated that war enmeshed with revolution systematized terror.[48] In the French case, war radicalized the republican center of Paris more fully, allowing its citizens to justify greater centralization of the whole nation, just as Britain grew more consciously "British" when Ireland exploded. The repression of the Vendée also galvanized opposition to the regime abroad, in ways similar to how France sympathized with a repressed Ireland. The British even considered intervening, as rebels from the Vendée contacted them for help. In the example of the Vendée insurgency, therefore, we see the difficult tightrope the French republican government had to walk if it wanted to channel forces without being consumed by them. As the Irish-British case would also testify, this proved a rule, rather than an exception, for the age.

War cost money. And though the Atlantic did not loom as large as before for the French, it still proved alluring. With war under way, the state needed the resources of the most profitable colony in the world. So, in 1792, the National Assembly sent commissioners to Saint-Domingue along with troops to try to reconstitute order. The commissioners traveled with hopes of enlisting free people of color in the revolutionary cause by mandating that they have full political rights. Perhaps in so doing the commissioners would conjure stability for the island, end the slave insurgency, and make the colony profitable once more.[49] What the commissioners did, though, was to heighten violence. Their efforts to restore order led to greater slave insurgency. The men and women of Saint-Domingue had become actors in the revolutionary crucible, and the status quo ante was no longer feasible.

In fact, the mission created a tangled quagmire. Because of its ties as an Atlantic node to other places, Saint-Domingue attracted the notice of France's rivals, in hopes that further destabilization would exacerbate France's troubles. Soon enough the Spaniards and the British proved willing to use the terrible dividing lines within Saint-Domingue for their own purposes. The Spanish found willing allies on the ground. Leaders of rebellion, especially Louverture and a man named Georges Biassou, encouraged their followers to flock to the Spanish cause once Louis XVI was executed, and Spain began courting them in its fight with the new republic. On allying with Spain, they argued they would "rather be slaves of the Spaniards than free with the French." That said, they never intended to be slaves again. In courting connections, the rebels would have to be adaptable. They struggled, like all players throughout the Atlantic, to maintain firm positions, as alliances shifted with revolution and war. While Spanish-supported troops had made inroads in Saint-Domingue, republican France turned the tables and took over control of Spanish Santo Domingo, adding to hopes of the enslaved but further complicating matters. Soon enough, the French left, compounding confusion.[50] The British used a different tack. White planters, now seeing the writing on the wall, turned to the British to cast off French sovereignty and place the island under the jurisdiction of Britain. Exploiting divisions and fears, therefore, the French, British, and Spanish sent Saint-Domingue into a tailspin of violence, one further compounded by the permeable border with Santo Domingo. As in Europe, war intensified differences just as it destabilized any form of order.[51]

Though the French vacillated when it came to emancipation, the tangles of warfare at this juncture pushed them to embrace the measure. No doubt, slavery ran afoul of fundamental notions of rights espoused by many, such as Marat. Jacobins now argued that the "aristocracy of the skin" rivaled that of the church and the nobility, and they purged pro-slavery people from their ranks. But it was pressure from Blacks playing against the backdrop of potential British support for white planters that sealed the government's support for general emancipation. Republican commissioners promised freedom for those who would help them root out royalist foes. Saint-Domingue would be free in theory, even as violence grew in intensity with war. The upshot? By no means was the move for emancipation inevitable. It became imaginable as a possibility because of aggression.[52]

The end of slavery was, in fact, "a prolonged and confused process."[53] For the French, wars had first to be won, against the British, against white royalists, and against free people of color who had allied themselves with the Spanish flag before the institution could be done away with. All of this would have required overwhelming force. Alas, warfare on the Continent would not allow the French to dispatch an army up to the task. For Saint-Domingue, the result was more chaos, and with no group able to make good on sovereign claims, many shifted allegiances. Chief among those moving between different sides in this kaleidoscopic struggle was Toussaint Louverture. Eventually, Louverture decided to cast his lot with republican freedom. Viewed within the moment, deserting the Spanish, really no more than a strategic ally and one that endorsed slavery, for the French made perfect sense. At least on paper, France now offered clarity. Like the French, Louverture was weighing his options in a highly volatile context, one made more complex still by the fortunes of war. He and his followers now fought against those they had fought with.[54]

Georges Biassou, now better known as Jorge, would never become the mythic hero that Louverture would. After the Spanish sued for peace with republican France in 1795, he and others would not be welcome in Santo Domingo. They would try to find a home in Cuba, where a large number would settle, but Spanish officials and local planters worried about the presence on the island of Black revolutionaries. Biassou eventually made his way to Spanish Florida. Like the Acadians who were rounded up by the British and sent all over North America during the mid-eighteenth century, Biassou's followers would be dispersed throughout the Caribbean regions of the Spanish Empire. Through such measures, Spain could keep war at bay. But only for a time.[55]

The last places to fracture from the War of the Revolutionary Age were those that had appeared the most liable to split apart years earlier but in fact had not: the Spanish and Portuguese Atlantic empires. They had held together because their weakness proved their strength. Reforms had made for a period of prosperity. In fact, Brazil's dependence on slavery and the riches it brought gave Portugal an edge in maintaining its empire despite the pressures from continual war, even if it was becoming a client state of Britain in the process. With the advent of the French revolutionary wars, the Spanish whipsawed between supporting Britain and backing revolutionary France, concerned as they were with maintaining the integrity of their empire and keeping it free from encroachments and from those who would exploit it. From the start of the French Revolution until 1807, Spain and Portugal and their empires held on. Ultimately, though, the two could not dodge the furies brought on by war.[56]

The end of empire in South America for both Spain and Portugal began when Napoleon invaded Portugal in 1807 and, then a year later in 1808, deposed the king of Spain and his son, installing his own brother instead. Invasion would imperil the veneer of metropolitan authority for both Portugal and Spain. More conspicuously, the concomitant challenge to sovereignty throughout both their empires would place provincials in all sorts of difficult dilemmas. It would pull them, on the one hand, between allegiance to their respective Crowns and the lure of further autonomy and, on the other hand, between worries about those below and the mastery of their provincial societies. Complicating this already kaleidoscopic picture were the templates for all now available. With revolution having occurred in North America, with the Great Nation of France turned upside down, and ominously or thrillingly with slave revolution in Saint-Domingue, all had models they could either emulate or try to short-circuit.[57]

First, the Spanish case. In what we could call the "1808 moment," war worked as "trigger" and "precipitant" to an almost overdetermined revolutionary process. It led to the teetering of imperial sovereignty and the dizzying competition to reconstitute it. The absence of authority set the stage for confusions, debates, experiments, and violence.[58] What follows is a complicated story of how revolutionary war brought an empire crashing down. We shall see many of the themes of revolution and war apparent earlier and in other places, the same bonds, dilemmas, crosscutting cleavages, competition, and bloodshed. We shall witness too how extensive the web of war in the Atlantic had become. It stretched from the centers of Europe to the very edges of South America, and once its threads were pulled none could escape the tangles of hopes and fears. The upshot was this: the empire's complexity, something that allowed the Spanish Empire to weather and even benefit from the earlier crisis of reform, proved its undoing once war entered the picture.

In 1808, when France invaded, Napoleon viewed Spain's empire as a potential bank for his war. He had long hoped to secure silver from Mexico to pay for his campaigns. Now he had his chance.[59] When he tried to install a puppet regime in Spain, he achieved his first step. But, of course, war created unanticipated consequences. Napoleon had to fight a nasty guerrilla campaign and would come to refer to the Iberian Peninsula as an "ulcer" that bled his army and "the fatal knot" in which "all the circumstances of my disasters are bound up."[60] As sovereignty collapsed in Spain, juntas emerged to fill the void. A Supreme Junta met at Seville, peopled by representatives from the other bodies. At first, the juntas served as placeholders for sovereignty.[61] The French vassal regime in Madrid may have claimed to be sovereign, but de facto sovereignty was scattered in localized militarized forms. With time, a new central government, now resisting the invaders and claiming authority, was situated in the Atlantic trading center of Cadiz.

French invasion and the incapacity of the Crown created a dangerous vacuum of sovereignty for the Spanish Empire. It acted as a virtual "shock" to the system. Would creoles see the new regime as legitimate? Who was sovereign? The deposed king? The Supreme Junta?[62] Turning sovereignty into a question confronted creoles with the sorts of issues that North Americans had grappled with. In the hyper-politicized world of the Atlantic, common men and women and those on the margins of society had templates of insurgency and resistance at hand that could be adopted but that would imperil elites. In the same breath, the crisis at the center afforded the opportunity to those on the periphery to reconfigure affairs in a way that finally gave them some parity with metropolitans and ensured that they would not bear—unfairly in their minds—the burdens of empire. The crisis of authority on the peninsula, therefore, became for Spanish America a crisis about legitimacy, both the empire's and that of creoles. It would finally force Spain's creoles to confront their provincial dilemmas, something they had been able to avoid for years.[63]

In the Latin American vacuum, juntas loyal to the deposed Crown also sprang up, just as they were doing in Spain and just as committees of correspondence had in North America. In April 1810, Caracas established a junta. In May 1810, Buenos Aires did the same. The latter represented a revolt against Spanish authority in the name of the Crown. Mexico City, viewing itself as almost the elder daughter of the Spanish Empire, proved the most audacious. It rejected the government put in place by Napoleon and called for the convocation of a "general junta." The city council argued that those in the provinces should have the same rights as subjects in the metropole. In making this claim, Fray Melchor Talamantes styled himself the Sieyès or Dickinson of Mexico. He made a clarion call to all his fellow Mexicans, arguing that because authority had disintegrated in the center, it should be reconstituted at the margins. Mexico City should replace Madrid as the new center of empire, though under the Crown. Creoles in Quito also announced themselves a junta and tried to declare themselves autonomous from Santa Fe de Bogotá and Lima. Quito had developed as a region with its own socioeconomic integrity, yet merchants and planters found themselves under the thumb of neighbors.[64]

These bodies became the chief vehicle by which creoles would deal with their dilemmas. The word "junta" conjures up images of generals and coups. Far better to consider the etymology of the word. It comes from a word that means meeting or joining. It suggests advisory committee or board. A junta could be and usually was ephemeral. It functioned much like the word "congress" in North America had. It, too, was not freighted with ideas about sovereignty. Just as in Spain, colonial juntas were designed as provincial forms of association that happened to step in to do the regular stuff of government while authority was uncertain. To creoles, the Crown—however compromised—still ruled the empire. As in Spain, juntas claimed only "provisional sovereignty."[65] But clutching at authority always meant addressing more than the issue of imperial governance. Juntas necessarily had to confront disorder in their own societies.

As if on cue, local tensions stirred to life. The same combination of hope and fear, problem and opportunity, that had visited other places now determined the fortunes of men and women in the Spanish world. The 1808 coup d'état in Mexico, with the viceroy deposed in favor of a junta, opened up a Pandora's box. Now old ways of accommodation could not keep social tensions in check.[66] Here and elsewhere, war and reactions to it were bringing old cleavages to the surface, generating the well-known mélange of revolutionary emotions and aspirations. In Upper Peru, creoles sought to reconstitute authority as quickly as possible to quell any unrest from below and to peel away control from Lima and from Buenos Aires. Farther north, locals viewed the crisis at the center "with a mixture of horror, despair, and incomprehension." They feared an America left "to its own devices." Soon, members of the Supreme Junta of Venezuela announced their allegiance to the Crown in its fight against France. The issue which this group faced, and which it fractured over, was the contraband trade along the South American coast. War had made such trade easier and more lucrative. The issue split those in Veracruz and Lima from those in Cartagena. The junta members from Cartagena used the moment to open their ports to all foreign goods. In Rio de la Plata, the moment gave some the possibility of doing the same, and soon goods of many nations flowed in. It also provided an opening for conquering neighboring provinces, as leading figures from the city of

Buenos Aires tried to extend their rule to the countryside. A junta also took shape in Santiago de Chile, pressing for its autonomy from other regions.[67]

War and reactions to it created seeming paradoxes. The creoles of South America did not throw off what they regarded as imperial shackles. Quite the opposite, in fact. They saw any attempts to govern their own communities through juntas as means to support the Crown in the face of invasion and occupation. They did not, at this point, aim for independence. They saw themselves as part of a composite monarchy, one that spanned the Atlantic. At this juncture they could imagine themselves only as subjects. The same, of course, could have been said for North America before 1774. The default position within the empire, even if compromised, was loyalty. The problem was, because of war, no one knew what or who represented established authority.[68]

In 1810, loyalty seemed to be paying off. In that year, the Spanish government in exile issued a proclamation, with the hope of holding onto the empire. It argued that all those in the colonies were to have nearly the same rights as those in the center. The word "nearly" matters. Spaniards were willing to see the New World as an integral part of "the Spanish Nation." In 1809, the Supreme Junta had declared that after elections the regions in Latin America were not to be considered colonies but territories. Those elected would form part of the Central Junta. Equality, though, had its limits. Those in the metropole were not willing to grant Americans a majority in the Cortes that was meeting in Cadiz. Natives would be allowed to vote. But those of African origin would not. Spaniards from the metropole worried that their inclusion would jeopardize their control of the Nation when it was struggling for its survival. Some Americans had their own reasons for supporting this measure based on race. They worried about control of their own societies. Nonetheless, this promulgation was followed by the announcement of the meeting of a new imperial Cortes that promised a power-sharing agreement between center and peripheries, the voting rights of most males, and a federated understanding of the empire under the Crown. Voting then began throughout the Spanish Nation.[69]

However limited the rights of Americans turned out to be in the Cortes at Cadiz, the wartime provincial regime was accomplishing what could be regarded as revolutionary aims. The rights that were discussed were unmistakably liberal. They suggested British, American, and French inspirations. National sovereignty was to be protected, the power of the church and the Inquisition was diminished, individuals were to enjoy rights, the press would have freedoms, and the government placed limits on the Crown—once it would be reinstated. This new constitution promulgated in 1812 bound old Spanish and newer enlightened ideas together into a whole for an empire reimagined as an Atlantic nation. Though it reflected the many tensions that had come to the fore in the age, especially over the status of Indigenous peoples and those of African descent, it was "the clearest attempt to transform, at least symbolically, an empire—the Spanish—into a nation—Spain." It could only have been imagined in the context of war and the dissolution of Crown sovereignty beginning in 1808. Its promise and appeal both in the Old World and the New suggested that perhaps the Spanish could avert the sort of crisis that had fractured the British Empire decades earlier.[70]

It was not to be. In 1814, once the king was back on his throne, he revoked the federal understanding. He also rejected the liberal tone of the constitution. He did so because of the fear of French-style radicalism and what he saw as an arrangement that could lead to greater disorder within the empire. Authoritarianism, he reckoned, could pull the empire back together.[71] Those in the provinces, politicized for so long, had other ideas. Some regions like Buenos Aires took over control of their own affairs without declaring independence. In Rio de la Plata, elites from Buenos Aires, many of whom espoused liberal ideas, hoped to hold on to the broader region. Those farther afield resisted. So, Buenos Aires sent armies to claim much of the royalist enclave of Upper Peru and the Banda Oriental, modern Uruguay, much as the French had marched forces into the Vendée. This was "a revolution on the offensive" led by urban creoles, who had seen merchants and smugglers across the Plata as rivals. Merchants in Caracas threatened to break away at this moment, as did those in Bogotá and in Cartagena.[72]

Intellectual ties reflected the refracted world the age of revolution had created. In Colombia, creoles published the American Declaration of Independence. Venezuelans translated the U.S. Constitution. After 1810, the parallels to North America now appeared compelling. Most menacingly or most promisingly, depending on perspective, French revolutionary constitutional models also inspired people throughout Spanish America.[73] Because of fears of France and the politicization of those lower down on the social ladder, the region's patriot leaders looked to Great Britain. Reformist notions gaining purchase in Britain spoke persuasively to creole elites, who also had to attend to concerns about home rule. France offered inspiration for tearing down an old regime. The United States spoke to hopes for autonomy. Only Britain promised stability through a time of war and revolution. The upshot was that all had to look somewhere.[74]

Elites were right to aim for British-like equipoise, as they imagined it. Civil war, as ever, also went hand in hand with struggles over home rule. Mexican Independence Day, September 16, 1810, commemorated an attempt by those below to rally to the Crown against Spaniards and whites. Under the leadership of a charismatic priest, Miguel Hidalgo, insurgents set up a junta and then called for a general uprising. Under the banner of the Virgin of Guadalupe, and fighting for the Crown, the rebels called for a new government that would return Native lands and end the rule of Spaniards. With fears of France and Saint-Domingue fresh in their minds, authorities struggled to suppress what they feared to be a race war. Others played upon fault lines to forestall such a possibility. Consider Venezuela. For a long time, the place had become politicized by rumors and bits of news, what officials called the revolutionary "disease." It also became the first place to make a bid for independence. The reasons stemmed from the earlier process of politicization, now brought to a head by French occupation of Spain. White creole leaders tried to enlist others in the bid for home rule, but they faced an uphill struggle. Some of the insurgent movements had embraced republican principles, the sorts that promised equality but that concerned elites.[75] In Caracas, white creoles, such as Simón Bolívar, a man who had traveled around the whole Atlantic, espoused radical principles and from early on favored independence. But he and other creole elites realized that South America's social characteristics could create what some saw as a "volcano at our feet." They favored a break and republican ideals, but they would limit rights to whites. Saint-Domingue cast a long shadow, both for those above and for those below.[76]

These daunting dilemmas, brought on by war, made independence for many self-evident. Independence had not been the goal when the crisis of 1808 appeared. At that moment, subjects in Spanish America considered themselves much as North American Britons had in 1763: loyal members of a nation that spanned the ocean. But as imperial ties tugged and pulled, they engaged in debates that revealed how the metropole, when push came to shove, viewed those in colonies far away. Thus began a fraught process of weighing options.[77] The state certainly could not protect them. So, like the North American case, declaring independence appeared, for those in Spanish America, "common sense." They had little choice, as disorder would bring France or Saint-Domingue. They rode, as did all provincials who became revolutionaries, on a wave of confidence in the maturity of their own societies and of dread of domestic and external threats, a wave that now impelled those who had been loyal to imagine independence.[78]

Few underestimated the challenges independence would bring. The age offered ample proof. Would their transition to independence lead to revolutionary chaos, or could they manage an orderly transition to a new form of sovereignty? Would Spain allow them to leave?[79] Most confounding, with the move to independence, was whether one idea binding all the potential fracture points would be found to replace the powerfully integrative idea of the Crown. "Patriarchal colonialism" had held the whole together. Not anymore. In other words, would they be visited by the sort of unrest that had gone hand in hand with American independence, with revolution in France and Saint-Domingue, with rebellion in Ireland, and with Europe's descent into chaos?[80]

Signs looked ominous. Spanish America was a far more complex place than British North America. Its societies had longer histories, its population was more diverse, its economy more sophisticated. Complexity underscored vexing concerns.[81] Tensions presented myriad challenges if unleashed, as they could be cross-cutting and thus unpredictable. The divisions between the very wealthiest and the poorest loomed large. Caste divided people into categories of status and wealth. And, of course, there was race. Regions within viceroyalties were ruled by rival factions, so even some elites hated one another. Most vexing were the confounding ways in which tensions expressed themselves. Many below, for instance, embraced traditionalist understandings of authority. Peasants in Mexico did not always support what we would consider the cause of republican liberation. They had, in fact, resorted to insurgency to protect their communities against change. The enslaved played many roles in society, and in some places, like Buenos Aires, they had even sided with creole elites to defend the city from the threat of Indigenous peoples from the Andes. In Peru, with so many potential flash points, elites dreaded any crisis of sovereignty, and they tended to cling to the Crown.[82]

Nonetheless, all old tensions and issues were channeled into the conflicts of the age. Ethnic and caste differences—a good example would be peasant Native communities in Bajío—were refashioned as race and class, and these categories proved explosive when sovereignty collapsed in the context of a revolutionary world. Social and racial animosities had extraordinary mobilizing power, and these could unleash violence that would have been unheard of before. In Bajio, this is the emotive transformation that Hidalgo tapped into and yoked to New World religious imagery and Enlightenment ideas coursing throughout the Atlantic. This fusion could focus both long-term discontents and more immediate concerns on the connection to Spain.[83]

History now bequeathed complexities that had to be confronted, all evident because of war. Look at just two last cases, examples at two extremes. These two, so different at face value, illustrate the myriad ways war mixed hope and fear together and how it could simplify aims or confuse them. Creole elites in a place like Rio de la Plata faced threats from the Andes and from insurgents. They worried about Indigenous peoples on the Pampas. They had to weigh threats from the British with global war raging. They struggled against penisulares in their midst who assumed a right to rule. They fretted about the enslaved, and these concerns were exacerbated by Saint-Domingue.[84] They were also concerned about their near neighbors. Already struggling with those they hoped to bring within the United Provinces, they found themselves fighting for supremacy of the Banda Oriental against incursions from Brazil. The area that would be Paraguay also became a disputed region. As much as any aspiration for freedom or autonomy, all of these considerations explain why creoles in Buenos Aires finally broke from the Crown in 1816. Things, for them, looked pretty straightforward.[85]

At another extreme, the fate of the Spanish colony of Santo Domingo, at the eastern end of the island of Hispaniola, demonstrated how the tangled nature of war could create Hobbesian realities. Though neglected and isolated, this place was as tied to Atlantic currents as Saint-Domingue. Fittingly, Santo Domingo had endured similar upheaval. It had serially been turned over to France in the early war years, conquered by Louverture and then occupied, reclaimed by France, blockaded by the British Navy, and re-reclaimed by Spain when it was without a king of its own. The barrage of takeovers and occupations eviscerated the island's economy. The inhabitants had witnessed the abolition of slavery, its reimposition, and its attenuation through circumstance. Santo Domingo had been unified to its neighbor to the west and then had become untethered again. Disorder, misery, and poverty prevailed. In 1810, in the wake of tumult, a disparate group of people—mercenaries who had served with French and Spanish armies who happened to be Italian; warlords sating

their own ambition; and some still enslaved—launched a bid for separa-
tion from Spain. They asked for help from the revolutionaries of Saint-
Domingue. Authorities arrested the ringleader of what they called "the
Italian revolution," one that never materialized in any way. Some insurgents were executed, their heads placed on pikes for all to see. Others
vanished from the island.[86]

Perhaps the most amazing story of these years involves the place that became more stable because of war: Brazil. Before the invasion crisis of
1807–8, the Portuguese found themselves in almost the same situation as
the Spanish, trapped between the Scylla of France and the Charybdis of
Britain. Like the Spanish, the Portuguese hoped to stay out of the conflict.
Increasingly bound to British might and protection, they were threatened
also by French saber-rattling. Neutrality seemed the only choice. On the
one hand, officials saw that war could help colonial trade. On the other,
they knew that war would fracture empire. The Portuguese tried to stay
balanced on the horns of their dilemma, caught between "terrors," as one
contemporary put it. With invasion by France, all bets were off.[87]

The empire was, in fact, already fractured. Continued warfare on the
Continent had plunged the metropole into an economic tailspin, quite a
reversal from the years just after the French Revolution had begun. At
the other extreme, some planters in Brazil were growing rich by warfare.
With no sugar leaving Saint-Domingue as it was rocked by revolutionary
violence, much of the world turned to the Portuguese Empire. Brazilian
exports of sugar skyrocketed, benefiting planters in one region of the
colony. Other creoles more reliant on the ties to the mother country had
not fared as well. With war, part of Brazil was growing wealthy, part was
languishing, and officials in Portugal fretted that warfare would turn it
into a vassal state of other powers.[88]

War demonstrated how the balance of power in empire had shifted
across the Atlantic. Wealthy planters in Brazil, from around the region of
Rio de Janeiro, took the initiative. Once it became clear that French invasion had compromised Portuguese sovereignty, they allied with one
another to propose a new vision of empire in which their concerns would
be central to imperial political economy. The great sugar planters argued
for a free trade arrangement within an empire still organized along mercantilist lines. They also warned that unless such an arrangement was put
in place, more disturbances like those in Minas Gerais would occur.
They believed that securing their hold of the empire and its trading

rules, and doing away with anachronistic regulations, would strengthen their hand and allow them to contain any contagion from below.

They would, in other words, refuse to weigh any sort of dilemma. Saint-Domingue explains why. It represented the specter that allowed these planters to make a case for greater control of empire. Even those who did not own vast sugar plantations had to agree. Some of them tended to see slavery as a scourge, and that as long as it existed they were holding a wolf by the ears, to use Jefferson's apt description. Even though some wanted to see an end to slavery in some fashion, all whites had to agree that what had occurred in Saint-Domingue was sobering, especially for a society in which the number of slaves dwarfed the number of whites and in a place so reliant on the export of products grown on plantations. The whites in Brazil, then, confronted the same concerns South Carolinians did in the 1770s. Just as those Americans had a sense of confidence in their ability to control the slaves in their midst, so too did the Brazilians. Greater autonomy from the imperial center, many creole planters were coming to believe, would provide a lasting basis for their ability to control their own society.

Events played into their evolving beliefs. After the French invasion, the British urged the Portuguese to shift their court from Portugal to Brazil. This new arrangement would ensure that France would not seize Portugal's navy and employ it against Britain. It would also allow the empire to survive the tumult unleashed by war. Britain's price was an end to the Portuguese trading monopoly within its empire, something that jibed with what the planter elite was clamoring for. On the face of it, moving a court to a colony seemed absurd. How could a creole tail wag an imperial dog? The empire, the British argued and creoles in Brazil had come to believe, had changed, and war only made such recognition urgent. Brazil's planters held the key to stability of the whole. With war, Portuguese officials found these ideas compelling.[89]

In 1808, the Portuguese ruler, John VI, moved his court to Brazil before he could be deposed by the French. British warships escorted him. In Rio, he established what was called "a Tropical Versailles." He did not regard this as a government in exile and hoped the arrangement would last only until stability came back to Portugal. Nevertheless, this drastic move recognized the simple fact that the seat of stability for the whole now resided in Brazil. Its elites remained about the only people in a world turned upside down that had the plan and the means to ensure that order would prevail. We could call this, as historians have, a "Brazilian inversion" of empire. Through it, the empire was able to avert revolution and independence movements and even strengthen the bases of order.[90] The upshot was this: the asymmetries of the Luso-Atlantic, exacerbated by reform, now saved the empire during war. While the Spanish Empire without sovereignty would descend into the abyss, Brazil and its empire would enjoy a veneer of unity and peace, even if whole swaths of people would never see the liberating potential of revolution because of it.[91]

The different fates of the two empires had one other telling consequence. War, of course, cut off markets, just as it opened others. Production in areas like Bajio in New Spain, which had prospered with silver, now saw production slump, as insurgencies crippled the local economy. Ships could not come or go. Soon the British looked elsewhere for hard specie. Now Brazilian gold seemed a good bet. Bajio lost out to Brazil just as the sugar production regime in Saint-Domingue did to Brazil. These changes triggered more seismic transformations. In both cases, neutral shippers like those from the United States and established powers like the British proved nimble enough to shift to new opportunities. In these circumstances, both pressed for freer trade. In this way, warfare and violence hastened a reconstitution of economic realities. War served to rationalize a new system of political economy that was emerging—one premised on the ideal of free trade—that benefited the most powerful on the ocean, like the British.[92]

The period's aggression also played upon age-old entanglements that had defined the consolidation phase of the Atlantic. What had been transpiring throughout the Atlantic was much discussed in African slaving ports. In fact, war and events throughout the Atlantic were catalyzing movements to overthrow slave-holding regimes in West Africa. Africans affected by the slave trade had, of course, reformed their states to compete. In the process, some had grown wealthy. Because of the warping effects of the slave trade, warfare was becoming perpetual in some regions. Maroon colonies in Africa—groups of men and women who had escaped the condition of slavery to set up their own communities—began to resist the powers-that-be. In the years of revolutionary war, regions in Senegambia and what is now northern Nigeria were also beginning to experience revolutionary ferment. Here, insurgents targeted ascendancies that had recently risen through the slave trade and the fallout from it. Just as had happened in France and in North America, insurgency was led by a disaffected merchant class. In this case, it was not reform that set them off but endemic war.[93]

Revolts took a religious cast, but what is just as interesting is how and why revolutionaries employed the ideas they did. Many of the merchants who resisted were Muslims with ties to the Mideast. They saw rulers as an aristocracy compromised by the trade in the enslaved. They allied themselves with those lower down the socioeconomic ladder who also resented the violence of the trade and the wars that followed in its wake. These people had borne the brunt of taxes and the dislocations of war. Slavery and Atlantic commerce had turned them into an underclass, and it seemed they had no way out but to revolt. The particulars, in other words, may have differed from North America, but the same dynamics held sway. Atlantic integration had benefited some at the expense of others. For both groups of the disaffected, embracing a set of powerful ideas that contested authority, in this case Islam, could be seen as form of resistance to the status quo. The parallels to France in this regard are notable, though the particulars differed. Islam seemed miles away ideologically from republicanism, but they both addressed the same concerns. Reform through Muslim purification became the ideal that people used to fill the vacuum caused by war. Jihad in the Hausa kingdoms of Nigeria represented the form revolution took. The end result was that a huge swath of West Africa saw the old order upended.[94]

The tangles of war and revolution in Africa extended farther still. War in Africa now connected the Atlantic to regions dominated by the desert trade. Those Muslims calling for a new jihad to manage the revolutionary Atlantic would help create a massive sovereign political entity: the Sokoto Caliphate. Its creation was not merely a parallel to the age. It stemmed from the massive growth of slavery in Brazil, the south of the United States, and the island of Cuba and from the warfare it occasioned in Africa. The emergence of a new superstate in Africa also remade the Atlantic, as whole regions became no-go areas for European slavers. They had to look increasingly to areas like the Bight of Biafra, the region Equiano claimed to have come from. Jihad, then, remade the shape of the Atlantic and the nature of what some historians have called "the second slavery" that would define Brazil, Cuba, and parts of the United States.[95]

Aggression in Africa would have dramatic implications for all of the Atlantic. What happened in Africa helped occasion resistance movements and rebellions that gripped the slave-holding circum-Caribbean. In the years of revolutionary warfare, Jamaica, Virginia, Santo Domingo, Louisiana, Brazil, and Cuba experienced slave revolts. In the cases of Brazil and Cuba, the connection between resistance and the warfare of the period is complex and variegated but was bound to what was happening in Africa. In Cuba in 1811, a free man of color, José Antonio Aponte, led a bold uprising against planters near Havana. He drew inspiration from Saint-Domingue but also to events as far off as Brazil and the United States. It was inspired too by a history of the enslaved serving in Cuba's militia. Hopes were stirred by the fact that the British had forbidden their subjects to engage in the slave trade. Aponte and his followers were conscious of the networks they were a part of. These included Africa. Insurgents relied on African traditions to organize and to resist, traditions that were at this very moment being reshaped.[96]

Similarly, in 1814, enslaved persons in Bahia rose up. These were new arrivals, many Hausa and Muslim. After war and revolution had closed off the trade in slaves and sugar to and from Saint-Domingue, the numbers of the enslaved brought to this region of Brazil exploded. Now many came as veterans of revolutionary campaigns in West Africa. Led by a Muslim preacher, rebels killed between fifty and a hundred men and women, shouting "Freedom" and "Death to whites and mulattos."[97] The rising failed. But it would not end there. In 1835, the enslaved rose up once more in Bahia. Once again, they were led by Muslims who had just arrived from Africa as veterans of jihad and revolution there. Similarly, insurgency in western Cuba in the 1830s also had roots in African conflict. Indeed, strategies and weapons appear to have been African in origin in both Cuba and Bahia. Though it is difficult to determine how many insurgents had been shaped by jihad, there is no doubt they came from regions reshaped by it. With African war in the Americas, the Atlantic had struck back.[98]

Even the Mideast was bound by this process. The French famously invaded Egypt in 1798. Why they did so points to the tangledness that still defined the revolutionary age. With trade cut off from its Atlantic colonies, with Saint-Domingue in flames, France had to look elsewhere for revenue in an era of war. Add to this the fact that France was caught in a death grip of sorts with Britain, a nation that had looked increasingly to Asia—India in particular—for its imperial future after the collapse of much of its Atlantic empire. Napoleon hoped that a French invasion of Egypt would destabilize Britain's growing Asian empire and its banking industry. He then convinced himself that with Ottoman power on the wane in the region, Egypt could be his for the taking. The French would try to do what they had done in the Rhenish confederation, remake the institutional structures of Egypt, all to make revenue hunting more efficient. They failed dismally, of course. With time, insurgency and British naval power—think here of Nelson—overwhelmed Napoleon's ever-diminishing number of troops. Napoleon would have been better off in Ireland.[99]

In the wake of the debacle in Egypt, Napoleon refocused his energies on the Atlantic. Infamously, he dispatched troops with the notion of reasserting French control of the island of Saint-Domingue. Most egregiously, he planned to reintroduce slavery in what he hoped to make once more a colony.[100] His efforts backfired. His forces found themselves fighting skirmishes against a skilled and elusive adversary. If the terrain or the former slaves did not kill them, disease did. In no way would Napoleon be able to restructure Saint-Domingue. Louverture and his followers were becoming de facto sovereign by virtue of living in the revolutionary crucible for so long and by creating the rudimentary institutions of authority. Soon they would make good on that pretension.[101] Under Napoleon's leadership, the French also set their eyes on Latin America even as it was lurching into instability, hoping that inroads there would provide answers to stability at home. Hopes in the networked world did not only transfix those seeking liberty; it also stirred the powerful who tugged at the web of war for their own purposes. Such was the case in Saint-Domingue, and such would be the case in Latin America.[102]

The tendrils of war extended far afield, leading men and women to reconsider fundamental questions about governance and self in just the way Europeans and Americans were doing. In China, in India, in Java, in Australia, in Persia, Britain and France engaged in direct conflict and in proxy wars with Indigenous peoples. These Europeans did so to weaken one another. In the process, they touched off revolutionary change in the Pacific. Men and women from all of these places had already been re-fashioning sovereignty to contest the intrusion of Europeans and the many settlers that came with them. With the extension of revolutionary warfare, that task grew more urgent. Peoples across the Pacific met their many challenges just as those in the Atlantic did, by fighting and reshaping who they were. Throughout Asia, revolutionary ferment would compel Europeans, especially the British, to try to assert imperial control.[103]

These many woven stories of war and uncertainty intersected in a place far from the Atlantic: Louisiana. Just before the Treaty of Paris in 1763, the French had turned the vast region, emptying into the all-important port of

New Orleans, over to the Spanish. When Napoleon turned Spain into a vassal state, he reassigned it, through treaty, to France. He harbored dreams of a reclaimed French American empire that would provide resources for his campaigns and bring glory to France. His plans ultimately hinged on reasserting control in Saint-Domingue or Latin America. Louisiana would serve as a base to retake what had been lost in the Caribbean. If this were to happen, France could once more lay claim to a productive and integrated Atlantic empire. Once Napoleon's dreams for Saint-Domingue died along with his troops, however, Louisiana appeared much less alluring.[104]

With his western design in tatters, Napoleon approached the United States to see if its officials would purchase the sprawling territory. He would need the money. The American government, now presided over by Thomas Jefferson, had long wanted New Orleans. It, he thought, held the key to unlocking the potential of the interior. But the land on offer could now prove more important, especially for Jefferson's western design. It would double the size of the United States, promising to sustain settlement, Jefferson hoped, for generations. With this land, he believed he could ensure the success of the American Revolution. For these reasons, the United States purchased Louisiana. Tensions in the east could be dispersed there. Independent yeomen, the paragons of republican virtue, could work the land. Just as important, "civility" could overcome "savagery." With this ideological and racist assurance, with time the new United States could and would put an end to the "native ground" west of the Mississippi.[105] The west was needed to ensure that disorder, either fomented by poorer whites or by Natives, would not revisit the United States in so destabilizing a time. Saving America's revolution depended on Louisiana and, therefore, hinged on what had transpired in Saint-Domingue, Egypt, and France in the preceding years of war.[106]

Yet, as also happened throughout the broader and much extended Atlantic, one decision for expansion set off a series of equal and opposite reactions. With more American settlement, new coalitions would emerge to contest what the expanding revolutionary state was trying to do, in this case the Comanches and the Sioux. They could be considered the Prussians of North America. Or maybe we should call the Prussians the Comanches or Lakotas of Europe. Each of these American polities developed into continental powers as the fledgling nation from the east, the United States, was expanding. Each of these states organized itself for total war in an era defined by aggression. These American continental empires would emerge as the new republican American government to the east tried to put the final piece of its revolution settlement in place.[107]

The best way to think of Jefferson and Napoleon is to consider them the Cromwells of a new revolutionary age. A century earlier, England's republican Lord Protector, after he had executed a king, invaded Ireland and Scotland and dreamt of a great western design to bring a semblance of order to a country reeling from civil war. Some things had not changed. In the new age, revolutions begot other revolutions through aggression because of the need for expansion to quell the voices unleashed by ferment. Even those revolutions touted as anti-imperial became imperial through this dynamic.[108]

   These plans never worked, even as they appeared endlessly alluring. In just the same way the frontier functioned as a safety valve in a mobilized United States, war offered a means of projecting and dispersing tensions. The tangles of the world, however, bound all together, and soon disorder in one place spread to another. This dynamic serves as a vivid reminder of how the integrated Atlantic was also bound in a system to other parts of the world, and as the Atlantic was thrust into turmoil, new regions in Asia, Africa, and the American west were brought under the imperial gaze. Aggression had another unanticipated consequence. With the failure of displacing chaos, state actors were forced to attend to the difficult task of addressing domestic tensions, of doing the hard work of bringing revolutions to an end. War had promised to do so on the cheap; it proved an illusion. War required everyone, eventually even Napoleon, to attend to first principles and to affairs at home.

   Wars would also provide the bases of a new form of order in places France tried to dominate. Eventually, Belgian independence, to cite just one example, which came in 1830, became imaginable because of how French invasion heightened the distinctiveness of the people there. War, of course, as it often does, served as a catalyst. But it was the particulars of the war that mattered to create Belgium. The people in the region were Catholic, but they were ethnically divided. Divisions could be overcome because of how they had become "Belgian" through war. War created the state, but it also created the nation, however unstable it would be.

   One people left without a nation, the Irish, also became the exemplars of the new sorts of entanglements that now animated the Atlantic in the years of war. At the earlier stages, the Catholic mercenary Thomas Conway fought for the French Crown, offered his services to American patriots, then rejoined the French, and finally would even fight for the British Empire as part of an Irish regiment. What a life of twists and turns, what a Barry Lyndon–like experience. But not an unusual one. This is what war and revolution did. If anything, as revolutionary conflict gripped the whole Atlantic, such boundary crossing became more pronounced. Later, as the British cracked down in Ireland and as radicals fled, Ireland exported more revolutionary adventurers. Some headed to the Continent, many more to America. Some of these then sailed to Latin America, to fight for independence movements there.[109]

The Irish, a people whose revolution, certainly in their eyes, had "failed," would foment revolution elsewhere. They were not alone. War had created more stateless people like these. "Rogue revolutionaries" moved from place to place, particularly in the Caribbean, to serve the cause of armies that fought under the banner of freedom. They took up arms as the Atlantic still heaved with aggression and revolution. They would do so even after general warfare ended. Their peripatetic existences demonstrated that war could not unmake the tangled bonds that tied the Atlantic together—bonds that war had, ironically, strengthened. Yet, most of these adventurers were destined to fail. The seeming futility of what they did suggested that these days of hope, fear, and aggression were coming to an end.[110]

CHAPTER SIX

# Singeing the Fray

## *The Vexed Task of Ending Revolution*

THE IRISHMAN DANIEL O'CONNELL spent much of his life living with the dashed hopes of the age of revolution and the new realities it gave rise to. O'Connell championed the rights of those the age had not liberated. The age served as his touchstone. He defined all through it. It explains why he channeled discontent into the political. If the revolutions that had just passed legitimated the state, then he would use the state to finish any task that had been left undone. He focused particularly on Catholics in Ireland, who had not been fully emancipated, and on the enslaved in America, who had not been freed. He committed his life to these causes. He did so without considering boundaries.[1]

In viewing the age through the prism of promise, O'Connell did not stand alone. He befriended those who fought for freedom, and famously his moniker—"the Liberator"—would grace the masthead of the most important abolitionist newspaper in America. He met Frederick Douglass on the latter's visit to Ireland in 1845. At a mass rally tying the causes of Ireland and of the enslaved together, he introduced Douglass as "the Black O'Connell of the United States." Both, as a newspaper covering the event recounted, "loved liberty and hated oppression the world over." For his part, Douglass was captivated by O'Connell. Ireland's influence on Douglass was profound and shaped his broader mission of freedom. "I live a new life," he recalled after his visit there.[2] Years earlier, O'Connell had become the chief supporter of another self-styled liberator, the great visionary for a republican Latin America, Simón Bolívar. O'Connell gave an address known today as "the Bolívar Speech," in which he hoped Ireland would find "a new Bolívar" to animate the nation. So deep was his devotion that he even sent one of his sons to fight for El Libertador. In a letter to Bolívar, O'Connell said he prayed "that my son may be enabled to form one link in that kindly chain which will, I hope, long bind in mutual affection the free people of Columbia [*sic*] and the gallant but unhappy natives of Ireland." Maybe Bolívar, O'Connell reckoned, could realize what so many other places touched by revolution had failed to achieve, a truly just and liberating settlement. Perhaps, as O'Connell wrote, Bolívar could "imitate the virtues of Washington."[3]

Though he styled himself a man of the broader Atlantic revolution, O'Connell also lamented a world marked by Jacobin excess. While he hoped to undo the rottenest aspects of the revolution settlement for the British Isles, he dared not propose anything that would generate the violence and uncertainty he and others had left behind.[4] He hoped that maybe Bolívar could accomplish something his and Douglass's societies had, in his eyes, failed to achieve. Maybe Bolívar could strike a balance between order and meaningful liberty. Bolívar would, of course, also prove unsuccessful, and this would haunt him until his death.[5] Although O'Connell did not know it, it was for the very same reasons revolution came up seemingly short for America and for Ireland.

No doubt, issues for many throughout the Atlantic remained unresolved. And this is the way that nearly everyone would give meaning to the challenging processes of the age. Those who lived through the period would use ideological yardsticks to measure how revolution in one place succeeded or failed to achieve some set of goals often set in another place. Nonetheless, it was also clear the settlements that had emerged and were emerging were best denominated in the plural. A whole array of distinctive settlements was now defining the political lives of nearly all in the Atlantic. Each differed from the other in ways that reflected the myriad experiences of different places with the integration, disintegration, and reintegration of the Atlantic. Catholics in Ireland had won some freedom for the age, and O'Connell pushed for more. Blacks in America had no such hope for incremental change. What would happen to Bolívar's world? Up to this point, each place realized a settlement that history would or could allow. The same fate would befall Latin America.

O'Connell's ambivalence also points to something else often over-looked when studying revolution. Ending a revolution, never mind an age, is no simple feat. Ending requires all sorts of trade-offs. It involves complex negotiations. It necessitates reconciliation when there can appear no possibility of finding common ground. It needs fatigue and res-ignation. The years of tangled hope, fear, and aggression had exhausted many. Nearly everyone dreaded revolutionary tumult and the competi-tion it entailed. Most important, and here is the vital ingredient, is that an authority has to emerge that can claim and make good on sovereignty. A power has to come into being, one that is stable and at least acceptable to a great many, that can act again as a magistrate after a state of war.

The end of revolution was the beginning of new sovereignties. The revolutionary settlements had to cohere to the distinctive natures of the societies in which they were hammered out. This is the world that O'Connell helped create and the one he had to work within. It was pop-ulated by discrete nations all touched by the period's uncertainties and haunted by their own histories, brought back once more into some state of equilibrium after the challenges of integration and the resulting cruci-ble of revolution.[6] Though each state looked different and had to man-age different tensions, they acted remarkably alike. The fact that many were republics was only part of the similarity. All these states, whether still monarchies or newly formed republics, bore the stamp of the age. All peoples had been mobilized and politicized to address the challenges of the day, and the state had to reshape itself accordingly. In most cases, these states acted imperially, even if some did so reluctantly. The older empires that stood when the age began could not do justice to the new pressures and tensions of a globalizing world. The new sort of state, with increased capacity, could.[7]

Therefore, the age of *revolution* became an age of *revolutions* to bring the period to a close and to canonize a new order in which the strong and agile could survive. It is not a mistake that singular settlements sup-planted an age marked by connections and entanglements. Connections in the unregulated system had fostered instability and conflict. Entangle-ments brought hope, fear, and war. The nation-state was best suited to managing the whole and the individual places that had been split open by revolution. The most powerful of these would become the successors of ancien régime empires.[8]

The age had its origins in connections. Its endings would only be found for each people trying to erect borders—between states, between peoples, between ideas, between the past and future, and between hopes and fears—yet recognizing that the world now was even more interconnected than before. With its emotive ties and its boundaries fixed to the state, the nation became the most effective means of sustaining sovereignty in a competitive world that had wrestled with dislocating mobilization on a mass scale. This reshuffling of space did not deny the transnational; it simply controlled and channeled. Bringing revolution to an end, despite the forlorn hopes of finding it in expansive war, required the hard and often dirty work of tussling with the past, recognizing some of it and turning away from other aspects. It meant grappling with the tensions that had become so explosive in the revolutionary crucible and placing limits on them. It meant compromising over how and where such limits should be set. Each people had its own fraught journey to walk to rebind what had been torn apart. Often, doing so meant excluding or coercing some groups.[9]

On this last point, we encounter the critical lesson of how the age came to a close. Even if O'Connell serves as the hinge point connecting Bolívar to Douglass, perhaps the latter, not O'Connell, should be the focus of this entangled story of endings. Of course, Douglass contested slavery in his own country, the main issue left unaddressed by revolution in America. He styled himself a reformer. He took principles seriously and wanted the United States to live up to them.[10] Yet, he would be written out of the American national story. In the short run, history would remember O'Connell and Bolívar, and in short order both would come to represent national aspirations. But the runaway slave from Maryland, though with time a celebrity, would be among the disappeared in his nation. Though as enmeshed as any other in a period defined by the transnational, he had to vanish in order for revolution to come to an end. His story, alas, would not be unique.

Douglass's America offers a template for the complex ways revolutions came to an end. We have witnessed, of course, Americans groping for endings in a number of ways. They did so as the rest of the Atlantic reeled from revolutionary dislocation. As Americans started experimenting with new institutions and new democratic sensibilities, that provisional, tentative, and improvisational search for order began to harden into the stuff of a durable settlement, one that would survive well into the nineteenth century. This hardening marked the period of the early republic and presaged what would happen throughout the Atlantic.

To be sure, the Constitution was a cornerstone of settlement. The republic would be composed of a union of smaller republics, all distinctive and bound together through a central government. The arrangement, as it took shape in the years after ratification, was sneakily efficacious and functioned like a system. In practice, the central state worked with and through its more willing and able constituent parts.[11] What emerged was a state that could ensure disorder did not return, just as it was designed to do. That said, the new American arrangement did not create a behemoth. It could be inefficient and ineffective, and was always improvised. Sometimes it was pulled along by the whims and wishes of the states and of its citizens. Yet, even if we admit as much, the state system could do enough to contain tensions within it. Centrifugal forces threatened to pull the nation apart. But it held. It did so by and large because of the way the federal arrangement legitimated power through the states and because the threats it faced were not as robust as those in places like France and Latin America.[12]

The developing federal system is only one part of the story. In the main, the settlement cohered because of boundaries. These were established through political culture. To maintain an acceptable level of debate, certain political stances would remain out of bounds. Radical republicanism, the sort espoused by Thomas Paine, could not be countenanced, even after revolution seemed in the proverbial rearview mirror. In fact, when Paine returned to America after a difficult patch in France when he was caught up in the Terror, he was considered a pariah. He seemed a harbinger of what could befall America once again if it did not protect its discursive bounds.[13] At the other end of the political spectrum, Loyalism or the idea of returning to Britain remained beyond the pale. As Loyalism appeared extinguished, some now considered those called Federalists outside the fence line of the acceptable as well. In a revolutionary age, they could now be likened to America's "aristocrats." Democracy relied on fixing the terms of legitimate debate. To be part of the American democratic nation necessitated ideological commitments to it. That meant limits.[14]

The settlement did not only set boundaries. It also recognized them. Most noticeably, it was bounded by what had happened over the intervening period. The settlement for America paid deference to the democratic ethos of the revolutionary era. In no way could deferential ways of organizing society be reimposed on a citizenry that had been mobilized.[15] Moreover, resurrecting older governing arrangements, in which elites controlled all local politics, could not be countenanced—at least officially. Elites could still rule. They had to recognize the ways political culture had been transformed, however. For instance, as new states were added to the union, such as Kentucky, all white men would enjoy the right to vote. Who received and who did not receive political rights followed the logic of what settlements were supposed to do: end the state of war and disorder. White men could not be overlooked.[16] In the new republic, popular voices were able to vent their grievances at state levels. Political culture remained boisterous but was channeled productively in a few institutional directions.[17]

The state sustained a new series of arrangements that allowed the United States to compete in the new Atlantic economic order and to provide "domestic tranquility." During their presidencies, Thomas Jefferson and James Madison pressed for the rights to trade freely. Though they bristled at the idea of Americans becoming urban creatures, they conceded that cities could serve as outlets for the trade of American-produced commodities abroad. The frontier proved critical for any American competitive advantage in this regard. What was grown there had great value in the Atlantic. The frontier also helped ensure postrevolutionary stability. The empire of and for liberty needed an open and moving frontier. That entailed the will and the capacity on the part of the state, at its multiple federated levels, to see to it that Natives would not inherit the land.[18] No doubt, the process would not be bloodless. With new Native American empires emerging, such as the Comanches, warfare and unrest would continue to define what officials and settlers called "the West." For decades the process stood, with local and federal officials using all means, fair and foul, to deprive Natives of their land. Officials often had to be dragged along to do so, but they knew they had to accede to the wishes of the people or risk a return to chaos. For Americans, this sort of empire was the answer to the problem of revolution.[19]

And so equilibrium returned, and Americans achieved the only sort of settlement they could have sustained: one unjust but efficacious. No doubt, the state was not as powerful as many in the age. But it had just enough power to coerce those groups whose liberty and autonomy would have threatened the return to order. Moreover, local authorities had a great deal of coercive power at their disposal, which they used to maintain the emerging settlement. When the central government did not or could not step in, the states could. All of this being said, people were not merely bystanders in the new republic. To the contrary, they accom-

plished settlement through vigorous debate, through the threats of violence, by compromising, by acquiescing, by coercing, and by cajoling.[20]

Most realized, as Jefferson had argued, that in this new postrevolutionary world Americans were still tussling with the defining entanglement of the age: slavery. On the one hand, most now reckoned that the
slave trade could not stand in this world. For some, its cruelty seemed
anachronistic in an age consciously defined by liberty. For others, a less
altruistic rationale prevailed. As many plantations transitioned to new
crops, fewer hands were needed. Surplus enslaved labor could be sold off
as the nation expanded westward. For both the principled and the oppor-
tunistic, the specter of race war in Saint-Domingue still haunted. What
had happened on the island was one more argument against the slave
trade.[21] The institution of slavery was another matter. To be sure, slavery
seemed to come from the old world of mercantilism.[22] But slavery
proved the only means to remain competitive in world markets, particularly as Americans tapped into the interior of the continent. Unfreedom
allowed burgeoning free trade. Postcolonial America, then, would still be
defined by that institution that had integrated the Atlantic.

This issue raises a critical variable when it came to bringing revolution
to an end: endings dovetailed with the possible. Perhaps if slavery would
have been outlawed throughout the United States, the states would not
have remained united. Some northerners hated the idea that much of the
south would remain a slave society. Nonetheless, they signed on to this
bargain to maintain union. Without union, they reckoned, the United
States would have been swallowed up in the geopolitical mess that was
much of the Atlantic world in a period of revolutionary intrigue. Allowing
slave owners to control the enslaved in their midst, as was the case in Brazil, seemed the only means of ensuring that the most fearful specter of the
age of revolution, slave revolt, did not visit the United States.[23] Slavery
persisted in those places wedded to plantation economies. Brazil was one
such place, as were some islands in the Caribbean, notably Cuba. The
American South was another.[24] Make no mistake about it: the suppression
of Blacks undergirded much of the stability of the new arrangement. It elevated the status of whites on even the margins of society, just as slavery
allowed the United States to compete economically.[25]

A boundary line provided the final bond of settlement. In the United
States, potential ideological problems were skirted because of a border between it and another state: Canada. For North America, two states lived
side by side, almost as mirror images of each other. Both were unmistakably

"American." Both places were peopled by many of the same sorts of men and women. One was republican, the other part of a British and Loyalist empire. Remember that in the aftermath of America's revolution, many Loyalists had fled. A good number went north.[26] The standoff between two Americas made for a stable arrangement. That is, until the revolutionary wars threatened it. Like much of the Atlantic, the United States and Britain's remaining North American provinces were drawn into the conflicts of the period. For the new United States, participation in the War of 1812 proved critical to its standing among other nations. Waging war ensured it would not be hemmed in by the great powers and could trade on its own terms. This chapter of the wider revolutionary conflicts of the age revolved around sovereignty. To sustain the American settlement entailed having access to the Atlantic economy and control of sailors and ships. The United States, in other words, needed the integrated Atlantic. This entailed war with British Canada.[27]

The War of 1812 gave Americans distinctive identities as a people in a still integrated world. Fittingly, the adversaries of the United States would discover in the war their identity as "Canadians." The conflict offered something to distinguish them from their relatives living to the south. They were no longer simply Loyalist Americans. For creoles in the United States, this event proved almost a second war of independence. It secured the borders of the new nation and gave them, as well, an experience as a people. Both states constructed a national sense of self from the war, and the boundary between the two became peaceful and secure. The North American border created mirror images of stability.[28]

Entanglements certainly persisted. The story of James Workman provides a case in point. Born in Ireland, Workman trained at Middle Temple in London to become a lawyer. Publishing pro–United Irish material, he had to flee to the United States. He chose Charleston, South Carolina, as his new base. He led a wandering existence, moving to Havana and then to Philadelphia, where he roomed with generals from France's revolutionary army. Eventually, he established his home in the Louisiana Territory, in the city of New Orleans, where he would support Liberian resettlement plans for the enslaved even though he owned two enslaved persons himself. He seemed to be everywhere and to know everyone. He collected money for Daniel O'Connell's Catholic emancipation efforts, funds O'Connell returned because they came from the slave-holding south. He also drafted a constitution for the united colonies of Spain in the New World. For this, he did his homework, studying the legal codes and social conditions of different regions of South America. When sovereignty collapsed in Spain with the Napoleonic invasion, Workman believed he could help create a federated state along the lines of the United States. He became a leader of a group called the Mexican Association, which aimed to help New Spain get out from under Spanish control. He even plotted with the former vice president Aaron Burr to carve out a new state in the American west with territory from the United States and New Spain. Believe it or not, Workman dreamt of using Irish Catholics to liberate Latin America and in so doing give Ireland a vaunted role in a reinvigorated British Empire. His plans did not eventuate in anything, but his varied experiences point to the ways the era of entanglements had not come to an end. They still could confound. They were just more effectively managed.[29]

Americans still believed they had served as Atlantic paragons. Holding a mirror up to themselves, they revived the conceit that maybe, just maybe, the United States still acted as a beacon of liberty. Earlier hopes about the age had been dashed when France and Saint-Domingue descended into violence. What happened in both places short-circuited the sense of Atlantic connectedness. Events in Latin America suggested that Americans still inhabited an entangled world. Independence there prompted citizens from the United States to toast their brothers and sisters to the south, to name children after their freedom fighters such as Simón Bolívar, and to rename towns after places in South America. Maybe France and Saint-Domingue were aberrations. Some even held out hope for Brazil. It seemed that Americans would no longer be alone.[30]

Americans had bounded their state and their people after a period when society had frayed. Because of this, the American story proved alluring to so many tussling with the fundamental dynamics of the period. Appearances deceived, however. Americans had a few advantages others did not. The white population was relatively homogenous, and the distance between rich and poor did not loom as large as it did in other regions of the Atlantic. No people with inherited titles lived there. Moreover, the new nation had land, which could function as a release for discontent. The War of Independence had also simplified and channeled tensions; the same sorts of appalling, civil war violence that gripped so many regions throughout the Atlantic did not visit most American communities. Finally, the greatest potential fracture points would not stymie settlement. To ensure order and an end to revolution, the enslaved would be placed on the wrong side of boundaries established by law and race;

for Indigenous peoples, lines would be geographic and cultural. To satisfy the majority, some groups would be placed beyond the pale of citizenship. Order mattered more to most.[31]

America would be prologue. In this story, gender may be the most significant feature. Through the years of revolution, women began to think of themselves in new terms. Some pressed for a greater share of political rights. Women had struggled and borne the burdens of revolution and war. It had become clear that they did not differ from men in their capacities. Yet, they would not enjoy formal political rights. States made no allowance for it, with the exception of New Jersey, which permitted unmarried independent women to vote during the war years. After the Revolution, New Jersey would follow the example of others. Why? Well, norms had been toppled, but not patriarchy. That had withstood the challenges of the time. That said, women did not go to their old roles unchanged.

Most of the poorer sort, those who had lived with the fears and uncertainties of armies and of material want, returned to the roles they had known before the War of Independence. Nonetheless, war had changed them. Through their sacrifice, they had a vested interest in the new nation and styled themselves its guardians. Academies for female education opened throughout the United States in the years after revolution. This represented an important feature of the postrevolutionary landscape in America and suggested women were the equals of men. This sentiment did not yet extend to political participation. The women who could afford to attend such schools rarely pushed for the same sort of political participation men enjoyed. Few made the arguments that Wollstonecraft did. At least for now. Revolution had transformed women, up and down the socioeconomic ladder. It had also turned subjects into citizens. These female citizens, though, still understood their primary status in terms of what they did. The greatest thing they could do for the revolutionary settlement was to serve as "republican mothers." In the United States, and by extension throughout much of the Atlantic, women would be valorized for what they could do for social virtue.[32]

Reining in those who had been politicized to bring an end to revolution, therefore, did not happen in straightforward or simplistic ways. Such would be the case throughout the Atlantic. Witness again the Dames des Halles in Paris. They would not enjoy full political rights as revolution came to an end in France—same thing as in the United States, of course, and throughout much of the Atlantic. It would be easy to say that political rights for men, which would with time become the norm, were borne on the backs of women. Inclusion, in other words, always created exclusion. But things are more complex. The Dames did not define themselves by voting; they based their rights on what they did and what they made. This conferred a claim to being part of the nation. The October Days, and the resulting fracturing of society, certainly gave them a political voice, as had happened throughout the Atlantic when sovereignty collapsed; but as authority was reconstructed, they were not simply shunted away. Women still remained citizens, even if the full measure of citizenship—what we conventionally look for—was not realized as revolution came to a close. Excluded? Perhaps. But the story is more complicated than what that single word conveys. After all, women had earned citizenship.[33] As was the case in America, partial exclusion was offset by the cultural cachet that women enjoyed throughout the Atlantic. They became defenders of the nation. This sort of trade-off, too, would make for a pattern that defined the lot of many people—men and women— throughout the Atlantic when it came to endings.[34]

The fate of women in the United States and in France reminds us of an important lesson in considering endings. For France, as had been the case in the new United States, exclusion was rarely absolute. Even if some people were written out of the formal political nation, order and exclusion did not necessarily go hand in hand. At this politicized moment, nearly everything revolved around negotiation. The most significant piece in the Atlantic puzzle, France, proves the rule. It cohered to the broad patterns evident in North America and to the oftentimes troubling prospect of striking a balance between order and inclusion.

The beginning of the end of France's revolution came with the adventure in Egypt and the debacle in Saint-Domingue. In the wake of these setbacks, and in the immediate aftermath of a disastrous naval loss to Nelson at the Battle of the Nile, Napoleon returned to France. With the tide turning against the republic internationally and still bedeviled by instability at home, Sieyès encouraged Bonaparte to take over the reins of power in France and so bring an end to the whipsawing effects of the period. After the Terror, government followed government. France was exhausted by war and conscription. It was exhausted by financial chaos and penury. It was exhausted by uncertainty and violence. Sieyès reckoned that the "saber" of leviathan had to be wielded by someone who could steer France between the extremes of the old Bourbon order and Jacobin Terror. Near the end of the 1799, after a coup, the new "Consul" Bonaparte, along with two others with no pretensions to power, took over control of the country. This move would end revolution in France. With a new focus on the metropole, Napoleon was able to do something no other individual or group could do: restore order.[35]

Myth surrounds Napoleon and how he ended a revolution. But he really did something quite simple. He enjoyed immense stature, and he combined what we would consider liberal and authoritarian sensibilities at just the moment France had had enough. He worked to suppress violence and lawlessness by using the powers of the state to establish security and stability. He aimed to end uncertainty. He knew his way around power. He had, after all, directed the very manifestation of popular mobilization, an army designed for total war. Yet, he did not intend to bring France back to ancien régime authoritarianism. Shrewdly, just as Americans had done, he welcomed all comers into the arena of political discourse, except for those on the very margins of right and left: unreconciled royalists and hard-core Jacobins. The space between the two represented the broad channel of political legitimacy. All, even Napoleon, had to recognize the substantive changes in political culture and to the practice of politics that revolution had wrought. He, therefore, promised to end revolution without overturning it.[36]

As was the case with America, he also instituted a new constitution of a sort, the so-called Napoleonic Code, and the institutions that would enforce it. This initiative became the basis for ensuring France would no longer be governed in arbitrary fashion, an important concession to the Revolution. But France would be ruled. Departments now had prefects, themselves elites, to guarantee that order prevailed throughout the country. They governed in the name of the republic and for its official ideology— still liberty, equality, and fraternity—but did so with an eye to bring the Revolution to a close.[37] Napoleon also used the code to lay out the outlines of a new settlement and who was in and who was out. The code instantiated family as the core unit of society. It hemmed in women's rights as political citizens and made patriarchal assumptions about the basis of the law and of social cohesion. This move, like all such exclusions, represented what those who could threaten order took to be the lowest common denominator for stability. Thus, Napoleon ended revolution by turning away from much of what the Revolution had accomplished. Though cloaking himself in its mantle, he curtailed what he took to be its destabilizing excesses.[38]

In other words, Napoleon found himself facing the same sorts of crisis that people like Washington and Jefferson had confronted. France's "founding father" also struggled to find a path through the constraints and possibilities of the moment with the context and ideas he inherited. This, as in the case of the American founders, represented Napoleon's genius. All testified to the truth that revolutions are difficult to end, yet men like Napoleon and Jefferson succeeded by using almost exactly the same means. These centered on setting limits and erecting all sorts of boundaries. Napoleon combined the ideas of people, nation, and state into one compelling settlement after a period of uncertain sovereignty. Americans like Jefferson had done exactly the same thing. They, too, just as Napoleon would do, used an idea of the nation to bind a fractured society together and to remake the state. All served sovereignty.[39]

The most critical limit that was established centered on the ideal of Revolution with a capital "R." The new French state, indeed the new French order, rested on the ideas of its Revolution. It made no difference if France played the part of an empire or if Napoleon styled himself an emperor. The ideals of the Revolution were not fully realized, of course, as was the case with the United States, but they formed the basis of appeals to the state, its resources, and its protection. There was no going back, even if the republic was to revert, as it did a few times, to a constitutional monarchy. Sovereignty had been reestablished through a crown and through empire, but a republican crown and republican understanding of empire.[40]

The settlements in America and France pointed out the nature of the negotiations and compromises over boundaries that necessarily went into creating a new order. Take the case of the Catholic Church in France. Decried from the early days of revolution as the epitome of all that was wrong with the ancien régime and French society, the church had effectively been destroyed in France. Many resisted, of course, particularly in the Vendée. It was clear that as Napoleon attempted to bring an end to the disorder of the period, some peace would have to be made with France's Catholic past. If he did not, he would be inviting unending trouble and a potential source for renewed revolutionary chaos in the guise of what officials tellingly thought of as "counterrevolution." So, against his instincts Napoleon signed a concordat with the Catholic Church, restoring many of its privileges. The agreement did not require him to hand over all the property that had been confiscated. That was gone forever. But the church could play a public role once more in French life. Napoleon saw some virtue in this. Religious belief could provide social and political benefits for a France that had fallen apart. This move may not have completely pleased rebels in thoroughly Catholic areas—they still hated the republic and wanted a restoration—but it offered a means for them to stomach the new regime. As was the case for women, what those in places like the Vendée lost in one area, their political allegiance to the Crown, they gained in another, their religious freedom. Though the move aided the stability Napoleon premised his rule on, it did not co-opt or marginalize Catholicism; it strengthened fervor for the faith and turned it into a political force.[41]

This sort of cross-trussing that bound everyone to the state in some way provided an ingenious basis for order. No group won everything it wanted. All had to compromise. But most won just enough to allow them to live with the new order. In this way, tensions did not need to be debilitating; they could sustain. War and revolution had not done away with old cleavages, but the resulting compromises reordered them and made them the stuff of more durable arrangements. Americans also had constructed their own cross-trussing. The state had to ensure that those who could undo a settlement could enjoy some rights. In the same way, men and women in France could at least hold on to the idea of liberty undergirded by order.[42]

The search for order ran through Napoleon, in France, in Europe, and in the Atlantic system as a whole. He was, after all, as Hegel asserted, the "spirit of the age on horseback." For most, order, of course, hinged on defeating Napoleon. There are many explanations for why he eventually lost. The allies finally learned to cooperate. The French, already sapped by years of war, attempted to invade Russia, a bridge too far. The other nations of Europe had come to see the value of the new force that Napoleon had unleashed: mobilization of the nation. Thus empowered, they could bring numbers to bear in 1815 when France no longer could. One other explanation offers a more prosaic reason: Napoleon lost because the British controlled the Atlantic. He had ceded the Atlantic to them by focusing his energies on the Continent. With a far superior navy and a savvy merchant class, with the fiscal-military state fully engaged, the British were able to endure a prolonged conflict more easily than the French. Wellington's famous victory at Waterloo in 1815, which actually turned on Prussian generalship and on allied numbers, was a fitting coda to the period.[43]

The end to the Continental chapter came in 1815 at the Congress of Vienna. Most of the actors present wanted to roll back the clock to rebind the frayed state of Europe after a period defined by what they regarded as dangerous hopes, real fears, and prolonged warfare. Try as they might, the genies could not be put back into the bottles, even as the delegates at the congress attempted to prop up the traditional social structures in each country. In fact, the men and women in and around the congress operated in the space between reaction and reform, hoping to piece Europe together again like Humpty Dumpty.[44] France itself offers an instructive example. With Napoleon's fall, the Bourbon monarchy had been reinstated, but the new king was no absolutist. He shared power with an elected assembly, abided by a written constitution, and allowed freedom of religion. The gist of the Revolution could not be revoked. The more significant result of Vienna was how the power of the state to control its peoples was canonized. A number of tiny statelets that existed before the age of war and revolution had been gobbled up. In their place a few larger states had come into being, and a great many others of the sort of size and composition that were apt to be able to survive in this more competitive world. By tapping into the popular energies of revolution and deploying them through warfare, the French had unearthed a new sort of power. Only a new order made up of more powerful legitimate states could hope to manage it.[45]

The congress achieved one other critical goal. From this point forward, states would not be drawn into imperial or colonial conflicts. The new system in Europe would seal off the tensions that had previously dragged them into war. They set up buffers between states, and they "fenced off" Europe from colonial, commercial, and maritime conflicts. Entanglements would not lead to war, because a new state system would not allow it.[46] Going to war over the Atlantic system, as had been the case at the time of the Seven Years' War or the first Atlantic war, would hopefully be a thing of the past.

The congress recognized the changed nature of the world but also realized that certain realities persisted. The world of commerce still resembled a state of nature. Mercantilism had served as the chief means for ordering the Atlantic before the age, but the consequences of trying to disentangle trade had proved catastrophic. Mercantilism could not survive in the new order. Free trade, an ideal well attuned to a competitive world of free agents, allowed those officials in Vienna to imagine a world in which entanglements would no longer lead to conflict. On the one hand, it seems Adam Smith had been prophetic when in 1776 he wrote *The Wealth of Nations*. The imperatives of the Atlantic had not changed. Only now states christened competition itself as the basis of the system and its chief attribute. Necessity was thus turned into virtue. On the other hand, the new series of arrangements taking shape saw the state play a mediating role in the Atlantic by supporting state actors to compete in the Atlantic economy. In reality, states would regulate the participation of merchants in the Atlantic economy through tariff policies. Even if the invisible hand did not propel all commerce, what emerged was a far cry from the older mercantilist ideals that had been behind reformist impulses earlier on. The new states had a stake in free flows of trade, but unsurprisingly they hoped to manage them for their benefit.[47] Now with much greater capacity because of all of those years of revolution and war, the state played a mediating role it could not have before, even if it had to bow to systemic constraints.[48]

If there was one winner that emerged through this period, it was Britain. The first place to experience the tumult of revolution and civil war at the opening of the period had lost some of its empire but grew stronger for the experience. We can point to a few reasons. First, perhaps by breaking off its most radical appendage before the era of French connections, the British ensured that the crisis of the Atlantic did not shatter the center. Far from it, in fact. After the loss of much of North America, empire expanded to global proportions. Second, the British had effectively retooled given the challenges of the age and given the changing nature of the Atlantic. The Houdini-like trick Britain managed was this: it had adapted by appearing not to change. After the "near-revolution" of the period, conservatives did what they could to shore up authority, while realizing that cautious reform was in order. As in other states where popular sovereignty was the ostensible basis of authority, the British also conceded that "consent" had to be at the root of governance, even if some came to this position grudgingly. Third, and most important, was how Britain accomplished both at once. The British ushered in domestic reform to sustain an old system; they then tied that reinvigorated system to a new vision of global empire.[49]

Even though officials of nearly all stripes had fulminated against the extension of political rights to the common sort, more and more realized that unless the state reformed and recognized the existence of a mobilized people by offering them a political voice, they would be courting chaos. No doubt, the Great Reform Act passed in 1832, opening the franchise to more men, passed with great reluctance. But it passed. Allowing for more and more people to vote and giving them certain civil freedoms, reform measures spoke to the ways the world had changed

since the eighteenth century. Popular sovereignty had become a fait ac-
compli throughout the Atlantic and in a now demilitarizing Europe. This
included Britain. In light of what had happened to the Atlantic, such
measures also allowed the British to claim they had achieved what others
aspired to: order and liberalization.[50]

The approach allowed Britain to manage another great transformation of the period: the so-called industrial revolution. The story of this
transformation is a complex one, bound to the political changes of the period and mobilization of people. Both political and industrial revolution
required people to be remade and to be marshaled. Of course, industrialization also created class antagonism, just as political revolution did. But
reform blunted conflict. Willy-nilly and not by design, reform worked as a
preemptive measure to stifle or co-opt worker discontent, as it gave common people both a legitimate voice in the system and a stake in it. They
had sacrificed for war and to defeat radicalism, and they secured some
rights, however modest, as a just reward. In other words, political change
paved the way for subsequent economic transformation, while bounding
social conflict.[51] All in all, the British would achieve if not, as Wellington
intoned, "a revolution by due process of law," at least stability.[52]

The most telling and perhaps significant reform that came at the
close of the revolutionary age added to the equilibrium of the state and
the broader system. More so than any other change, it was altruistically
framed but attuned to the changing system. In the years after revolution,
a growing chorus of men and women in England were pressing for an
end to the greatest outrage of the old system: slavery. No doubt, leaders
such as William Wilberforce believed that the end of slavery and the
trade that sustained it would be a crowning achievement of Christian virtue and of Enlightenment thought. Politically, it had become more than
palatable to argue against the institution, particularly because Britain had
lost so much of its slave-owning empire when the United States broke
away. For both idealists and the practically minded, Saint-Domingue
provided motivation. Abolitionists could tap into the fears it still engendered to suggest that if slavery remained, all risked a replay of Saint-
Domingue. Unending war and revolution would be the result if this
vestige of an older world were left untouched.[53]

Yet, the end of the slave trade and slavery played into an emerging
system in which those who could compete in a free market would thrive.
An Atlantic free of slavery gave Britain, with its mature merchant community, a comparative advantage over those places that still relied on the

institution. Free movement of goods, of people, and of capital advantaged the nimble and the maritime. Even those calling for an end to an institution so seemingly out of touch with the age did so only when abolition could prove consonant with the demands of the market. The colony of Sierra Leone on the West African coast, for instance, long dreamt of as a refuge for freedom, could only be countenanced so long as it turned a profit.[54] Similarly, abolitionists and officials worried that plantations would not have enough laborers, even as they worked to abolish the slave trade. Abolitionism, too, cohered to systemic imperatives.[55]

Abolitionism, yoked to trade for profit, would also define the British approach to much of the rest of the Atlantic, including patriot movements in Spanish America. If creoles expected support, they would have to play by the new rules of the game, many of which were set by the British and would benefit the British handsomely. The British did not always hold this abolitionist line, but they did so for what had been Spanish America. In the still entangled Atlantic, Britain now pulled a great many strings. Slavery no longer represented one of them, but only insofar as profitability was not compromised.[56]

The British, therefore, were among the first to recognize the shifting parameters of a changing world and so retool for new constraints and possibilities. This was their genius. The British, of course, did not turn their backs on what could be called territorial forms of empire—think here of India—but they coupled these older forms with a newer emphasis on extensive networks of trade. Far from being altruistic, free trade was a strategy of power. It allowed the British to expand empire from the Atlantic to the entire globe. It would demand that they contest revolutionary movements throughout Asia by creating a consciously counterrevolutionary global empire as the age came to a close. This would be one of the chief implications of the age, one that would remake connections between East and West and that would shape the global system.[57] This is the story of the Pacific. For the Atlantic, commerce, not conquest, sustained a British "informal empire." Through trade, shipping, and banking, London and Liverpool held sway over both the United States and Latin America and would make Britain a force to be reckoned with for generations to come.[58]

The whole was still entangled, only newly rationalized. In fact, the postrevolutionary United States still depended on ongoing ties with Britain. America could only disperse revolutionary energies in an "empire of liberty" with the impunity that was supplied by British power. Americans traded within the parameters of the new Pax Britannica. The new nation slotted itself into the global economy in the ways most colonies did in a mercantilist political economy: its farmers produced goods destined for metropoles in exchange for finished products and capital investment. These also included goods produced by slave labor. The Royal Navy protected the newly independent nation and this arrangement.[59] Moreover, the City of London provided a great deal of the financing for westward movement. Ironically, Americans did much of what they did to bring their Revolution to a close with British help.[60]

There were two final connected pieces to the British postrevolutionary puzzle. The first was movement. In the years the age was coming to a close, Britain experienced a "settler revolution." The term "settler colonialism" is one scholars employ to describe the newly independent United States. The concept suggests how common men and women led the way in conquering the lands of Indigenous peoples in the west. In fact, it became a global phenomenon with the close of the age of revolution. The British perfected it. They fetishized movement as a virtue, just as merchants waxed rhapsodic about free trade. Upon this idea Britain would construct the contours of a vast global empire of settlers. This amounted to their version of the empire of liberty, one based on the ideology of extending civilization and commerce and that would march forward on the feet of soldiers as well. It served the same stabilizing purposes as it did for Jefferson's empire.[61] Many would be more invested in Britain because of their active participation in the state and in the project of ruling British India and creating a "Greater Britain." If the people of Britain were now bound to the state, they were unbound to move through the world, and Indigenous peoples around the world from South Asia and Australia to South Africa and North America would suffer because of it.[62]

This brings us to the other missing puzzle piece. The British had also integrated, albeit imperfectly, the most vexing region remaining of the old empire: Ireland. Reform on this front was achieved in two steps. The first involved the Union itself. After the failed rising of 1798 and the sectarian violence and suppression that followed, officials decided that Ireland had to be part of a United Kingdom. They hoped that doing so would dilute Catholic and incendiary voices in a broader Protestant and stable whole. So, after 1801 Ireland lost its constitutional autonomy. Its Parliament voted itself out of existence aided by all sorts of incentives to do so. Britain could not countenance an independent Ireland in a world still reeling.[63]

The second reform measure took shape grudgingly. Eventually, Britain's government recognized that Catholics could not remain second-class subjects within the United Kingdom. Recognition came after years of struggle and after extraordinary pressure was brought to bear. At first Catholics were placed beyond the pale of full citizenship. No doubt, they won some concessions. Those with enough property could vote. Catholics could now bear arms. They could officially serve in the ranks of the military. But they could not sit in a Parliament into which Ireland was now bound. They remained Britain's excluded: the sort shut out from the political nation for the short-term stability of the whole. Nonetheless, given the new realities of the age and the threat to order that disaffected Catholics represented, full emancipation was a matter of time. It was passed by someone adamantly opposed to the idea, none other than the Duke of Wellington. He sponsored a bill in the wake of O'Connell's campaign to see to it that Catholics should enjoy the right to sit in Parliament.

That struggle and the bitterness it engendered tainted the bonds between Britain and Ireland. It also poisoned relationships within Ireland, as confessional identities hardened. The result was that Britain and Ireland were fundamentally compromised as a unit. Because the British failed to remake Ireland in any fundamental way and did not bind Catholics to the British state, Ireland remained an underdeveloped hinterland of Britain and the Atlantic. The military provided a safety valve. Movement offered a surer means of relieving pressures. The Irish participated in Britain's settler revolution. They, too, moved to places like Australia, even if some did so as convicts. Many, many more migrated across the Atlantic to the United States. Most left from regions dealing with the dislocating effects of modernization in Ireland. Because of its insecure fit in the Union, Ireland suffered through a warping form of modernity. Ultimately, these were the premodern people who built the canals and infrastructure that made the world modern and that tied the United States more securely into the global economy. Ireland's most important role then was to serve the labor needs of places like New York.[64] The movement of the Irish in no small part stemmed from Britain's need for stability. Irish migration would come to be one of the defining characteristics of the nineteenth-century Atlantic, just as Britain's search for order would be played out across the world.

Britain's efforts to remake itself in a postrevolutionary world led to tumult in South America. With Spanish sovereignty in ruins, the British saw an opportunity to tap into the resources of South America. They did not want rivals to benefit from any sort of imperial Spanish crisis. The

British would act under the banner of trade. So anxious were British merchants to extend their reach to South America that the government sacked Buenos Aires when Napoleon invaded the Iberian Peninsula. In so doing, they destabilized the region. British moves emboldened creole elites there to seek to expand their hinterland to the region of Paraguay and into Brazil. We could say in light of this example that the British, near the end of their age, were helping to initiate another.[65]

South Americans, therefore, found themselves unraveling while the world around them reknit. But there is another and more significant reason to study Latin America and to consider it in terms of the age. We see in what happened there how the tangles implicit in revolutionary origins foreshadowed the difficulties of bringing revolution to a close. Latin America is, in fact, the ideal case study for appreciating endings or, as we shall see, nonendings. For what vexed men and women there challenged those everywhere throughout the Atlantic.

The story begins in a way we would expect. Independence, as some prophesied, heralded uncertainty and led to bloodshed as it had in other places. The order that would emerge would be shaped and haunted by the violence, mass mobilization, and politicized fragmentation that emerged when sovereignty collapsed. The dilemmas that creoles faced when addressing home rule proved much more complex than those that British Americans and the Irish Ascendancy had dealt with. Allegiances and affiliations were in flux because of dramatic changes initiated by reform and by integration. All was complicated further still by race and status. When the fault lines cracked, no one could predict what direction revolution would take. Whereas bids for independence would channel potentially revolutionary impulses in North America into a clear-cut set of allegiances, in Spanish America independence dispersed such energies. Independence furthered the fracturing in this society and created more opportunities for revolutionary violence.[66] In such a world, the inheritors of revolution would find bounds difficult to erect.

As a rule, the sequence went thus: independence "led to disunity, and disunity to destruction."[67] Then, many actors competed to fill the sovereign void. In some regions, irregular forces and warlords, what were referred to as caudillos, emerged in the maelstrom of collapsing authority. They sided with causes most likely to provide paths to power. So, too, did juntas. Some of these bodies declared independence from the Crown and also from competitors who claimed sovereignty over the regions in which they lived. Juntas could be loyal to the Crown or try to take the place of the Crown. They could appear progressive or conservative. Some, such as those in Colombia, courted free Blacks to depose Spanish governors. Others, as in Peru, latched on to the royalism of Indigenous peoples. Natives were convinced the Crown could right wrongs and protect their interests, especially as institutions failed to do so. In other places, creoles held fast to lines of caste.[68]

Historians have long debated whether ideas or circumstances propelled action. Lately, circumstances seem to have the upper hand. As we have seen elsewhere, with no authority, in a hyper-politicized context, and with perceived threats and potential possibilities for liberation just around the corner, violence had a revolutionary edge. Unlike with France, though, the state did not sponsor the lion's share of the violence. It was the absence of the state that made bloodshed so frightening, and its scale unprecedented.[69] As was the case with North America, programs of sovereignty did take shape—broadly patriot and royalist—but most of the fighting between the sides, and people could change allegiances just as they had in Saint-Domingue, had a civil war quality. Amid a power vacuum, much of Spanish America became like the American south, the Vendée, or Wexford. Spanish America, under such pressures, disintegrated.[70]

Trying to characterize the violence would suggest how difficult it would be to bring it to an end. Violence could take the form of large-scale insurrections, as would be the case for Mexico, a society with an Indigenous majority. It could appear in the guise of royalist insurrections, as would occur in Venezuela, the place with the largest slave society in Spanish America. Some regions would be marked by unending insurgencies, as in Upper Peru. Others still would be plagued by provincial revolts or would suffer under the thumb of royalist suppression. In Buenos Aires, local elites wanted to reclaim silver-mining regions that were so important to their Atlantic fortunes, setting off a conflagration. Soon Indians rose up to contest what was happening. In Cartagena, faction fighting spread to the countryside, and soon the larger viceroyalty was in tatters. When Spanish expeditionary forces would finally come to try to reknit the fabric of empire, they would only add to the intractability of the situation. They, too, became trapped, especially as all sides tried to mobilize everyone—rural and urban, enslaved and free, Native and creole—into simmering civil wars. The result was fragmentation throughout the continent.[71]

South America, without sovereignty, had become a Hobbesian world of violence erupting along fracture points. Much of South America reeled from unresolvable conflict. Spanish forces employed draconian means to win hearts and minds, hoping to secure one region after another and return to some imagined past in which centralized sovereignty reigned. Doing so heightened violence.[72] Even Peru, more loyal and more stable than most, where a small group of former imperial officials had been able to use force to maintain some semblance of authority, experienced substantive popular insurrection.[73]

Though some hoped for a seamless transition from older imperial viceroyalties to a new order, any sort of integrated vision seemed an unattainable dream. Some, such as Bolívar, wanted to create independent superstates that would combine older administrative units, such as, say, merging New Granada and Quito with Venezuela. Called the Liberator for his fight for independence for all of South America, he also wanted to contain the many pressures that were blowing societies into pieces.[74] Venezuela offers an apt example of the furies he was trying to cage. Here he had a hand in creating a republic. He then lost it to royalists and insurgents, after which he launched the "liberation" of New Granada. He followed this up with an invasion of Venezuela to create a second republic, only to see all collapse into internecine violence as all strata of society became politicized. With the crisis of sovereignty, "civic wars" turned into "civil wars" once all were mobilized. Venezuela proved impossible for Bolívar to control, even as he employed more and more violence in calling for a "War to the Death" against his enemies there, particularly peninsulares. He hoped to style himself a Bonaparte and deliver the order necessary to restore governance. But the chaos was too great, and his methods only added to the morass. His Gran Colombia fell to pieces. Bolívar grew convinced that what had been Spanish America needed independence with strong government.[75]

In North America, the bid for independence muted revolutionary violence. In South America, it had the opposite effect. The civil war nature of the revolution combined with independence wars to create a maelstrom. Chile offers a microcosm of sorts of the way revolution and independence confounded each other. After the collapse of Spanish rule with Napoleon's invasion, a junta in Santiago claimed to establish control in the name of the Crown. As Spanish-allied officials attempted to assume power once again, a military man named José Miguel Carrera declared Chile would not come to heel. The Spanish viceroy then called on royalist troops from Peru to put down what he called a rebellion. All hell then broke loose, and the region was engulfed in civil war. Collapse of sovereignty brought further disorder and violence, as happened all throughout the Atlantic. In the political vacuum, conflicting ideals of sovereignty soon emerged, and competition became intense. Provinces took up arms against one another. Different visions of republicanism vied. Royalists held whole swaths of the country.[76] The great warlord José de San Martín sent troops to Chile, hoping like Bolívar to tie much of South America together through aggression. The "liberator of the south" focused on establishing Buenos Aires along the lines of the old viceroyalty. To achieve this goal, he thought he had to do exactly what Bolívar advocated to the north. He had to "liberate" the regions around Buenos Aires, as well as that royalist bastion of peasant resistance and center of Spanish power, Peru, and Chile. Bernardo O'Higgins, the son of a Spanish official turned revolutionary, skillfully worked with San Martín to restore order in Chile. The only sort that could be established here, however, was a Roman-style dictatorship, and even with that they could not bring the royalist and Indigenous south to heel.[77]

In a last-ditch attempt to try to win the wars, the Spanish regime hoped to break the back of rebellion in Buenos Aires, the great entrepôt tying the Atlantic to the Continent. The attempt resulted in a virtual coup in Spain, forcing the king to rely more on liberal methods to entice the colonies back into empire rather than ruinously expensive force. But it was too late. Rebel armies, now fully mobilized, were marching across South America, far from the former viceroyalties that had given birth to them. The Spanish state, even after Napoleon had been defeated, did not have the capacity to bind the whole together, especially in the face of so much patriot resistance across so many places and after a long war of attrition.[78]

The wars and revolutions in Spanish America, and the relationship between them, revealed features of the quest for order not immediately evident elsewhere. Violence deepened regional cleavages, as the dreams of grand republics died. The many hatreds of the past were resurrected by disorder and made reestablishing boundaries within societies almost impossible. For the few, creole elites, this proved exasperating. For many, just as in other places, this state of affairs offered liberation or autonomy. When the empire dissolved and order fell apart, Natives and Blacks now made their choices as well. In many cases, they sided with royalist forces. The Crown, to many of them, was the only thing that stood between their fortunes and rapacious local elites. The parallels to North America in these instances are compelling. Blacks and Natives in what had been British North America tended to side with the Crown against white creoles. In both North and South America, in the midst of revolutionary uncertainty, declaring for the Crown against local oppressors could make perfect sense.[79]

Sometimes creole leaders of independence movements appreciated these realities. Bolívar declared that all enslaved males who took up arms in support of patriots would win their freedom in Venezuela. He also pushed for slavery to be abolished throughout Gran Colombia, though he failed. He did so partially out of principle. He thought independence should undo the corruptions of the past. Moreover, he and patriot leaders like him knew that if they ever expected British support, they would be wise to toe the abolitionist line. He also did so because he feared Saint-Domingue. In his Chilean campaign, San Martín did much the same from the get-go, enlisting in his army those who had been enslaved and trying to channel angers.[80] The decisions of so many creole actors to mobilize the enslaved in the civil wars of the period would pave the way for abolition at war's end in many places. Eventually, that is. In some regions, like Venezuela, where war had torn the fabric of society to shreds and where the economy was still reliant on the enslaved more as collateral than for their labor, slavery limped along before it was finally extinguished.[81]

The search for order seemed quixotic. South America fell apart along its regional fault lines, and only on smaller scales could sovereignty be reconstituted. Even these would be dogged by instability, confusion, and division. Though small in comparison to prerevolutionary political units, they would prove extraordinarily difficult to manage. For many, authoritarianism and the myth of republican unanimity could place only a fig leaf over the divisions that remained. Even if strong men could impose authority, divisions like race remained so powerful that they could not be recognized. Such would be the case for Colombia, where it became taboo to mention race even though it cast a shadow over all relations. War and revolution left marks that could not be effaced.[82]

Mexico offers perhaps the best example of how the process of revolution made binding frays a fraught exercise. In Mexico, the imposition of order in the short run proved less elusive than in other places. Society there did not immediately descend into the crucible of violence between 1810, when insurgency began, and 1814, when independence was declared. At first, most pressed for autonomy to support the king, but soon different groups were vying to put in place their own vision for what autonomy would mean.[83] Royalists realized what a vacuum of power could entail, and they pushed for greater local control, all with an eye to buttressing their authority in an uncertain world. The imbroglio over sovereignty provoked the same sort of crisis that had afflicted France in 1789. The early phase, we know already. Those peasants who were increasingly marginalized by a creeping commercial economy pressed for their traditional rights when the state was incapacitated, doing so in ways distinctive to the culture and traditions of New Spain. As opposed to the case of Buenos Aires, this was a popular movement, leading to mass mobilization. Mobilization stoked older hatreds, turning them into fracture points, and fomented frightening levels of violence. Miguel Hidalgo and his followers may have opened "a Pandora's box"; but they promised liberation.[84]

They would not win the fight for sovereignty. In the wake of the Terror in France, the toppling of regimes across Europe, and slave revolution in Saint-Domingue, creole elites tried to co-opt peasant-led movements into a broader push for independence. They countered popular insurgency with one of their own. Under the leadership of Agustín de Iturbide, a creole who had been recruited to suppress Hidalgo's rebellion, Mexico became independent without major bloodshed. Iturbide was deeply conservative and hoped to install an independent monarchy. Yet, he became an agent of order. With good reason, Bolívar would characterize him, along with O'Higgins and San Martín, as one of "the Three Caesars" of Latin America. He offered Mexico an authoritarian route out of the age. The route served to keep potentially explosive tensions in check.[85] In 1814, when Mexico became independent, the new order did not differ that much from the old order.[86]

The long run proved more vexing. The search for ultimate stability in Mexico, even if independence was achieved, would be long and violent. The most marginal provinces split off. The centrifugal much more than the centripetal defined the tenor of revolution in Mexico. All of Central America broke away and became a feuding, violent mess of states without authority and nations without histories once Iturbide came to power and then fell from it. This occurred not by design or because of any sort of vision of revolution or independence. It happened by default. The same could be said for a great deal of Spanish America. Mexico was also hamstrung by economic dislocation from the Atlantic. Wars, independence, and revolution had compromised its productive ties to the Atlantic, particularly textile manufacturing and silver production. Defining the nation, and calming conflict, would prove all the more difficult because of stagnation. Mexico would also not be alone in this regard.[87]

The end result was that in Mexico old tensions lived on in new guises. Order, in the immediate wake of independence, may have been reinstituted. But authorities had not addressed, much less rectified, the old fracture points that had erupted. They had just put a lid on them. Revolution did not vanquish the old, especially its most egregious injustices. In fact, the dislocations of the period only amplified them. The roots of unresolved issues that would plague Mexico throughout the nineteenth century lay in how insurgents acted upon older frustrations in new ways during the age.[88]

Mexico was not unique. The emerging new order in Latin America looked as mosaic-like as the revolutions themselves. Argentina would with time become stable and prosperous. So would Chile. They would find a fit into the Atlantic economy. In doing so, they would be aided by British support. Yet they were still wracked with tensions, even if they were becoming more orderly. Order could mask oppressive measures and, as was the case with Mexico, could create the energy for future explosions of discontent. Other places did not have it so good in the short run. Royalist Peru was, as Bolívar admitted, "a corpse." It was resurrected not as one but as two impoverished states, Peru and Bolivia. Stability remained elusive. In the new Peru, officials and elites regarded Natives as second-class citizens. Natives continued to resist what could be regarded as a neocolonial regime, as they had since the time of Túpac Amaru. Here, as in the United States, the stability of the state depended on their marginalization. Complicating matters further, Peru could not strike the balance between military and civilian control. In this region, still simmering with division and discontent, voices cried out for a confederation that would benefit everyone. The violence of the preceding period, and the deep divisions remaining, precluded such a course. In still other areas, like Colombia, dreams for unity foundered because regional elites refused to cede any power to rivals. With no legitimate force that could bind the forces of disintegration together, the integrity of the whole would prove futile.[89]

Cuba proved an outlier. The tumult of the period and the collapse of empire did not lead to independence, revolution, or mobilization here; in fact, it bound the island more closely to Spain. Fear of what had happened on the neighboring island of Saint-Domingue, to be sure, drove planters to remain loyal to Spain, as had the Aponte Rebellion of 1811. So too did self-interest. Loyalty allowed "the ever-faithful isle" to thrive. With the abolition of the slave trade throughout much of the Atlantic,

planters picked up the pace, and soon they were importing unprecedented numbers of men and women from Africa. Despite a growing chorus of voices throughout the Atlantic condemning slavery and the trade,
slave traders grew rich, and whole regions, especially around the western
province of Matanzas, were turned over to sugar. Meanwhile, creoles
could point to dreaded Saint-Domingue to garner support from the
metropole and to buttress their rule. Planters had to be vigilant. With rumors of slave risings in other places, they clamped down on anyone
preaching liberty, doing what they could to cordon Cuba off from the
wider revolutionary Atlantic. In the mid-1840s, the enslaved on a number
of plantations rebelled in a wave of uprisings known by the brutal suppression that followed as La Escalera. Notably, a few women from Africa,
including one called Carlota, played critical roles in the rising. This episode proved an aberration. With time, planters secured control of their
slave societies and displayed a self-confidence found in few other places.
While the rest of Latin America broke from Spain and fell apart, Cuba
remained a colony. Its stability allowed it to be as enmeshed in the Atlantic economy as the United States and Brazil—two other places known for
reliance on chattel slavery.[90]

However exceptional it might have appeared, Latin America was, in
fact, not. The difficulties of reestablishing frayed sovereignties just appeared more apparent here than in other places. The era had unraveled
all societies, especially where states lacked the will or capacity to impose
order. France had found itself whipsawed in such a way until a warlord,
Napoleon, could impose himself on a nation, and even his rule ultimately
failed. The many sovereign inheritors of empire in South America
looked so modest in size because of the vaunted ambition of quixotic
characters like the Liberator and because of the sheer size and complexity of the empire that collapsed. The divisions that remained in Spanish
America resembled those of other places bedeviled by tensions that were
not rectified by the age. The United States and Ireland come to mind.
The failures of states to rebind frays in Central and South America, then,
point to the incomplete and flawed nature of revolutionary endings for
all who were touched by the Atlantic age. Bolívar was speaking for the
whole revolutionary age when he declared, in exasperation, "America is
ungovernable. Those who have served the revolution have ploughed
the sea."[91]

What of Spain? It remained an empire and a place globally connected, but in a much diminished capacity. Now shorn of its possessions

in South America, the jewels of its imperial crown, it held only Cuba and Puerto Rico in the New World. For most of the nineteenth century, until 1898 when its imperial days formally ended, Spain and its remaining American subjects still tussled over authority. American subjects pushed for autonomy. Those back in the metropole, which had reverted to absolutism in the wake of war, refused. Drawing on what the British had done to secure their so-called second empire, as well as what Napoleon had tried to do to bring revolution to an end in France, Spanish officials devised an imperial regime that resembled a "liberal dictatorship." The slave regime in Cuba had to be protected, and officials proposed a plan of imperial centralization. Planters acquiesced to metropolitan demands. They traded autonomy and representation for security. Meanwhile, the enslaved on the island were ruled with a "healthy terror." This arrangement never became as stable as those at the center hoped, but it did last until 1898.[92]

Brazil had nothing to end. In fact, it averted revolution while gaining independence. Although even under the relocated Crown Brazil experienced some social instability, especially when slaves rose up in 1814 in Bahia, disturbances to the social order were generally and ruthlessly crushed. A replay of Saint-Domingue never represented a remote possibility in Brazil. Here elites firmly controlled the slave population. Nonetheless, as far as Brazilian creoles were concerned, retaining ties to a troubled Europe could only embroil Brazil in the cycle of fear, hope, and aggression seen elsewhere. In light of their reluctance to see connections generate instability, creoles embraced a conservative conception of nation. They would clamor for a monarchy untethered from Portugal and its ongoing problems. This would, they reckoned, allow them to maintain control of their societies as the world swirled around them.[93]

Independence also grew from Portugal's inability to hold on to its empire. Ultimately, the Portuguese state did not have the capacity to control Brazil. The war and the period of revolution had irrevocably shifted the balance between Old World and New World. Brazil could trade throughout the Atlantic without the help of Portugal; it relied on the slave trade and resented any interference with it. In effect, the pressures on the trade revealed two things: Brazil could now manage the Atlantic on its own, and Rio de Janeiro had become the political and economic force of the empire. Increasingly seeing themselves as different from the Portuguese, Brazilian creoles thought they could do what former British subjects in North America had accomplished: claim nationhood without upsetting their ability to rule at home. They could have the best of all possible worlds amid crisis.[94]

The moving of the court to Brazil became the occasion for imperial dissolution. While Portugal had been incapacitated by invasion by France and then by dependence on Britain—and with the empire's ruler relocated in Brazil—the court declared Brazil a kingdom on par with Portugal. In theory, the empire henceforth would be a commonwealth of kingdoms. The removal of the Portuguese court to Brazil, some believed, would help foster a transition from absolutism to a more enlightened approach to governance that many throughout the Atlantic now embraced. Or so it was predicted. The Portuguese hoped to create an accommodation between the Old World and the New that could, in theory, offer regeneration in an age of tumult.[95]

The hybrid imperial response to the crisis of sovereignty throughout the Atlantic was meant to ensure order, but this arrangement did not last. Eventually, given the pressures of the age, the Portuguese empire split in two. In 1815, with peace established in Europe, King John headed back to Lisbon. His son Pedro remained in Rio to rule Brazil. Fixing the relationship between the two conjoined kingdoms made the next few years vexing. Fearing that Portugal intended to reinstitute the old colonial relationship, many creoles began clamoring for formal independence. Vacillation and uncertainty were especially dreaded by Brazilians. They fretted over what was happening around them in Spanish America, just as they worried that some sort of reversion to colonial status would threaten their ability to take advantage of what the Atlantic had to offer. Pedro agreed. He declared Brazil independent in 1822, just as chaos was engulfing the rest of South America. Untying the New World from the Old seemed the only sensible way of steering clear of the sort of sovereign crisis that had ensnared so many. Brazilians, therefore, used the tools of independence to forestall revolution. Independence in the Brazilian case did not depend on the sort of mobilization that could liberate individuals but that proved so difficult for the state to contain.[96]

Not all went smoothly. After independence, the new Brazilian Empire controlled the area around Rio. There is no question that independence favored planters there, just as autonomy had. Other regions hoped to remain part of a Portuguese Empire. Portugal, though, did not have the ability to hold on to any of Brazil. Those supporting independence fought and concluded a short conflict against some Portuguese holdouts in recalcitrant regions, even dispatching a small armada in the process. In 1825, Portugal formally recognized Brazil's full independence. The Portuguese won an indemnity in doing so, some trading rights, and at least the surety that Brazil would not go the republican route. Brazil would be a monarchy ruled by a Braganza, just like Portugal. The two were still entwined, even if now separate sovereign entities.[97]

The new form of Brazilian sovereignty resembled that of the republic in North America. Brazil's stability would be premised on some of the same forms of exclusion for the same ends. Blacks, for instance, would not enjoy rights. The fact that Brazil could control a large landmass, just like the United States, speaks to the power of elites there and the lengths they would and could go to in order to sustain their rule and avoid the tortuous dilemmas that caused fits for so many others throughout the Atlantic.[98] This is not to say that Brazil avoided all intrigue. As in other places in South America, regions in Brazil would vie with one another for supremacy. Here, though, the southeast would be able to retain dominance through fearmongering about potential slave insurrection and through the use of force to put down any regional rebellions. By the 1840s the period of uncertainty had come to an end, and the economy was prospering.[99]

Brazilian creoles, therefore, used sovereignty as a cordon sanitaire to isolate themselves from the political currents of the Atlantic and to control their population. They did not cut the cord to the Atlantic, though; far from it. Sugar was joined increasingly to coffee as a principal export. Of all places, Brazil was more reliant on the Atlantic economy for its survival. But it would not go it alone. In fact, British capital and trade sustained this slave-based production economy. Abolitionism notwithstanding, British protection—much in the way it fostered the development, trade, and expansion of the United States—secured Brazil's continuing engagement with the Atlantic. Though the British insisted on outlawing the slave trade, and the Brazilian legislature promised to do so, more and more slaves entered the empire. British banks and merchants proved complicit, just as the British government winked and nodded. Slavery remained good for business, both for the British and for Brazilian planters. When the British did police the Atlantic to try to clamp down on the slave trade, Brazilian traders resorted to the age-old strategy of smuggling. At the same time, they tended to sell the enslaved from less productive regions to those that needed labor, just as was happening in the United States. Brazil's independence, then, allowed its elites to tie themselves into the new economy that emerged through and from the age.[100]

Brazil had become, in fact, the Atlantic entrepôt par excellence, a place defined by that institution that had brought the Atlantic into being. With independence, Brazil's creoles were now prepared to compete in an Atlantic in which mercantilist ideals were an anachronism. They were a free-trading, New World ancien régime. Their reliance on slavery allowed them to be so. In Brazil, merchants in Rio were strong enough to keep the slavery channel between Angola and Brazil open and to protect their commerce. Economic interests went hand in hand with social and political goals. In pulling off what they did, they proved as entrepreneurial and adaptable as their peers in North America.[101]

No doubt, planters held fast to the memory of slave rebellion, such as failed risings in Minas Gerais and Bahia, both of which saw people of color press for emancipation amid calls for a break from Portugal. The fears of their own past and those of the present in Saint-Domingue mobilized elites to police the enslaved with vigor. Like planters in Cuba, they did so with confidence. They were an anomaly, therefore, but one that cohered both to the imperatives of the broader system and to the rule of Atlantic sovereignty, as it was taking shape after revolution.[102] Sovereignty and entanglement no longer presented those in the Atlantic with either-or propositions.

In accomplishing this feat, Brazil was not aberrational, just more perniciously successful than most. All strove for it. Bounds and barriers went hand in hand with permeability. The new system demanded a new order, and given the fact that states now engaged with one another more systematically and that such competition required the mobilization of men and women for armies, farms, and factories in order to do so, states that hoped to survive had little choice but to promote order and openness. To the states that could adapt belonged the spoils of the system. Of course, adaptation and order—bounding and remaining entangled—necessitated coercion just as much they depended on negotiation. Equilibrium took shape around these new realities.[103]

What of Portugal? Well, it did not follow the British model of successfully navigating the system's new imperatives. As in many other things, Portugal followed Spain's lead. Both were greatly diminished by what they had lost. But Portugal differed from Spain in that there was precious little left to be despotic about. The Portuguese state liberalized through what was called the Porto revolution of 1820, adopting a set of reforming measures. The reality of the unbinding to Brazil, however, and the fact that Brazil—not Portugal—had served as the hub of empire for some time, determined the nation's imperial fortunes. Portugal would provide Brazil with members of its royal family until Brazil declared itself a republic in 1889. But the two remained separate and sometimes competing entities. Portugal, on paper, still called itself an empire and claimed to rule "all Portuguese citizens" in the metropole and in its remaining holdings in Africa. It still retained trading posts here and in Asia, but these proved insignificant. Brazil had been the keystone that held empire together.[104] Portugal, thus, held onto what it could as an empire in name only and did so anxiously, fearful that perhaps the loss of Angola might be next. All too fittingly, rumors stirred from time to time that Benguela, the most important center for the slave trade in Angola, aimed to become a province of Brazil.[105]

Saint-Domingue stood as almost the anti-model of how the age came to a conclusion. It proved unable to secure the paradox of disconnection and entanglement that Brazil had. This is why it deserves the pride of place of concluding this discussion of conclusions. It was the one place revolution proved truly revolutionary. But Saint-Domingue could find no easy fit either in the new international order or in the new Atlantic equilibrium. The issue came down to race and, once again, to the entangledness of hope, fear, and aggression.

Louverture had seemed destined to play the role of Napoleon for Saint-Domingue. He, too, hoped to bring order by using the language of republican liberty, as he was fighting for control of the colony. He knew that Saint-Domingue had to be made productive once more after the chaos of war and destruction, but he had problems envisioning anything beyond the production of sugar and coffee, both of which meant the return to plantations of those who had gained their freedom. Such was, as far as he could see, the cost of order and of orderly integration into the Atlantic economy. He did not want slavery to return, however. Nor did he envision independence, even if he pushed for autonomy within the republican French Empire. Napoleon's invasion and his attempt to reinstitute slavery there put paid to such concerns.

As Saint-Domingue was plunged into yet another chapter of revolutionary chaos, Louverture became a standard-bearer for independence. The dilemmas that had dogged so many creoles throughout the whole period now were obviated. What emerged was a clear dividing line between white and Black and between subservience and independence. Freedom for Blacks could not come without independence. At this moment the idea of a free Black republic became imaginable. Employing the word "Haiti," an Indigenous word for the new nation denoting the topography of the place, those fighting for freedom imagined a new destiny for their people, however difficult that road would be.[106]

In 1804, the Haitians had their freedom, after vanquishing the French. On January 1 of that year, the leader of the rebel army, Jean-Jacques Dessalines, declared Haiti an independent state. All Haitians, no matter the color of their skin, were enshrined in the new nation's constitution of 1805 as "Black." In much the same way the Constitution of the United States had laid to rest some of the uncertainty of the period by proclaiming new certainties, and by laying out new bases for inclusion and exclusion, Haitians were looking back on the violent years of revolution to enshrine their boundaries. To be "white" was to be excluded.[107] The creation of Haiti represented a summit of sorts for the age, as all of its most radical aspirations were now—in theory—realized.

Unlike, say, Brazilians, Haitians had fashioned the most radical transformation of the whole age; yet, they could not enjoy the best of all possible worlds. They would not achieve freedom and independence. Warlords who had arisen in the tumult now became a new band of oligarchs. They controlled the plantation economy and the politics of the newly independent state. In fact, for a while two independent Haitis were forming amid the chaos of the period, one ruled by a king and the other by a president. Competition to create sustainable sovereignty still shaped the search for endings, as it would in places like Mexico. As did crushing poverty and division. Those who had once toiled as the enslaved found themselves with little opportunity aside from working as field hands on plantations. Ironically, the people of Saint-Domingue had achieved all that revolution had promised: even the most downtrodden, those who had sustained the changing Atlantic economy and system on their very backs, had used the uncertainty of revolution and of war to declare their own independence, to earn their freedom despite all sorts of obstacles. But the world would not cooperate with this conceit. Louverture, who had withstood and taken advantage of the furies for so long, ended up dying in a jail in France while his hope for an independent and flourishing Haiti, a Black republic standing among the nations of the earth, was undone.[108]

The story of Haiti's relationship to the rest of the Atlantic after independence in 1804 is more complex than we would believe. The British, the Danes, the Dutch, and even the Americans, who still had a slave system ascendant in part of their republic, viewed Haiti with fear but also with ambivalence. Because its leaders set themselves against France in a world defined by war, the British did what they could to support the new state without granting it diplomatic recognition. The Americans, as neutrals, had even less reason to secure diplomatic relations with the state, but U.S. merchants looked for opportunities for trade. No doubt, they feared what the example of Haiti would mean to their own enslaved labor force. They also saw in the fluid Atlantic how this seeming pariah could prove an ally or at least a pawn. For the French, there was no ambiguity. The regime that emerged from revolution would levy a settlement we can only call extortionist on Haiti. For their freedom in the new world of imperial states and for diplomatic recognition by their former colonial masters, Haitians would have to indemnify France for the losses it claimed it had suffered. Haiti, in fact, would be crippled by "double debt." Not only was the new nation forced to pay back slaveowners for their losses, officials had to take out loans from French banks to pay the ransom. One estimate puts the subsequent losses to the economy at $21 billion in 2022 dollars.[109]

There is no denying that fear and racism lay at the root of Haiti's distinctive experience. In the supercharged Atlantic world, now just leaving a period defined by tumult and war, Haiti represented a troubling example of endless unsettledness in the minds of contemporaries. It remained a place that could not be disentangled from racist assumptions about human difference and about the perceived bonds between Blackness and violence. Haitians were, as some theorists of the day believed, a strange people that had sought, and would perpetually seek, vengeance. What made Haitians seem distinctive was that in the imaginations of most, more confounded than ever by racist assumptions, they would remain "monstrous hybrids," liberated as men and women but violent by their very nature.[110]

Though producing by far the most liberating revolution of the revolutionary era, Haiti could not be fully countenanced by the new order. Diplomatically, even if merchants and some officials hoped to make use of Haiti in the competitive Atlantic, it became a negative example of all that could happen if places like the United States and Brazil failed to keep the lid on the greatest of all disturbances: slave revolt. And so the boundary between Haiti and the rest of the Atlantic was policed.[111] Nations, most especially the United States, would not recognize the new nation. Diplomatic recognition would only come in 1862, when Americans—from the North—were engaged in a civil war with the slave system of the South.

This new Atlantic world was now made up of republics of different sizes and reformed empires. Both had to recognize the power of people. In the New World, the successor states of old empires tended to take on republican forms. For them, revolution and independence were bound together. Most of these, even the United States, tended to be unstable. These were, after all, new creations, conjured ex nihilo, with none of the accretions of tradition that underscored legitimacy. They were filled with the politicized, who were also tasked with helping to create institutions of governance. The Old World was now made up of a constitutional monarchy in France and dynastic states that had also been reformed and transformed by revolution. Both the new and the old states had managed the feat of providing internal stability and allowing external competitiveness for their people. All remained intertwined within the Atlantic system, with the notable exception of Haiti. Within the system, only sovereignty could rescue people from the abyss. Only states with capacity and with enough legitimacy to act could keep in check unresolved tensions still present in each place. Even some of the new states of Latin America fitted the bill, though for many more it would take time. The new Atlantic world was inhabited by a new sort of leviathan. No doubt, each bore the distinctive stamp of the society from which a given state emerged. Those included in or excluded from the political nation also differed from place to place. Some of these states were larger and some smaller. Some enjoyed more stability than others. But they all arose from revolution and were fairly well suited to managing the continuing entanglements of the Atlantic system. Haiti, again, proved an outlier.[112]

Some of the hallmarks of the new equilibrium still mark the modern world. Political economy would be premised, with time, on free trade. The movements of free people proved critical for the stability of the whole, and now regions with surplus labor, and potential sources of instability, were tied to centers in more free-flowing ways or to lands held for the moment by Indigenous peoples. Enlightenment ideas offered the chief means for rationalizing these imperatives. The Atlantic still demanded men and women in motion, moving from the labor rich to the labor starved, from the land poor to the land wealthy. To develop, the system needed people freed from the constraints of older obligations. It demanded citizens, not subjects. The invisible hand nodded to this new reality, as did the political ideal of popular sovereignty. Only a state organized to mediate such systemic demands could compete in the new post-revolutionary world.

The new settlement was also sustained by what we would regard as anachronistic social relations, ones seemingly better attuned to the world that revolution had vanquished. To be sure, unfree labor seemed to be a thing of the past, certainly for some areas. But in others, it thrived, even if people seemed uncomfortable living with the galling hypocrisies it confronted all with. In fact, slavery grew more pronounced in some places. Most turned their heads the other way, even if they valorized the idea of freedom. But slave labor was now only bound to plantation economies, which increasingly were tied to the world through free markets. Slavery allowed states with plantation economies to compete. Such was the case, especially, for Brazil and for the North American south. In both places, officials and planters employed ideas rooted in the Enlightenment to justify slavery's existence.

More daunting would be yoking "nation" to state.[113] In Latin America, again a place dogged by bringing an end to tumult, the new states that were emerging had no intrinsic emotional appeal to new citizens. What did it mean to be Bolivian? Or Mexican? Most of the markers of national attachment—say, religion, ethnicity, or language—were shared by so many states that had warred with each other. In most cases, states were built because of the practical considerations of the moment, but belonging and attachment required more. Those in the successor states of the Spanish Empire were not alone in this regard. The new United States would struggle with similar issues. Ultimately men and women carved out a volitional and prescriptive understanding of what it meant to be an American citizen. One chose and performed American nationality. But this was not the sort of sensibility on which to build a state. This conundrum of attachment even affected the old. The ideals of monarchy and traditional hierarchies had been discredited in theory and compromised in fact by the tumult of the period. They confronted the same dilemmas as new states. The successors of the revolutionary generation in both the Old World and the New would face the challenge of creating consciousness where none had existed before or of sustaining what had been tarnished.[114]

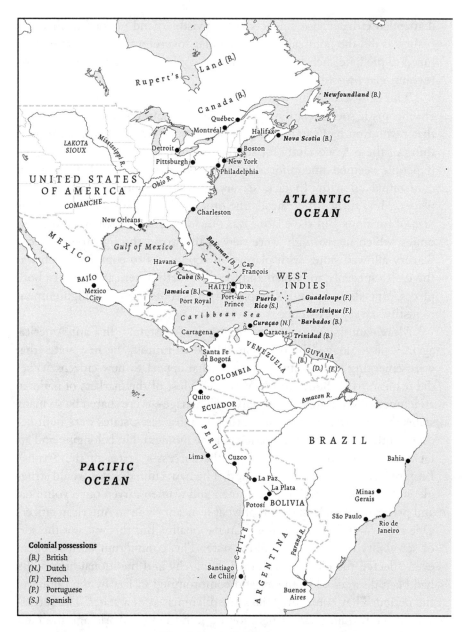

The Atlantic, late 1850s.

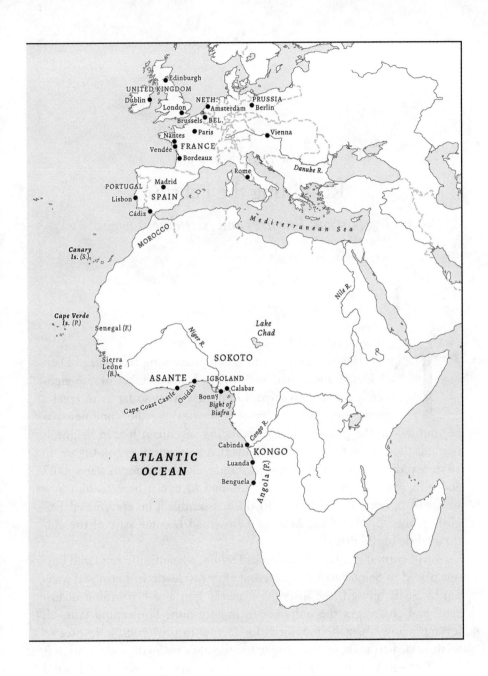

Edinburgh

UNITED KINGDOM

Dublin
London
Nantes
Vendée
FRANCE
Bordeaux

NETH.
Amsterdam
Brussels BEL.
Paris

PRUSSIA
Berlin

Vienna

Rome

Danube R.

PORTUGAL
Madrid
Lisbon
SPAIN
Cádiz

MOROCCO

Mediterranean Sea

Canary
Is. (S.)

Nile R.

Cape Verde
Is. (P.)
Senegal (F.)

Lake
Chad

Niger R.

SOKOTO

Sierra
Leone
(B.)

ASANTE
Cape Coast Castle
Ouidah

IGBOLAND
Bonny
Bight of
Biafra
Calabar

Congo R.

Cabinda
KONGO
Luanda
Benguela
Angola (P.)

ATLANTIC
OCEAN

CHAPTER SEVEN

# Reknitting the Fabric

## *Nation, Empire, and Settlement*

THE CITIES OF LONDON and Dublin have long recognized Daniel Defoe and Jonathan Swift as leading lights of the eighteenth century. In 1870, Londoners went so far as to erect a granite obelisk—"a sort of Cleopatra's needle," one newspaper put it—on the grave of Defoe. Standing seventeen feet in height, it reminds those passing by Bunhill Fields that he wrote *Robinson Crusoe*. In 1870, seventeen hundred people—including, as the memorial states, boys and girls who raised sixpence each—hoped to pay tribute to him as a writer of "a book for all time." To those assembled, he epitomized English genius. By this time, *Robinson Crusoe* had become part of the cultural fabric of the British nation.[1]

Swift earned similar adulation. In Dublin, a beautifully rendered bust was placed in Saint Patrick's Cathedral after his death. In Latin and written by Swift himself, the inscription marks him as a "champion of liberty" and challenges the onlooker to imitate him. The setting is much less auspicious than the memorial for Defoe. In the 1760s, a devotee of Swift hoped to make a monument for the ages to Swift and to place it near College Green in Dublin's most public space. Swift would stand with an equestrian statue of King William III, an Irish riposte to British supremacy over the kingdom. But the vision for a great public memorial never got off the ground. Later, a niche was carved out in the cathedral,

Grave memorial to Daniel Defoe in Bunhill Fields,
London, United Kingdom. Image from iStock
.com/stevenallan.

where the bust was placed.[2] The setting is appropriate. Swift came to define national aspirations before there was a nation. The memorial does
not nod to *Gulliver's Travels*. Then again, who would need to be told that
Swift wrote it? He is a founding father of an Irish literary canon that ties
him to such figures as Wilde and Joyce. And this canon is as tethered to
Irish sense of self as Defoe is to British. Both are memorialized as national champions.

These memorials privilege certain themes and let others slip into
oblivion. Swift and Defoe, for instance, are not remembered as two men
whose work vividly chronicled the excitement and the trepidation that

Bust of Jonathan Swift in Saint Patrick's Cathedral,
Dublin, Ireland. Image from Attila JANDI/
Shutterstock.com.

made the Atlantic what it was on the eve of a cataclysm neither could
have predicted. They are not seen as the prophets of entanglement. They
remain in memory products of the nation. In other words, some things
about them are remembered, some are forgotten. And some are invented.

In playing such roles, the two epitomize the spate of memorialization
that gripped the Atlantic just as the age was coming to an end or, better,
just as men and women wanted to declare the revolutionary era over.
Many have noted that the end of the eighteenth century and the early part
of the nineteenth witnessed what can be described as a statue mania. Memorials to Swift and Defoe, though rooted in the nationhood of Ireland

and Britain, suggest a transnational process. All cloaked under the mantle of nation the many settlements that had been achieved. All would mythologize contested memories. Accordingly, those remembering this period would be bound in a process of "perpetual memorialization."[3]

All of this is fitting. Monuments say more about who is doing the memorializing than who is being remembered. The memorialized Swift and Defoe speak to the way Britons and the Irish, in their own ways, could lay claim to the most important epoch in Atlantic history as theirs, a time that transformed how states fitted into a system and how people related to the state. Memorials did so much more than salve national honor, as was the case with Swift, or fire the national imagination, as Defoe did for Britain. Memorials offered for men and women a way to valorize suffering, to psychically deal with fear and death, to explain how they moved from one form of sovereignty to another and the trauma that went hand in hand with the transition. Remembering allowed them to forget and, in the process, to invent a new national narrative. Societies, as well as people, conspired to consign troubling parts of the past to collective oblivion. Through this complex process, memorialization became the stuff that bound new nations to a new order.[4]

All followed cosmopolitan scripts but rooted them in the local or the national. Most tended to look to classical antiquity for inspiration. Rome was especially alluring.[5] Memorialists also emulated each other. Consequently, they used the same sort of Enlightenment sensibilities and practices that had given birth to imperial reforms a generation earlier. In what they shared, memorials offered silent testimony to how deeply connected the Atlantic remained. They also spoke of supposed national distinctiveness. Though born of Atlantic bonds, they eschewed the ties that had twisted and contorted local tensions that had given rise to the fears and pressures of the age but that in reality still persisted.[6] Memorials arose to anoint the only thing that could provide a basis of order for the continued entanglements of the age: the nation-state. Monuments, therefore, also differed, as they each had to address different histories, anxieties, and revolutionary trajectories. Things made of metal and stone were the final pieces of an age of revolution. The upshot was that each nation came up with an understanding of itself rooted in the exceptional even if none was really distinctive, and they used the same tools and moment to do so.[7]

All societies need to note certain foundational moments, those things that tie people to a story line and allow them to make sense of the tangles of history with a straight narrative arc. Each of the places touched or devoured by revolution had, of course, such foundations before. In many cases, these had come tumbling down. In the interregnum between meaningful sovereignties people lived either with improvised forms of nation or with unsustainable ones. Hand in hand with the rise of sovereignty arose memorials that announced new foundational myths that took the place of those wiped away by revolution and war. These knit people to the state. The same went for those who had evaded the furies. For them, new moments were tethered to older narratives to reinscribe the ideal of continuity. Monuments demonstrated the creative capacity of men and women to sanctify new orders or rechristen old ones that had endured.[8]

Monuments can be likened almost to new covenants for a new age. They became so by creating and then strengthening the idea of nation. But they did not do so perfectly, even if they worked to convince viewers they did. What they also reveal is that the new settlements were always fragile. Memorials took on an air of permanence because the forces they were trying to contain remained potentially volatile. All memorials worked to manage tensions. They simplified and sometimes oversimplified. They excluded, just as settlements did. Beneath them, in their silences and their occlusions, lay those rotten bargains that had been struck, those groups that had been singed and ruled outside the bounds of new settlements, and the violent pasts, deeply rooted and recently forgotten, that such resolutions gestured toward. They all pointed out how endings proved more aspirational than actual.[9]

Consider the ways those of the United States observed their revolution. Many lessons we can apply elsewhere are evident in what they did. The successors to British Empire in North America christened theirs the "American Revolution" by arguing that it somehow differed in fundamental ways from others. Theirs had been a reasonable event. It centered on founders. It eschewed the tumult and radicalism that defined the age for others. Americans seemed to be saying that they had escaped the disorder that had devoured so many places. They were able to comprehend their many differences, a great number exacerbated by revolution and violence, through recourse to an idealized vision of these few men and the roles they had played. Or so they insisted.[10]

One of the most iconic images created in the wake of the age tells the story of how revolution became Revolution. John Trumbull, the son

*The Declaration of Independence*, by John Trumbull. Image from iStock.com/
Keith Lance.

of a governor of Connecticut, and an aide-de-camp to George Washington during the war, painted an image that hangs now in the Capitol rotunda in Washington, D.C., and that speaks to how Americans had come to view their experience. Entitled *The Declaration of Independence*, it offers a myth of foundation. In a room in Philadelphia, members of what had been a creole elite look out from the painting toward a desk where Thomas Jefferson hands John Hancock, the president of the Continental Congress, a draft of the Declaration. This is the moment the nation was born. Without exaggeration, one art historian has called it "a secular creche" that "reenacted the nativity of the United States." The new nation was born without the typical birth pangs that defined the experience of others. The peaceful and deliberative would be American epic.[11] The founders served as midwives to an event that emerged from the most rational principles of the Enlightenment through a document that spoke to the highest aspirations of the period. Americans had a restrained revolution. The story is clear. Independence is won, order is established, and the founders bear responsibility.

This ideal of the Revolution stands as the nation's source of self-understanding. It functions as either a demonstration of all that was achieved or that which has not been fully realized. It serves as a national "vanishing point," a moment to which all previous experience gestures toward and to which all subsequent experience harkens back.[12] Tellingly, that national moment of conception hinges on document writing, not warfare, insurgency, or popular action. Myth sanitized everything, allowing Americans to see themselves as liberty loving but also as a reasonable people.

The new myths, then, sustained order and solidified the new bargains that had been struck to bring the tumult of revolution to a close. The idea of the founders allowed both of these ends to be accomplished. This is why Jefferson, more than nearly any other founder, matters. He epitomized the way Americans, in the wake of their Revolution, could construe themselves as a people of contradiction. They could explain away negotiations and live with the glaring inconsistencies of the age. For their part, Americans at large could fob off their complicity in these contradictions by pointing to the founders, most especially Jefferson. Jefferson did not speak to paradoxes and injustices in the United States alone but in the Atlantic as a whole. He could, as he did, claim that all he worked for was premised on a belief in enlightenment progress. He did so even as he assumed the role of patriarch, and even if the most retrograde form of labor and exploitation would serve the cause of progress.[13]

The cult of the founders that emerged at the moment of memorialization also speaks to the ways Americans would with time come to terms with what Trumbull's image obscured, denied, or avoided. By gesturing toward a consensual moment and a foundational scripture, Americans could tell themselves that liberation would come when it could to those left out of the room. Even those critics who assailed the idea of exclusions still pointed to the founders and to the Declaration of Independence in particular as legitimizing criticism. America was always in a sense becoming, trying to live up to its true principles. In many ways, this simple idea suggested a postrevolutionary politics focused on the measuring stick of the revolutionary moment. The invocation and reinvocation of one simple date, July 4, would ritualize the act of paying deference to the founders and the centrality of their Revolution. The nation was made by commemorating the social contract, when the revolutionary state of nature was bound in a new understanding of citizen and state, one that later generations could claim would be more fully realized with time.[14]

The great fudge over remaining tensions that American nationhood rested upon allowed different regions with distinctive social configurations to tweak the narrative as they saw fit and to emphasize certain aspects of the American story at the expense of others. For some, say, in New England, the American nation stood for the federal union. For those farther south, the founders had built a nation premised on state sovereignty. The ideal of nation that the American Revolution, with a capital "R," created proved plastic enough to incorporate interpretations that would seem contradictory, at least for the moment.[15]

Such vanishing points would shape space and subsequent memorialization. The greatest monument to the founders and their Revolution would be the city named after the figure who emerged "first in war, first in peace, and first in hearts of his countrymen," George Washington. Washington, D.C., was a bold experiment in Enlightenment engineering. Hoping to create a capital ex nihilo or from a tabula rasa, Washington himself came up with the scheme that envisioned a capital that could be freed from the fetters of older ways and older places, yet that would become a grand national city that could stand beside Europe's great capitals. It would, he hoped, reflect the aspirations of a new nation dedicated to international commerce and to growth to the west. This would be a city built from scratch out of a state of nature, a place not weighed down with the accretions of the old. It, like the new nation, would be singular and distinctive. Washington's name was not chosen for the city only because he was seen as the liberator of much of North America. More to the point, he had almost been deified by Americans after his death in 1799. In fact, he would be resurrected over and over and reinvented as well, all for men and women to consider themselves citizens. The same had happened to Franklin. It would be the fate of other founders too. These men, Washington chief among them, had become American supermen.[16] Fittingly, once the cupola of the new Capitol building was erected, it would be decorated with a fresco of the apotheosis of George Washington.

The structures of the city would look like an enlightened capital should look like. The neoclassical would hold sway. Jefferson believed the style could serve a number of functions. It could harken back to the glories of Rome and declare that Americas were heirs of that legacy. In the city, liberty and power could be balanced. This would be the center of the new empire of liberty. The sorts of buildings imagined suggested solidity and permanence. Form followed function. They signaled that sovereignty would be durable, even if early on it was more aspiration than fact. Washington would, after the tumult, stand the test of the ages. The city also suggested how entanglements of the age remained but were muted. Architects in Washington consistently looked to Paris for inspiration, well into the twentieth century, even as they tried to gesture to the New World distinctiveness of the city rising on the Potomac.[17] Its monuments spoke to continuing ties, even as they heralded new national ideals that seemed to obviate connectedness.

Fittingly, those excluded or those whose marginalization would make way for the empire of liberty would disappear. The enslaved, unsurprisingly, did not feature in memorials. Natives offer a more complicated story, albeit one centering on vanishing. Natives, who had remade themselves in the face of extraordinary challenges, had their memorials too. Theirs turned on expulsion, both geographical and cultural. The Trail of Tears, the most infamous episode in the removal of Indigenous peoples from the southeast, is dotted by monuments and remembrances. It is also marked by cemeteries, for those who died and those who suffered to make the founders' vision a reality. One such memorial arose at New Echota, where a pillar was erected a century after the fact, ironically, by the U.S. government. Even as the trail was remembered, the damage was not undone. Settlers did not leave Cherokee lands. This monument thus justified and continues to justify the land grab. For those who resisted, like Tecumseh and Tenskwatawa, memorialization was wrapped up in the nostalgia of the "vanishing Indian." In fact, the most famous monument to Tecumseh sits not in the United States but just across the border in Canada. But his presence, even in the United States, would not threaten the settler republic. Even the Daughters of the American Revolution, those who would keep the flame of the founders alive, could fund a marker for the site where the prophet called for resistance to the United States. Natives could then be remembered only in their vanishing. They belonged to the past. They did not have a place in nation, or they could only insofar as they remained romanticized but gone.[18]

As the case of the United States suggests, memorials could not be unbound from the idea of nation. In doing this work, though, American monuments had one distinct advantage. The white inheritors of revolution did not have to include those who stood outside the political nation. For order, they did not have to incorporate the excluded or the vanished. When tensions could not be wished away, memorials of the age did more creative work. They had to tussle with tangled presents as well as legacies of the past. In this way, memorials could often become tension points themselves, as they would have to allow for different visions of the nation to sit side by side.

Monument to Jacob van Artevelde in Ghent,
Belgium. Image from Sergei Afanasev/
Shutterstock.com.

Take the case of Belgium. Belgians had to create a new past for a new state. To justify its existence, the people living there held onto the idea that they were somehow descended from an ancient group of tribes that lived in northern Gaul, the Belgae. That proved challenging enough. The more critical issue was how to bind together this place with two different ethnic traditions. To some extent, French annexation did some of the work for them. Statues did the rest. Monuments here worked like "ciphers" that could speak to any number of different conceptions of the nation. For the Flemish in Bruges and Ghent, for instance, locals with the blessing of the new monarch festooned the main squares with statues of local freedom fighters who fought for autonomy against encroaching powers. These monument builders went back to the Middle Ages for such examples, to a period all could agree was a moment of "grandeur" for Belgians. In Bruges, Jan Breydel and Pieter de Coninck, for instance, had worked as a butcher and weaver, respectively, before they took on French aggressors. They and Jacob van Artevelde of Ghent had in the fourteenth century fought for Flemish rights against French would-be conquerors. In the nineteenth century, a people calling themselves Belgians resurrected the trio as resisters against French republican aggression. These figures from centuries past offered, so those who erected the statues believed, a vision of Belgian distinctiveness built on anti-French animus.[19]

In French-speaking Brussels, by contrast, memorials celebrated the same events but did so with a completely different cast of characters and implications. In this case, they celebrated French speakers who had died as martyrs to create a new nation. In Brussels, hundreds of those slain in 1830 in the fight for independence lay buried in a crypt beneath the Place des Martyrs. The crypt memorializes the nation, or Patria, as a statue on the plaza announces. At her feet, the lion of Belgium snaps the chains of oppression.[20] Francophone Belgians tended to emphasize not anti-Frenchness but such themes as subjugation, sacrifice, and redemption—ideals sure to resonate with a Catholic people. These themes, they argued, underwrote Belgianness. For all the tensions between regions, these memorials spoke to how the idea of nation had to be created in some cases out of little more than invented pasts and traditions and the memory of suppression during the age. This is the same work the founders did for the United States.

In other words, memorials gave birth to nations, even if groups held contending interpretations of nation. Canada follows this model as well. It more or less declared its sovereign status through the so-called War of 1812. Participants in the westernmost theater of the War of the Revolutionary Age differentiated themselves from their republican relatives to the south and from Britons through experience in wartime. In this crucible, they began to emerge as Canadians. Events like the war gave them an identity as a people. It still does. Memorials proliferated throughout the province that would be known as Ontario. The most recent memorial installed in Ottawa, the War of 1812 Monument, presents a group of statues engaged in battle. It stands as both an assertion of Canadian nationhood and, because it lionizes the "diversity" of the cause, a rebuke to the behemoth and oftentimes race-addled state to the south. Entitled

Place des Martyrs in Brussels, Belgium. Image from agefotostock/Alamy
Stock Photo.

*The Fight for Canada*, its statues recover the moment "people from various walks of life came together—men and women; military personnel
and civilians; English, French and Aboriginal peoples." The band united
"to defeat the American invasion." Canadian national unity stems from
both the moment and the subsequent experience of living in the shadow
of the republican United States.[21]

Yet, the memorials of the age in another part of Canada also demonstrate the difficulties of creating nations, of achieving what Belgians tried
to accomplish. The age reordered tensions; it did not erase them. Just
consider Quebec. In Montreal, the inhabitants who considered themselves proudly British erected a column to the memory of Lord Nelson.
On the top of it, they placed a statue of the hero. So anxious were they to
establish their Britishness, they were the first people to raise money for
and the second to construct such a memorial after Nelson's death.
Glasgow had beaten them to it. They constructed it in the old French
part of the town right near the waterfront on Place Jacques Cartier, historically a central meeting place for Francophones. Some members of
the Catholic Church supported the monument, since it stood as a rebuke
to the anti-religious tendencies of the French Revolution. Yet, other

French men and women would not have it, and the installation of the column started an uneasy game of chess for the spatial soul of the city. Francophones erected statues of their own to the founders of the old colony just outside their mother church, Notre Dame, on the Place des Armes. What is now a basilica stares down the headquarters of the Anglo-dominated Bank of Montreal across the plaza. In 2013, a Canadian sculptor fittingly added two statues to the plaza, now called the "two snobs": one a woman holding a French poodle, staring disdainfully at the bank; the other a man holding an English pug glowering at the basilica. Here the truce between the city's growing number of "stony standoffs" would hold. Amazingly, the column to Nelson, though galling to Francophones, did not come tumbling down, even if some who were angry over its presence threatened to destroy it or have it moved.[22]

In one instance, the truce failed in Quebec City; in another, it worked. Here, in the wake of the age, consciously British subjects placed a column on the exact spot General James Wolfe had died on the Plains of Abraham. Quebecois nationalists toppled it. The latest monument, erected in 1965, recounts in detail the history of the memorial in two languages, with words of conquest removed, to at least recognize the cultural complexities of national sentiments in the province. A more successful attempt at memorialization of the age would be a monument that was put up at the same time those in Montreal memorialized Nelson. Here, on Governor's Square, citizens put up a granite obelisk to both Wolfe and the Marquis de Montcalm. One name appears on one side, and the other on the opposite side. The marble entablature speaks of the "common" fate, fame, virtue, and history of the two men, and by extension the common future of two peoples with very different ideas of nationhood. The uneasy truce implicit in juxtaposing two martyrs recognized the tangled nature of national identity in the period ending the age, even if these places were now unambiguously British. The monument demonstrates the need to root a people in the nation, particularly in this moment when nations were coming into being, but also how some places could hold contending visions of what the nation meant.[23]

For all these places, whether the job proved simple or complex, nationalism provided the string that fastened new states together. States could manage the tangles of the new international order and the realities of change in the Atlantic system more effectively than the antiquated empires of the past. Nation did much of the same work domestically. In societies torn by war and revolution, both of which depended on the mo-

Wolfe-Montcalm Monument in Quebec City,
Quebec. Image from iStock.com/ilbusca.

bilization of the "people," the idea of nation could contain such energy and employ it for the service of the state. The equation of "nation-state," then, hinged on the hyphen. Through it, the state could safeguard the nation, just as the nation could buttress the state. Tying the two together prepared citizens and states for the competitive and combative world that the era of revolution had created. The marble and paint and granite that inscribed nation gave the state the legitimacy it needed to do the work it had to do.[24]

The nation-state seems almost natural because nationalism was the most transnational of phenomena. What was most universal was the fact that all nations were invested in the same task of defining their people as distinctive. Such an impulse did not emerge only in France or the Americas. It arose throughout the Atlantic as men and women were engaged with similar issues and in conversation with other places. Nationalisms arose in parallel fashion to root states in populations that increasingly had sovereign power. Nationalisms all insisted on the particularities of identity, claiming that a people through their past were "exceptional." Yet, all peoples embraced such a conceit, even those who lived in empires.[25] Through monuments, national sentiment tied people to an imagined past and rooted communal imagination in this experience of looking back to key distinctive moments.[26] Nation did so as it beckoned toward the future. The state had a stake both in looking backward and in glancing forward. The national ideal—as imagined past and as aspiration—wedded people to the state. And this was imperative in the aftermath of war and revolution.[27] It is no mistake, therefore, that we begin the study of nation and of nationalism with the age, just as we do for the state and the new system it was embedded in.[28]

Monuments proved more than window dressing or props. Places or realms of memory, "les lieux de mémoire," turned history, though often contested, into a coherent narrative of social belonging. Soon "memory places" took on a life of their own and became the very substance of national identity. They also represented the stuff of the new order. Of course, the nature of memory places differed from place to place because they were always rooted in specific history. But what bound all the various places together was the fact that specifics were tied to the age. The age of revolution was also an age of the national, even for those societies like Belgium and Canada that tried to create nations despite divisions.[29]

The inheritors of Spanish empire in America also had complex divisions that needed binding. These divisions, though, proved more difficult to tie together for the new states that emerged. With reason, they have been seen "as incomplete nations at best," places where the process of nation building grew in tension with the difficulty of reestablishing state sovereignty amid the chaos of war. People throughout Latin America also faced the challenges of sustaining distinctive identities vis-à-vis neighbors who spoke the same language, had the same essential history, and practiced the same religion. Finally, in new republics, anyone aspiring to lead—the few—had to appeal to those they would lead—the many—without courting more instability. More often than not, the many differed with the few on the meanings of the recent past.[30] Memorialization reflected these realities.

State iconography played a critical role in Spanish America after independence. It was fundamental to the state and the nation-building exercise. In some cases, though, memorials could not perfectly bind funda-

Monumento a la Independencia in Mexico City, Mexico. Image from
iStock.com/atosan.

mental tensions. In Mexico, for instance, memorials vied with one another
for the mantle of official narrative. In the years after independence, two
sets of memorials were erected, suggesting different vanishing points. One
set focused on independence. These memorials tended to lionize those
former royalists who claimed to have led the push for Mexican statehood.
In Mexico City, one famous memorial was constructed to the memory of
Agustín de Iturbide, the emperor of Mexico, in the Metropolitan Cathedral. In one of the side chapels, his remains can be found surrounded by
Mexican flags. The setting suggests that the transition from old imperial
order to statehood went smoothly, without disrupting the social order, and
that the old symbiotic relationship between church and state would remain unchanged after independence. For more conservative-leaning Mexicans, September 27 became the anniversary of the birth of the nation, the
day in 1821 when Iturbide entered Mexico City and independence was
achieved and recognized. This was a new "national holy day." For some.[31]

Another monument, far more popular than the one found in the cathedral, would offer another vision of the moment. Called the Column of Independence but usually known as the Angel, because of the bronze statue at the top, and erected in the wake of another revolution, this one referred back to a very different ideal of what independence meant. It was modeled after the column on Place Vendôme in Paris, itself harkening back to Trajan's column in Rome. In the base of the Angel, the remains of great leaders of popular rebellions are to be found, most especially Miguel Hidalgo. Iturbide is not mentioned. As one official put it, pointing to the cathedral, "I left Iturbide there among those of his kind, where he belongs." The Angel memorial speaks of the possibilities missed and roads not taken in the early nineteenth century, making the point that what had been begun with the collapse of Spanish sovereignty was only finished after the bloodshed that followed later in the century. Fittingly, those who hail Hidalgo as founder look to September 16 as the nation's most important day, recognizing Hildalgo's 1810 call for an uprising. Like the other interpretation, this one is rooted in the age. It, too, has had great staying power in Mexico.[32]

Memorials, as binding agents, then, were meant to—at the very least—paper over fault lines that remained after revolution or—at their very best—try to address and heal the rifts that revolution did not or could not rectify. The remaining cleavages reveal what we could call a bifurcated sense of memory.[33] Either way, memorials were designed to claim and sustain order, even if people could use them for different ends. Because the idea of revolution gave rise to hopes and dreams, as well as fears, and because this moment would remain for each nation the moment all subsequent history would pay deference to, memorials had almost talismanic power. So powerful have they been for the formation of memory and narratives that they become the physical sites where the people of a nation debate who they are. Such has certainly been the case in Buenos Aires. Like Mexicans, Argentinians have been painfully divided over the meaning of the age. But in the case of Argentina the ruling elites were able to keep tensions under wraps throughout the nineteenth century, and the new state was able to find a fit in the Atlantic economy. Argentinians, too, had two sets of dates, one for independence and one for the republic, and monuments gesture to both, but in the case of Argentina the state created by revolution managed the disjunction.

A cathedral features as well in Argentinian memory. In the Metropolitan Cathedral of Buenos Aires, completed only in the period after in-

Tomb of San Martín in the Metropolitan Cathedral
of Buenos Aires, Buenos Aires, Argentina. Image
from iStock.com/mercedeslorenzo.

dependence, lie the remains of the great liberator of much of Latin
America, José de San Martín. His remains were moved from France,
where he died, to the cathedral in 1880. Draped in the flag of the nation
and guarded by statues representing other regions he "liberated" from
Spain, the memorial speaks to transnational visions and national realities.
San Martín had a more conservative notion of what he hoped "revolution" would achieve. Independence and the liberation of other regions
in the war with Spain mattered more than the sort of change that turned
a world upside down. The dates invoked follow San Martín's wars of

liberation and the achievement of formal independence. Like the Mexican monument to Iturbide, this one also tells a story of continuities, of how independence was achieved without the tumult of French-style revolution. Hence the siting of it in the cathedral. Placing the monument in the cathedral sanctifies the emergence of an orderly nation as an ideal. This is more than fitting. After all, San Martín himself said: "The external signs adopted by governments are the only language appropriate for explaining to the multitude the principles that animate them."[34]

Whereas in Mexico this narrative based in a cathedral proved unsustainable, in Argentina it worked. But only for so long. And this brings us back to bifurcated memory. Outside the cathedral, in the plaza leading up to the presidential palace, one other memorial was erected. On the famous Plaza de Mayo stands the May Pyramid. This one gestures to a date of conception different from San Martín's "liberating" moments: May 25, 1810—when the May Revolution began, not when independence was formally won or even proclaimed. The nation, the pyramid announces, was born of insurgency. It also gestures to the transnational context, how the nation came into being during an age of revolution. It is an obelisk topped by a statue of a figure representing liberty and nationhood replete with symbols of the age: one hand clasping another in a gesture of reconciliation after civil conflict and a Phrygian cap. Not grandiose at all, it nonetheless has captured the imagination of many in the nation, right up to this very day. Ostensibly, it implies that unity was and is won by independence and the birth of the republic. In reality, it has become a site of contestation or "memory struggles." It has witnessed massive demonstrations and the sorts of political conflict that have defined so much of twentieth-century Latin America, and groups with varied agendas ranging from Peronists and liberals to Marxists have appropriated this founding moment to assert their legitimacy.[35]

Of all the Latin American liberators, none would have an afterlife that could rival that of Simón Bolívar. Streets were named after him. Statues were erected. Towns would bear his name. Indeed, a nation-state would take its name from his, something that even Jefferson and Napoleon could not boast. In nearly every nation shaped by revolution, Bolívar has been memorialized, most notably in Paris near the Seine not far from the Arc de Triomphe and in New York where Central Park meets the Avenue of the Americas. Even in London he is memorialized with a statue in Belgrave Square, one that portrays wise England as a protector of states. The reason for the mania across the ideological spectrum and around the Atlantic is easy to understand. Bolívar seemed to epitomize a notion of revolution in which order featured as much as liberty. He also spoke to a transnational dream. He was and remains a romantic figure, the founder who never truly liberated and never achieved his vision. Hence, he could be safely memorialized by nearly all, hailed by conservatives and liberals alike. Even populists, socialists, and Marxists indulged in the cult of Bolívar. He could serve contending notions of memory that the inheritors of Spanish empire in the Americas reaped through revolution.[36]

Memorialization for Latin America spoke to the uneasy issue of endings and how difficult it was to bind everyone to the state through invocation of the nation. All of this pertains for Spanish South America, with a notable exception: Chile. Memorials in Santiago do not offer two narratives but focus on one set of powerful ideas: independence coupled with order. They do not recall revolution, and they present a more unified sense than those found in Mexico City and Buenos Aires. They underscore an official consensus that emerged by the 1830s. The first monuments in Santiago were put up in the 1850s, as veterans of the independence struggles hoped "the echo of the tombs of emancipation" would awaken all to the common good in the present and heal the wounds of the past.[37] In public plazas, such as that in front of La Moneda, the presidential palace, the most notable statue is that of Bernardo O'Higgins. In a sculpture by the Frenchman Albert Ernest Carrier-Belleuse, the figure of O'Higgins vanquishes chaos and the Crown in one instant beneath his horse's hooves. Mounted and separated from the palace by a main artery bearing his name and declaring him "Libertador," he tramples over a Spanish soldier to achieve order. With independence, not revolution, Chile was able to right fundamental wrongs and check chaos. Around the statue on the pedestal are bronze reliefs of his signal deeds. They proclaim that order is realized by sacrificing individual wants for the good of the republic.

Memory here is not bifurcated but tells one story. In the Plaza de Armas, for instance, visitors will see just one statue to the period. Erected in 1870, after more than thirty years of postrevolution stability, it is inscribed to "the Glory of Bolívar" and portrays a female figure representing civilization and order holding a scepter over the head of a kneeling Native. Bolívar, of course, is a safe, consensual figure. Yet, the monument does much more. Civilization uplifts the Native, whose chains drop to the ground as she stands. The message could not be clearer. Order is what the Europeans promised, and order is what independence realized.

Statue of Bernardo O'Higgins in Santiago, Chile. Image from Diego Grandi/Shutterstock.com.

The use of the preconquest past proved a bit unusual. As a rule, the postindependence successor states of Spanish empire tended to focus on founding fathers like O'Higgins and San Martín—and San Martín would feature in Chilean iconography of the age as well—and eschewed Indigenous peoples. Such images had played an important role in the early phase of revolution, but not at the end, when men and women had to search for distinctiveness to bring order. Postindependence Chilean nation builders remained comfortable enough to continue boldly connecting the nation to an imagined Native past. To make connections even more evident, bas-reliefs around the statue conjoin the discovery of the New World with the wars that Bolívar led to win independence. One act in the civilizing mission presaged its fulfillment in the next.[38]

The simplicity of Chilean memorialization underscores Chilean exceptionalism. Its officials prided themselves on the distinctive republic they had created. They were at pains to declare that the new nation was not fractured over the moment, and so independence predominates and revolution is muted. In fact, actors like O'Higgins worked to ensure revolution would not follow independence as it did in other nations. Accordingly, Chile, through an authoritarian state, would not reckon with

Monumento a la Libertad Americana in the Plaza
de Armas, Santiago, Chile. Image from iStock.com/
AlexandreFagundes.

tumult and insurrection for quite some time. When some in the country
would rise up to imperil that state, the champions of liberation would
find it difficult to find meaningful symbols from the revolutionary past.
Authoritarians would have an easier time.

O'Higgins would be resurrected throughout Chile's history to do just
that. In 1979, the Pinochet regime moved his tomb of elaborately carved
marble with Roman statuary from a cemetery to an underground crypt
below the presidential palace. In 1973, La Moneda had featured in the
coup that brought Salvador Allende down, as fighter jets attacked the palace and set it ablaze. Now, in this most sacred secular space, O'Higgins

would be put to rest, "in the hope of the resurrection." He would lie at the heart of a state anxious to maintain order at all costs and to claim some mantle of legitimacy. General Augusto Pinochet had an obsession with O'Higgins. He looked to the moment of independence for inspiration and to justify the coup and his mania for order. O'Higgins seemed to speak to his vision for Chile. Today, the crypt remains inviolate, even after Pinochet was ousted by plebiscite. In memory, O'Higgins has no rivals. He became and still is Chile's Washington, not only in being considered the chief father of the new nation but also because he epitomized a republicanism that was premised on order.[39]

As these cases demonstrate, memorials do difficult and complex work, usually by trying to disentangle independence from revolution. Not so for Brazil. The most important monument to be erected to independence, the rather unimaginatively named Monument to the Independence of Brazil in São Paulo, suggests freedom came without revolutionary baggage. Built to commemorate the hundredth anniversary of independence from Portugal, this massive and impressive memorial is an avowedly Catholic monument, one in which an altar would be later installed. Buried deep within the monument itself lies Pedro I, hailed as the "founder of the empire, first constitutional emperor and perpetual defender of Brazil." Even though Brazil would become a republic in 1889, the memorial salutes the royal family of Brazil's empire, and it announces how Brazil confidently escaped the challenges of the age. It had, of course—led by a slave-owning planter and mercantile elite. Therefore, there was little to memorialize.[40]

However it differs from other memorials, the São Paulo monument offers a profound, and invented, understanding of nationhood that reaches fruition only with the age. The viewer is told a story of how Pedro I's declaration of independence at this site by a small stream called the Ipiranga represented the culmination of earlier bids for independence. The 1789 revolt in Minas Gerais is recast as the first nation-building attempt. In what is almost a side altar to the main statue, a determined and defiant Christ-like Tiradentes is held bound by Portuguese soldiers. A statue of later "revolutionaries," who in fact had led a localist revolt, flank the monument, as well as key "patriarchs" of independence. None of these feature the enslaved whom planters found so troubling. They are erased from this narrative of nationhood, as well they had to be, given how the nation itself was built to ensure that planters would guide a state that would take as its motto "order and progress." The monument is topped by a large group of figures surrounding a chariot carrying a woman, repre-

Monumento à Independência do Brasil in São Paulo, Brazil. Image from
Alf Ribeiro/Shutterstock.com.

senting Brazil, grasping the flag of sovereign nationhood in one hand and
a cross in the other. The entourage proclaiming the fame of the new
nation as it marches into the future includes an Indian stoically picking up
the rear. The front of the monument, by far the most striking part, is a
relief of charging cavalry shouting, as the legend tells us, "independência
ou morte." They were in fact doing nothing more than rallying to the new
self-proclaimed king of Brazil. The monument, thus, not only creates a
largely invented apostolic succession of national heroes but also hopes to
transform a promulgation into high drama. It intends to do what Trumbull tried to accomplish for the United States: to turn a declaration or a
proclamation into the stuff of myth.

For those who would lose these empires, the Spanish and the Portuguese, memorials mingled victory with a sense of loss. Like Belgian memorials, theirs tended, understandably, to invoke the experience of war
against the French republican foe. Spanish monuments—some simple in
their classical lines, others more baroque in design—sprang up in nu-

merous cities. They uniformly sang of the glories of Spanish nationhood. Nation, in fact, is lionized, largely through the use of columns and arches and the invocation of the people who rallied to the cause. They often use images of the Spanish lion conquering a French republican eagle. They do not, as a rule, invoke the Crown; rather, heroes and defenders are featured. These are now the exemplars of nation. The emphasis is appropriate, as much of this fighting was done without the Crown. In essence, such memorials try to recapture a past that is irrevocably lost even as Spanish forces proved victorious over France. They resisted and they endured. Just like their empire, but in a much-diminished capacity.[41] Many of these went up to commemorate the centennial of what those from across the political spectrum called the "war of independence" against France. The "disaster" of 1898 and the need to respond to it, rising Catalan and Basque nationalist movements, and the conflict between liberal and traditional Catholic understandings of Spain's past preoccupied those who were building these monuments. Constructed in a moment of anxiety, Spanish monuments sought to inspire a sense of confidence that could somehow be recaptured by invoking a long-gone age.[42]

Portuguese monuments also touch on greatness, and one in Porto—the Monumento aos Heróis da Guerra Peninsular—also incorporates the lion standing atop a French bird of prey, but in most cases they revel in nostalgia for the age of Atlantic empire. A stirring memorial in Lisbon called the Monumento ao Povo e aos Heróis da Guerra Peninisular does what it says on the proverbial tin: it focuses on people and everyday heroes. But it juxtaposes these with waves and images like a group of subjects swearing to defend the nation at Vasco da Gama's tomb. It also ties the alliance with the British to fight the Peninsular War to exploration in the early modern period, the glory days when empire arose. Glory is still rooted in the Atlantic, even if this war would put an end to the Portuguese Atlantic empire.[43]

This last monument, as were many of those in Spain, was constructed to commemorate the hundredth anniversary of the start of the war and of the move to "national independence." It also went up around the time Portuguese soldiers were preparing to fight in the First World War, when the state hoped to use that moment to step out from under the British shadow, a place Portugal had been trapped in since the revolutionary age. So it speaks to aspirations not of the revolutionary moment but of the period following it; nevertheless, it still ties meaning into the nostalgia of greatness that the age represented to many in both countries.[44] Victories

Monumento aos Heróis da Guerra Peninsular in
Porto, Portugal. Image from iStock.com/
Sergey_Peterman.

over the French proved, in both the Spanish and the Portuguese cases,
Pyrrhic. The monuments reflect the victories won but empire and first-
rank status lost in the age. They suggest imperial grandeur, but of the
diminished kind, of rekindling that which cannot be recaptured. These
nostalgic sentiments would also shape nation in both places.

As a rule, memorialists subscribed to the idea that the bonds to the old
had to be broken; what had come immediately before the age could exist
only to instruct.[45] With an older order discredited, revolutionary regime

builders throughout the Atlantic would look further back to what they regarded as an untainted and instructive age: the classical period. Classical forms became the new historical "referents" for nearly all states. Straight lines and classical examples would be employed to make arcane complexities a thing of the past. This sentiment shaped monuments and streetscapes.[46]

Most followed these rules about ending an age. The French established them. Out with the old and in with the new animated the invocation of "1789." France's new birthday bespoke the frightening character of wiping the slate clean as well as the difficult dismantling of an old order. Americans had chosen the moment of the birth of the new as their national reference point, and they rooted that moment in a myth of consensus, of drafting a document. The French chose a very different image, of the storming of a prison dating from the Middle Ages. Their invocation of killing the old pointed to the necessity of profound violence in making straight the tangledness of history. Violence purged and cleared away the debris of the old, so that the rational could reign. In this way, the French could recover of the virtues of republican Rome. For the French, "1789" became the vanishing point. Indeed, in the case of the Bastille, the symbols of the old age became fetishes of the new order. Famously, the blocks of the Bastille were carved into keepsakes. Images of it appeared everywhere.[47] One of its keys had even been given to George Washington.

Another way of addressing the great upheaval was to insist that France's revolution had been exceptional. Memorials—and again these tended to be classical in form—suggested that this event had remade the world. Modernity began in 1789 on a monumental scale. That such a great and awful thing had been created by one people meant that the violence, suffering, and fear had not been in vain. The Great Nation had given "the West" the modern world and the rebirth of classical virtues.[48] The memorials gestured toward this sense of self-understanding. For this reason, rather ironically, French memorials would serve as inspirations for others intent on characterizing their revolutions as singular.

Because so much of the action and drama of the French Revolution happened in the streets of Paris, the city became the site on which the memory of the Revolution would be performed from this point forward. "Paris could represent the Revolution," a literary critic writes, "because the Revolution, in its turn, remade Paris in its image." Paris was no tabula rasa.[49] Monuments from this period claimed space by overtaking and overawing the past and its allegiances. The Pantheon, in which the great heroes of republican France are buried and remembered, had just recently been completed as a Catholic church to honor the patroness of Paris, Saint Genevieve. By taking over such a structure, and fittingly and fortunately it was classical in style, the republican state was making a grand statement. It would be the new church of the nation, once the older religious vestiges were purged. Napoleon considered the paving over of the old in the service of the new critical for his regime. A key to doing so was ensuring that his cult and that of the "grands hommes" who remade France would be sacralized. Only part of the Pantheon, in particular the altar, would be subject to the iconoclastic energies of the period. The rest was tailor-made for a new republican church. Fittingly, Voltaire, that great enemy of the church, would be placed there, as would Jefferson's friend Condorcet—symbolically, at least; for his remains were lost.[50]

Violence had done much of the work in vanquishing what had come before and been overturned; the state would do the rest. In Paris, space was punctuated by memorials, all with the idea of offering a new narrative for a new people. The Arc de Triomphe heralded the greatness of the nation and the sacrifice needed to bring it into being by tying the nation to Rome. On it, the names of all the battles the French had won create an intimidating and impressive litany of the Great Nation's martial accomplishments. It honors battles and anonymous common soldiers. It does one other piece of work: it suggests how liberty and efficacy within a republican tradition, vying with each other, could be balanced. The French and others used arches and obelisks, going back to classical antiquity, not only to claim that imagined past for themselves but also to demonstrate how they could somehow resolve the tensions they had conjured up during the age. The tensions were now managed by the imperial state in republican form.[51]

French monuments were meant to almost "boulevardize." We should think of the term literally. They uprooted and overturned an old order and they used streetscapes to do so. New straight lines through the city would be created to tether all to a new rational narrative. The Arc became a nexus or focal point of the new city. Paris, of course, had been the living embodiment of the old order, a ramshackle medieval city. The Arc had to be retrofitted into the old, offering a new way of imagining space for a people remade in the cauldron of revolution. Out from it radiated a new historical axis, or "axe historique," one that ran from the l'Étoile straight up the old Champs Élysées to the Arc de Triomphe du Carrousel. The

The Champs Élysées and Arc de Triomphe during a Bastille Day parade.
Image from REUTERS/Alamy Stock Photo.

arches were based on older Roman ones, of Titus and Constantine, respectively. So they used the permanence and greatness of the Roman
past to suggest the beginning of a new epoch based on a very different set
of ideas.[52]

Monumentalism asserted, as officials now insisted, that the state had
mastered the difficulties of the new age and was christening a new sacred
center for the nation.[53] With the historical axis in Paris, we encounter a
carefully orchestrated use of space in the cruciform that demonstrates
the state's insistence in its supremacy, that through its authority the nation dominates all. All civic engagement and subsequent development
were to be imaginatively tied to this line running from the Arc de Triomphe to the Arc de Triomphe du Carrousel. Arches, columns, neoclassical edifices, and obelisks stemming off from the line worked together as a
"monumental system" whose meaning could be subtly redefined but that
from this point forward drew its inspiration and legitimacy from the age.
This system included a column that would be later put up at Place de la
Bastille. The very center of the axe historique had initially been named
for Louis XV, with his equestrian statue reminiscent of the one in

New York to George III at the center. The statue had gone up in 1748. It came down on August 10, 1792. Its toppling left a "sacred void." But not for long. It was replaced by a statue called Liberty. Place Louis XV then would be named Place de la Révolution in honor of the new national narrative emerging. It witnessed the executions of many, including the grandson of Louis XV, Louis XVI. Then it would be renamed yet again Place de la Concorde for the peace that anxious Parisians hoped could wash away the Terror. The center of the axis, then, encapsulated all of revolution, both its hopes and its fears.[54]

Things, of course, are never quite so simple. The vision of new lines could not put the old completely to rest. If we view the obelisk at Place de la Concorde as the center of a cross, on the arms sit the National Assembly, the former Palais Bourbon, and a Catholic church called La Madeleine. They are almost exactly alike. Indeed, they were designed to be. The tangled relationship between the two speaks to how the French saw and lived with the tensions that boulevardization would seem to obviate. The church was originally built to serve as a memorial to Napoleon's soldiers, and it would, in perfect republican fashion, serve as a balance to the forces of the demos, the people. The National Assembly had originally been a palace and was given a new neoclassical facade to match the temple to Napoleon's soldiers and to speak to the republican regime. It is more fitting that the former became a Catholic church. As an orator put it, on this urban cross "two temples correspond to each other: one is that of laws, the other that of God." The state could, through the memory of the Revolution, overturn the old, but aspects of the ancien régime also held on, despite attempts to create new narratives that erased them.[55]

Think, too, of one of the iconic images of the period, that of Marianne. Marianne also yoked older sensibilities to new republican realities. Bells rang out to her, just as they had to the Virgin Mary in the time of the ancien régime. Marianne was also venerated. Thus, she could subsume the old by appropriating its symbolism, in just the same way the Virgin Mary had superseded older pagan symbols centuries earlier. The sensibilities of the old, then, could be marshaled to defeat the symbolic importance of the old. Marianne did other work as well. Her image also made the point that women represented virtue. Marianne, of course, would be identified as a spirited martial leader too, bestowing courage on the men who followed her into combat.[56]

In making this move, the French did exactly what Americans in the United States did when they employed the image of a woman to symbolize

liberty or Brazilians did when they used the female form to represent progress. In a world still tied together symbolically, perhaps even more so because of parallel memorialization projects, nation builders used women to
symbolize the chief virtues that sustained order in their respective societies,
thereby granting them symbolic inclusion.[57] The age thus canonized often
contradictory impulses into a coherent whole—such as the new and the
old—and, needless to say, the many tensions that still remained, not least of
all the imperfect inclusion of women in the narrative of the age.

To say that French revolutionary memorialists did not fully achieve a
unified vision of monumentalization misses the point. In fact, they accomplished some extraordinary things. The tossing out of the old and its
tangled ways to lay out rational and straight new lines did not only lay
claim to the Revolution; doing so also insisted that revolution had come
to an end. Monuments announced that the state, wrapped in national
identity, has solved the riddle of sovereignty. To boulevardize did something else. Even walking the city of Paris reinforced the connection between nation and state, strengthening both in the process in just the
same way anniversaries of dates—July 4 and July 14—and of the years—
1810 and 1821—did. Space was as ritualized as the calendar. In this way,
Revolution with a capital "R" became the time in space that all history
moved to and moved from. When urban reformers, in particular Napoleon III and Baron von Haussmann, tried to remake the city of Paris,
they began where Napoleon left off. They hoped to cut swathes through
old medieval neighborhoods, all with an eye to modernizing, but also to
turn memorials into reference points for the whole city. Just as the Revolution had become for all of France.[58]

Let's throw out all the rules we've just discussed. Sometimes memorials
fetishized the old and condemned the new. Revolution, of course,
touched all Atlantic societies and even some far removed from the ocean,
particularly as all were drawn into war. Some societies, like France, were
overturned in the process. But others, if anything, saw the ancien régime
nature of their states strengthened through the age. These, too, would
memorialize in almost the same way the French did. They did so for
many of the same reasons. They, too, had to tether mobilized people to
the state, and now the state had to prove ever vigilant against the forces
of hope and fear that could continually disrupt. For these people, memorials did not so much try to vanquish the old through the use of new
lines; rather, they laid out lines to gesture to the old, to highlight it and

the stability it provided. The old would be made monumental, and many of the tricks the French used would be employed to very different purposes. In Austria, for instance, statues went up extolling the emperor and his army. The martial became much more prominent in memorials, stemming from the need to invoke the power of the state both in sustaining order and in valorizing a people who had mobilized for war.[59]

Prussians had a similar, if more dramatic, story. Prussia emerged as one of the winners of the age. The government had learned to mobilize and to use a democratized people for state purposes. Indeed, the ruling elite, whose fortunes had risen in the eyes of the people through war making during the age, had become synonymous with the state. No doubt, Prussians had done so by avoiding revolution. The monarchy had not fallen. The old order remained. People had rallied to the idea of the efficacious state. In the process, the state itself became the emotive basis of nation. Prussia, then, is best construed as the state-nation. After the Congress of Vienna, the Prussian state-nation could present itself as epitomizing German national aspirations in much the way Austria had.[60]

Prussians experienced nothing short of a mania for remembering their "Wars of Liberation," as officials declared them, or, as some of the mobilized argued, "Wars of Liberty." The Crown and the popular were melded together through memory. Nothing out of the ordinary, in other words.[61] Yet, the Prussians did something rather different with memorials. They reinvented or rechristened the old to speak to the new. The iconic monument to Prussian aspirations for all of Germany only became such in the wake of the age. Berlin's Brandenburg Gate had been constructed earlier in the eighteenth century as a functioning entryway and as a peace memorial. Napoleon, after he had taken Berlin, turned it into his own triumphal arch. He even took the quatrain of horses atop the arch to Paris to commemorate his victories over Prussia. With his eventual defeat, the quatrain was returned, readorned with a Prussian eagle and Iron Cross, and put aloft once more on the gate. The Prussians then recast it as a "Gate of Victory." What had been something consecrated to peace became one that spoke to the nation at war and the centrality of the state's victory in the German saga.[62]

The act of rechristening or "layering" during the age would mark later memorialization for Prussians and, with time, Germans. They would use, reuse, and reinvent the meanings of monuments in just the way they had with the Brandenburg Gate.[63] The best example lies just half a mile from the gate. On the famous eighteenth-century avenue Unter den

Neue Wache in Berlin, Germany. Image from Ilari Nackel/Shutterstock.com.

Linden sits the Neue Wache, or New Guardhouse. This neoclassical structure was designed to honor Prussian soldiers who fought in the Napoleonic Wars and as a paean to Prussian militarism. On this Prussian Champs Élysées or axis of power, this "guardhouse" served much the same function the earlier incarnation of La Madeleine did. But it would prove even more plastic, reflecting the terror and tragedy of German history since this moment of national greatness. The Neue Wache would first serve as a Prussian memorial to the wars with Napoleon, then as a Weimar monument to the First World War to remember those who fell. After the Second World War, and since the building sat in East Berlin, authorities would redefine it yet again, as a reminder of the brutality of fascism. Since the fall of the Berlin Wall, it has housed a simple, but powerful, pietà-like statue of a mother cradling a dead son. The coupling does not so much evoke salvation as suffering. The Neue Wache now stands as a memorial for all victims of war and tyranny in Germany's past, a past littered with atrocities. What had been a memorial to the glories and omnipotence of the Prussian state, and of victory, became a means of addressing German national trauma and, as some critics would say, victimhood.[64] The forms of these memorials, then, unlike the French versions, served more as shells that could be suffused with new meaning.

Britain far outpaced Prussia in memorializing the age; in fact, the British rivaled the French in their enthusiasm for remembering what had happened through the construction of monuments. "There was a constant demand for them," William Thackeray noted in 1847, "during the first fifteen years of the present century," so much so that sculptors were kept quite busy.[65] In Britain, monuments went up soon after the wars to honor those who had triumphed in defending an ancien régime. The conceit they memorialized characterized Britain as a nation of continuities, the one state that had skillfully negotiated the age and all its tangles. From the simplest perspective, memorials served as a rebuke of, or reaction to, the very idea of the revolutionary age. Yet, the British did not do so in a simplistic way. The story of memorialization for them during the long age, one that began with their imperial crisis in 1763 and that for them ended with Wellington's victory in 1815, played on the theme of redemption.[66]

The drama British memorials prescribe is suffused with scriptural overtones. On one hand, Britons looked back at the age nostalgically to gesture to what was gone. A number of them, for instance, lamented the loss of much of America. In such a telling, William Pitt represented the sane and enlightened road not taken, the virtuous way through the age that was eschewed and that led to American loss. In John Singleton Copley's great painting of the period, *The Death of the Earl of Chatham*, Pitt stands for what could have and maybe should have been—and what could be and would once more. His stand for an empire bound to the Crown-in-Parliament but rooted in consent represented a road not taken at the time that would lead to imperial tragedy, exemplified in his collapse at the moment American independence was realized.[67] This image and others like it would have served as national rebukes, if not for victory that was achieved later. Far from a memorial of despair, Copley's image would be vindicated as a monument of prophecy.

In Westminster stand the fulfillments of such prophecies. In the Royal Gallery of the House of Lords, great murals of Wellington meeting the Prussian field marshal Blücher after Waterloo and the death of Nelson dominate the space. Painted by the Irishman Daniel Maclise in 1861, these broke new ground in the world of decorative art, combining artwork and space in conscious ways to create a panoramic statement of permanence and power. They offer a story of Britain as a unified entity culminating in Trafalgar and Waterloo. All the kingdoms are represented in these allegorical battle scenes. In fact, they point toward this moment

*The Death of the Earl of Chatham,* by John Singleton Copley. Image from
PRISMA ARCHIVO/Alamy Stock Photo.

as an apogee of the consensual unity of the British Isles and when constituted authority—in the person of the two national heroes—overcame
chaos.[68] Carnage apparent in the murals ensured that violent change
would not visit Britain. The Christlike dead on battlefields far away have
sacrificed their lives to ensure that radicalism did not visit home. They
are martyrs of and for an age. Ultimately, the murals suggest that these
men ensured that Britain had withstood the revolutionary era unchanged
and unscathed, even if this, of course, was pious myth.

In doing such work for the British nation, Nelson stands above all
others. We could and should call him "Saint Nelson." Indeed, the ubiquity of Nelson's image on everything from mugs to paintings casting him
as British national messiah mimicked the Wolfe mania after the victory
in Quebec in 1759. Both epitomized nation, but they did so in subtly different ways. Wolfe's time had passed. Like Saint John the Baptist, Wolfe
merely prefigured he who was to come. It is clear who it is Nelson plays
in the drama. In London, Nelson inhabited two central places. He would
be entombed in one of the great pantheons to the age, Saint Paul's Cathedral. Here, the civic and sacred, the nation and faith, were united in
his person. The other, of course, is the most famous square in London.

Nelson's Column in Trafalgar Square, London, United Kingdom. Image
from iStock.com/lachris77.

Trafalgar Square still serves as the city's chief meeting place. Central to
it, of course, is the column that Lord Nelson tops. In the 1820s, as the
British were trying to make traffic more manageable in their bustling
capital, they used the refurbishment of the Charing Cross area to memorialize properly one of the two people that everyone looked to as the sav-
iors of the British nation. To that end, King George IV commissioned an
architect named John Nash. Finally, in 1840 the square was laid out. Fittingly, it would be Wellington who helped dedicate the monument to
Nelson. Napoleon's Paris, it should be said with a touch of irony, served
as an inspiration for Nash, only in this case to enhance the Crown and
tradition.[69]

Trafalgar Square also suggests how London, as much as Paris or
Washington, reordered itself through memorials. Nelson's monument
became a hinge point between the past that was nostalgically recalled, on
the one hand, and the new that was integrated into the national story by
invoking the old, on the other. It does not stand as an axial point for a
new order, like the Arc de Triomphe, but is one that brings together an
old site of commerce—in this case the City of London up through the
Strand—with the ancient seat of political power—Westminster. It ties

the economic center of empire and docklands farther to the east, with their ships going all over a world now redesigned for free trade, with the older institutions that Britain had retained through the tumult of war.[70]

London is not unique in this. So central had he become to the new British biblical narrative, Nelson became after his death a postrevolutionary Saint Simeon Stylites, so often was he perched atop a column. A monument to his memory would rise in both Scotland and Ireland too, just as it had in Montreal. Scotland's tower to Nelson does not incorporate a statue, but its verticality stands as a vivid reminder of how Scotland has been enmeshed to the center. On a hill over the city of Edinburgh, this monument to Nelson stands amid an uncompleted temple to the memory of the wars, in all of which from this point forward Scots would play leading roles. At Calton Hill, military monuments mingle with the memory of Enlightenment figures. Scotland would still be a provincial society but would be tied to the state through the memory of service and martial sacrifice and would demonstrate its distinctive genius by gesturing to the preeminent role it played in the Enlightenment.[71] Nelson, then, towers above the city and this narrative.

Dublin's monument to Nelson was meant to do the same dovetailing work for the Irish. It, in theory, bound them as well to a national narrative, in which the Irish were supposed to play supporting roles. Indeed, the Irish could boast that they beat Londoners to the punch. Their modern Trajan's Column topped with a statue went up years before the one in Trafalgar Square to remember, as its plaque declared, "the Transcendent Heroic Achievements" of the man. It would be easy to say that this act of construction amounted to the last gasp of the Protestant Ascendancy in Ireland. In fact, middle-class Catholics, in the wake of the aborted rising of 1798, proved anxious to support the erection of England's new worthy and for Dublin to be considered the "second city" of empire. The column would become a focal point of Dublin's urban streetscape.[72]

Even in the provinces Nelson did not stand alone. Wellington too was lionized in stone and metal for all he had done. In Dublin, where he had been born, citizens raised funds to honor their "heroic countryman" with a massive obelisk in Phoenix Park, laying the cornerstone in 1817 to memorialize his victory at Waterloo. Height for this and for Nelson's was "the cheapest way and one of the most certain of obtaining sublimity." The Irish also erected a metal bridge across the Liffey in his honor, known today as the Halfpenny Bridge.[73]

Wellington's image performs the same heroic service in England. Wellington's home, Apsley House—with an address of Number 1, London—was refitted into what would become a shrine to all he had accomplished. Rooms were festooned with images that recalled all he had done to maintain the line against radicalism. Nearby, he could look out of his window to see a statue of himself on horseback surrounded by a Welsh fusilier, an Irish dragoon, a Scottish Highlander, and an English guardsman. Wellington had sealed the union by relying on the manpower of the four nations. Fittingly, he would be laid to rest in the same Saint Paul's pantheon close to Nelson. Meanwhile, two large triumphant arches, Waterloo Arch and Marble Arch, were erected near Hyde Park Corner to commemorate his victories. Marble Arch was the work of the same John Nash charged with Trafalgar Square.[74]

The arches in London were similar to those being erected all over the Atlantic world, but the London ones differed from the others in one critical way: they pointed the viewer toward royal power. They were positioned with the intention of drawing the person walking beneath them to Buckingham Palace. The palace, not the monument, served as focal point. Unlike the Arc de Triomphe, these monuments reflected power and glory; they did not bring it into being. All beckoned to the Crown and the notion of tradition and progress it underscored. Monuments, thus, embodied hierarchy, order, and legitimacy. They stood as examples of stability in the face of the chaos of the age. Fittingly, it would be the king's birthday and coronation day that would serve the purpose of national commemoration in much the way July 4 and July 14 did for the Americans and the French, respectively.[75]

The Irish case, unsurprisingly, could not quite fit this redemptive narrative. National memorialization tells this tale as well. Ireland's Nelson column would serve at first as a focal point on a street destined to be named after Daniel O'Connell, where his statue would also stand. At this very site, coincidentally, O'Connell and Frederick Douglass had first met.[76] O'Connell was one revolutionary the British could incorporate into the monumental canon. He rejected radical approaches to change, opting instead for reforming the new system rather than trying to tear it down for something more perfect. For this reason, he could stand with Nelson. In fact, he also contested him. The two titans, on their pedestals, with O'Connell turning his back on Nelson, would face off for decades. The Irish, their juxtaposition seemed to suggest, were members of the

Photo of O'Connell Street in Dublin, Ireland, taken in 1927, showing the
O'Connell Monument and Nelson's Pillar. Image from SOTK2011/Alamy
Stock Photo.

United Kingdom but often neglected partners of the union. The face-off
also pointed out the fact that, for better or often worse, Ireland's history
was now to be incorporated into the story of greater Britain.[77]

Of the two, Nelson loomed larger. The neoclassical column suggested how Ireland was part of the nation- and state-building project that
defined the whole Atlantic in the wake of revolution, one that engrafted
Ireland to Great Britain in a broad United Kingdom. The transnational
form suggested that Ireland could also lay claim to being part of a newly
invigorated nation-state. Irish particulars, past grievances, and distinctive
dilemmas of remaining a kingdom-colony could be obviated in the multinational state. Fittingly, Nelson's memorial was erected not at the center
of Ascendancy life, Saint Stephen's Green, but at a more "plebeian" site
where ordinary Dublin came and went.[78] Later monuments further
bound Ireland to the Union. They, too, took their inspiration in form and
intent from the age. The triumphal arch on Saint Stephen's Green, for
instance, was modeled like many others on Rome's Arch of Titus. It was
built to memorialize the Dublin Fusiliers, who had fought for Britain in
the Boer War, and so would tie Ireland into the national canon more

completely.[79] The Irish, the tale went, had fought against the forces that sought to overturn the ancien régime, and for doing so they had secured a place under the umbrella of the Pax Britannica.

The afterlife of Nelson's monument in Dublin, however, speaks to how Irish tensions could not be effectively subsumed into the British state. Nelson's Pillar would befall a fate similar to George III's in New York and Louis XV's in Paris. In 1966, members of the outlawed Irish Republican Army blew the top off the Nelson Pillar in what they called, appropriately, Operation Humpty Dumpty. With its fall, they erased this part of their history. The nation, they declared, belonged to those who had perished on Vinegar Hill, and they traced a direct path of national apostolic succession from those rebels. Canceling Nelson announced that the Irish too stood as inheritors of an age that made republics. The story of the remnants also resembles the tale of George III's head, ironically sent to a former lord lieutenant of Ireland. Today, all that remains of the column is the head of Nelson. It rests hidden away as a curiosity in Dublin's Pearse Street Library, never to be put atop a statue again, its nose smashed.[80]

For the Irish, the most salient memorials of the age would go up long after it was over and would eschew the forms and themes evident in British Dublin. In general, they would focus on the meaning of loss within a broader Atlantic story of liberation, one the Irish had a hand in. A memorial finished in 1998 on Vinegar Hill, where the 1798 rebellion had come to its bloody end, stands as a circle of anonymous bronze pikemen, alone in a lonely spot. They commemorate defeat and the idea of Ireland as an Atlantic outlier. The most vivid reminders of these themes are found in Mayo, where the French had landed in 1798. Late in the nineteenth century and early in the twentieth, monuments went up in and around Castlebar to commemorate what had transpired there. Here the French and Irish defeated British troops, even if the broader Irish republican cause foundered. The notion of the aborted nation resonated as Catholics in Ireland pressed for rights and home rule later in the nineteenth century. Across from Christ Church, whose Church of Ireland parishioners had in 1844 erected a statue to a local officer who had fought at Waterloo for the Crown, in 1953 Catholics erected a simple monument on the mall with harp and fleur-de-lis facing the church. Clericalist in intent, it invoked the French connection and the patronage of Mary to lead the righteous cause of nationhood. Even in defeat, a Catholic God stood on their side, and now history vindicated this belief.[81] The monument encourages

1798 Rebellion memorial at the Mall, Castlebar, County Mayo, Ireland.
Image from Keith Heneghan/Alamy Stock Photo.

viewers to consider time as they think about Ireland's relationship to the age. The age would inspire the nation finally born in the future. The placement facing Christ Church spoke of a counternarrative to the state's story, that even in defeat the nation was culturally constructed and was realized in God's time, not man's.[82]

One other theme would also focus on loss and eventual redemption but would do so geographically. The Irish, after all, may have failed at home, but they succeeded elsewhere. With good reason, they styled themselves revolutionary exiles. In Dublin and in Mayo, monuments would note the connection of the Irish to the story of Latin American independence, for instance, with a bust of O'Higgins placed in Merrion Square in Dublin and a statue erected in Foxford of Admiral William Brown, the Mayo-born founder of the Argentinian Navy, who had served in the United States beforehand. Even if the nation in Ireland proved elusive, the Irish served as midwives to freedom elsewhere. Consider in this vein the memorial to the Irishman John Barry in Wexford, the father of the American Navy, which President Eisenhower lauded for the "intermingling" of Irish and American history. Failure at home brought vindication elsewhere.[83]

Perhaps the most significant story of the Irish age of revolution was what was forgotten. In the aftermath of violence, the descendants of those Protestants who had conspired to rise against the British Crown tended to embrace the cause of the union. As they did so, they remade the past, expunging or downplaying revolutionary radicalism, especially that associated with the failed rising in Ulster, and embracing, of all things, Orangeism. To be fair, Catholics indulged in selective remembrance as well, positing that what happened in the southeast of the country was inspired by republican nationalism and not by sectarian hatreds. By forgetting, the Irish—now far from united—became two camps formed by different visions of a shared past. Memorials to 1798, then, arose in areas dominated by nationalists. They were not erected in unionist areas. Those that were put up were defaced.[84]

For the nineteenth century, between 1798 and 1916, only the duel in stone between a conjoined Nelson and O'Connell stood as official, yoked as they were to the state. In these years, the counternarrative lived, but not in marble. If anything, it epitomized the inability to fit Ireland into the patterns of endings. It was the image of what would come to be known as "the Fenian." After the dust had settled from a revolutionary age, the Irish had emerged as an almost stateless proletariat, expatriated exiles. They peopled armies and canal-building sites. They did so from Britain to the United States and Argentina, a mass movement that began in earnest after the Treaty of Ghent, signed in 1814, and that accelerated to an industrial scale after the Famine, which began the very year Douglass visited Ireland. The emergence of the violent image of the Fenian marked another iconic development of the period after the age. It served as the antithesis to the stability that had been sustained by the state. Even though the Irish constructed the stuff of the Atlantic economy and pushed the bounds of empire, they portended mobility and rebellion, when all was settlement. Ever lurking on the edges, the Fenian threatened a return to the furies. The image stood as a reminder of how all could not necessarily be bound up in new myths and in new settlements.[85]

The act of building monuments bound all to new historical narratives. The state had, through monuments, become the guardian of that history and would be tied to it from this point forward. Enlightenment thinkers like Kant, and much later Alexis de Tocqueville, suggested that history could be understood and so harnessed, that the jumble of the past could be appreciated, and that state power could derive from the act of imposing order on it. The states that were the inheritors to the age of revolution robed themselves in this understanding. Offering new vanishing points, they affirmed themselves as the sum total of history. They asked people to fix themselves, though nationalism, to the narrative of progress. History made the state, just as the state made history.[86] Even those states that questioned the liberating logic of revolution, such as Britain, found they had to be yoked to the past in ways they had not been before.[87] Similarly, weaker leviathans that stepped onto the stage with some reluctance, as was the case with the United States, had to figure creative ways to manage a democratized people.[88] The idea of the American Revolution as exceptional served such a purpose.

The new nations, therefore, had new dates they were beholden to, new moments that spoke to the revolutions they emerged from or evaded. They were sustained by new myths, but ones that conjured a belief in a more just order than those they replaced. This is not to say that dissent did not capture imaginations. It most certainly did. But myth served as a powerful counterpoise. It also established the terms of national debate from this point forward. Myth suggested that the alluring ideas the promise of the age memorialized were never completely realized. In fact, dissent, if framed within the new mythic paradigm, could serve to strengthen the very institutions and sensibilities it was contesting.

It's no surprise that all states in the wake of revolution looked alike. Yet, the monuments, like the dilemmas faced by creole elites a generation earlier, pointed toward confidence and anxiety. They proclaimed new bases of sovereignty and of authority. But their grandiosity belied fears of tumult returning once more. They were designed to hold hopes and fears in balance. For the new states, or those that had survived the furies, had to rely on subjects and citizens as never before to survive. Popular mobilization gave states the sort of power that officials in 1750 could not have imagined. It also ever threatened the new order. All states had to manage and acknowledge this reality, even if they did so distinctively and with different sets of challenges and advantages. The specter of revolution now lurked, especially for those states that based their legitimacy on the idea of revolution. Monuments both dwarfed and paid deference to the faceless many who had made revolution. They had to if the new states were to be able to thrive.

As had been the case throughout the age, Haitians would be the most prominent outliers. Today, many memorials to the age can be seen in

Haiti. But for a long time, few monuments went up. The explanation tells us a great deal about the hurdles Haitians faced in sealing their revolution. For a start, the outside world tried to isolate the place and its revolution, a strategy that would shape much of the nation's subsequent history. In Haiti's success, the rest of the Atlantic saw the failure of the whole and the specter of revolution returning. If Haiti could stand and be recognized as an equal, all the work that the memorials throughout the Atlantic did could be imperiled.[89]

This is not to say that Haitians did not memorialize. Of course they did, and they had ample reason to do so. As early as the late 1790s, they erected a Greco-Roman temple to commemorate emancipation and national liberty. It was destroyed in 1802 when Napoleon dispatched French troops to retake the island. Haitians then appropriated metropolitan forms even as they scorned French sovereignty. Smaller commemorative columns and altars to liberty, as well as temporary triumphal arches, arose throughout the country. Visual expression in the first years after revolution also took Native or African forms, especially after Haitians won independence. Most of these were modest in size.[90] It just took much longer to memorialize revolution on a large scale in Haiti. To gain their independence, Haitians had to pay France a massive indemnity, one that subsequent generations claimed hobbled the future prospects of the nation. Partially cut off from the Atlantic because of the threat it represented, Haiti struggled with isolation and poverty. In 1954, the state constructed a spate of official memorials to recognize the 150th anniversary of freedom. Others came later. Natural disasters and relentless poverty made marking independence and freedom less pressing than in other regions.

But marginalization and impoverishment are only part of the explanation. In light of Haiti's postrevolutionary history, no one knew how to consider founding fathers of the state like Louverture. Louverture had made decisions that compromised freedom, and in so doing, he and others like him had doomed many to a form of vassalage on the land, made all the more impossible to escape by poverty and international isolation. Fittingly, more statues of Louverture appeared in Communist Cuba than in most other places. Over the past generation these views have changed. Men and women are more comfortable noting the ambivalence of the moment, how the circumstances that people like Louverture faced were extraordinarily fraught. He is now recognized by Haitians—and by the French, who have had an inscription to him rendered in their Pantheon—as the founding father of a nation consecrated to the idea of freedom and

The Sans-Souci Palace in Milot, Haiti. Image from Rotorhead 30A
Productions/Shutterstock.com.

to the end of that peculiar institution that had defined the eighteenth-
century Atlantic. Thankfully, the French sent the remains of Louverture
back to be reinterred in the Haitian Pantheon, where he is revered as the
founding father of the nation.[91]

The most fitting memorial to what happened in Haiti in the immediate aftermath of the age, and one that dovetails with the tragic history
of the place, was not meant to be a memorial at all. The place is called
the Sans-Souci Palace.[92] Sans-Souci, French for "without cares or worries," was constructed by Henri Christophe, one of the actors vying to
bring control and authority back to the island in the midst of the tumult
of revolution and the self-styled king of the north of the island. Christophe had fought with the French on the side of American revolutionaries at the Battle of Savannah. He then returned to Saint-Domingue and
became one of the chief fomenters of insurrection. He tried to establish
his power ruthlessly, and after suppressing a rising among the formerly
enslaved and terrifying rivals, he hoped to declare himself king of Haiti,
even if he controlled only the north. Part of his plan to demonstrate his
sovereign control involved erecting a fitting symbol of that authority.

The name Sans-Souci conjures a number of different ideas. The palace of Christophe more than likely took its name from Frederick the
Great's ode to Versailles in Potsdam. Really more of a summer palace—

the small place was always overcrowded—it was nonetheless used by Frederick to do much of his official business. Its day-to-day functioning epitomized the image of "state" that Frederick wanted to project.[93] Christophe as well styled himself almost a Prussian-like figure in trying to overawe with the power of the state. The name and allusion to Prussia demonstrated how he hoped to make Haiti a nation to be reckoned with, a Black nation standing as an equal to the white powers of the Atlantic and of Europe.

Yet, the name has other resonances too, the sort that speak to the difficult struggle that defined the revolutionary years in Haiti. Christophe had built his power on the suppression of the formerly enslaved, one of whom was nicknamed Sans Souci. Sans Souci had come to Saint-Domingue from the Kongo, where he had gained military experience. He would not compromise with the French or with those who would re-impose slavery once it was abolished. He found himself confronting Christophe in the revolutionary contest over power. Eventually Christophe killed him. The monument, then, was literally built on the backs of the oppressed. Black laborers constructed it, and Christophe, though he did not reintroduce slavery, wanted to put in place a brutal labor regime to make the island profitable after the tumult of revolution. The construction of Sans-Souci, then, epitomized the tangled nature of state formation and nation building.

Sans-Souci never really fulfilled its function as a palace. It only ended up as a monument to the age because of Haiti's difficulty binding society back together. Christophe did not fare well after the construction. Fearing a coup, he took his own life, and days later his son, whom he had designated as his heir, was assassinated. Haiti had an extraordinarily difficult time reestablishing legitimate authority, and the very term Sans-Souci speaks to its plight. Today, what remains of it stands as a ruin. An earthquake brought much of it down in the mid-nineteenth century. The lessons of Sans-Souci should give us pause. The ruin, perhaps more than any other memorial, recognizes the tragic reality of Haiti, and by extension many others gone missing from official narratives of nationhood, during and after the age.

It has taken nations much more time to memorialize the most traumatic aspect of the age of revolution: slavery. That legacy was forgotten, or better, un-remembered. Un-remembering has led to haunting, for Africans and for the other Atlantic societies that imported the enslaved or were complicit in the trade in humans. Even attempting to remember slavery does not work in normal ways. The act is best characterized as touching a "wound" that can only be described and never understood or fully healed. Maybe men and women in the societies where the enslaved toiled cannot come to terms with remembering because of racist assumptions that still have a hold on some. Nonetheless, scholars, artists, and the general public throughout the Atlantic are beginning to work through the difficult process of trying.[94]

Cubans struggled for a long time to characterize their Atlantic story. On the grounds of one of the plantations where the 1843 rising near Matanzas took place, known as La Escalera, the regime of Fidel Castro finally tried to do so, building a stunning monument to the men and women who resisted. In fact, the enslaved woman Carlota, who played such an important role in the insurrection, features. While others forgot, Castro and his followers needed to remember. He had sound political reasons for doing so. Cuba's rulers used the memory of the enslaved, and their ties to Africa, to insist on a role for a Communist Cuba in a wider world. The narrative Castro fastened on announced that the oppressed would overcome the oppressors. The monument mimics the heroic style of statues in the Soviet Union. The rebel in front has broken his bonds and wields a stick that he will use against his oppressors. Carlota, too, holds weapons. She is an equal in the drama. Castro would proclaim in 1991 at this site that Cubans "would never return to the slave barracks." Fittingly, he would in 1975 call his intervention in Angola Operation Black Carlota. It suited his political purposes in many ways to tie Cuba to Africa. Of course, in so doing, he was also paying homage to the African roots of slave resistance in Cuba, as well as to the identity of so many of those descended from the enslaved in the island country. All Cubans, all Communist ones in any event, could consider themselves the emancipated.[95]

Africa would memorialize slavery and the age around the same time Cuba did, but for different reasons. In the twentieth century, particularly in the wake of the civil rights struggles in much of the Western world, African states sponsored the construction of monuments to their experience during the age. These tended to be placed at slaving factories. These places that more than any other represented the entangled nature of the Atlantic and became the engines that drove what enlighteners called "progress" now offer silent testimony to the traumas of the age and how Africans experienced it. In Ghana, Cape Coast Castle brandishes the flags of the nations complicit in the trade. In Benin, the Door of No Return, a

The Door of No Return in Ouidah, Benin. Image from StreetVJ/
Shutterstock.com.

broad arch, frames a view of the sea from Ouidah. This was the last sight
those in chains saw of their homeland. One such door on Gorée Island in
Senegal tries to make the same point. These speak to narratives that people in Africa are now willing to entertain after a period characterized by
"amnesia."[96]

Arches and statues conjure loss and victimhood. They recognize
those gone and the trauma of those left behind. They tend to be focused
on the ocean, the great beyond where so many would be bound. Like
Native American memorials, they tend to be faceless. They speak not of
deeds but of experience. This was West Africa's age, and these memorials
offer unvarnished and simple truths that many other monuments miss or
ignore. States struggling economically in West Africa built these for the
diaspora to tie the descendants of those who were captured and enslaved
back to Africa imaginatively. They are made of the transnational for the
transnational.[97]

Like others, nonetheless, these memorials are rooted in nation. Nation-states that had won independence in the twentieth century put them
up to suggest that slavery formed the vanishing points for West Africa's
nations. More than any date, slavery marked Africans and those of the

diaspora. They call on the world, as UNESCO has done, to see these places as integral to the Atlantic story of the age. Though these memorials offer a rebuke to those of other nations throughout the Atlantic, though they were addressing the age of revolution much later than others did, they still do the same work as other monuments.[98]

Sometimes, therefore, those that don't fit the conventional script offer the best means to appreciate fundamental principles. And maybe on this note we should end with someone with whom we started this story: Olaudah Equiano. No statue to Equiano exists from the period, though a few small memorials can be seen in London. Some have called for a statue to him to be made and erected on the famous fourth plinth, the empty one, at Trafalgar Square. Those who support the move note that in today's climate Nelson would not be honored. He had, after all, employed naval power to protect the interests and property of slaveholders. How fitting it would be to have Equiano stand at that historic place. Nothing as yet has come of this.[99] Equiano's life and toils did earn a plaque in 2009 in Saint Margaret's next to Westminster Abbey, where "the African" was baptized in 1759.[100] The City of Westminster placed a green plaque at 73 Riding House Street, where he lived and worked, though some complained that Equiano's exploits have not been put on a more prestigious blue plaque.

More recently another memorial has arisen. On Telegraph Hill, near a swing set, children from the Edmund Waller School created a garden dedicated to the end of the slave trade and a small monument to Equiano's memory. It features a colorful bust atop a pedestal festooned with images of Africa and the Atlantic. The children made the garden in the shape of Africa, and they planted flowers reminiscent of the greater Caribbean. Many of the children had come from Africa and the Caribbean, reflecting how multicultural England had become in the years since the age.[101] The children's monument does far more than any plaque. Kitschy to be sure, and clearly the handiwork of the unskilled, it speaks of Equiano as adventurer, sailor, abolitionist, writer, campaigner, and survivor of the horrors of his age. It also recounts his imagined African past. Though the work of children, it captures in some sense the tangled world that he gave birth to and that gave birth to him.

We should be thankful that the children remembered Equiano. For many years he went unrecognized. He was the living manifestation of the perfidy that went into creating the Atlantic system and the creative capacities of people to act when sovereignty teetered. He epitomized the

Plinth to Olaudah Equiano in Telegraph Hill Park,
London, United Kingdom. Image from Bill Brand/
Alamy Stock Photo.

system's imperatives, just as he was product and producer of the entanglements of the period. Also fitting, painfully so, is the late recognition
he has been accorded. For many decades, his accomplishments have been
written out of the Atlantic story. Only recently have we discovered how
characters such as Equiano better represented the age than nearly any
others. The Atlantic now belongs to him.

For all of this, Equiano remains a complicated figure that reflects the
realities of a complicated age. Some now reckon that parts of his story
may have been fabricated, which has led to a furious row among scholars.
Equiano, some believe, was born in South Carolina, not Africa. But from

surviving testimony of others, we know his narrative spoke to many dynamics we know to be true. In fact, his reconstructed life appears as a
pastiche of the experiences of so many others, and this fact leads many to
think there is still great value in his story and in the narrative he wrote.
Most scholars think we need Equiano. The stain that remained from the
age, experienced by so many as a moment of liberation, illustrates the
Janus-faced nature of the age, memorials to the contrary. To those who
created the memorials to bring the age to an end and to begin the re-
weaving needed for new nations to thrive in a competitive Atlantic,
Equiano was deeply troubling. The idea of liberation, after all, became
the stuff of national narratives. Equiano points out the limitations of the
stories we tell. He reminds us of the age's most pronounced limits, its
singeing realities. Equiano also has no fitting memorial because he is a
vivid reminder of how it was that certain groups, most especially the enslaved in places like Brazil, Cuba, and the United States, remained excluded from national settlement as the price of stability.[102]

There is one other reason. The pull of the nation, the mythic construct that arose from this period and that has subsequently obscured the
deeper story of Atlantic connectedness, also makes it hard to memorialize someone like Equiano. His is a transnational tale. Every nation and
no nation can claim him. Statues are the stuff of nation-states. It will be
challenging to find a plinth that can belong to him.

# Epilogue

WHEN DID AN AGE of Revolution, with a capital "R," and revolutions, with a lowercase "r," conclude? Well, the last Spanish troops left Latin America in 1826.[1] That would seem a fitting endpoint to an era that began in 1776 with a rope and a statue. Fifty years from start to finish. How about a hundred years, an era of change lasting in the Atlantic from—ballpark—1750 to about 1850, from when the Atlantic was becoming a complex and contested space until things throughout the Atlantic seemed settled?[2] Those who cut out Latin America could argue for 1799, with the rest being "climax and denouement," or, perhaps, 1804 with the end of the Haitian Revolution.[3] There is even a case for the very beginning of the twentieth century, after the last republics in the Americas, Brazil and Cuba, came into being. By that time, even those places that had experimented with or reverted to monarchical government in the wake of revolution—Mexico, France, and Haiti—had declared themselves, irrevocably, republics. Those states that had not experienced revolution, like Britain, were republics in all but name. From this point on throughout the Atlantic, there was no going back.[4] Common sense, though—pun intended—seems to push against a neat and tidy chronology. So many subsequent events became realizations of or reactions to the age that they defy enumeration. Fixing endings gets tricky, trickier even than pronouncing a beginning date.

Just think of what appeared to be the most perfectly packaged revolution, America's. The cause of Revolution lived on even if revolution had ostensibly ended. In the United States, common men would use the invocation of the moment to parade in the streets and to push for their rights. They would also do so to justify filibustering in Latin America and the land grab of Texas and later much of northern Mexico. In the early republic, the idea of the American Revolution could be used to distinguish Americans from the rest of the world, to exclude some deemed to be inferior, and to conquer others.[5]

A good case can be made that the American Revolution concluded in 1865. Americans from the North and the South still used the same revolutionary ideas and events to define and articulate their aspirations. Both states' rights and the ideal of union were hoisted on the shoulders of the founding fathers; in fact, both sides fought to vindicate what they believed the founding vision had been, to achieve what was promised. The fraying of order, and the violence that ensued, reflected how the earlier revolution settlement both framed debate and proved, ultimately, unable to contain the tensions that had been simmering since. When Lincoln spoke of "four score and seven years ago" at Gettysburg, he was referring to 1776 in order to make sense of what he deemed to be "sacrifice" on the altar of the American Revolution.[6] The Civil War, of course, proved to be the crucible in which the rottenest aspect of the negotiations that went into bringing the Revolution to a close were rectified. Only violence could undo the settlement and fix it.[7] The American war to end slavery, the great engine and stain of Atlantic integration, initiated the final process to kill off an institution that contradicted the spirit of the age and that represented the last vestige—with the notable exceptions of the slave systems of Cuba and Brazil—of an old and vanquished world.[8] The United States would finally become a stable polity.

When all is said and done, for Americans at least, endings lay in the eye of the beholder. For Europe, the case proves more fraught. The age echoed beyond those places that had emerged from the crucible of revolution. In 1821, Greeks staged an uprising against the Ottoman Turks that would lead to independence, an event that would make manifest the new promethean power of nationalism. It also rode on the same mixture of hope, fear, and violence that marked what had happened throughout the Atlantic just years earlier. However far Greece lay from the Atlantic, participants considered the movement part of the age. "There are famous epochs which seem marked by Providence," like the times of Alexander and Caesar, a booster of Greek independence wrote in 1822. "Such, too, is our own."[9] Europe reeled from revolutionary "aftershocks" in the early 1830s, in risings and independence movements that stretched from Belgium and France in the West to Poland and Russia in the East. These paled in comparison to the earthquake that was 1848. The year alone conjures an image of the return of revolutionary hopes and fears. Lincoln saw the many risings as part of the "general cause of Republican liberty," a continuation of all that had happened half a century before. The revolutions of 1848 were attempts of some people to try to realize the true promise of the age, especially in the wake of conservative retrenchment that kept the furies in a cage.[10] These events served as vivid reminders that politicized people had to be recognized, and that the age had turned the idea of popular sovereignty into a reality that could not be undone. A mobilized citizenry could be yoked to the state, or co-opted, but it could never be ignored. This is exactly how Otto von Bismarck construed the moment. Under his watch, the resurrected forces of the age "continued to flow through the public life of the Prussian state, even if the channels that connected them to the political executive were narrow."[11] Instability would ever lurk if these forces were given short shrift. Moreover, the events of 1848 and how what happened in one place electrified others reminded all how imbricated the system remained even if the idea of the nation had become yoked to state power.

The year 1848, like America's Civil War, was unambiguously bound to the promise and missed opportunities of the era of revolution.[12] For this reason, it resonated far and wide. Those North Americans most vocal for seizing parts of South America, "Young America" as they called themselves, took inspiration from the headiness of 1848. They tied race and nation together in a toxic mix, but they took themselves to be part of a connected world of revolutionary ferment. Events and debates in Europe over 1848 reverberated in South America from Colombia to Chile. They sustained hopes of liberation and fears of the masses. All saw things through the lens of what had happened in the Atlantic a generation earlier. Brazilians, too, hailed 1848. It encouraged some to launch a regional uprising, even if the government put it down. Nonetheless, the government, at the same time, ended the state's involvement in the slave trade, particularly the smuggling that went hand in hand with it, bringing Brazil in line with the prevailing Atlantic vision of political economy.[13]

Karl Marx, too, saw 1848 as a continuation of what had begun earlier. Fittingly, it would be these events that so terrified and enthralled Europe that gave rise to his understanding of what revolution could and should do. Marx had grown up in a region of Germany that had been occupied by the French during the revolutionary years. The age formed his intellectual inheritance. Not coincidentally, Marx and Friedrich Engels drafted the *Communist Manifesto* in the very year of 1848. Marx saw the events that transfixed the world in the late eighteenth century as a model for revolution in the nineteenth.[14]

Maybe the "1848–1865 moment" would be the most appropriate term for a closing act. A few consciously drew the two codas together to try to recapture the age of revolution and help all realize what it had promised. One of American's Civil War heroes, the founder of the famed Irish Brigade, took his inspiration from 1848. Thomas Francis Meagher traveled to Paris to meet with self-styled revolutionaries, bringing back a tricolor to Ireland, and then launched an abortive rising against British power. Disavowing the constitutional means of Daniel O'Connell, this member of "Young Ireland" believed that only the sword of revolution could undo the tie to Britain. Indeed, we could style this abortive rebellion Britain's "1848 revolution." Meagher would then fight in America for much the same cause, employing Irish-born veterans of the wars of the revolution from Europe and Latin America. These Fenians believed that if the Union fell, the hopes of all republicans would be dashed. In seeing things this way, they drew a straight line from the American Revolution through the French Revolution, the United Irish Rising, and Latin American independence to 1848 and the American Civil War.[15]

These episodes and actors—from Marx to the American Civil War and all points in between—reminded everyone that endings were at best provisional and always plastic. The plight of the North Atlantic differed little from that of the South Atlantic in this regard. Those in Latin America may have wondered why it seemed North America had enjoyed stability and prosperity while they struggled with unresolved endings. The Civil War put paid to that assumption. Endings perplexed all.[16] The great rebinding was never perfect. Ends proved aspirational, even if states considered them definitive. Memorials may have tried to make a case for permanence and to canonize new origin myths, but the unresolved tensions of the age would come back to haunt or enthrall the heirs of revolution, especially in those places that had created states just efficacious enough to end revolution but not powerful enough to keep in check in perpetuity the tensions that stemmed from revolution.

The age continued to inspire and could occasion new instances of violence, liberation, and state formation. The great nineteenth-century nation-building experiments in Europe grew from the age. Italy and Germany became nations because of the inspiration of what had happened in the late eighteenth and early nineteenth centuries. They both emerged from "the will of the people."[17] The Brandenburg Gate thenceforth would become the most vivid symbol of Germanness.[18] Italians would create monuments to the idea of unification that drew inspiration directly from the age. Witness the neoclassical monument next to the forum, the shrine to unification and to the rule of Victor Immanuel II. It announced that Italy, too, was a nation born of a broader moment of change, and that it was the most vivid and direct link to the glories of Rome. Above the Vatican itself, on the Janiculum Hill, busts of the heroes of unification, tying Italy to the revolutions that remade Europe and the Atlantic, were erected.

The notion of the age reverberated well into the twentieth century and even the twenty-first, as the story of nation building and memorial building in Africa suggests. All the great anti-imperial movements in the twentieth century that freed India and much of Africa and Southeast Asia from European rule also owed allegiance to the age. All history thereafter deferred to the moment or seemed to emerge from it, as each nation was either born at the momentous conception or claimed it if born after. Mexicans would struggle with revolution in the nineteenth century, reflecting the bifurcated memory of the age. Some fought to realize what they now regarded as the vision of Hidalgo. In later years, he was turned into a modern freedom fighter, a Marxian champion for the rights of the oppressed. He featured in paintings as an artisan, a simple farmer, an intellectual, an insurgent, an incendiary, a freer of the enslaved, and heir to Mexico's deep pre-Spanish history.[19] For Mexicans, the idea of the age and the notion of rights at its heart proved expansive, able to amalgamate new ideas, like those of Marx, which themselves owed their all to the age. In places like Mexico and Argentina, where memory had been frayed from the very moment of national birth, it did not take much for the whole to unravel, and new concepts of the person, of society, and of governance—themselves born through reverberations of the age—could pull settlements apart.

Much of Latin America, then, faced a prolonged crisis because of how the age was understood. By the 1870s, the great hopes of the age, and the idea that Latin America represented the place where "republican modernity" could be most fully realized, were clearly dashed amid vying interpretations and the rise of an exploitative capitalism. In some places, distinctive and conflicting visions of Revolution sat side by side, almost just waiting to be reanimated by any new eventuality. Contradictory narratives, both rooted in the same period, made appeals to national ideals that much more powerful. Conflicted interpretations of the age would make for violent nineteenth and twentieth centuries.[20]

In other words, settlements could confound. State actors knew this. Monumentalization institutionalized memory, of course. It also institutionalized forgetfulness. Some things from the period could be dwelt upon; others could not. In France, concord and victory wiped away terror and religious conflict. In America, the founders effaced the tensions over slavery. In both places, memory focused imaginations and the idea of nation itself on certain key aspects at the expense of others, especially those that could fundamentally disrupt the state. In much of Latin America, if anything, too much was remembered. Bifurcated memorialization made for competing vanishing points and vying occlusions. Their permanent duel made for a chronic instability. In the case of France and of America, forgetfulness, in the short term, made for a collective "amnesia or denial" that allowed for the more problematic and traumatic to be shunted away and the process of nation building to go on. Yet, too much forgetfulness and "social forgetting," in particular—and this was certainly the case in Ireland and its persistent "Troubles"—created susceptibility to explosions and aftershocks.[21]

Maybe we are wrong even thinking in terms of echoes, epilogues, and aftershocks. Perhaps the age of revolution did not end at all. The French have, to be sure, argued over this very point. They still do. In 1989, the bicentennial of the fall of the Bastille, historians debated whether or not it had ended. François Furet, who had by this time fought on all sides of the battles over revisionism and Marxism, famously suggested that it had indeed finished by that time. He was probably wrong. Certainly if we gauge a thing by how often it is invoked, the Revolution is still alive and well.[22] Witness the 2021 firestorm set off by President Emmanuel Macron invoking Napoleon as "a part of us." One scholar, citing Napoleon's attempt to reinstitute slavery in Saint-Domingue, found it "particularly galling" that many in France still deferred to his national vision. Whatever perspective embraced, he—and by extension the Revolution—still matter.[23] Perhaps Haiti's revolution continues as well. After the Civil War in the United States and into the twentieth century, Black intellectuals in America still looked to it for inspiration. They also suggested that it had not been completed. In a still entangled world, Haiti still stood at the very center of the idea of an age, even if its revolution was still in the offing.[24]

A few other sets of memorials encourage us to conceive of endings—
or better, nonendings—in this light. Just consider the afterlives of two
people as deeply enmeshed as any in the origins and outcomes of the age,
two who were not considered nation builders worthy of memorialization
as the age seemed to come to an end. In the nineteenth century,
O'Connell's friend Frederick Douglass was not hailed as one of the ava-
tars of American nationhood. Of course, he famously took issue with the
national day of founding, the Fourth of July, because the Revolution was
premised on the exclusion of his people. He would not celebrate the date
until the injustice of slavery ended and the hypocrisy that went hand in
hand with it. He delivered his most pointed salvo in Rochester on a fifth
of July. "What to a slave," he thundered, "is the Fourth of July?" For him,
the American Revolution represented a "touchstone," but one that had
not achieved its potential. He was then a critic.[25]

Now? Douglass's statues adorn American cities. Two have been
erected in New York alone, including one in Central Park not far from
likenesses of the heroes of Latin American independence. You will find
monuments to Douglass in Baltimore and in Annapolis. Maryland, in fact,
seems to have cornered the market on memorials to him. The most famous statue stands in Rochester to commemorate his call for the nation to
realize the promise of the revolutionary era. It is the earliest piece to memorialize an African American in the United States. Thirteen more statues
went up to recognize the two hundredth anniversary of his birth, all to
help citizens remember how Douglass called all to live up to what the idea
of the age in the minds of most promised. This is how he is remembered.
In 2013, Joe Biden dedicated a statue of Douglass in the U.S. Capitol.
Here, in the same building in which hangs the famous painting by John
Trumbull of Jefferson handing over his draft of the Declaration, Biden declared that though "he was born in horrific circumstances sanctioned by
the laws passed in this very building," Douglass had no intention of "condemning the nation who made him a slave." Instead, he "embraced the
sustaining principles and used them as a sword to try to free others." He
struggled to make the nation live up to what the age demanded.[26]

The revolutionary period is now incomprehensible without him, so
much so that people from across the spectrum can count Douglass as a
founder of the nation. He was and is a radical who "loved" the Declaration
of Independence.[27] His story promotes a by now almost self-evident truth
that some of those excluded could employ the legitimacy of the age also to
press for inclusion. Most notably, African Americans would use the ideals

Statue of Frederick Douglass in the United States
Capitol Visitor Center, Washington, D.C., United
States. Image from UPI/Alamy Stock Photo.

of 1776 to make the case that they too deserved rights, that even the most
iniquitous holdovers of the age could and should be rectified because the
logic of the age dictated as much. Frederick Douglass, who would go on to
become ambassador to Haiti once it was recognized by the United States,
hailed "the black sons of Haiti" who had "struck for freedom" during the
age. The self-styled "black O'Connell" saw the nineteenth century as the
playing out of themes that had begun in the eighteenth century. He was
prophetic. Now nearly all Americans subscribe to his vision.[28]

A similar fate awaited Mary Wollstonecraft. She earned a blue plaque
on Dolben Street in the Borough of Southwark in London in 2004. Finally
in 2020 she was recognized with a sculpture erected on Newington Green

in London, right near where she lived, wrote, and attended church. Not a statue per se, the monument tries to capture in shimmering silver what she represents for women today. The long emergence through struggle to a place of standing and equality in society is epitomized by the small nude figure atop "a Milton flank of silvered bronze." On it, the viewer reads a quotation from her seminal work *A Vindication for the Rights of Woman*: "I do not wish women to have power over men; but over themselves." The campaign to erect a statue, Mary on the Green, was organized around the ideas of diversity, equity, and inclusion, ideas that speak to many today but that are also rooted in the age of revolution. The sculpture has, rather famously, generated all sorts of controversy. At issue is the statue of a nude to represent all women. As a writer for the *Guardian* put it, would the same fate befall a man's statue? Nonetheless, what was not controversial was placing a monument to one of the heroes of the revolutionary Atlantic on the Green. Wollstonecraft, too, is considered a central character in the British national story, a story inconceivable without invoking the age and all it promised. Like Douglass, Wollstonecraft now is seen as a figure who presaged the more complete fulfillment of revolutionary promises, one that was only achieved though time and great effort.[29] As with Douglass, we cannot invoke the age of revolution and what it meant without including her, even if women were written out of political life with the initial national settlements.

The two, then, represented peoples explicitly excluded or only imperfectly included. Now they have also become symbols of nation and of its evolving ties to the age of revolution. In this way, for both Americans and Britons, but more fully for many elsewhere, the age is premised on the idea of becoming and redemption. These ideas have, in fact, become inscribed in the very concept of the age, and they now underscore the national narrative of so many places. The national vanishing points excluded in the past. Now they have finally been enlarged to bring into the fold those who had been on the outside looking in. This myth of expansive rights now is as powerful as the ones reified in stone and metal at the beginning of the nineteenth century.[30]

Maybe Paine was right after all. The age did and still does revolve around ideas. Perhaps we should denominate it with a capital "A" to distinguish this usage from simply employing the word to describe a period that most somehow thought of as connected. The Age reverberated for a long period, and it continues to do so because the Age became the vanishing point for all nations of the Atlantic. The Age created aspirations, and these ideas promised a new world. They were rooted in the progressive

*A Sculpture for Mary Wollstonecraft* in Newington
Green, London, United Kingdom. Image from
marc zakian/Alamy Stock Photo.

vision of history that posited that things could be improved only if people
had more freedom. Beguilingly, Paine's Revolution—and here the term
suggests a program for progressive change—seemed to represent a leap
forward in the development of our more liberal, tolerant world. It still
does. We live with the illusions of unending, that because 1776 or 1789 or
1810—pick your totemic date—ushered in a new Age, a time "to begin
the world anew," freedom always just lay around the corner. The moment
of birth was not so much ended as unfulfilled. The quest for fulfillment
echoes down from the age—and from the Age—to us today.

Burke still argues otherwise. He stays squarely with the lowercase "a" age, the use of the word that focuses on connection in the past and one that had to end for order. It centers on revolution as process. The process of revolution suggests a different sort of narrative to Paine's Age. States limit rights, even if they gain their legitimacy from them, to ensure that citizens are not thrust back into the crucible of violence. While governments had to be of the people, by the people, and for the people, they also had to do all in their power to protect the new equilibrium, the integrity of the system, and manage the many tensions that still remained in each respective society. States were and are all remarkably distinct, but the realities that states faced were and are remarkably alike. When order breaks down, no one enjoys rights. Fear dominates. Even if the state could instantiate the illusion of unending, especially through the invocation and reinvocation of the Age as foundational moment, the state had to ensure the age did come to an end. The Atlantic needed and still needs stable sovereignty and equilibrium.

Edmund Burke, then, serves as the fitting counterpoise to Thomas Paine. Like Paine, he uttered some uncomfortable truths. He focused on institutions and on traditions, of the role they played in maintaining balance in society. Take what restrains away, and you open Pandora's boxes. But, and this gets us back to Paine, place people in oppressive boxes, and they will awaken. Order cannot be fetishized as an end unto itself. Such a solution to the challenges of politicization inevitably leads to the diminishment of human dignity. The collective must leave space for the individual to flourish. Just as the individual must, from time to time, sacrifice some rights for the stability of the whole and the integrity of the common fabric. Paine and Burke, then, must be held in tension, just as the Age of Revolution must never end and the age of revolution had to end.

Fittingly, it was the great nineteenth-century student of Atlantic revolutions who appreciated that the age could only be understood if Paine was tied to Burke. Alexis de Tocqueville believed that the future lay with democracy. He also conceded that societies needed some semblance of order rooted in the past. Democracy demanded both rights and sovereignty that worked. Tocqueville had seen revolutionary hopes in America when he toured there in the early 1830s. He also had learned about revolutionary fears from his parents, who had suffered a great deal during the Terror. The same man who lauded the nature of democracy in America cautioned about what had happened to France after its revolution. He shared Paine's enthusiasm and Burke's concerns. Ties had to bind, but they could not chafe.[31]

On this point, Tocqueville proved prophetic. Because nations knit or re-knit themselves around one moment, it is unsurprising that two connected and dueling characters like Paine and Burke would themselves take on iconic meaning for us. They are two sides of the same coin, both indispensable even to this day. Indeed, the more we fight over them, invoke them as civic saints, and champion the different visions they seem to represent, the more we bind ourselves to the Age and the evolving bargains that ever go into bringing it to an end. Through Burke and Paine we continue to reenact the completion of an age that never has really closed. By tethering our different interpretations about citizenship and nationhood to it, we reconsecrate it. The very quest for endings, then, ties us together as people of the Age and as inheritors of the age.

To close, let's view one last memorial. One other monument was erected to the glory of Wellington. Right behind Apsley House stands a large statue of a naked Achilles, one whose graphic anatomical detail shocked Londoners at the time it went up. More scandalous still was the fact was that it was erected by Wellington's "countrywomen," as it says on the plinth. All of this matters a great deal less than what the statue was made of. It was made of the weapons of war. It was produced of French cannon melted down, in fact twelve four-and-twenty pounders leavened with other metal to make the material more pliable.[32] So too, fittingly, were the bronze reliefs attached to the base of Nelson's Column in London.

There was nothing unusual, of course, in tying together monuments and armaments. The New Yorkers in 1776 had done much the same. But whereas they tore down a monument, sustaining an old myth of sovereignty, to produce the bullets to destroy an ancien régime, the Wellington Monument and Nelson's reliefs used the weapons of destruction to create a new myth.

Today, these moments, and the statues, are almost lost in time. In New York where the statue of George III once stood tourists rush by with cellphone cameras to see the Raging Bull and nearby Defiant Girl, both potent symbols of our time. In Hyde Park, the Achilles is little more than a curiosity of some bygone war, something passed by tourist and Londoner alike out on a stroll to and from places like Harrods or Piccadilly Circus. Yet, the world the age created has stood the test of time. The Age has proven remarkably durable and produced a powerful and still entangled international system and resilient national settlements. Its mythic invocation also ensures that the violence of the eigh-

The Achilles statue in Hyde Park, London, United Kingdom. Image from chrisdorney/Shutterstock.com.

teenth century does not come back to haunt the world. Its symbols are so omnipresent as to be almost imperceptible.

And that is just the point. Whether they realize it or not, all in today's Atlantic, and most around the world, still take their meaning from the Age, every bit as much as those who created monuments in the nineteenth century to end the age. When we push to enjoy the full promise of the Age, we are pressing to see just how elastic its limits really are. Sometimes the process is consensual, sometimes combative. At times, it can revolve around pleas to tear down the very statues and symbols that the era of revolution bequeathed us. Nonetheless, through such acts, even acts of ostensibly refuting the darker aspects of the age, we reinforce the central status of the Age in national life and strengthen its hold over us, just as we consecrate the idea that its understandings of liberty and of order can and do evolve.[33] The age may have come to a close, as Burke would have demanded, but its implications live on, as Paine foresaw. The settlement managed, despite Marx's predictions, to make it past the era of industrialization. It has lived through the great tests of two world wars, as well as a Cold War. It's a good bet the Age will survive our day, too. It still ties us together.

# Notes

## Prologue

1. Alexander J. Wall, *The Equestrian Statue of George III and the Pedestrian Statue of William Pitt Erected in the City of New York, 1770* (New York, 1920), 52; *New York Gazette*, 30 June 1766; John Adams to L. H. Butterfield, *Diary and Autobiography of John Adams*, vol. 2 (Cambridge, 1961), 103; *The Journal of Lieutenant Isaac Bangs, 1 April to 29 July 1776* (Cambridge, 1890), 57; *Maryland Journal and the Baltimore Advertiser*, 17 July 1776. On the toppling, see Patrick Griffin, *America's Revolution* (New York, 2012), 137–38; and Brendan McConville, *The King's Three Faces: The Rise and Fall of Royal America, 1688–1776* (Chapel Hill, 2007), 309–11.
2. On the many complexities of iconoclasm, see Wendy Bellion, *Iconoclasm in New York: Revolution to Reenactment* (Philadelphia, 2019).

## Introduction

1. *Temple of Reason*, 15 November 1800; John Adams to James Lloyd, 29 March 1815, in *The Works of John Adams*, ed. Charles Francis Adams, 10 vols. (Boston, 1850–56), vol. 10, 149. I am indebted to José Gleeson and David Armitage for bringing these quotes to my attention.
2. Jean-Jacques Rousseau quoted in David Armitage and Sanjay Subrahmanyam, "Introduction," in *The Age of Revolutions in Global Context, c. 1760–1840* (Basingstoke, 2010), xiii; Voltaire quoted in Keith Baker, *Inventing the French Revolution: Essays on French Political Culture in the Eighteenth Century* (Cambridge, 1990), 203; Thomas Jefferson quoted in Sarah Knott, "Narrating the Age of Revolution," *William and Mary Quarterly*, 73, no. 1 (2016), 4; Lyman Beecher, "Something has been done, during the last forty years," *Christian Pamphlets*, vol. 4 (S.I., 1800–1844), 6.

3. Thomas Paine, *The Rights of Man* (New York, 1995), 162. Paine has had commentators who argue that his vision was never fully realized. See, most notably, Jonathan Israel, *The Expanding Blaze: How the American Revolution Ignited the World* (Princeton, 2017). Paine has also had his detractors. For this take, see J. C. D. Clark, *Thomas Paine: Britain, America, and France in the Age of Enlightenment and Revolution* (New York, 2018). Perhaps, another suggests, the prevailing interpretation of Paine misconstrues how he changed his views over the course of the French Revolution; some think he was repulsed by the violence and developed a more nuanced interpretation of the period. See Adam Lebovitz, "An Unknown Manuscript on the Terror, Attributed to Thomas Paine," *William and Mary Quarterly*, 3rd ser., 75 (2018), 685–714.

4. For a look at such metaphors, and the limitation of using them to establish connections, see J. C. D. Clark, "How Did the American Revolution Relate to the French? Richard Price, the Age of Revolutions, and the Enlightenment," *Modern Intellectual History*, 19 (2020), 105–27. For an explanation of how naturalistic metaphors were employed to make sense of revolution, see Mary Ashburn Miller, *A Natural History of Revolution: Violence and Nature in the French Revolutionary Imagination, 1789–1794* (Ithaca, 2011).

5. For this formulation, see C. A. Bayly, *The Birth of the Modern World, 1780–1914* (London, 2003); and Anne Sa'adah, *The Shaping of Liberal Politics in Revolutionary France* (Princeton, 1990), 21. On how France led the way, see Ferenc Feher, ed., *The French Revolution and the Birth of Modernity* (Berkeley, 1990). For just a partial list of what this age achieved and what "modernity" can mean, see Michael Levin, *Political Thought in the Age of Revolution, 1776–1848: Burke to Marx* (London, 2010), 13–16. On the idea that democracy was created by actors during this period, see James Livesey, *Making Democracy in the French Revolution* (Cambridge, MA, 2001). For how Latin America also shared in this modern moment, in opposition to what he regarded as traditional, see Francois-Xavier Guerra, *Modernidad e independencias: Ensayos sobre las revoluciónes hispanicas* (Madrid, 1992).

6. An excellent biographical study that says we must incorporate Latin America to make sense of the age is John Lynch, *Simón Bolívar: A Life* (New Haven, 2006), 30. He is writing against Eric Hobsbawm's contention that the dual transformation of the age was the French Revolution and the industrial revolution in Britain, See Eric Hobsbawm, *The Age of Revolution, 1789–1848* (New York, 1962). For a view that rejects the wave or sequence model (or, better, complicates it), see Roberto Breña, "The Cadiz Liberal Revolution and Spanish American Independence," in John Tutino, ed., *New Countries: Capitalism, Revolutions, and Nations in the Americas, 1750–1870* (Durham, NC, 2016), 98.

7. Kate Fullagar and Michael McDonnell, "Introduction: Empire, Indigeneity, and Revolution," in *Facing Empire: Indigenous Experiences in a Revolutionary Age* (Baltimore, 2018), 4; Sujit Sivasundaram, *Waves across the South: A New History of Revolution and Empire* (Chicago, 2020).

8. For an interpretation that stresses the ugly aspects, and even the birth of "a racist world order" that emerged from the age, see Kehinde Andrews, *The New Age of Empire: How Racism and Colonialism Still Rule the World* (New York, 2021). The more sobering side is also covered by Sarah Knott, "Narrating the Age of Revolution," *William and Mary Quarterly*, 3rd ser., 73 (2016), 3–36.

9. Seamus Deane, "Down on the Plantation," *Dublin Review of Books* (2019). For a view of Burke as a critic of imperial hubris, see Luke Gibbons, *Edmund Burke and Ireland: Aesthetics, Politics and the Colonial Sublime* (Cambridge, 2003); and, most important, Richard Bourke, *Empire and Revolution: The Political Life of Edmund Burke* (Princeton, 2015). For a brief and perceptive account of how and why Paine's and Burke's visions are diametrically opposed, see Thomas Sowell, *A Conflict of Visions: Ideological Origins of Political Struggles* (New York, 2007), 21.

10. See, for instance, R. R. Palmer in his classic two-volume study of the idea of democracy entitled *The Age of Democratic Revolution* (Princeton, 1969–70). An updated version pursuing the same sorts of these would be James Kloppenberg, *Toward Democracy: The Struggle for Self-Rule in European and American Thought* (New York, 2016). For the global, the best statement is Armitage and Subrahmanyam, "Introduction," in *The Age of Revolutions in Global Context*. On the bringing together of global and Atlantic, and why the Atlantic should be privileged as a context, see Trevor Burnard, *The Atlantic in World History, 1490–1830* (London, 2020), 119, 298–99. For a hemispheric study, see Lester Langley, *The Americas in the Age of Revolution, 1750–1850* (New Haven, 1996); and Caitlin Fitz, *Our Sister Republics: The United States in the Age of American Revolutions* (New York, 2017). Then there is the comparative, of which there is a great deal. Among the best is Patrice Higgonet's, which focuses on republicanism as an idea tying together the American and French Revolutions. See *Sister Republics: The Origins of French and American Republicanism* (Cambridge, MA, 1988). A pioneering tour de force in this regard would be J. Godechot and R. R. Palmer, "Le problème de l'Atlantique du XVIIIeme au XIXeme siècle," *Storia contemporanea: Relazioni del X Congresso internazionale di scienze storiche*, 5 (Florence, 1955), 175–239. For an estimation of how this work shaped the ways we think of the revolutionary age, refer to Philippe Bourdin and Jean-Luc Chappey, *Révoltes et révolutions en Europe et aux Ameriques (1773–1802)* (Paris, 2004), 1–12. For a detailed discussion of the stormy reception it engendered at the time, see Bernard Bailyn, *Atlantic History: Concept and Contours* (Cambridge, MA, 2005), 24–30. On how Latin America does and does not fit the model, see Roberto Breña, *El primer liberalismo español y los procesos de emancipación de America, 1808–1824* (Mexico City, 2006), 177–87. Breña has his doubts, but this book tries to address them.

11. See Edward Gray, *Tom Paine's Iron Bridge: Building a United States* (New York, 2016) for the details of their friendship, and for their falling out. For the quote see p. 128.

12. Edmund Burke to French Laurence, 18 August 1788, in Thomas Copeland, ed., *The Correspondence of Edmund Burke* (Chicago, 1958), vol. 5, 412. The best work on their connections is Thomas Copeland, *Edmund Burke: Six Essays* (New York, 1950), 146–89; and Kloppenberg, *Toward Democracy*, 506–9.

13. *Rights of Man*, 88; Burke to the Sheriffs of Bristol, 3 April 1777, in Warren Elofson et al., eds., *The Writings and Speeches of Edmund Burke* (Oxford, 1996), vol. 3, 305; Armin Mattes, *Citizens of a Common Intellectual Homeland: The Transatlantic Origins of American Democracy and Nationhood* (Charlottesville, VA, 2015), 21.

14. Edmund Burke to Earl Fitzwilliam, 4 August 1791, in Copeland, ed., *The Correspondence of Edmund Burke*, vol. 6, 312–13.

15. For a model of this world of ideas, see Clement Thibaud, "Pour une histoire polycentrique des republicanismes atlantiques (années 1770–années 1880)," *Revue d'histoire du XIXe siècle*, 56 (2018), 151–70.

16. For the best statement on doing this sort of history, see Michael Werner and Bénédicte Zimmerman, "Beyond Comparison: Histoire Croisée and the Challenge of Reflexivity," *History and Theory*, 45 (2006), 30–50; and Thibaud, "Pour une histoire polycentrique des republicanismes atlantiques," 159. For a look at how imperial history can help with such an approach, see Paul Kramer, "Power and Connection: Imperial Histories of the United States in the World," *American Historical Review*, 116 (2011), 1348–91. A good recent example of such a connected history examines how the links between social movements in one place inspired radicalism in other places. See Micah Alpaugh, *Friends of Freedom: The Rise of Social Movements in the Age of Atlantic Revolutions* (New York, 2022).

17. On this idea, see Josep Fradera, *The Imperial Nation: Citizens and Subjects in the British, French, Spanish, and American Empires* (Princeton, 2018). This book makes great use of the idea of connection, tying, and binding. For the use of these in metaphor, see Ralph Metzner, "Knots, Ties, Nets, and Bonds in Relationships," *Journal of Transpersonal Psychology*, 17 (1985), 41–45.

18. On connective and contextual, see Nathan Perl-Rosenthal, "Atlantic Cultures and the Age of Revolution," *William and Mary Quarterly*, 3rd ser., 74 (2017), 667–96. For a similar take on how men and women lived in a connected Atlantic and had to confront diseases in ways that compromised plans and shaped what they could hope to do, see J. R. McNeill, *Mosquito Empires: Ecology and War in the Greater Caribbean, 1620–1914* (Cambridge, 2012).

19. Think here of the famous link between international war and revolutionary crisis, which is covered in Theda Skocpol, *States and Social Revolution: A Comparative Analysis of France, Russia, and China* (New York, 2015).

20. Heinrich Greeven, "The Gospel Synopsis from 1776 to the Present Day" (translated by Robert Althann), in Bernard Orchard and Thomas Longstaff, eds., *J. J. Griesbach: Synoptic and Text-Critical Studies, 1776–1976* (Cambridge, 1976), 23.

21. For a similar approach to seeing things this way, see the remarks by Clement Thibaud, Manuel Covo, and Jack Rakove (chaired by Bertrand Van Ruymbeke) in a roundtable entitled "Les indépendances dans l'espace atlantique, v. 1763–v. 1829," *Annales historiques de la Révolution française*, 384 (2016), 167–98.

22. A terrific taste of primary sources for the period, and an Atlantic interpretation that accords with this one, can be found in Rafe Blaufarb, *The Revolutionary Atlantic: Republican Vision, 1760–1830: A Documentary History* (New York, 2018).

23. On the pitfalls and the possibilities of doing this sort of history, see the essay by Thibaud, "Pour une histoire polycentrique des republicanismes atlantiques," 151–70. For a thoughtful discussion of these tensions, I am indebted to Roberto Breña, "The Cadiz Liberal Revolution and Spanish American Independence," in John Tutino, ed., *New Countries: Capitalism, Revolutions, and Nations in the Americas, 1750–1870* (Durham, NC, 2016), 93–98.

24. Moreover, what could be called "intertwinements" did not just involve space. "Linked processes" also involved men and women in new connections with local, national, and imperial regimes and the systems each tried to manage. On this, see Cyrus Schayegh, "Transpatialization: A New Heuristic Model to Think about Modern Cities," at https://globalurbanhistory.com/2017/12/14/transpatialization-a-new-heuristic-model-to-think-about-modern-cities, 17 December 2017, for a breakdown of the idea he fleshes out in *The Middle East and the Making of the Modern World* (Cambridge, MA, 2017).

25. Jürgen Kocka, "Comparison and Beyond," *History and Theory*, 42 (2003), 44.

26. On the idea of equilibrium and sovereignty, and the resulting crisis that led to the transition from empires to nations, see Jeremy Adelman, "An Age of Imperial Revolutions," *American Historical Review*, 113 (2008), 319–40. In making this case, I am not alone; in fact, across fields usually cordoned off from one another we see an exciting conjuncture on just these points. For those doing so in quite innovative ways, some lately and others some time ago, which have proven the most helpful in thinking through the problems this book grapples with, see Jeremy Adelman, *Sovereignty and Revolution in the Iberian Atlantic* (Princeton, 2006); Wim Klooster, *Revolutions in the Atlantic World: A Comparative History* (New York, 2018); William Doyle, *The Oxford History of the French Revolution* (New York, 2018); Colin Jones, *The Great Nation: France from Louis XV to Napoleon* (New York, 2003); Anthony McFarlane, *War and Independence in Spanish America* (New York, 2013); and John Lynch, *The Spanish American Revolutions, 1808–1826* (New York, 1986). Such a focus has defined the way scholars see the American Revolution of late. See especially T. H. Breen, *The Will of the People: The Revolutionary Birth of America* (Cambridge, MA, 2019); Alan Taylor, *American Revolutions: A Continental History* (New York, 2016); and Patrick Griffin, *America's Revolution* (New York, 2012). The best statement on the possibilities of seeing Atlantic development and revolution across empires this way is Bailyn, *Atlantic History*.

27. For an in-depth study of this question, see Anna Vincenzi, "Imagining an Age of Revolutions? Interpretations of the American Revolution in the Italian States (1765–1799)" (Ph.D. diss., University of Notre Dame, 2020).

28. On the puzzle of how to define the age, see Michael McDonnell, "Introduction," in McDonnell, ed., *Rethinking the Age of Revolution*, 1.

29. Crane Brinton, *The Anatomy of Revolution* (New York, 1938), 3, 259. A more up-to-date take on how revolutions as processes work would be Jack Goldstone, *Revolutions: A Very Short Introduction* (New York, 2014). On how the definition is changing for France, see Silvia Marzagalli, "Economic and Demographic Developments," in David Andress, ed., *The Oxford Handbook of the French Revolution* (New York, 2019), 5. On the revolution/Revolution distinction, see Keith Baker, "Revolutionizing Revolution," in Keith M. Baker and Dan Edelstein, eds., *Scripting Revolution: A Historical Approach to the Comparative Study of Revolutions* (Stanford, 2015), 71–102; and David Bell, "Global Conceptual Legacies," in Andress, ed., *The Oxford Handbook of the French Revolution*, 653–58.

30. This phrase belongs to Eammon Duffy. See "Rites of Passage," in *Times Literary Supplement*, 10 February 2017. On how American networks inspired French versions, see Alpaugh, *Friends of Freedom*.

31. One other reason we keep coming back to the age: most would agree or suggest, though they might not employ the terms, that this moment was what one scholar called a "sattelzeit," a saddle period or middle time, in which so many of our categories of belonging, understandings of the person, and ideas about governance came into being. On this, see Jürgen Osterhammel, *The Transformation of the World: A Global History of the Nineteenth Century* (Princeton, 2014), 58. For ideas, see the classic by J. G. A. Pocock, *The Machiavellian Moment: Florentine Political Thought and the Atlantic Republican Tradition* (Princeton, 1975); and the recent book by Israel, *The Expanding Blaze*. This "critical juncture" witnessed a crisis to one part of a global system, as well as a way of conceiving of power and territory, and a transition that would give rise to new organizing principles for space and for authority. See Matthias Middell and Katja Naumann, "Global History and the Spatial Turn: From the Impact of Area Studies to the Study of Critical Junctures of Globalization," *Journal of Global History*, 5 (2010), 162–70.

## Chapter One. A Tangled World

1. Daniel Defoe, *Robinson Crusoe* (Oxford, 2007), 5; Jonathan Swift, *Gulliver's Travels* (Oxford, 2005), 71, 15. On the particular ways travel literature holds a mirror up to society, see Daniel Carey, "Swift, Gulliver, and Travel Satire," in *the Oxford Handbook of Eighteenth-Century Satire*, ed. Paddy Bullard (Oxford, 2019). I am indebted to Professor Carey for showing me an early version of this essay. For Defoe and the sea, see Jamie Bolker, "Lost at Sea:

*Robinson Crusoe* and the Art of Navigation," *Eighteenth-Century Studies* (2020), 589–606. On comparisons of the two works, see John Mullan, "Swift, Defoe, and Narrative Forms," in *The Cambridge Companion to English Literature, 1650–1740*, ed. Steven N. Zwicker (Cambridge, 2004), 250–75. My thanks to Chris Fox for this reference.

2. Swift, *Gulliver's Travels*, 47, 17; Christopher Fox, "Introduction: Biographical and Historical Contexts," in *Gulliver's Travels: Complete, Authoritative Text with Biographical and Historical Contexts, Critical History, and Essays from Five Contemporary Critical Perspectives*, ed. Christopher Fox (Boston, 1995), 7.

3. My reading of these is indebted to Daniel Carey, "Reading Contrapuntally: Robinson Crusoe, Slavery, and Postcolonial Theory," in Daniel Carey and Lynn M. Festa, eds., *Postcolonial Enlightenment: Eighteenth-Century Colonialisms and Postcolonial Theory* (Oxford, 2009), 105–36.

4. Olaudah Equiano, *The Interesting Narrative of the Life of Olaudah Equiano*, ed. Robert Allison (Boston, 1995), 53, 197.

5. For the lure of the sea in the eighteenth century, see Stephen Taylor, *The Common Seaman in the Heroic Age of Sail* (New Haven, 2020). For an account that balances the romance with the terror of the sea, see James Lundberg's review of the book in *Wooden Boat Magazine*, 280 (2021).

6. Equiano, *Life of Olaudah Equiano*, 204–5, 94.

7. Equiano, *Life of Olaudah Equiano*, 99.

8. Changes to the space were "lodged in an economic and a social context which gave them significantly greater cumulative force for change than was the case in . . . the rest of the world." See C. A. Bayly, *The Birth of the Modern World, 1780–1914* (London, 2003), 59, 62, 243; A. G. Hopkins calls this process in this period "proto-globalization" in *American Empire: A Global History* (Princeton, 2018), 34.

9. See Philip J. Stern and Carl Wennerlind, "Introduction," in Philip J. Stern and Carl Wennerlind, eds., *Mercantilism Reimagined: Political Economy in Early Modern Britain and Its Empire* (New York, 2014), 3–24.

10. Anthony Pagden, *Lords of All the World: Ideologies of Empire in Spain, Britain and France c. 1500–c. 1800* (New Haven, 1998); Bernard Bailyn, *Atlantic History: Concepts and Contours* (Cambridge, 2005), 51; Edwin Williamson, *The Penguin History of Latin America* (London, 1992), 92–93, 96.

11. Lauren Benton, *A Search for Sovereignty: Law and Geography in European Empires, 1400–1990* (New York, 2009); Williamson, *Penguin History of Latin America*, 164–65.

12. Williamson, *Penguin History of Latin America*, 179; Kenneth J. Banks, *Chasing Empire across the Sea: Communications and the State in the French Atlantic, 1713–1763* (Montreal, 2002), 27–28. On imperial grandeur, see Jack Greene, *Evaluating Empire and Confronting Colonialism in Eighteenth-Century Britain* (New York, 2013), 84–119.

13. Peter Coclanis, "Atlantic World or Atlantic/World?" *William and Mary Quarterly*, 3rd ser., 63 (2006), 725–42.

14. On Spain, see Kenneth Andrien, "The Spanish Atlantic," in Jack P. Greene and Philip D. Morgan, eds., *Atlantic History: A Critical Appraisal* (Oxford, 2009), 55–57.

15. Ian K. Steele, *The English Atlantic, 1675–1740: An Exploration of Communication and Community* (New York, 1986); Banks, *Chasing Empire*, 32–42.

16. Zara Anishanslin, *Portrait of a Woman in Silk: Hidden Histories of the British Atlantic World* (New Haven, 2016), 13.

17. Andrien, "Spanish Atlantic," in Greene and Morgan, eds., *Atlantic History*, 62–66.

18. Peter Wood, *Black Majority: Negroes in Colonial South Carolina from 1670 through the Stono Rebellion* (New York, 1996).

19. T. M. Devine, *The Tobacco Lords: A Study of the Tobacco Merchants of Glasgow and Their Trading Activities* (Edinburgh, 1975); Silvia Marzagalli, "The French Atlantic World in the Seventeenth and Eighteenth Centuries," in Nicholas P. Canny and Philip D. Morgan *The Oxford Handbook of the Atlantic World, c. 1450-c.1850* (New York, 2013), 244–50; Colin Jones, *The Great Nation: France from Louis XV to Napoleon 1715–99* (New York, 2002), 355; Banks, *Chasing Empire*, 32–37. On the percentages, see Paul Cheney, *Cul de Sac: Patrimony, Capitalism, and Slavery in French Saint-Domingue* (Chicago, 2017), 1; Laurent Dubois and John Garrigus, *Slave Revolution in the Caribbean, 1789–1804: A Brief History with Documents* (New York, 2006), 8; Laurent Dubois, *Avengers of the New World: The Story of the Haitian Revolution* (Cambridge, MA, 2004), 18–21; Jeremy Popkin, *A New World Begins: The History of the French Revolution* (New York, 2019), 3. For an interesting study of how Atlantic history has and has not been applied to France, see Alain Cabantous, "Résistance de principe ou lucidité intellectuelle? Les historiens et l'histoire atlantique," *Revue historique*, 663 (2012), 705–26.

20. Carolyn Fick, "From Slave Colony to Black Nation: Haiti's Revolutionary Inversion," in Tutino, ed., *New Countries*; Ferrer, *Freedom's Mirror*, 1.

21. Cecile Vidal, *Caribbean New Orleans: Empire, Race, and the Making of a Slave Society* (Chapel Hill), 6–9, 14, 44–46.

22. Trevor Burnard, *Planters, Merchants, and Slaves: Plantation Societies in British America, 1650–1820* (Chicago, 2015), 7.

23. Trevor Burnard and John Garrigus, *The Plantation Machine: Atlantic Capitalism in French Saint-Domingue and British Jamaica* (Philadelphia, 2016), 4; Williamson, *Penguin History of Latin America*, 172–77, 184–85; Kirsten Schultz, "Atlantic Transformations and Brazil's Independence," in Tutino, ed., *New Countries*, 204–5; Gabriel B. Paquette, *The European Seaborne Empires: From the Thirty Years' War to the Age of Revolutions* (New Haven, 2019), 86–87.

24. Walter Hawthorne, *From Africa to Brazil: Culture, Identity, and an Atlantic Slave Trade, 1600–1830* (New York, 2010), 6. On the massive growth in numbers to Bahia, see Alexandre Vieira Ribeiro, "The Transatlantic Slave Trade to Bahia," in David Eltis and David Richardson, eds., *Extending the Frontiers: Essays on the New Transatlantic Slave Trade Database* (New Haven, 2008), 133–35.

25. Cheney, *Cul de Sac*, 1–2, 6.

26. For what the trade did to Africa, see Cécile Fromont, *The Art of Conversion: Christian Visual Culture in the Kingdom of Kongo* (Chapel Hill, 2014). Also see Hawthorne, *From Africa to Brazil*, 208–47; and Joseph C. Miller, "The Dynamics of History in Africa and the Atlantic 'Age of Revolutions,'" in David Armitage and Sanjay Subrahmanyam, eds., *The Age of Revolutions in Global Context, c. 1760–1840* (New York, 2010), 101–24.

27. John Thornton, *Africa and Africans in the Making of the Atlantic World, 1400–1800* (Cambridge, 1992), 304–10; James Searing, *West African Slavery and Atlantic Commerce* (Cambridge, 1993), 63–74.

28. This calculation drove the period, according to Charles Maier, in *Leviathan 2.0: Inventing Modern Statehood* (Cambridge, 2014); and Bernard Bailyn, *The Peopling of British North America: An Introduction* (New York, 1988).

29. John Lynch, *The Spanish American Revolutions, 1808–1826* (New York, 1986), 16; Jaime Rodríguez O., *The Independence of Spanish America* (New York, 1998), 11, 35; Brian Hamnett, *The End of Iberian Rule on the American Continent, 1770–1830* (New York, 2017), 138. On the economic and cultural development of Greater Pennsylvania and Philadelphia, see James Lemon, *The Best Poor Man's Country: A Geographical Study of Early Southeastern Pennsylvania* (New York, 1976); and Sally Schwartz, *"A Mixed Multitude": The Struggle for Toleration in Colonial Pennsylvania* (New York, 1989).

30. For one such fascinating portrait of this, see Anishanslin, *Portrait of a Woman in Silk.*

31. T. H. Breen, *Marketplace of Revolution: How Consumer Politics Shaped American Independence* (New York, 2004); Lauren Klay, "The Bourgeoisie, Capitalism, and the Origins of the French Revolution," in David Andress, ed., *The Oxford Handbook of the French Revolution* (New York, 2015), 27.

32. Rodríguez O., *Independence of Spanish America*, 36.

33. Christopher M. Clark, *Iron Kingdom: The Rise and Downfall of Prussia* (Cambridge, 2006), 224. One of the most concise and insightful excavations of the overlapping and "polycentric" nature of the Atlantic can be found in Bailyn, *Atlantic History*, 84–85.

34. Michael Kwass, "The Global Underground: Smuggling, Rebellion, and the Origins of the French Revolution," in Suzanne Desan, Lynn Hunt, and William Max Nelson, eds., *The French Revolution in Global Perspective* (Ithaca, 2013), 15–31; Banks, *Chasing Empire*, 31, 39; John Shovlin, *The Political Economy of Virtue: Luxury, Patriotism, and the Origins of the French Revolution* (Ithaca, 2006), 15. Also see Paul Cheney, *Revolutionary Commerce: Globalization and the French Monarchy* (Cambridge, 2010), 22, 26–28. I am indebted to Paul Hanson for bringing this to my attention at a roundtable discussion at Notre Dame on 4 May 2017.

35. Vidal, *Caribbean New Orleans*, 70.

36. Jeremy Adelman, *Sovereignty and Revolution in the Iberian Atlantic* (Princeton, 2006), 21. Jones, *The Great Nation*, 345, 361–62.

37. John Tutino, "Introduction," in Tutino, ed., *New Countries*.
38. D. W. Jones, *War and Economy in the Age of William III and Marlborough* (Oxford, 1998). I thank Joanna Innes for this reference. Also see Schultz, "Atlantic Transformations," in Tutino, ed., *New Countries*, 204–5. On smuggling and precious metals, see Bailyn, *Atlantic History*, 88.
39. Wim Klooster, *Revolutions in the Atlantic World: A Comparative History* (New York, 2018), 122; Eliga Gould, "Entangled Histories, Entangled World: The English-Speaking Atlantic as a Spanish Periphery," *American Historical Review*, 112 (2007), 764–86; Williamson, *Penguin History of Latin America*, 106, 184; Jesse Cromwell, *The Smugglers' World: Illicit Trade and Atlantic Communities in Eighteenth-Century Venezuela* (Chapel Hill, 2018), 13.
40. Klooster, *Revolutions in the Atlantic World*, 122; Gould, "Entangled Histories, Entangled World"; Williamson, *Penguin History of Latin America*, 106, 184; Banks, *Chasing Empire*, 35.
41. Mark Peterson, *The City-State of Boston: The Rise and Fall of an Atlantic Power, 1630–1865* (Princeton, 2019), 249, 174–77.
42. Anishanslin, *Portrait of a Woman in Silk*, 10. Also see T. H. Breen, "The Baubles of Britain: The American and Consumer Revolutions of the Eighteenth Century," *Past and Present*, 119 (1988), 73–104; Breen, "Narrative of Commercial Life: Consumption, Ideology, and Community on the Eve of the American Revolution," *William and Mary Quarterly*, 3rd. ser., 50 (1993), 471–501; Jorge Canizares-Esguerra, "Introduction," and Ernesto Bassi, "Enabling, Implementing, Experiencing Entanglement," in Jorge Canizares-Esguerra, ed., *Entangled Empires: The Anglo-Iberian Atlantic, 1500–1830* (Philadelphia, 2018), 3, 219; Gould, "Afterword," in Canizares-Esguerra, ed., *Entangled Empires*, 256. On how the idea of connected history works, though without an in-depth discussion, see the series of essays by Sanjay Subrahmanyan entitled *Explorations in Connected History: From the Tagus to the Ganges* (Oxford, 2005).
43. Eliga H. Gould, *Among the Powers of the Earth: The American Revolution and the Making of a New World Empire* (New York, 2012), 87, 90. These merchants had become "citizens of the world," as opposed to British subjects, according to David Hancock, *Citizens of the World: London Merchants and the Integration of the British Atlantic Community, 1735–1785* (New York, 1995). For a look at networks in Boston, see John Tyler, *Smugglers and Patriots: Boston Merchants and the Advent of the American Revolution* (Boston, 1986).
44. Hamnett, *End of Iberian Rule*, 91; Jane T. Merritt, *The Trouble with Tea: The Politics of Consumption in the Eighteenth-Century Global Economy* (Baltimore, 2017), 4–5, 29, 52–53; Huw David, *Trade, Politics, and Revolution: South Carolina and Britain's Atlantic Commerce, 1730–1790* (Columbia, SC, 2018), 64, 99; Mary Beth Norton, *1774: The Long Year of Revolution* (New York, 2020), 4–7.
45. For this dynamic, see William Pettigrew, *Freedom's Debt: The Royal African Company and the Politics of the Atlantic Slave Trade, 1672–1752* (Chapel Hill, 2013);

and Dylan LeBlanc, "Empire in Chains: British Government Men in the Atlantic Slave Trade, 1670–1700" (Ph.D. diss., University of Notre Dame, 2019). On creoles, and their outsized role, see Ira Berlin, *Many Thousands Gone: The First Two Centuries of Slavery in North America* (Cambridge, MA, 1998); and Jane Landers, *Atlantic Creoles in the Age of Revolution* (Cambridge, MA, 2010).

46. Paquette, *European Seaborne Empires*, 85–86; Emily Berquist Soule, "The Spanish Slave Trade during the American Revolutionary War," in Gabriel Paquette and Gonzalo M. Quintero Saravia, eds., *Spain and the American Revolution: New Approaches and Perspectives* (New York, 2020), 102.

47. Williamson, *Penguin History of Latin America*, 142. On the complexities occasioned by the Asiento, see Adrian Finucane, *The Temptations of Trade: Britain, Spain, and the Struggle for Empire* (Philadelphia, 2016). Some argue it was the British who would introduce ten thousand slaves into Cuba, making its sugar economy. On this, see Julius Scott, *The Common Wind: Afro-American Currents in the Age of the Haitian Revolution* (London, 2018), 5.

48. Elena Schneider, *The Occupation of Havana: War, Trade, and Slavery in the Atlantic World* (Chapel Hill, 2018), 3–9; Ada Ferrer, *Freedom's Mirror: Cuba and Haiti in the Age of Revolutions* (New York, 2014), 18–20; Dubois, *Avengers of the New World*, 32–33.

49. On these themes for the French, see Michael Kwass, "The Global Underground," and Lynn Hunt, "The Global Financial Origins of 1789," in Desan, Hunt, and Nelson, eds., *The French Revolution in Global Perspective*, 15–44.

50. Robin Law, *Ouidah: The Social History of a West African Slaving Port, 1727–1892* (Athens, OH, 2004), 7, 126, 156.

51. John Thornton, "African Dimensions of the Stono Rebellion," *American Historical Review*, 96 (1991), 1101–13; Jeroen Dewulf, *Afro-American Catholics: The Catholic Roots of African American Spirituality* (Notre Dame, 2022).

52. Marzagalli, "Economic and Demographic Developments"; and Lauren Klay, "The Bourgeoisie, Capitalism, and the Origins of the French Revolution," Andress, ed., *Oxford Handbook of the French Revolution*, 15, 27.

53. Klooster, *Revolutions in the Atlantic World*, 6; Thomas Truxes, *Defying Empire: Trading with the Enemy in Colonial New York* (New Haven, 2008), 7.

54. For a provocative look at this, and the centrality of the Caribbean in the crisscrossed world of the Atlantic, see Ernesto Bassi, *An Aqueous Territory: Sailor Geographies and New Granada's Transimperial Greater Caribbean World* (Durham, 2016).

55. Nicholas Canny, "How the Local Can Be Global and the Global Local: Ireland, Irish Catholics, and European Overseas Empires, 1500–1900," in Patrick Griffin and Francis Cogliano, eds., *Ireland and America: Empire, Revolution, and Sovereignty* (Charlottesville, VA, 2021), 31–37. On cities and the changing tenor of the eighteenth century because of trade, see David Dickson, *The First Irish Cities: An Eighteenth-Century Transformation* (New Haven, 2021).

56. On changes in the North, see Dickson, *The First Irish Cities,* 73–79; and Patrick Griffin, *The People with No Name: Ireland's Ulster Scots, America's Scots Irish, and the Creation of a British Atlantic World, 1689–1764* (Princeton, 2001). The flax-migrant-linen connection is explored in Thomas Truxes, *Irish-American Trade, 1600–1783* (New York, 1989).

57. For the best study on the hyper-networked nature of the Caribbean in general, and specifically Saint-Domingue, see Scott, *Common Wind.*

58. Fink, "From Slave Colony to Black Nation," in Tutino, ed., *New Countries,* 139.

59. See Janet L. Polasky, *Revolutions without Borders: The Call to Liberty in the Atlantic World* (New Haven, 2015).

60. Katherine Smoak, "The Weight of Necessity: Counterfeit Coins in the British Atlantic World, 1760–1800," *William and Mary Quarterly,* 3rd ser., 74 (2017), 467–502.

61. Fabrício Pereira Prado, *Edge of Empire: Atlantic Networks and Revolution in Bourbon Rio de la Plata* (Oakland, 2015), 14, 24, 103–4; Williamson, *Penguin History of Latin America,* 132.

62. Forrest Hylton, " 'The Sole Owners of the Land': Empire, War, and Authority in the Guajira Peninsula, 1761–1779," in Michael A. McDonnell, ed., *Rethinking the Age of Revolution,* (New York, 2017), 15.

63. David Dickson, *Old World Colony: Cork and South Munster, 1630–1830* (Madison, WI, 2005), 152–54; also see Dickson, *Dublin: The Making of a Capital City* (Cambridge, MA, 2014), 125–28. Also refer to Orla Power, "Irish Planters, Atlantic Merchants: The Development of St. Croix, Danish West Indies, 1750 to 1766" (Ph.D. diss., National University of Ireland, Galway, 2011). My thanks to Nicholas Canny and Jim Smyth for help on these points. Thanks, too, to Michael Gibbons with his help on Connemara smuggling networks. On this, see Tim Robinson, *Connemara* (Roundstone, Galway, 1990), 167–68. On Montrose, I am indebted to Colin Barr and also to Duncan Fraser, *The Smugglers* (Montrose, Scotland, 1978).

64. Michael Kwass, *Contraband: Louis Mandrin and the Making of a Global Underground* (Cambridge, MA, 2014); John Banks, *Smugglers and Smuggling in Sussex* (London, 1873).

65. Bailyn, *Atlantic History,* 90–91.

66. The Danes may have made a claim to this title in the way Saint Thomas, a failed slave society, became a center of clandestine trade and attracted a smorgasbord of peoples from every corner of the Atlantic. See Johan Heinsen, *Mutiny in the Danish Atlantic World: Convicts, Sailors, and a Dissonant Empire* (London, 2017).

67. Benjamin Schmidt, "The Dutch Atlantic," in Greene and Morgan, eds., *Atlantic History,* 176–77; Truxes, *Defying Empire,* 2–3, 51; Gert Oostindie, "Slave Resistance, Colour Lines, and the Impact of the French and Haitian Revolutions in Curaçao," and Linda Rupert, "Inter-Colonial Networks and Revolutionary Ferment in Eighteenth-Century Curaçao and Tierra Firme," in Wim Klooster and Gert Ooostindie, eds., *Curaçao in the Age of Revolutions,*

*1705–1800* (Leiden, 2011), 2–3, 75–92; and Bram Hoonhout, *Borderless Empire: Dutch Guiana in the Atlantic World, 1750–1800* (Athens, GA, 2020).

68. On this see, Wim Klooster and Gert Oostindie, *Realm between Empires: The Second Dutch Atlantic* (Ithaca, 2018).

69. For this, I am indebted to William Smith, "A Heavenly Correspondence: Benjamin Colman's Epistolary World and the Dissenting Interest" (Ph.D. diss., University of Notre Dame, 2017); and Caroline Winterer's "Mapping the Republic of Letters" database at Stanford University. On this see Dan Edelstein, Paula Findlen, Giovanna Ceserani, Caroline Winterer, and Nicole Coleman, "Historical Research in a Digital Age: Reflections from the Mapping the Republic of Letters Project," *American Historical Review*, 112 (2017), 400–424.

70. Lindsay O'Neill, *The Opened Letter: Networking in the Early Modern British World* (Philadelphia, 2015).

71. Carla Mulford, *Benjamin Franklin and the Ends of Empire* (New York, 2015). On the roles of the news in shaping the very content of networks, see Joseph Adelman, *Revolutionary Networks: The Business and Politics of Printing the News, 1763–1789* (Baltimore, 2019), 19–50.

72. This perspective owes a great deal to Jan Stievermann. He is now working on a volume of how the ideas of Protestantism and even of "religion" took shape because of Atlantic networks. "A Syncretism of Piety: Imagining Global Protestantism in Boston, Tranquebar, and Halle," unpublished essay. My thanks to Professor Stievermann for sharing his work with me. On Boston's ties, see Peterson, *The City-State of Boston*, 234–46.

73. Shovlin, *Political Economy of Virtue*, 2, 14–15, 213.

74. Francisco Bethencourt, *Racisms: From the Crusades to the Twentieth Century* (Princeton, 2013), 255.

75. Rebecca Earle, "The Pleasures of Taxonomy: Casta Paintings, Classification, and Colonialism," *William and Mary Quarterly*, 3rd ser., 73 (2016), 427–66; Antonio Feros, *Speaking of Spain: The Evolution of Race and Nation in the Hispanic World* (Cambridge, MA, 2017), 189–231 For Venezuela, see John Lynch, *Simón Bolívar: A Life* (New Haven, 2006), 10–11. On this and the ideal of classification, see Bethencourt, *Racisms*.

76. John Robertson, *The Enlightenment: A Very Short Introduction* (Oxford, 2015), 60–72; Richard Bourke, "Political Theory and the Philosophy of History" (lecture, University of Notre Dame Department of Political Science, Notre Dame, IN, 10 April 2018).

77. Robertson, *Enlightenment*, 2–4, 13; Ritchie Robertson, *The Enlightenment: The Pursuit of Happiness, 1689–1790* (New York, 2021), 1–41; John Crowley, *The Invention of Comfort: Sensibilities and Design in Early Modern Britain and Early America* (Baltimore, 2000).

78. On Frederick as historian and friend of Voltaire, see Christopher Clark, *Time and Power: Visions of History in German Politics, from the Thirty Years' War to the Third Reich* (Princeton, 2019), 72–98.

79. Ulrich Lehner, *The Catholic Enlightenment: The Forgotten History of a Global Movement* (New York, 2016); Jorge Canizares-Esguerra, *How to Write a History of the New World: Histories, Epistemologies, and Identities in the Eighteenth-Century Atlantic World* (Stanford, 2001); Williamson, *Penguin History of Latin America*, 162–63; Rodríguez O., *Independence of Spanish America*, 37, 15; Cheney, *Revolutionary Commerce*, 14.

80. On this, see Franco Venturi, *The End of the Old Regime in Europe, 1768–1776* (Princeton, 1991).

81. With the period's transformations, something we could call "public opinion" could claim a sort of authority to articulate or make imaginative space for new tensions of the period. See Keith Michael Baker, *Inventing the French Revolution: Essays on French Political Culture in the Eighteenth Century* (New York, 1990), 115–16, 199.

82. Kehinde Andrews, *The New Age of Empire: How Racism and Colonialism Still Rule the World* (New York, 2021).

83. Linda Kerber, *Women of the Republic: Intellect and Ideology in Revolutionary America* (Chapel Hill, 1980), 13–32.

84. Teresa Ann Smith, *The Emerging Female Citizen: Gender and Enlightenment in Spain* (Berkeley, 2006), 40–73; Rosalind Carr, *Gender and Enlightenment Culture in Eighteenth-Century Scotland* (Edinburgh, 2014), 73–101; Katie Jarvis, *Politics in the Marketplace: Work, Gender, and Citizenship in Revolutionary France* (New York, 2019), 27; Saran Knott and Barbara Taylor, "General Introduction," xvi; and Karen O'Brien, "Introduction," in Knott and Taylor, eds., *Women, Gender, and Enlightenment* (New York, 2005), xvi, 3.

85. Karen O'Brien, *Women and Enlightenment in Eighteenth-Century Britain* (Cambridge, 2009), 3.

86. Andrien, "Spanish Atlantic," in Greene and Morgain, eds., *Atlantic History*, 66; Ida Altman, "The Spanish Atlantic, 1650–1780," in Canny and Morgan, eds., *Oxford Handbook of the Atlantic World*, 183–92; and especially Elena Schneider, *The Occupation of Havana: War, Trade, and Slavery in the Atlantic World* (Chapel Hill, 2018), 9.

87. A. J. R. Russell-Wood, "The Portuguese Atlantic," in Greene and Morgan, eds., *Atlantic History*, 81–104; Russell-Wood, "The Portuguese Atlantic World, c. 1650–c. 1760," in Canny and Morgan, eds., *Oxford Handbook of the Atlantic World*, eds. 201–18.

88. Roquinaldo Ferreira, *Cross-Cultural Exchange in the Atlantic World: Angola and Brazil during the Era of the Slave Trade* (New York, 2012), 7–9, 221–23.

89. Griffin, *The People with No Name*; Alexander Byrd, *Captives and Voyagers: Black Migrants across the Eighteenth-Century British Atlantic World* (Baton Rouge, 2008); Hawthorne, *From Africa to Brazil*; Walter Hawthorne, *Planting Rice and Harvesting Slaves: Transformations along the Guinea-Bissau Coast, 1400–1990* (Athens, OH, 2003); Ferreira, *Cross-Cultural Exchange in the Atlantic World*.

90. On this story, see Sophie White, *Voices of the Enslaved: Love, Labor, and Longing in French Louisiana* (Chapel Hill, 2019), 134. On these themes, see Jane Landers, *Atlantic Creoles*; Hawthorne, *From Africa to Brazil*, 18–19; and Philip Morgan, *Slave Counterpoint: Black Culture in the Eighteenth-century Chesapeake and Lowcountry* (Chapel Hill, 1998).

91. Frank Lambert, *"Pedlar in Divinity": George Whitefield and the Transatlantic Revivals* (Princeton, 1993); Timothy Hall, *Contested Boundaries: Itinerancy and the Reshaping of the Colonial American Religious World* (Durham, 1994). On similar dynamics in Ireland and Scotland, see James Livesey, *Civil Society and Empire: Ireland and Scotland in the Eighteenth-Century Atlantic World* (New Haven, 2009).

92. Gregory Dowd, *A Spirited Resistance: The North American Indian Struggle for Unity, 1745–1815* (Baltimore, 1993); James Merrell, *The Indians' New World: Catawbas and Their Neighbors from European Contact through the Era of Removal* (Chapel Hill, 1989); Timothy Shannon, "Dressing for Success on the Mohawk Frontier: Hendrick, William Johnson, and the Indian Fashion," *William and Mary Quarterly*, 3rd ser., 53 (1996), 13–42.

93. See Sean Connolly, *Religion, Law and Power: The Making of Protestant Ireland, 1660–1760* (Oxford, 1992).

94. George Goodwin, *Benjamin Franklin in London: The British Life of America's Founding Father* (New Haven, 2016); Carla Mulford, *Benjamin Franklin and the Ends of Empire* (New York, 2015).

95. Timothy Shannon, *Indian Captive, Indian King: Peter Williamson in America and Britain* (Cambridge, MA, 2018).

96. Rebecca Earle, "The Pleasures of Taxonomy"; Jane Kamensky, *A Revolution in Color: The World of John Singleton Copley* (New York, 2016). On this dynamic in Virginia, see Kathleen Brown, *Good Wives, Nasty Wenches, and Anxious Patriarchs: Gender, Race, and Power in Colonial Virginia* (Chapel Hill, 1996), 247.

97. The best statement on this remains E. P. Thompson's classic, *The Making of the English Working Class* (New York, 1964); Gary Nash, *The Urban Crucible: The Northern Seaports and the Origins of the American Revolution* (Cambridge, MA, 1986).

98. Paul Langford, *A Polite and Commercial People: England 1727–1783* (New York, 1989); Perry Gauci, *William Beckford: First Prime Minister of the London Empire* (New Haven, 2013).

99. Williamson, *Penguin History of Latin America*, 154; Lynch, *Spanish American Revolutions*, 4.

100. John Clive and Bernard Bailyn, "England's Cultural Provinces: Scotland and America," *William and Mary Quarterly*, 3rd ser., 11 (1954), 200–213; Craig Yirush, *Settlers, Liberty, and Empire: The Roots of Early American Political Theory, 1675–1775* (New York, 2011); Andrew Shankman, Ignacio Gallup-Diaz, and David Silverman, eds., *Anglicizing America: Empire, Revolution,*

*Republic* (Philadelphia, 2015), 1–2, 243–46. For a critique of Anglicization, one positing that colonists had a sophisticated understanding of geopolitics and Britain's role in the world, see D. H. Robinson, *The Idea of Europe and the Origins of the American Revolution* (Oxford, 2020).

101. Rodríguez O., *Independence of Spanish America*, 13; Jim Smyth, " 'Like Amphibious Animals': Irish Protestants, Ancient Britons, 1691–1707," in *Historical Journal*, 36 (1993), 785–97.

102. Patrick Griffin, *The Townshend Moment: The Making of Empire and Revolution in the Eighteenth Century* (New Haven, 2017); Joshua Simon, *The Ideology of Creole Revolution: Imperialism and Independence in American and Latin American Political Thought* (Cambridge, 2017).

103. On how an area in Europe not on the littoral was gripped by change, but also was culturally prepared to adapt, see James Livesey, *Provincializing Global History: Money, Ideas, and Things in in the Languedoc, 1680–1830* (New Haven, 2020).

104. Richard Dunn, *Sugar and Slaves: The Rise of the Planter Class in the English West Indies, 1624–1713* (Chapel Hill, 1972), 11–12.

105. On this, see Robertson, *Enlightenment*, 71, 78.

106. Matthew Dziennik, " 'Under ye Lash of ye Law': The State and the Law in the Post-Culloden Scottish Highlands," *Journal of British Studies*, 60 (2021), 1–23.

107. John Shovlin, *Trading with the Enemy: Britain, France, and the Eighteenth-Century Quest for a Peaceful World Order* (New Haven, 2021), 150, 3.

108. John Brewer, *The Sinews of Power: War, Money, and the English State, 1688–1783* (New York, 1989).

109. Adelman, *Sovereignty and Revolution*, 17. On how men in armies were drawn into conflicts over global capitalist development, see Peter Way, "Militarizing the Atlantic World: Army Discipline, Coerced Labor, and Britain's Commercial Empire," in McDonnell, ed., *Rethinking the Age of Revolution*, 45–69; Cheney, *Revolutionary Commerce*, 197. For the ways the economy was bound to lethality and how the wars of the Atlantic grew in intensity because of that link, culminating in the Seven Years' War, see Geoffrey Plank, *Atlantic Wars: From the Fifteenth Century to the Age of Revolution* (New York, 2020), 228, 242–49.

110. Josep Fradera, *The Imperial Nation: Citizens and Subjects in the British, French, Spanish, and American Empires* (Princeton, 2018), 2.

111. The war also centered on rivalries in places such as Nova Scotia. This was an important site of future settlement and for naval protection of British Atlantic commerce. This is the view of Steve Pincus in a talk entitled "Do Wars Make States and States Make War? Rethinking the Origins of the Seven Years' War," Notre Dame International Security Center, 6 April 2021.

112. Robinson, *The Idea of Europe and the Origins of the American Revolution*, 157–68.

113. On this place in time, see Michael McConnell, *A Country Between: The Upper Ohio Valley and Its Peoples, 1724–1774* (Lincoln, NE, 1997); and Richard White, *The Middle Ground: Indians, Empires, and Republics in the Great Lakes Region, 1650–1815* (New York, 2010).

114. On "war capitalism," see Sven Beckert, *Empire of Cotton: A Global History* (New York, 2014); and Tutino, "Rise of Industrial Capitalism," in Tutino, ed., *New Countries*, 33, 40–41. Also see Vincent Brown's essay in Joseph Miller et al., eds., *The Princeton Companion to Atlantic History* (Princeton, 2015), 36–46.

115. On this, see Bailey Stone, *The Genesis of the French Revolution: A Global-Historical Interpretation* (Cambridge, 1994).

116. For the war, and its tangled origins, see Fred Anderson, *Crucible of War: The Seven Years' War and the Fate of Empire in British North America, 1754–1766* (New York, 2000). What follows is based on this study.

117. Brewer, *Sinews of Power*; Clark, *Iron Kingdom*, 206–29.

118. Richard White, *The Middle Ground: Indians, Empires, and Republics in the Great Lakes Region, 1650–1815* (New York, 1991), 243–47.

119. Griffin, *Townshend Moment*.

120. Adelman, *Sovereignty and Revolution*, 18–20.

121. Sergio Serulnikov, *Revolution in the Andes: The Age of Túpac Amaru* (Durham, 2013), 21–23.

122. Martyn Powell, *Britain and Ireland in the Eighteenth-Century Crisis of Empire* (London, 2003), 149–50; Vincent Morley, *The Popular Mind in Eighteenth-Century Ireland* (Cork, 2017), 217–25; Morley, *Irish Opinion and the American Revolution, 1760–1783* (Cambridge, 2002), 48–50.

123. Gregory Evans Dowd, *War under Heaven: Pontiac, the Indian Nations and the British Empire* (Baltimore, 2002).

124. Burnard and Garrigus, *Plantation Machine*; Trevor Burnard, "Settlement, Security and the British Imperial System" (lecture, University of Melbourne, Melbourne, 10 November 2018); Vincent Brown, *Tacky's Revolt: The Story of an Atlantic Slave War* (Cambridge, MA, 2020). For rebellions simmering in South America, see Anthony McFarlane, *War and Independence in Spanish America* (New York, 2014), 25–26.

125. Marjoleine Kars, *Blood on the River: The Untold Story of the Berbice Rebellion* (New York, 2020).

## Chapter Two. Disentangling the Atlantic

1. On these debates, see Jack Greene, *Evaluating Empire and Confronting Colonialism in Eighteenth-Century Britain* (New York, 2013); and Eliga Gould, *The Persistence of Empire: British Political Culture in the Age of the American Revolution* (Chapel Hill, 2000).

2. Gabriel Paquette, The *European Seaborne Empires: From the Thirty Years' War to the Age of Revolution* (New Haven, 2019), 77, 116; Gabriel Paquette,

*Enlightenment, Governance, and Reform in Spain and Its Empire, 1759–1808* (New York, 2008).

3. On this theme, see David Bell, *The Cult of the Nation in France: Inventing Nationalism, 1680–1800* (Cambridge, MA, 2001), 78–106.

4. On the challenge of using early modern sovereignty, see Lauren Benton, *A Search for Sovereignty: Law and Geography in European Empires, 1400–1900* (New York, 2010), 279–82.

5. On reform and disequilibrium, see Jeremy Adelman, "Empires, Nations, and Revolutions," *Journal of the History of Ideas*, 79 (2018), 73–88.

6. Bernard Bailyn, *Atlantic History: Concepts and Contours* (Cambridge, 2005), 104–5.

7. Toby Green, *A Fistful of Shells: West Africa from the Rise of the Slave Trade to the Age of Revolution* (Chicago, 2019), 9, 296–300.

8. Sophus Reinert, *Translating Empire: Emulation and the Origins of Political Economy* (Cambridge, MA, 2011), 2–3; John Brewer, *The Sinews of Power: War, Money, and the English State, 1688–1783* (London, 1989).

9. Marc Raeeff, *The Well-Ordered Police State: Social and Institutional Change through Law in the Germanies and Russia, 1600–1800* (New Haven, 1983), 146–66, 221–50. On Prussia, see Christopher Clark, *Iron Kingdom: The Rise and Downfall of Prussia, 1600–1947* (Cambridge, MA, 2006), 239–46. On Austria, see John Deák, *Forging a Multinational State: State Making in Imperial Austria from the Enlightenment to the First World War* (Stanford, 2015); Jon Singerton, "The Residue of Revolution: Experiencing the Age of Revolution in Habsburg Lands, 1763–1815" (lecture, University of Oxford, Oxford, 14 September 2019).

10. On Belgium, see Janet Polasky, *Revolution in Brussels, 1787–1793* (Brussels, 1987), 36–37; Jane Judge, *The United States of Belgium: The Story of the First Belgian Revolution* (Leuven, 2018).

11. On this, see Franco Venturi, *End of the Old Regime in Europe, 1776–1789* (Princeton, 1991).

12. For this tangled tale, see John Shovlin, *The Political Economy of Virtue: Luxury, Patriotism, and the Origins of the French Revolution* (Ithaca, 2006). The debt percentage comes from p. 92. Also see Michael Kwass, "The Global Underground: Smuggling, Rebellion, and the Origins of the French Revolution," in Suzanne Desan, Lynn Hunt, and William Max Nelson, eds., *The French Revolution in Global Perspective* (Ithaca, 2013), 24–28.

13. Kwass, "Global Underground," 24–28; Shovlin, *Political Economy of Virtue*, 105.

14. Bailey Stone, *The Genesis of the French Revolution: A Global-Historical Interpretation* (Cambridge, 1994), 32–33, 44, 98–103. Also see Shovlin, *Political Economy of Virtue*, on these debates.

15. Bell, *Cult of the Nation*.

16. Lauren Clay, "The Bourgeoisie, Capitalism, and the Origins of the French Revolution," in David Andress, ed., *The Oxford Handbook of the French Revolution* (Oxford, 2015), 22.

17. On this, see Rafe Blaufarb, *The Revolutionary Atlantic: Republican Visions, 1760–1850* (New York, 2018), 51–55.

18. Laurent Dubois, *Avengers of the New World: The Story of the Haitian Revolution* (Cambridge, MA, 2004), 33; Trevor Burnard and John Garrigus, *The Plantation Machine: Atlantic Capitalism in French Saint-Domingue and British Jamaica* (Philadelphia, 2016), 154–91; Manuel Covo, "Race, Slavery, and Colonies in the French Atlantic," in David Andress, ed., *The Oxford Handbook of the French Revolution* (New York, 2015), 292.

19. John Garrigus, *Before Haiti: Race and Citizenship in French Saint-Domingue* (New York, 2006), 109–39. For how this strategy was employed elsewhere, see Edmund Morgan, *American Slavery, American Freedom: The Ordeal of Colonial Virginia* (New York, 2003).

20. Laurent Dubois, "The French Atlantic," in Greene and Morgan, eds., *Atlantic History*, 143–44; Burnard and Garrigus, *Plantation Machine*, 24; Dubois, *Avengers of the New World*, 33, 39, 62–64; Paul Cheney, *Cul de Sac: Patrimony, Capitalism, and Slavery in French Saint-Domingue* (Chicago, 2017), 8–9; Banks, *Chasing Empire*, 218–220; Jeremy Popkin, "Saint-Domingue, Slavery, and the Origins of the French Revolution," in Thomas Kaiser and Dale Van Kley, eds., *From Deficit to Deluge: The Origins of the French Revolution* (Stanford, 2011), 221.

21. Kenneth Maxwell, *Conflicts and Conspiracies: Brazil and Portugal, 1750–1808* (Cambridge, 1973), 1–32; Paquette, *European Seaborne Empires*, 92; Jorge Miguel Viana Pedreira, "From Growth to Collapse: Portugal, Brazil, and the Breakdown of the Old Colonial System (1750–1830)," *Hispanic American Historical Review*, 80 (2000), 840–41.

22. Gabriel Paquette, *Imperial Portugal in the Age of Atlantic Revolutions: The Luso-Brazilian World, c. 1770–1850* (Cambridge, 2013), 17–21, 25–32, 52; A. J. R. Russell-Wood, "The Portuguese Atlantic World, c. 1650–c. 1760," in Canny and Morgan, eds., *Oxford Handbook of the Atlantic World*, 214–17.

23. Walter Hawthorne, *Africa to Brazil: Culture, Identity, and an Atlantic Slave Trade, 1600–1830* (New York, 2010), 45–62.

24. Maxwell, *Conflicts and Conspiracies*, 33–60.

25. Edwin Williamson, *Penguin History of Latin America* (London, 1992), 208–9.

26. Ida Altman, "The Spanish Atlantic, 1650–1780," in Canny and Morgan, eds., *Oxford Handbook of the Atlantic World*, 192–97. On the process, see J. H. Elliott, *Empires of the Atlantic World: Britain and Spain in America, 1492–1830* (New Haven, 2006), 365.

27. Wim Klooster, *Revolutions in the Atlantic World: A Comparative History* (New York, 2018), 122–24; Jaime Rodríguez O., *Independence of Spanish America* (New York, 1998), 19–20; Monica Ricketts, *Who Should Rule? Men of Arms, the Republic of Letters, and the Fall of the Spanish Empire* (New York, 2017), 23–28, 34–39.

28. Valentina Tikoff, "Spanish Orphans, British Prisoners, and the American Revolution: Warfare, Social Welfare, and Technical Training," *Studies in Eighteenth-Century Culture*, 47 (2018), 34–37; Andrien, "Spanish Atlantic," in

Greene and Morgan, eds., *Atlantic History*, 65–69; Paquette, *Enlightenment, Governance, and Reform*, 128. For military reform, see Anthony McFarlane, *War and Independence in Spanish America* (New York, 2014), 15–22.

29. Rodríguez O., *Independence of Spanish America*, 7; Lester Langley, *The Americas in the Age of Revolution, 1750–1850* (New Haven, 1996), 148–49.

30. On this, see Paquette, *Enlightenment, Governance, and Reform*, 39–45. On parallels to the British case, see Elliott, *Empires of the Atlantic World*.

31. Kathleen DuVal, *The Native Ground: Indians and Colonists in the Heart of the Continent* (Philadelphia, 2006), 118–27.

32. Fidel Tavarez, "The Commercial Machine: Reforming Imperial Commerce in the Spanish Atlantic, 1740–1808" (Ph.D. diss., Princeton University, 2016). My thanks to Dr. Tavarez for sharing with me the introduction to his new book of the same title. On negotiation, see Paquette, *Enlightenment, Governance, and Reform*, 127–30. Also see Rodríguez O., *Independence of Spanish America*, 20–22; and Jeremy Adelman, *Sovereignty and Revolution in the Iberian Atlantic* (Princeton, 2006), 23–29.

33. Klooster, *Revolutions in the Atlantic World*, 125; Elena Schneider, *The Occupation of Havana: War, Trade, and Slavery in the Atlantic World* (Chapel Hill, 2018), 262–65, 270–74; Williamson, *Penguin History of Latin America*, 198–99.

34. Adelman, *Sovereignty and Revolution*, 29–39.

35. Rodríguez O., *Independence of Spanish America*, 30–31; McFarlane, *War and Independence in Spanish America*, 22–24; Paquette, *European Seaborne Empires*, 90.

36. Lyman Johnson, *Workshop of Revolution: Plebeian Buenos Aires and the Atlantic World, 1776–1810* (Durham, 2011), 8–11; Elliott, *Empires of the Atlantic World*, 357.

37. Carlos Marichal, *Bankruptcy of Empire: Mexican Silver and the Wars between Spain, Britain, and France* (Cambridge, 2007), 16–47. On silver and how it shaped a community and its culture and politics, see John Tutino, *Mexico City, 1808: Power, Sovereignty, and Silver in an Age of War and Revolution* (Albuquerque, NM, 2018), 6–10, 30–41.

38. Marichal, *Bankruptcy of Empire*, 50; Rodríguez O., *Independence of Spanish America*, 24–25; Langley, *Americas in the Age of Revolution*, 150–51; Forrest Hylton, " 'Sole Owners of the Land': Empire, War, and Authority in the Guajira Peninsula, 1761–1779," in Michael McDonnell, ed., *Rethinking the Age of Revolution* (New York, 2017), 33–34.

39. Scarlett O'Phelan quoted in Brian Hamnett, *End of Iberian Rule, 1770–1830* (Cambridge, 2017), 65; Elliott, *Empires of the Atlantic World*, 357.

40. Sinclair Thomson, *We Alone Will Rule: Native Andean Politics in the Age of Insurgency* (Madison, WI, 2002), 10; Sergio Serulnikov, *Revolution in the Andes: The Age of Tupac Amaru* (Durham, 2013), 125–33; Anthony McFarlane, *War and Independence in Spanish America*, 25–26.

41. On this, and how reform stirred the movement, see Charles Walker, *The Tupac Amaru Rebellion* (Cambridge, MA, 2016); Serulnikov, *Revolution in the*

*Andes*, 21–23. For this understanding of Pontiac, see Gregory Evans Dowd, *A Spirited Resistance: The North American Indian Struggle for Unity, 1745–1815* (Baltimore, 1992). I thank Professor Walker for making this connection evident to me in the course of a conversation.

42. Charles Walker, *Smoldering Ashes: Cuzco and the Creation of Republican Peru, 1780–1840* (Durham, NC, 1999), 16–54.

43. Adelman, *Sovereignty and Revolution*, 49–53; Serulnikov, *Revolution in the Andes*, 1–3; Klooster, *Revolutions in the Atlantic World*, 127; Williamson, *Penguin History of Latin America*, 200–201; Rodríguez O., *Independence of Spanish America*, 4. Adelman considers this a reaction to imperial reform. On this see Jeremy Adelman, "An Age of Imperial Revolutions," *American Historical Review*, 113 (2008), 319–40.

44. Jesse Cromwell, *Smugglers' World: Illicit Trade and Atlantic Communities in Eighteenth-Century Venezuela* (Chapel Hill, 2018), 271–301; John Leddy Phelan, *The People and the King: The Comunero Revolution in Colombia, 1781* (Madison, WI, 1978), 3–35. On conquest, see John Lynch, *Spanish American Revolutions, 1808–1826* (New York, 1986).

45. This is the interpretation of Lynch, *Spanish America Revolutions*, 7–24.

46. Hamnett, *End of Iberian Rule*, 125.

47. Langley, *Americas in the Age of Revolution*, 153, 159. For similar dynamics, albeit in a different setting, see Paul Lovejoy, *Jihad in West Africa during the Age of Revolutions* (Athens, OH, 2016).

48. Elliott, *Empires of the Atlantic World*, 353; Carlos Marichal, *Bankruptcy of Empire: Mexican Silver and the Wars between Spain, Britain, and France, 1760–1810* (New York, 2007), 48–80. For the success of reforms, and how they did not destabilize empire, see Gabriel Paquette and Gonzalo Quintero Saravia, "Introduction: Spain and the American Revolution," in Paquette and Quintero, eds., *Spain and the American Revolution: New Approaches and Perspectives* (New York, 2020), 2–11.

49. Edmund Morgan, *The Birth of the Republic, 1763–89* (Chicago, 2013), 13–14.

50. Patrick Griffin, *The Townshend Moment: The Making of Empire and Revolution in the Eighteenth Century* (New Haven, 2017), ch. 2.

51. See Gould, *Persistence of Empire*, 110–22. On the centralizing thrust, see Jack Greene, "State Formation, Resistance, and the Creation of Revolutionary Traditions in the Early Modern Era," in Michael Morrison and Melinda Zook, eds., *Revolutionary Currents: Nation Building in the Transatlantic World*, (Lanham, MD, 2004), 16–17.

52. See Greene, *Evaluating Empire*, 84–91; Patrick Griffin, *America's Revolution* (New York, 2012), 65–70; Richard Bourke, *Empire and Revolution: The Political Life of Edmund Burke* (Princeton, 2015), ch. 6.

53. Thomas Truxes, *Defying Empire: Trading with the Enemy in Colonial New York* (New Haven, 2008), 189.

54. Gould, *Among the Powers of the Earth*, 83, 86, 91.
55. Truxes, *Defying Empire*, 226; Fred Anderson, *Crucible of War: The Seven Years' War and the Fate of Empire in British North America* (New York, 2000), 563.
56. Amy Dunagin, "A Nova Scotia Scheme and the Imperial Politics of Ulster Emigration," *Journal of British Studies*, 58 (2019), 519–42.
57. Gregory E. O'Malley, *Final Passages: The Intercolonial Slave Trade of British America, 1619–1807* (Chapel Hill, 2014), ch. 8; John Shovlin, *Trading with the Enemy: Britain, France, and the Eighteenth-Century Quest for a Peaceful World Order* (New Haven, 2021), 195–206; Francis Armytage, *The Free Port System in the British West Indies* (London, 1953). Ernesto Bassi, "Enabling, Implementing, Experiencing Entanglement," in Jorge Canizares-Esguerra, ed., *Entangled Empires: The Anglo-Iberian Atlantic, 1500–1830* (Philadelphia, 2018), 221–22.
58. R. Grant Kleiser, "An Empire of Free Ports: British Commercial Imperialism in the 1766 Free Port Act," *Journal of British Studies*, 60 (2021), 334–61.
59. Griffin, *Townshend Moment*; Gould, *The Persistence of Empire*.
60. Paquette and Quintero Saravia, "Introduction: Spain and the American Revolution," in *Spain and the American Revolution*, 7.
61. Patrick Griffin, *American Leviathan: Empire, Nation, and Revolutionary Frontier* (New York, 2007), 19–45. For the broader context, see Eric Hinderaker, *Elusive Empires: Constructing Colonialism in the Ohio Valley, 1673–1800* (New York, 1997), 134–75.
62. T. H. Breen, *Marketplace of Revolution: How Consumer Politics Shaped American Independence* (New York, 2004), 196.
63. T. H. Breen, *The Will of the People: The Revolutionary Birth of America* (Cambridge, MA, 2019); Griffin, *America's Revolution*, 51–55, 71.
64. Griffin, *Townshend Moment*, 151–64.
65. Like the great upheaval of the "Reformation," a period of reform that resurrected all sorts of ghosts from the late medieval world, rode on the webs of new communication networks that reached to the farthest corners of Europe, and grew from new geopolitical pressures that states now confronted, this new moment of reformation forced all to wrestle with the implications of Atlantic consolidation. On this idea, I am indebted to John Watts, who is completing a book provisionally entitled *Renaissance England* for the New Oxford History of England series.
66. On the dilemma, see John Clive and Bernard Bailyn, "England's Cultural Provinces: Scotland and America," *William and Mary Quarterly*, 3rd ser., 11 (1954), 200–213. For the various issues faced by colonists, see Gary Nash, *Urban Crucible: The Northern Seaports and the Origins of the American Revolution* (Cambridge, MA, 1986); T. H. Breen, *Tobacco Culture: The Mentality of the Great Tidewater Planters on the Eve of Revolution* (Princeton, 2001); and Woody Holton, *Forced Founders: Indians, Debtors, Slaves, and the Making of the American Revolution in Virginia* (Chapel Hill, 1999).
67. Voltaire, *Candide* (New York, 2005), 4. For how reform shaped policy, see Steven Pincus, *The Heart of the Declaration: The Founders' Case for an Activist*

*Government* (New Haven, 2016), 53–68; Jacques Léon Godechot, *Les révolutions, 1770–1799* (Paris, 1970), 94–96. Usually, as one historian notes, this dilemma underscored a metropolitan understanding that "negotiation" with a creole elite could secure goals. So long as these elites had a sense that give-and-take defined the rules of the game, they would not question empire. See Klooster, *Revolutions in the Atlantic World*, 5.

68. Eric Hinderaker, *Boston's Massacre* (Cambridge, MA, 2017), 106–19, 168–73.

69. Griffin, *Townshend Moment*, 217–27.

70. Thomas Bartlett, *Ireland: A History* (New York, 2010), 153–58; Ian McBride, *Eighteenth-Century Ireland: Isle of Slaves* (Dublin, 2009), 273–320.

71. Matthew Dziennik, *The Fatal Land: War, Empire, and the Highland Soldier in British America* (New Haven, 2015), 24–30, 124–28; Stephen Brumwell, *Redcoats: The British Soldier and War in the Americas, 1755–1763* (New York, 2002), 268–80; Andrew Jackson O'Shaughnessy, *An Empire Divided: The American Revolution and the British Caribbean* (Philadelphia, 2000); Brad Jones, *Resisting Independence: Popular Loyalism in the Revolutionary British Atlantic* (Ithaca, 2021), 141.

72. See Bernard Bailyn, *The Ideological Origins of the American Revolution* (Cambridge, MA, 2017), 55–93; Woody Holton, *Forced Founders*; Matthew Mulcahy, *Hubs of Empire: The Southeastern Lowcountry and British Caribbean* (Baltimore, 2014), 205–14. For a thorough account that emphasizes how reform measures impinged on provincial smuggling, land hunger, and rule over enslaved persons, see Woody Holton, *Liberty Is Sweet: The Hidden History of the American Revolution* (New York, 2021).

73. Griffin, *American Leviathan*, 84–88.

74. Richard White, *The Middle Ground*, 323; Colin Calloway, *The American Revolution in Indian Country*; Dowd, *War under Heaven*, 264–75.

75. This was not unusual. Very often reform measures, and their provincial implications, set groups that subsequent historians would call "aristocrats" and "democrats" against each other. See Godechot, *Les révolutions*, 104–5. On the alliance between traders, smugglers, and some of the rioters, see John Tyler, *Smugglers and Patriots: Boston Merchants and the Advent of the American Revolution* (Boston, 1986).

76. Craig Yirush, *Settlers, Liberty, and Empire: The Roots of Early American Political Theory, 1675–1775* (New York, 2011), 229–33.

77. Pierre Serna, "Every Revolution Is a War of Independence," in Suzanne Desan, Lynn Hunt, and William Nelson, eds., *The French Revolution in Global Perspective* (Ithaca, 2013), 165–82.

78. John Murrin, "1776: The Countercyclical Revolution," in Morrison and Zook, eds., *Revolutionary Currents*, 67. Also see Hopkins, *American Empire*, 8. For the latest study to focus on secession, one that suggests Americans broke away because of how their visions of engaging Europe diverged from Britain's, see D. H. Robinson, *The Idea of Europe and the Origins of the American Revolution* (Oxford, 2020).

79. Mary Beth Norton, *1774: The Long Year of Revolution* (New York, 2020).
80. For a recent recasting of the American Revolution within the broader revolutionary age, see Thomas Bender, *A Nation among Nations: America's Place in World History* (New York, 2006). For the crisis and how it fitted into broader British patterns, see Pincus, *Heart of the Declaration*.
81. Peter Thompson "The 1776 Moment" (lecture, Rothermere American Institute, Oxford, U.K., 11 July 2018). On the declaration in general, see David Armitage, *The Declaration of Independence: A Global History* (Cambridge, MA, 2007); and Pauline Maier, *American Scripture: Making the Declaration of Independence* (New York, 1998).
82. Griffin, *America's Revolution*, 93–124; Jay Fliegelman, *Prodigals and Pilgrims: The American Revolution against Patriarchal Authority, 1750–1800* (New York, 1982). My thanks to Peter Thompson for bringing the Friday parallel to my attention.
83. On these varied experiences, and the common themes they encourage us to see, see Rosemarie Zagarri, "Introduction," in Barbara Oberg, ed., *Women in the American Revolution: Gender, Politics, and the Domestic World* (Charlottesville, VA, 2019), 1–16.
84. Carol Berkin, *Revolutionary Mothers: Women in the Struggle for America's Independence* (New York, 2005), 26–49; Mary Beth Norton, *Liberty's Daughters: The Revolutionary Experience of American Women, 1750–1800* (Ithaca, 1996), 155–77; Linda Kerber, *Women of the Republic: Intellect and Ideology in Revolutionary America* (Chapel Hill, NC, 1980), 73–113; T. H. Breen, *Marketplace of Revolution*, 230–34, 279–89; Griffin, *America's Revolution*, 95; Vivian Conger, "Reading Early American Women's Political Lives: The Revolutionary Performances of Deborah Read Franklin and Sally Franklin Bache," *Early American Studies*, 2 (2018), 317–52; Patricia Cleary, *Elizabeth Murray: A Woman's Pursuit of Independence in Eighteenth-Century America* (Amherst, MA, 2000); Susan Brandt, " 'Getting into a Little Business': Margaret Hill Morris and Women's Medical Entrepreneurship during the American Revolution," *Early American Studies*, 13 (2015), 774–807; Holton, *Liberty Is Sweet*, 99–102.
85. Sarah Knott, "Female Liberty? Sentimental Gallantry, Republican Womanhood, and Rights Feminism in the Age of Revolutions," *William and Mary Quarterly*, 3rd ser., 71 (2014), 455.
86. Arno Mayer, *The Furies: Violence and Terror in the French and Russian Revolutions* (Princeton, 2002). For the violent American Revolution, see Holger Hoock, *Scars of Independence: America's Violent Birth* (New York, 2017); T. Cole Jones, *Captives of Liberty: Prisoners of War and the Politics of Vengeance in the American Revolution* (Philadelphia, 2020); Breen, *Will of the People*, 218; Alan Taylor, *American Revolutions: A Continental History* (New York, 2016). For the classic statement of the enslaved revolting by declaring independence, see Gary Nash, *Red, White, and Black: The Peoples of Early America* (New York, 1974), 277.
87. Griffin, *America's Revolution*, chs. 4–6.

88. Adelman, *Sovereignty and Revolution*, 7.
89. I refer to this as their "provincial dilemmas" in *Townshend Moment*. Joshua Simon sees it as the ideology of what he calls "Creole Revolution." See Joshua Simon, *Ideology of Creole Revolution: Imperialism and Independence in American and Latin American Political Thought* (Cambridge, 2017), 28, 32.

## Chapter Three. The French Connection

1. The best treatment of the many seeming paradoxes of Thomas Jefferson would be Annette Gordon-Reed and Peter S. Onuf, *"Most Blessed of Patriarchs": Thomas Jefferson and the Empire of Imagination* (New York, 2016).
2. Nathan Hatch, *The Sacred Cause of Liberty: Republican Thought and the Millennium in Revolutionary New England* (New Haven, 1977), 36–54.
3. See Johnathan Israel, *The Expanding Blaze: How the American Revolution Ignited the World, 1775–1848* (Princeton, 2017) for this connection. For a thorough examination of the idea of revolutionary connections, see Annie Jourdan, "Tumultuous Contexts and Radical Ideas (1783–89): The 'Pre-Revolution' in a Transnational Perspective," in David Andress, ed., *The Oxford Handbook of the French Revolution* (New York, 2015), 92–108.
4. Philipp Ziesche, *Cosmopolitan Patriots: Americans in Paris in the Age of Revolution* (Charlottesville, VA, 2010), 15–38.
5. Thomas Jefferson to Eliza House Trist, 18 August 1785, in *The Papers of Thomas Jefferson, Vol. 8*, ed. Julian P. Boyd (Princeton, 1953), 403–5; Israel, *Expanding Blaze*, 252, 255.
6. See Thomas Jefferson to Tench Coxe, 1 June 1795, in *The Papers of Thomas Jefferson, Vol. 25*, ed. John Catanzariti (Princeton, 1992), 14–17.
7. Jefferson quoted in Adam Lebovitz, "An Unknown Manuscript on the Terror, Attributed to Thomas Paine," *William and Mary Quarterly*, 3rd ser., 75 (2018), 712; Thomas Jefferson to George Mason, 4 February 1791, in *The Papers of Thomas Jefferson, Vol. 19*, ed. Julian P. Boyd (Princeton, 1974), 241–43; Armin Mattes, *Citizens of the Common Intellectual Homeland: The Transatlantic Origins of American Democracy and Nationhood* (Charlottesville, VA, 2015), 143.
8. Marquis de Condorcet, "The Influence of the American Revolution on Europe," trans. Durand Echeverria, in Durand Echeverria, "Condorcet's *The Influence of the American Revolution on Europe*," *William and Mary Quarterly*, 3rd ser., 25 (1968), 85–108; Israel, *Expanding Blaze*, 253–54; Condorcet to Jefferson, 21 December 1792, in *The Papers of Thomas Jefferson, Vol. 24*, ed. John Catanzariti (Princeton, 1990), 760–62.
9. On this, see Bernard Bailyn, *Ideological Origins of the American Revolution* (Cambridge, MA, 1968), 160–61. For the most penetrating statement on the intellectual connections, epitomized by the Jefferson-Condorcet connection, see James Kloppenberg, *Toward Democracy: The Struggle for Self-Rule in European and American Thought* (New York, 2016), 465–67, 472–75. Micah

Alpaugh examines the ways that networks created almost a chain reaction of social movement formation in *Friends of Freedom: The Rise of Social Movements in the Age of Atlantic Revolutions* (New York, 2022). The resulting movements, he finds, inspired "enlightenment though activism" (p. 7).

10. Sylvana Tomaselli, *Wollstonecraft: Philosophy, Passion, and Politics* (Princeton, 2021), 145, 147, 69. Wollstonecraft quoted in Thomas Furniss, "Mary Wollstonecraft's French Revolution," in *The Cambridge Companion to Mary Wollstonecraft* (Cambridge, 2002), 61. For ties to the Declaration, see Susan Manning, *The Poetics of Character: Transatlantic Encounters, 1700–1900* (Cambridge, 2013), 117. On the connections between categories, see Denise Davidson, "Feminism and Abolitionism: Transatlantic Trajectories," in Suzanne Desan, Lynn Hunt, and William Max Nelson, eds., *The French Revolution in Global Perspective* (Ithaca, 2013), 101–11.

11. For a compelling interpretation on this complex intertwining, see Manuel Covo, "Race, Slavery, and Colonies in the French Atlantic," in David Andress, ed., *The Oxford Handbook of the French Revolution* (New York, 2015), 290–310.

12. James Roger Sharp, "France and the United States at the End of the Eighteenth Century," in Manuela Albertone and Antonio De Francesco, eds., *Rethinking the Atlantic World: Europe and America in the Age of Democratic Revolutions* (New York, 2009), 203.

13. C. A. Bayly, *Birth of the Modern World, 1780–1914* (London, 2003), 101. Ideology, Anne Sa'adah writes, served as "the catalyst through which other, more basic but often more diffuse causes became politically operational." It mediated "between multiple 'structural' causes and the actual choices made by historical actors." So the process of making meaning worked at this moment. See Anne Sa'adah, *The Shaping of Liberal Politics in Revolutionary France* (Princeton, 1990), 26.

14. Charles Maier, *Leviathan 2.0: Inventing Modern Statehood* (Cambridge, MA, 2014), 15.

15. For how the idea of revolution led people to search for precedents and definitions, see Annie Jourdain, *La révolution, une exception française?* (Paris, 2003), 282–312.

16. Janet Polasky, "Revolutionaries between Nations, 1776–1789," *Past and Present*, 232 (2016), 165–201, 166–70. On the American connections, see Maria O'Malley and Denys Van Renan, eds., *Beyond 1776: Globalizing the Cultures of the American Revolution* (Charlottesville, VA, 2018).

17. For this, see Anna Vincenzi, "Imagining an Age of Revolutions? Interpretations of the American Revolution in the Italian States (1765–1799)" (Ph.D. diss., University of Notre Dame, 2020).

18. Jon Singerton, "The Residue of Revolution: Experiencing the Age of Revolution in Habsburg Lands, 1763–1815" (lecture, University of Oxford, 14 September 2019).

19. Emilia Viotti da Costa, *The Brazilian Empire: Myths and Histories* (Chicago, 1985), 5.

20. Jeremy Adelman, *Sovereignty and Revolution in the Iberian Atlantic* (Princeton, 2006), 51; Adelman, "An Age of Imperial Revolutions," *American Historical Review*, 113 (2008), 326.

21. For perceptive studies of the eighteenth century, see Ian McBride, *Eighteenth-Century Ireland: Isle of Slaves* (Dublin, 2009), 51–91; and David Dickson, *New Foundations: Ireland 1660–1800* (Dublin, 1987). Also refer to Griffin, *The Townshend Moment*. For Ireland as laboratory, see Nicholas Canny, "The Ideology of English Colonization: From Ireland to America," *William and Mary Quarterly*, 3rd ser., 30 (1973), 575–98.

22. Vincent Morley, *Irish Opinion and the American Revolution, 1760–1783* (Cambridge, 2002), 184–85; Ian McBride, *Scripture Politics: Ulster Presbyterians and Irish Radicalism in the Late Eighteenth Century* (Oxford, 1998); Steve Pincus, "The Irish Revolution of 1782 and the Age of Revolutions" (a talk at the Keough-Naughton Institute, University of Notre Dame, 25 January 2019).

23. For this complicated story, see Thomas Bartlett, *The Fall and Rise of the Irish Nation* (Dublin, 1992).

24. Ireland's case revolved around the realities of demographics: a settler minority with power over a native and Catholic majority. See Michael Brown, *The Irish Enlightenment* (Cambridge, MA, 2016).

25. Janet Polasky, "Revolutionaries between Nations, 1776–1789," *Past and Present*, 232 (2016): 165–201, 170–75; Richard Whatmore, "Saving Republics by Moving Republicans: Britain, Ireland and 'New Geneva' during the Age of Revolutions," *History: The Journal of the Historical Association*, 102 (2017): 386–413.

26. Israel, *Expanding Blaze*, 3, 5.

27. On the Dutch, see Israel, *Expanding Blaze*, 226, 82; R. R. Palmer, *The Age of Democratic Revolution*, vol. I (Princeton, 1969), 324, 325–340; Janet Polasky, *Revolutions without Borders: The Call to Liberty in the Atlantic World* (New Haven, 2015), 32–36.

28. John Lynch, *Spanish American Revolutions, 1808–1826* (New York, 1986), 24–29; Lynch, *Simón Bolívar: A Life* (New Haven, 2006), 13; Jaime Rodríguez O., *Independence of Spanish America* (New York, 1998), 39; Karen Racine, " 'This England and This Now': British Cultural and Intellectual Influence in the Spanish American Independence Era," *Hispanic American Historical Review*, 90 (2010), 428. "Common cause" comes from Robert Parkinson, *The Common Cause: Creating Race and Nation in the American Revolution* (Chapel Hill, 2016).

29. Anthony McFarlane, "The American Revolution and Spanish America, 1776–1814," in Gabriel Paquette and Gonzalo Quintero Saravia, eds., *Spain and the American Revolution: New Approaches and Perspectives* (New York, 2020), 41.

30. Serna, "Every Revolution Is a War of Independence," 177.

31. Kloppenberg, *Toward Democracy*, 457.

32. Kathleen DuVal, *Independence Lost: Lives on the Edge of the American Revolution* (New York, 2015), 125–28; Gabriel Paquette and Gonzalo Quintero

Saravia, "Introduction: Spain and the American Revolution," in Paquette and Quintero, eds., *Spain and the American Revolution*, 11–26.

33. Luke Ritter, "The American Revolution on the Periphery of Empire: Don Bernardo de Galvez and the Spanish-American Alliance, 1763–1783," *Journal of Early American History*, 7 (2017), 177–201.

34. Eliga Gould on the treaty and its international implications in his forthcoming book tentatively entitled *Crucible of Peace: The Turbulent History of America's Founding Treaty* (forthcoming, Oxford University Press). I am thankful for his help on these issues. On the tangles and the war, see Piers Mackesy, *The War for America, 1775–1783* (Cambridge, MA, 1964); P. J. Marshall, *The Making and Unmaking of Empires: Britain, India, and America, c. 1750–1783* (New York, 2005), 363–64; and Andrew O'Shaughnessy, *The Men Who Lost America: British Leadership, the American Revolution, and the Fate of Empire* (New Haven, 2013).

35. Simon Schama, *Citizens: A Chronicle of the French Revolution* (New York, 1990), 62–64.

36. Colin Jones, *The Great Nation: France from Louis XV to Napoleon* (New York, 2003), 341.

37. On this, see John Shovlin, *Political Economy of Virtue: Luxury, Patriotism, and the Origins of the French Revolution* (Ithaca, 2006), 9–10.

38. For the importance of Saint-Domingue to the metropole, see Manuel Covo, "Race, Slavery, and Colonies in the French Revolution." For a counterargument, one that focuses on continuities and downplays how changing notions of political economy transformed some old regime ways, see Clare Haru Crowston, *Credit, Fashion, Sex: Economies of Regard in Old Regime France* (Durham, 2013).

39. Paul Cheney, *Revolutionary Commerce: Globalization and the French Monarchy* (Cambridge, MA, 2010), 195–96, 201. On this and what follows, see William Doyle, *Origins of the French Revolution* (Oxford, 1999).

40. On this, see Anthony Hopkins, *American Empire: A Global History* (Princeton, 2018), 52; and Carlos Marichal, *Bankruptcy of Empire: Mexican Silver and the Wars between Spain, Britain, and France* (Cambridge, 2007), 81–118.

41. Doyle, *Origins*.

42. On Franklin and mania for America at this moment, see Schama, *Citizens*, 27–28, 42–43; Jeremy Popkin, *A New World Begins: The History of the French Revolution* (New York, 2019), 71.

43. Richard Whatmore, "The French and North American Revolutions in Comparative Perspective," and Antonio De Francesco, "Federalist Obsession and Jacobin Conspiracy: France and the United States in a Time of Revolution, 1789–1794," in Manuela Albertone and Antonio De Francesco, eds., *Rethinking the Atlantic World*, 219–23, 239–40.

44. Jeremy Popkin, "Saint-Domingue, Slavery, and the Origins of the French Revolution," in Thomas Kaiser and Dale Van Kley, eds., *From Deficit to Del-*

*uge: The Origins of the French Revolution* (Stanford, 2011), 220–21; Suzanne Desan, "Internationalizing the French Revolution," *French Politics, Culture and Society*, 29 (2011), 137–160.

45. "Introduction: Beyond Atlantic History," in Manuela Albertone and Antonio De Francesco, eds., *Rethinking the Atlantic World: Europe and America in the Age of Democratic Revolutions* (New York, 2009), 2–3. This volume has a number of essays that explore these connections. For a study that looks at how global smuggling had a role to play in the origins of the French Revolution, largely by undermining faith in institutions and in the fairness of the regime, see Michael Kwass, *Contraband: Louis Mandrin and the Making of a Global Underground* (Cambridge, MA, 2014).

46. Jones, *Great Nation*, 423.

47. Charles Walton, "The Fall from Eden: The Free-Trade Origins of the French Revolution," in Suzanne Desan, Lynn Hunt, and William Max Nelson, eds., *The French Revolution in Global Perspective* (Ithaca, 2013), 46, 55. On Calonne, see Jones, *Great Nation*, 343–48.

48. On this, see Jones, *Great Nation*, 363. Also see Walton, "Fall from Eden." For a comparative interpretation that explores structural differences, and the divergent paths two liberal experiments would take, see Sa'adah, *The Shaping of Liberal Politics in Revolutionary France*.

49. For this synopsis, I am indebted to Bill Doyle and a paper he delivered entitled "Delusions of Despotism: Absolutism in Retreat before 1789" (New History of the State Conference, University of Notre Dame, 2018).

50. See Doyle, *The Oxford History*, 101–11; and Jones, *Great Nation*. For Louis XVI's failures to govern, see Popkin, *A New World Begins*.

51. Jones, *Great Nation*, 404–5. For the tensions this move unleashed, see John Hardman, "The View from Above," in Andress, ed., *Oxford Handbook of the French Revolution*, 132–148.

52. Jones, *Great Nation*, 411.

53. Schama, *Citizens*, 379.

54. François Furet, *Revolutionary France, 1770–1880* (Oxford, 1988), 41.

55. On this, see Keith Baker, *Inventing the French Revolution: Essays on French Political Culture in the Eighteenth Century* (New York, 1990), 16, 124–25. On the older idea of nation now resurrected, see David Bell, *The Cult of the Nation in France: Inventing Nationalism, 1600–1800* (Cambridge, MA, 2001) (p. 22 for Sieyès quote). On Sieyès, see Furet, *Revolutionary France*, 45–51; and Popkin, *A New World Begins*, 105.

56. Jones, *Great Nation*, 400.

57. Lauren Klay, "Origins of the French Revolution," in Andress, ed., *Oxford Handbook of the French Revolution*, 21–22.

58. Peter McPhee, "A Social Revolution? Rethinking Popular Insurrection in 1789," in Andress, ed., *Oxford Handbook of the French Revolution*, 167; Schama, *Citizens*, 387.

59. Jones, *Great Nation*, 415.
60. Silvia Marzagalli, "Economic and Demographic Developments," in Andress, ed., *Oxford Handbook of the French Revolution*, 5; and McPhee, "A Social Revolution?" 172.
61. Thomas Kaiser and Dale Van Kley, "Introduction," in Kaiser and Van Kley, eds., *From Deficit to Deluge*, 1–8; Jones, *Great Nation*, 397, 377. For the vacuum idea, see William Doyle, *The French Revolution: A Very Short Introduction* (New York, 2001), 36.
62. Peter McPhee, *Liberty or Death: The French Revolution* (New Haven, 2016), 56–57; Keith Baker, "Enlightenment Idioms, Old Regime Discourses, and Revolutionary Improvisation," in Kaiser and Van Kley, eds., *From Deficit to Deluge*, 165–97.
63. McPhee, *Liberty or Death*, 72–73. For a description of the event as well as the way the event became symbol, see Schama, *Citizens*, 399–409.
64. Katie Jarvis, *Politics in the Marketplace: Work, Gender, and Citizenship in Revolutionary France* (New York, 2019), 58–73; D. M. G. Sutherland, "Urban Violence in 1789," and David Andress, "Politics and Insurrection: The Sans-Culottes, the 'Popular Movement,' and the People of Paris," in Andress, ed., *The Oxford Handbook of the French Revolution*, 282–83, 404.
65. Suzanne Desan, "Recent Historiography on the French Revolution and Gender," *Journal of Social History*, 52 (2019), 568.
66. Patrick Griffin, *America's Revolution* (New York, 2012), 199–228.
67. For the debates in context, see Jonathan Gienapp, *The Second Creation: Fixing the American Constitution in the Founding Era* (Cambridge, MA, 2018).
68. Maya Jasanoff, *Liberty's Exiles: American Loyalists in the Revolutionary World* (New York, 2011); Rebecca Brannon, *From Revolution to Reunion: The Reintegration of the South Carolina Loyalists* (Charleston, 2016).
69. Alan Taylor, *American Revolutions: A Continental History* (New York, 2016), 437–40; George Van Cleve, *A Slaveholders' Union: Slavery, Politics, and the Constitution in the Early Republic* (Chicago, 2011). Also see, most provocatively, David Waldstreicher, *Slavery's Constitution: From Revolution to Ratification* (New York, 2009).
70. On this, see McPhee, *Liberty or Death*; Furet, *Revolutionary France*, 3.
71. McPhee, *Liberty or Death*, 82.
72. On the idea of the creation of an age, see Vincenzi, "Imagining an Age of Revolutions?"
73. François Furstenberg, *When the United States Spoke French: Five Refugees Who Shaped a Nation* (New York, 2014).
74. Alfred Young, *The Democratic Republicans of New York: The Origins, 1763–1797* (Chapel Hill, 1967); Alpaugh, *Friends of Freedom*, 366–94.
75. See, in particular, *Rights of Man*. The quote comes from his dedication to George Washington.
76. Marianne Elliott, *Partners in Revolution: The United Irishmen and France* (New Haven, 1982); Thomas Bartlett, *Ireland: A History* (New York, 2010), 206–11.

77. Jim Smyth, *The Men of No Property: Irish Radicals and Popular Politics in the Late Eighteenth Century* (New York, 1992).

78. Maurice Bric, *Ireland, Philadelphia, and the Re-Invention of America, 1760–1800* (Dublin, 2008).

79. See James Sheehan, *German History, 1770–1866* (Oxford, 1989), 208–18. Kant quoted by McPhee, *Liberty or Death*, x. On this view of ideas, see Ritchie Robertson, *The Enlightenment: The Pursuit of Happiness, 1689–1790* (New York, 2021).

80. Christopher Clark, *Iron Kingdom: The Rise and Downfall of Prussia, 1600–1947* (Cambridge, MA, 2006), 284–85.

81. David Cannadine, *Victorious Century: The United Kingdom, 1800–1906* (London, 2017), 13.

82. Arthur Burns and Joanna Innes, "Introduction," in Arthur Burns and Joanna Innes, eds., *Rethinking the Age of Reform: Britain, 1780–1850* (Cambridge, 2003), 4–10.

83. William Selinger, *Parliamentarianism: From Burke to Weber* (Cambridge, 2019), 75–79.

84. For a longer explanation of this take, see Matthew Lockwood, *To Begin the World Over Again: How the American Revolution Devastated the Globe* (New Haven, 2019), 76–82.

85. Lynch, *Spanish American Revolutions*, 24–29; Rodríguez O., *Independence of Spanish America*, 36–41.

86. Anthony McFarlane, *War and Independence in Spanish America* (New York, 2014), 27.

87. Laurent Dubois, *Avengers of the New World: The Story of the Haitian Revolution* (Cambridge, MA, 2004), 1–2, 21. The classic statement on the connections remains C. L. R. James, *The Black Jacobins* (New York, 1938). A newer one that masterfully explores the many complexities of connection is Jane Landers, *Atlantic Creoles in the Age of Revolution* (Cambridge, MA, 2010). For the latest approach bringing France and Saint-Domingue together, see Popkin, *A New World Begins*; and Covo, "Race, Slavery, and Colonies in the French Revolution."

88. Laurent Dubois and John Garrigus, *Slave Revolution in the Caribbean, 1789–1804: A Brief History with Documents* (New York, 2006), 18. For what the enslaved knew of France, see Landers, *Atlantic Creoles in the Age of Revolution*, 59.

89. John Garrigus, *Before Haiti: Race and Citizenship in French Saint-Domingue* (New York, 2006), 229–35.

90. Cheney, *Revolutionary Commerce*, 205–6.

91. For this narrative of events, see Dubois, *Avengers of the New World*, 60–90.

92. On these connections, see Julius Scott, *The Common Wind: Afro-American Currents in the Age of the Haitian Revolution* (New York, 2018), 77. For the pamphlets, see Landers, *Atlantic Creoles in the Age of Revolution*, 62.

93. McFarlane, *War and Independence in Spanish America*, 27–28.

94. Garrigus, *Before Haiti*, 236–37, 249.
95. Dubois, *Avengers of the New World*, 87–88.
96. On cane burning, see Dubois, *Avengers of the New World*, 90–96.
97. Jones, *Great Nation*, 433.

## Chapter Four. The Gordian Knot of Fear

1. As one scholar of the Caribbean argues, in general slaves feared masters, and with good reason. The violence they could employ could be terrifying. But at certain moments, slaves could terrify their masters. Trevor Burnard, "Settlement, Security and the British Imperial System" (lecture, the University of Melbourne, 10 November 2018).

2. Jean-Paul Marat, *Ami du peuple*, in Laurent Dubois and John Garrigus, eds., *Slave Revolution in the Caribbean, 1789–1804: A Brief History with Documents* (New York, 2006), 111–112; Laurent Dubois, *Avengers of the New World: The Story of the Haitian Revolution* (Cambridge, MA, 2004), 129; Alex Dupay, "Toussaint Louverture, the Haitian Revolution, and Negritude: A Critical Assessment of Aime Cesaire's Interpretation," in *Haiti: From Revolutionary Slaves to Powerless Citizens: Essays on the Politics and Economics of Underdevelopment, 1804–2013* (London, 2014), 42.

3. On Louverture, see Dubois, *Avengers of the New World*, 171–76.

4. Toussaint Louverture, quoted in Dubois and Garrigus, eds., *Slave Revolution*, 146–53.

5. On this, see Arno Mayer, *The Furies: Violence and Terror in the French and Russian Revolutions* (Princeton, 2002), 30.

6. On this, I am following the line of Jean-Clement Martin, *Violence et révolution: Essai sur la naissance d'un mythe national* (Paris, 2006).

7. For this interpretation, see Timothy Tackett, *The Coming of the Terror in the French Revolution* (Cambridge, MA, 2015).

8. Mayer, *Furies*, 172–73.

9. For this view on the Terror, see Colin Jones, "Did Emotions Cause the Terror?" Review of *The Coming of the Terror in the French Revolution*, by Timothy Tackett, *New York Review of Books*, 64 (June 2017), 38–40; and most provocatively Jones's study of the Revolution in one day, *The Fall of Robespierre: 24 Hours in Revolutionary Paris* (Oxford, 2021), 2.

10. For a summary of the view that the state had a critical role to play, as well as the different position taken by Jean-Clement Martin, see Jennifer Ngaire Heuer, "Did Everything Change? Rethinking Revolutionary Legacies," in David Andress, ed., *The Oxford Handbook of the French Revolution* (Oxford, 2015), 637.

11. François Furet, *Revolutionary France, 1770–1880* (Oxford, 1988), 111.

12. Katie Jarvis, "The Cost of Female Citizenship: How Price Controls Gendered Democracy in Revolutionary France," *French Historical Studies*, 41

(2018), 647–80; David Andress, "Politics and Insurrection: The Sans-culottes, the 'Popular Movement,' and the People of Paris," in David Andress, ed., *The Oxford Handbook of the French Revolution* (Oxford, 2015), 404–5.

13. Sylvana Tomaselli, *Wollstonecraft: Philosophy, Passion, and Politics* (Princeton, 2021), 120; Thomas Furniss, "Mary Wollstonecraft's French Revolution," in Claudia L. Johnson, *The Cambridge Companion to Mary Wollstonecraft* (Cambridge, 2002), 63, 64.

14. For this, see Martin, *Violence et révolution*; Dan Edelstein, "What Was the Terror?" in David Andress, ed., *The Oxford Handbook of the French Revolution* (Oxford, 2015), 453–54.

15. Mary Ashburn Miller, *A Natural History of Revolution: Violence and Nature in the French Revolutionary Imagination, 1789–1794* (Ithaca, 2011).

16. Dan Edelstein, *The Terror of Natural Right: Republicanism, the Cult of Nature, and the French Revolution* (Chicago, 2009), 128. Edelstein covers the historiographical debate over the Terror as well (chap. 3).

17. William Doyle sees these at work in *The Oxford History of the French Revolution* (New York, 2002).

18. Peter McPhee, *Liberty or Death: The French Revolution* (New Haven, 2016), 141–63.

19. For this shift, see Dan Edelstein, "Do We Want a Revolution without Revolution? Reflections on Political Authority," *French Historical Studies*, 35 (2012), 269–89.

20. For the mind-set, see McPhee, *Liberty or Death*, 149.

21. On Louis, and the indignities he experienced, see Simon Schama, *Citizens: A Chronicle of the French Revolution* (New York, 1991), 653–63.

22. Doyle, *Oxford History*, 174–96. "Revolutionary intolerance and popular bloodlust," writes Peter McPhee, were driven by "the menace of counter-revolution and the mixed emotions of panic, outrage, pride and fear that it arouses." See *Liberty or Death*, 163. For the people as playing the role as lead actors, see Jones, *The Fall of Robespierre*.

23. Schama, *Citizens*, 623, 665; Mayer, *Furies*, 49, 186.

24. Marisa Linton, "Terror and Politics," and Jennifer Ngaire Heuer, "Did Everything Change? Rethinking Revolutionary Legacies," in David Andress, ed., *The Oxford Handbook of the French Revolution* (Oxford, 2015), 472, 476, 635.

25. For a piece laying out the parameters of different views, see Samuel Moyn, "Mind the Enlightenment," *Nation*, 29 June 2015. On the problems scholars confront explaining the Terror, see Schama, *Citizens*, 631; Tim Blanning, *The Pursuit of Glory: Europe, 1648–1815* (New York, 2007), 344; James Kloppenberg, *Toward Democracy: The Struggle for Self-Rule in European and American Thought* (New York, 2016), 457, 530, 541; Jeremy Popkin, *A New World Begins: The History of the French Revolution* (New York, 2019), 417.

26. Mayer, *Furies*, 71, 87. I am especially reliant on the work of Timothy Tackett on these points. See *The Coming of the Terror in the French Revolution*, 12.

27. Colin Jones, *The Great Nation: France from Louis XV to Napoleon* (New York, 2003), 449–56.

28. Jones, *Great Nation*, 471, 476, 480–81.

29. Edelstein, *Terror of Natural Right*, 260. Terror as an idea did not always have the negative associations we associate with it today. The church employed the term to speak of salvation. Kings and laws could be terrible because of their majesty and because of the need for order. Terror could be and was "salutary." It was those who sent people to the guillotine that gave Terror a bad name. But it was already part of the French lexicon. On this, see Ronald Schechter, *A Genealogy of Terror in Eighteenth-Century France* (Chicago, 2018). The trajectory violence took used universalized ideals as the justification. In other words, the symbols would appeal far beyond France—and far past the eighteenth century. They would cast an immense shadow. See Julia Douthwaite, *The Frankenstein of 1790 and Other Lost Chapters from Revolutionary France* (Chicago, 2012), 153–227.

30. What follows owes a great deal to Dubois's narrative in *Avengers of the New World*, 97–114. For the best study on the networks that sustained news to and from Saint-Domingue, and that stoked fears throughout the Atlantic, see Julius Scott, *The Common Wind: Afro-American Currents in the Age of the Haitian Revolution* (New York, 2018). On the *Rights of Man*, see Dubois, *Avengers of the New World*, 105.

31. John Garrigus, *Before Haiti: Race and Citizenship in French Saint-Domingue* (New York, 2006), 250–51.

32. Adom Getachew, "Universalism after the Post-Colonial Turn: Interpreting the Haitian Revolution," *Political Theory*, 44 (2016), 821–45.

33. On this, see John K. Thornton, " 'I Am the Subject of the King of Congo': African Political Ideology and the Haitian Revolution," *Journal of World History*, 4 (1992), 181–214.

34. Carolyn Fick, *The Making of Haiti: The Saint Domingue Revolution from Below* (Knoxville, 1990), 75, 137–38, 237.

35. Garrigus, *Before Haiti*, 260.

36. Dubois, *Avengers of the New World*, 116.

37. Ada Ferrer, *Freedom's Mirror: Cuba and Haiti in the Age of Revolution* (New York, 2014), 3.

38. Malick Ghachem covers the tangled categorization of race in *The Old Regime and the Haitian Revolution* (New York, 2012), 13, 104. The best account of the cross-cutting binds, and how what we would expect did not necessarily happen, is Jane Landers, *Atlantic Creoles in the Age of Revolution* (Cambridge, MA, 2010), 71.

39. William Doyle, *The French Revolution: A Very Short Introduction* (New York, 2001), 72–73; Dubois, *Avengers of the New World*, 151.

40. On this broad theme, see Robin Blackburn, "The Force of Example," in David Geggus, ed., *The Impact of the Haitian Revolution in the Atlantic World* (Columbia, SC, 2001), 15–22.

41. For this narrative, see Dubois, *Avengers of the New World*, 125–31.

42. Dubois, *Avengers of the New World*, 302; Marlene Daut, *Tropics of Haiti: Race and the Literary History of the Haitian Revolution in the Atlantic World, 1789–1865* (Liverpool, 2015), 63–72. Of course, what transpired involved a great deal more than violence, including subtle shifts in understandings of race and law. See Ghachem, *Old Regime*, 5–6, 10.

43. See David Brion Davis, "Impact of the French and Haitian Revolutions," in Geggus, ed., *Impact of the Haitian Revolution*, 3–9; Gert Oostindie, "Slave Resistance," in Gert Oostindie and Wim Klooster, eds., *Curaçao in the Age of Revolutions*, 6–10; John Lynch, *Simón Bolívar: A Life* (New Haven, 2006), 97–100.

44. Dubois, *Avengers of the New World*, 305.

45. For how the rebels were dealt with, see Lynch, *Simón Bolívar*; Trevor Burnard and John Garrigus, *The Plantation Machine: Atlantic Capitalism in French Saint-Domingue and British Jamaica* (Philadelphia, 2016), 139–42.

46. On connections in the Caribbean and throughout the Atlantic in this period, see David Barry Gaspar and David Patrick Geggus, eds., *A Turbulent Time: The French Revolution and the Greater Caribbean* (Bloomington, IN, 1997); and Dubois and Garrigus, eds., *Slave Revolution*, 34.

47. David Patrick Geggus, *Haitian Revolutionary Studies* (Bloomington, 2002), 171–76, quote on p. 175; David Geggus, "The Exile of 1791 Slave Leaders: Spain's Resettlement of Its Black Auxiliary Troops," *Journal of Haitian Studies*, 8 (2002), 52–67.

48. Mathieu Ferradou, "Introduction: L'Irlande et la France à l'Époque de la République Atlantique: Historiographie et nouvelles approches," *La Révolution Française*, 11 (2016), 2–26. For the twisted nature of allegiances, and how they would play out civil-war-like, see David Dickson, *New Foundations: Ireland 1660–1800* (Dublin, 1987), 170–96.

49. Peter Linebaugh, " 'A Dish with One Spoon': American Experience and the Transformation of Three Officers of the Crown," in Thomas Bartlett et al., eds., *1798: A Bicentenary Perspective* (Dublin, 2003), 644.

50. On this idea and the link with South America and United States, see José Shane Brownrigg-Gleeson Martínez, "Irlanda, los Irlandeses en los Estados Unidos y las independencias iberoamericanas: Una interpretación transatlántica (1808–1820)," (Ph.D. diss., University of Salamanca, July 2017).

51. Dickson, *New Foundations*, 206–7.

52. Thomas Bartlett, *Ireland: A History* (New York, 2010), 211–16.

53. Arthur Burns and Joanna Innes, "Introduction," in Arthur Burns and Joanna Innes, eds., *Rethinking the Age of Reform: Britain, 1780–1850* (Cambridge, 2003), 12–14.

54. David Cannadine, *Victorious Century: The United Kingdom, 1800–1906* (London, 2017), 14–15.

55. Karin Schuller, "From Liberalism to Racism: German Historians, Journalists and the Haitian Revolution from the Late Eighteenth to the Early Twentieth Centuries," in Geggus, ed., *Impact of the Haitian Revolution*, 23–43.

56. On this, see James Sheehan, *German History, 1770–1866* (New York, 1989), 208–18.

57. On this, see Janet Polasky, *Revolution in Brussels, 1787–1793* (Brussels, 1987); Jane Judge, *The United States of Belgium: The Story of the First Belgian Revolution* (Leuven, 2018).

58. Matthew Rainbow Hale, "Regenerating the World: The French Revolution, Civic Festivals, and the Forging of Modern American Democracy, 1793–1795," *Journal of American History*, 103 (2017), 891–920; Gordon Wood, *The Empire of Liberty: A History of the Early Republic, 1789–1815* (New York, 2009), 203–4; Stanley Elkins and Eric McKitrick, *The Age of Federalism: The Early American Republic, 1788–1800* (New York, 1993), chs. 8, 15.

59. Michel-Rolph Trouillot, *Silencing the Past: Power and the Production of History* (Boston, 2015), 87–88.

60. For such "transcoloniality," see Sara Johnson, *The Fear of French Negroes: Transcolonial Collaborations in the Revolutionary Americas* (Berkeley, 2012).

61. Simon Newman, "American Political Culture and the French and Haitian Revolutions: Nathaniel Cutting and the Jefferson Republicans," in Geggus, ed., *Impact of the Haitian Revolution*, 72–89; Ashli White, *Encountering Revolution: Haiti and the Making of the Early Republic* (Baltimore, 2010), 2.

62. White, *Encountering Revolution*, 5; Jane Landers, *Atlantic Creoles in the Age of Revolution* (Cambridge, MA, 2010), quote on page 5; James Dun, *Dangerous Neighbors: Making the Haitian Revolution in Early America* (Philadelphia, 2016), 87–92, 143–48; David Wilson, *United Irishmen, United States: Immigrant Radicals in the Early Republic* (Ithaca, 1998).

63. On this, see Elkins and McKitrick, *The Age of Federalism*.

64. Colin Calloway, *The American Revolution in Indian Country: Crisis and Diversity in Native American Communities* (Cambridge, 1995), 279–89. On the wider west in this period, see Gregory Nobles, *American Frontiers: Cultural Encounters and Continental Conquest* (New York, 1997).

65. Alyssa Mt. Pleasant, "Independence for Whom? Expansion and Conflict in the Northeast and Northwest," in Andrew Shankman, ed., *The Worlds of the Revolutionary American Republic: Land, Labor, and the Conflict for a Continent* (London, 2014), 116–33.

66. Kathleen DuVal, *Independence Lost: Lives on the Edge of the American Revolution* (New York, 2015), 268–69.

67. Alan Taylor, *The Divided Ground: Indians, Settlers, and the Northern Borderland of the American Revolution* (New York, 2006), 114–17.

68. DuVal, *Independence Lost*, 292–312.

69. Christian Ayne Crouch, "The French Revolution in Indian Country: Reconsidering the Reach and Place of Atlantic Upheaval," in Matthias Middell and

Megan Maruschke, eds., *The French Revolution as a Moment of Respatialization* (Berlin, 2019), 85–105. On the confederacies, see Richard White, *The Middle Ground: Indians, Empires, and Republics in the Great Lakes Region, 1650–1815* (New York, 1991), 413–48. For reinvention in the face of renewed invasion, see Christina Snyder, "Native Nations in the Age of Revolution," in Shankman, ed., *The Worlds of the Revolutionary American Republic*, 77–94.

70. On this and what follows, see Thomas Slaughter, *The Whiskey Rebellion: Frontier Epilogue to the American Revolution* (New York, 1986); Patrick Griffin, *American Leviathan: Empire, Nation, and Revolutionary Frontier* (New York, 2007).

71. Ira Berlin, *Many Thousands Gone: The First Two Centuries of Slavery in North America* (Cambridge, MA, 1998), 290–324.

72. Burnard and Garrigus, *Plantation Machine*, 139.

73. Colin Calloway, *The Indian World of George Washington: The First President, the First Americans, and the Birth of the Nation* (New York, 2018); Drew McCoy, *The Elusive Republic: Political Economy in Jeffersonian America* (Chapel Hill, 1996).

74. On some of these ideas, see Mayer, *Furies*, 119.

75. Mayer, *Furies*, 98. As one historian who has spent a great deal of time studying the phenomenon argues, it "had ideological antecedents and circumstantial catalysts, and the emotional condition of its leaders and supporters helps to explain their actions." See Schechter, *Genealogy of Terror*, 200.

76. Jeremy Adelman, *Sovereignty and Revolution in the Iberian Atlantic* (Princeton, 2006), 64; Lester Langley, *Americas in the Age of Revolution, 1750–1850* (New Haven, 1996), 168, 175; John Lynch, *Spanish American Revolutions, 1808–1826* (New York, 1986), 29.

77. Adelman, *Sovereignty and Revolution*, 140.

78. Gabriel Paquette, *Enlightenment, Governance, and Reform in Spain and Its Empire, 1759–1808* (Cambridge, 2008), 127–30; Anthony McFarlane, "The American Revolution and Spanish America, 1776–1814," in Gabriel Paquette and Gonzalo Quintero Saravia, eds., *Spain and the American Revolution: New Approaches and Perspectives* (New York, 2020), 49.

79. Cristina Soriano, *Tides of Revolution: Information, Insurgencies, and the Crisis of Colonial Rule in Venezuela* (Albuquerque, NM, 2018).

80. Lynch, *Spanish American Revolutions*, 28–29; Juan González Mendoza, "Puerto Rico's Patriots and the Slave Trade after the Haitian Revolution," in Geggus, ed., *Impact of the Haitian Revolution*, 58–71; Anthony McFarlane, *War and Independence in Spanish America* (New York, 2014), 27–28, 413; Soriano, *Tides of Revolution*.

81. Ferrer, *Freedom's Mirror*, 5, 9, 10.

82. Roderick Barman, *Brazil: The Forging of a Nation, 1798–1852* (Stanford, 1988), 9, 34.

83. On this history, see Kenneth Maxwell, *Conflicts and Conspiracies: Brazil and Portugal, 1750–1808* (Cambridge, 1973), 218–28.

84. Eliga Gould, *Among the Nations of the Earth: The American Revolution and the Making of a New World Empire* (Cambridge, MA, 2008); McCoy, *The Elusive Republic*.

85. Seth Cotlar, *Tom Paine's America: The Rise and Fall of Transatlantic Radicalism in the Early Republic* (Charlottesville, VA, 2011), 211–14.

86. Cecile Vidal, *Caribbean New Orleans: Empire, Race, and the Making of a Slave Society* (Chapel Hill, 2017), 511.

87. Quote in letter to Adams in Griffin *America's Revolution*, 284–85.

88. Thomas Jefferson, *Notes on the State of Virginia* (London, 1787). My thanks to Andrew O'Shaughnessy for bringing this to my attention.

## Chapter Five. The Web of War

1. For this sort of interpretation, one that regards the American Revolution as an awful cataclysm for most of the world because of the war it unleashed, see Matthew Lockwood, *To Begin the World Over Again: How the American Revolution Devastated the Globe* (New Haven, 2019).

2. Indeed, we could refer to the period between 1756 and 1815 as one continuous war. I owe this idea to Tom Bartlett and a talk he gave entitled "Viewing and Acting: Irish Revolutionaries and South America, 1780–1820" (Pontifical University of Chile, 4 December 2018).

3. Arno Mayer, *The Furies: Violence and Terror in the French and Russian Revolutions* (Princeton, 2002), 33, 533. For this view of the period, see Michael Rapport, *The Napoleonic Wars: A Very Short Introduction* (Oxford, 2013). Anthony Page goes even further back, to the Jacobite Rising in 1745 as the starting point to a Seventy Years' War. See *Britain and the Seventy Years' War, 1744–1815: Enlightenment, Revolution, and Empire* (London, 2015). Or we could go back further still and say that Continental rivalries, which then became Atlantic in extent, had France and England—and then Britain—warring from 1689 to 1815, a "hundred years' war" that straddled the early modern and modern periods. See Alexander Mikaberidze, *The Napoleonic Wars: A Global History* (New York, 2020), xiii. Francis Cogliano suggests that when we incorporate America, the best number of years is sixty. See "The Sixty Years' War in North America," in Geoff Mortimer, ed., *Early Modern Military History* (London, 2004), 155–76.

4. Napoleon to the national guards of the Cisalpine Republic, 14 May 1797, quoted in Bruno Colson, *Napoleon: On War* (Oxford, 2015), 169; Mayer, *Furies*, 538; Patrice Gueniffey, *Bonaparte: 1769–1802* (Cambridge, MA, 2015), 294; David Bell, *The First Total War: Napoleon's Europe and the Birth of Warfare as We Know It* (Boston, 2007), 233. This is what we could call the "internalist" interpretation. See Mikaberidze, *Napoleonic Wars*, 3. For how his ambitions shaped his actions—and the whole of the period—see Rapport, *Napoleonic Wars*.

5. David Cannadine, *Victorious Century: The United Kingdom, 1800–1906* (London, 2017), 54, 74; Kevin Linch, *Britain and Wellington's Army: Recruitment, Society, and Tradition, 1807–1815* (New York, 2011), 56–82. On mobilization, its economic costs, and how it was critical to both waging war and determining the wages of war, see Eric Hobsbawm, *The Age of Revolution, 1789–1848* (New York, 1962), 77–98.

6. Nicholas Nicolas, ed., *The Dispatches and Letters of Vice Admiral Lord Viscount Nelson, with Notes*, 7 vols. (London, 1845–46), vol. 6, 100; Arthur Richard Wellesley, ed., *Supplementary Dispatches and Memoranda of Field Marshal Arthur Duke of Wellington, K.G.*, 15 vols. (London, 1858–72), vol. 7, 41 and 259; John Cartwright, *The Commonwealth in Danger* (London, 1795; reprint, New York, 1968), 17; Wellesley, ed., *Supplementary Dispatches*, vol. 6, 593, quoted in Linch, *Britain and Wellington's Army*, 125–26. On these themes, see J. E. Cookson, *The British Armed Nation, 1793–1815* (Oxford, 1997), 20–24; and James Davey, *In Nelson's Wake: The Navy and the Napoleonic Wars* (New Haven, 2015), 20–25. On Britain's fixation with Napoleon, see Tim Clayton, *This Dark Business: The Secret War against Napoleon* (London, 2018).

7. Even if they were bound together, it is clear that Napoleon did not think much of Wellington as a commander. See Andrew Roberts, *Napoleon: A Life* (New York, 2014), 759. For a recent study that suggests how war was central to the long history of the Atlantic and that its tangled nature only came to an end with the age, see Geoffrey Plank, *Atlantic Wars: From the Fifteenth Century to the Age of Revolution* (New York, 2020), 275–76.

8. For challenges to idea of knowledge, see Anders Engberg-Pedersen, *Empire of Chance: The Napoleonic Wars and the Disorder of Things* (Cambridge, MA, 2015). As Alexander Mikaberidze writes, for many "Revolution posed a threat not because it was impelled by powerful ideas but because those ideas carried guns." See *Napoleonic Wars*, 48. For this view of the warfare in the period, see Richard Evans, *The Pursuit of Power: Europe, 1815–1914* (New York, 2016), 1–20. For the way war played on tangles of the period, see John Tutino, "Introduction: Revolutions, Nations, and the New Industrial World," in Tutino, ed., *New Countries: Capitalism, Revolutions, and Nations in the Americas, 1750–1870* (Durham, NC, 2016), 8–9. For a study that views the period through the "prism of warfare," see Anthony McFarlane, *War and Independence in Spanish America* (New York, 2014).

9. Alan Forest, Karen Hagemann, and Michael Rowe, "Introduction: War, Demobilization and Memory in the Era of Atlantic Revolution," in Alan Forrest, Karen Hagemann, and Michael Rowe, eds., *War, Demobilization and Memory: The Legacy of War in the Era of Atlantic Revolutions* (New York, 2016), 5–9. Also see Plank, *Atlantic Wars*.

10. On this, see Thomas Slaughter, *The Whiskey Rebellion: Frontier Epilogue to the American Revolution* (New York, 1986). For the west in these years, see Patrick Griffin, *American Leviathan: Empire, Nation, and Revolutionary Frontier*

(New York, 2007), 222–49; and Gregory Nobles, *American Frontiers: Cultural Encounters and Continental Conquest* (New York, 1997).

11. On settler colonialism in this era, see Walter Hixson, *American Settler Colonialism: A History* (New York, 2013); Michael Witgen, "A Nation of Settlers: The Early American Republic and the Colonization of the Northwest Territory," *William and Mary Quarterly*, 3rd ser., 76 (2019), 391–98; Jeffrey Ostler, "Locating Settler Colonialism in Early American History," *William and Mary Quarterly*, 3rd ser., 76 (2019), 443–50; and Bethel Saler, *The Settlers' Empire Colonialism and State Formation in America's Old Northwest* (Philadelphia, 2015).

12. Sandra Moats, *Navigating Neutrality: Early American Governance in the Turbulent Atlantic* (Charlottesville, VA, 2021).

13. Gary Gerstle, *Liberty and Coercion: The Paradox of American Government from the Founding to the Present* (Princeton, 2015), 25.

14. On this and its implications, see Pekka Hämäläinen, *Lakota America: A New History of Indigenous Power* (New Haven, 2019); John Nelson, "The Geography to Command a Continent: Native Peoples, Europeans, and the Chicago Portage" (Ph.D. diss., University of Notre Dame, 2020); Alan Taylor, *The Divided Ground: Indians, Settlers, and the Northern Borderland of the American Revolution* (New York, 2006).

15. Peter Onuf, "Preface to the 2019 Edition," in Peter Onuf, *Statehood and Union: A History of the Northwest Ordnance* (Notre Dame, 2019), xiii–xx. For Jefferson's vision, see Onuf, *Jefferson's Empire: The Language of American Nationhood* (Charlottesville, VA, 2000).

16. On how development across space displaced tensions, see Drew McCoy, *The Elusive Republic: Political Economy in Jeffersonian America* (Chapel Hill, 1996). For the reluctance of the state and its weakness in the face of settlers, see Gerstle, *Liberty and Coercion*, 50–52.

17. Onuf, *Jefferson's Empire*, 46–49; Francis Cogliano, *Emperor of Liberty: Thomas Jefferson's Foreign Policy* (New Haven, 2014). Peter Onuf was especially helpful on these points.

18. Kathleen DuVal, *The Native Ground: Indians and Colonists in the Heart of the Continent* (Philadelphia, 2006), 158–63.

19. Claudio Saunt, *Unworthy Republic: The Dispossession of Native Americans and the Road to Indian Territory* (New York, 2020).

20. David Bell, *The First Total War: Napoleon's Europe and the Birth of Warfare as We Know It* (New York, 2007), 304, 77, 115. I am also indebted for the application of this notion to Ireland in the period to Tom Bartlett, "Ireland and Total War, 1793–1815" (lecture, Princess Grace Library, Monaco, 20 October 2018). On ideology and war, see Dan Edelstein, *Terror of Natural Right Republicanism, the Cult of Nature, and the French Revolution* (Chicago, 2009), 260. For how ideological commitment transformed the tenor of Atlantic warfare, see Plank, *Atlantic Wars*, 271.

21. Christopher Clark, *Iron Kingdom: The Rise and Downfall of Prussia, 1600–1947* (Cambridge, MA, 2006), 287.

22. The above is based on William Doyle, *Oxford History of the French Revolution* (New York, 2002), 197–219. For the diplomatic ins and outs, see Rapport, *Napoleonic Wars*.

23. Colin Jones, *The Great Nation: France from Louis XV to Napoleon* (New York, 2003), 450.

24. Edward Kolla, *Sovereignty, International Law, and the French Revolution* (Cambridge, 2017), 121–59.

25. Joris Oddens and Mart Rutjes, "The Political Culture of the Sister Republics"; and Andrew Jainchill, "The Transformation of Republicanism in the Sister Republics," in Joris Oddens, Mart Rutjes, and Erik Jacobs, eds., *The Political Culture of the Sister Republics, 1794–1806: France, the Netherlands, Switzerland, and Italy* (Amsterdam, 2015), 25–26, 43–47.

26. Pepijn Brandon and Karwan Fatah-Black, " 'The Supreme Power of the People': Local Autonomy and Radical Democracy in the Batavian Revolution (1795–1798)," in Michael McDonnell, ed., *Rethinking the Age of Revolution* (New York, 2017), 70–88. The episode, finally, marked the end of what scholars call "the second Dutch empire," that which had epitomized and thrived in the entangled Atlantic. War brought the clarity that did not permit ambiguous arrangements to survive. See Wim Klooster and Gert Oostindie, *Realm between Empires: The Second Dutch Atlantic, 1680–1815* (Ithaca, 2018), 224–25, 244–49.

27. Annie Jourdan, "The National Dimension in the Batavian Revolution Political Discussion, Institutions, and Constitutions," and Pierre Serna, "Small Nation, Big Sisters," in Oddens, Rutjes, and Jacobs, eds., *The Political Culture of the Sister Republics*, 183–84, 199.

28. Jones, *Great Nation*, 457.

29. All this is covered in Doyle, *Oxford History*, 200–201; and Kolla, *Sovereignty, International Law, and the French Revolution*, 280. On the Rhine and the ways locals came to cooperate because they could hold on to local customs, see Michael Rowe, *From Reich to State: The Rhineland in the Revolutionary Age, 1780–1830* (New York, 2003).

30. Jones, *Great Nation*, 455–57. On the levée, see Alan Forrest, "The French Revolution and the First Levée en Masse," in Daniel Moran and Arthur Waldron, eds., *The People in Arms: Military Myth and National Mobilization since the French Revolution* (New York, 2003), 8–32; Kolla, *Sovereignty, International law, and the French Revolution*, 172; Gunther E. Rothenberg, *The Art of Warfare in the Age of Napoleon* (Bloomington, IN, 1978), 100.

31. For dynamic destabilization, see Roy Foster, *Vivid Faces: The Revolutionary Generation in Ireland, 1890–1923* (New York, 2015).

32. James Sheehan, *German History, 1770–1866* (New York, 1990), 218–50. For an in-depth appreciation of these complexities, see Rowe, *From Reich to State*; Clark, *Iron Kingdom*, 284–96.

33. Sheehan, *German History*, 274–310; Michael Rowe, "The French Revolution, Napoleon and Nationalism in Europe," in John Breuilly, ed., *The Oxford Handbook of the History of Nationalism* (Oxford, 2013), 134–38; Karen

Hagemann, *Revisiting Prussia's Wars against Napoleon: History, Culture, and Memory* (New York, 2015), 47–60; Clark, *Iron Kingdom*, 331, 373–75; Karen Hagemann, "A Valorous Nation in a Holy War: War Mobilization, Religion and Political Culture in Prussia, 1807 to 1815," in Michael Broers, Peter Hicks, and Agustín Guimerá Ravina, eds., *The Napoleonic Empire and the New European Political Culture* (Basingstoke, 2012), 186–98.

34. DuVal, *The Native Ground*, 158. For the deep history of the Shawnees, see Peter Cozzens, *Tecumseh and the Prophet: The Shawnee Brothers Who Defied a Nation* (New York, 2020). For similar dynamics in North America, see Pekka Hämäläinen, *The Comanche Empire* (New Haven, 2008).

35. Charles Tilly, "Reflections on the History of European State-Making," in Charles Tilly, ed., *The Formation of National States in Western Europe* (Princeton, 1975), 42. My thanks to John Deak for this reference.

36. Mayer, *Furies*, 601.

37. Thomas Bartlett, " 'Total War' and Ireland, 1793–1815," *Irish Sword*, 31, 101–7.

38. For the ways political and confessional ideals entwined, for many groups, see Ian McBride, *Eighteenth-Century Ireland: Isle of Slaves* (Dublin, 2009), 406–33. The melding of French revolutionary ideas and sectarian views is captured in James Smyth, *Men of No Property: Irish Radicals and Popular Politics in the Late Eighteenth Century* (New York, 1992).

39. On this rising and its relationship to Continental intrigue, see Hugh Gough, "The Crisis Year: Europe and the Atlantic in 1798," in Thomas Bartlett et al. eds., *1798: A Bicentenary Perspective* (Dublin, 2003), 538–48. On the relationship between France and the United Irishmen, see Marianne Elliott, *Partners in Revolution: The United Irishmen and France* (New Haven, 1988). For Napoleon, see Roberts, *Napoleon*, 329–30. On Ulster, see Marianne Elliott, "Religious Polarization and Sectarianism in the Ulster Rebellion," in Bartlett et al., eds., *1798*, 288–89.

40. Tom Bartlett quoted in Kenan Malik, "The Great British Empire Debate," *New York Review of Books* (26 January 2018).

41. Bartlett, " 'Total War' and Ireland."

42. Linda Colley, *Britons: Forging the Nation, 1707–1837* (New Haven, 2009); Brad Jones, *Resisting Independence: Popular Loyalism in the Revolutionary British Atlantic* (Ithaca, 2021).

43. Linch, *Britain and Wellington's Army*, 56–72.

44. Scholars have long argued, as did the French who came to see Ireland as a place of potential destabilization for Britain, that Ireland could be Britain's Vendée. See Matthew Dziennik, "Peasants, Soldiers, and Revolutionaries: Interpreting Irish Manpower in the Age of Revolutions," in Patrick Griffin and Francis Cogliano, eds., *Ireland and America: Empire, Revolution, and Sovereignty* (Charlottesville, VA, 2021), 116.

45. Colin Jones, *The Fall of Robespierre: 24 Hours in Revolutionary Paris* (Oxford, 2021), 4–5; Jeremy Popkin, *A New World Begins: The History of the French Revolution* (New York, 2019), 323–25.

46. On this figure, see Tim Blanning, *Pursuit of Glory: Europe, 1648–1815* (New York, 2007), 345.

47. See Bell, *Total War*, 154–85. Marisa Linton puts the numbers at two hundred and fifty thousand insurgents and two hundred thousand republicans. See "Terror and Politics," in David Andress, ed., *The Oxford Handbook of the French Revolution* (Oxford, 2015), 472.

48. Mayer, *Furies*, 535.

49. Jones, *Great Nation*, 538.

50. Jane Lander, *Atlantic Creoles in the Age of Revolution* (Cambridge, MA, 2010), 60, 71; Graham Nessler, " 'They Always Knew Her to Be Free': Emancipation and Re-Enslavement in French Santo Domingo, 1804–1809," *Slavery and Abolition*, 33 (2012), 87–103.

51. Laurent Dubois, *Avengers of the New World: The Story of the Haitian Revolution* (Cambridge, MA, 2004), 152–54.

52. Dubois, *Avengers of the New World*, 129, 161–70; Popkin, *A New World Begins*, 388–89; David Patrick Geggus, *Haitian Revolutionary Studies* (Bloomington, 2002), 171–76; Jeremy Popkin, *You Are All Free: The Haitian Revolution and the Abolition of Slavery* (New York, 2010), 246–88.

53. Philippe Girard, "What's in a Name? Slave Trading during the French and Haitian Revolutions," *William and Mary Quarterly*, 3rd ser., 76 (2019), 763–96, 767.

54. All this is based on Dubois, *Avengers of the New World*; and Jane Landers, *Atlantic Creoles in the Age of Revolutions* (Cambridge, MA, 2010), 76.

55. Landers, *Atlantic Creoles*, 79–86; David Geggus, "The Exile of 1791 Slave Leaders: Spain's Resettlement of Its Black Auxiliary Troops," *Journal of Haitian Studies*, 8 (2002), 52–67. For this story, and for the ambiguities of status, see Rebecca Scott, "Paper Thin: Freedom and Re-enslavement in the Diaspora of the Haitian Revolution," *Law and History Review*, 29 (2011), 1061–87.

56. Brian Hamnett, *The End of Iberian Rule, 1770–1830* (Cambridge, 2017), 97–99; J. H. Elliott, *Empires of the Atlantic World: Britain and Spain in America, 1492–1830* (New Haven, 2006), 372–73; Jorge Miguel Viana Pedreira, "From Growth to Collapse: Portugal, Brazil, and the Breakdown of the Old Colonial System (1750–1830)," *Hispanic American Historical Review*, 80 (2000), 846.

57. Lester Langley, *The Americas in the Age of Revolution, 1750–1850* (New Haven, 1996), 166–67. Britain as well as France had a stake in what happened not only in the peninsula but in the empires too. They viewed the American peripheries of empire, reasonably, as parts of the whole that could be mobilized for the war effort. They also saw, particularly the British, that with empire adrift because of war, Latin America could be an extraordinary prize, especially for trade in the future. See Wim Klooster, *Revolutions in the Atlantic World: A Comparative History* (New York, 2018), 127–29. On the vacuum, see Elliott, *Empires of the Atlantic World*, 374–75.

58. Jaime Rodríguez O., The *Independence of Spanish America* (New York, 1998), 2; John Lynch, *Spanish American Revolutions, 1808–1826* (New York, 1986), 23–24. On the precipitant idea, now prominent in the literature, as well as the 1808 moment, see Gabriel Paquette, "The Dissolution of the Spanish Atlantic Monarchy," *Historical Journal*, 52 (2009), 197–98. José Portillo Valdés begins the first sentence of the body of his book with a simple statement about the significance of 1808. It was primum mobile. See José Portillo Valdés, *Crisis atlántica: Autonomía e independencia em la crisis de la monarquía hispana* (Madrid, 2006), 29; and Roberto Breña, *El primer liberalismo español y los processos de emancipacíon de America, 1808–1824* (Mexico City, 2006), 181.

59. McFarlane, *War and Independence in Spanish America*, 31, 45. On how war touched off "the western question," which in turn stirred tumult in South America, see Mikaberidze, *Napoleonic Wars*, 501.

60. Jeremy Adelman quotes Napoleon's use of the term "Spanish ulcer" in *Sovereignty and Revolution in the Iberian Atlantic* (Princeton, 2006), 179. On the war here, see Bell, *Total War*, 279–84. Anthony McFarlane sees war as a critical catalyst for the continent and 1808 as the critical moment. See *War and Independence in Spanish America*. Also refer to Roberts, *Napoleon*, 464.

61. Edwin Williamson, *Penguin History of Latin America* (London, 1992), 210–11. For the nature of juntas, see McFarlane, *War and Independence in Spanish America*, 42. For the latest on this line of thought, see Paquette, "The Dissolution of the Spanish Atlantic Monarchy," 175–212.

62. The pioneering study of uncertainty, debate, ideological ferment, and paradox, all stemming from the shock of 1808, is François-Xavier Guerra, *Modernidad e independencías: Ensayos sobre las revoluciones hispanicas* (Madrid, 1992).

63. John Lynch, *Simón Bolívar: A Life* (New Haven, 2006), 12–13. On the crisis of legitimacy, see Hamnett, *End of Iberian Rule*.

64. McFarlane, *War and Independence in Spanish America*, 51–57; Lynch, *Spanish American Revolutions*, 58; Hamnett, *End of Iberian Rule*, 119–126.

65. Williamson, *Penguin History of Latin America*, 211. On these, see McFarlane, *War and Independence in Spanish America*. This interpretation, focused on sovereignty, is that of Jaime Rodriguez O. in *The Independence of Spanish America*.

66. John Tutino, *Mexico City, 1808: Power, Sovereignty, and Silver in an Age of War and Revolution* (Albuquerque, NM, 2018). The year 1808, not 1810, represents the key turning point for Mexico, Tuntino argues. New Spain had become a virtual tax treasury for the Crown as it fought successive wars. So, while Spain could shunt the burden of war to the colonies, which France could not, in the process it had stripped some of the most productive regions bare. No money meant no resilience. Also see Carlos Marichal, *Bankruptcy of Empire: Mexican Silver and the Wars between Spain, Britain, and France* (Cambridge, 2007).

67. Hamnett, *End of Iberian Rule*, 127–41; Lynch, *Spanish American Revolutions*, 58–71.

68. Portillo, *Crisis atlántica*; Guerra, *Modernidad e independencías*, 127; Hamnett, *End of Iberian Rule*, 127–141.

69. Jaime Rodriguez O., " 'Equality! The Sacred Right of Equality': Representation under the Constitution of 1812," *Revista de Indias*, 68 (2008), 97–122; Portillo, *Crisis atlántica*, 29, 31; Antonio Feros, *Speaking of Spain: The Evolution of Race and Nation in the Hispanic World* (Cambridge, MA, 2017), 229–30, 232–77. My thanks to Fidel Tavarez for guidance on these points.

70. Roberto Breña, "The Cadiz Liberal Revolution and Spanish American Independence," in John Tutino, ed., *New Countries: Capitalism, Revolutions, and Nations in the Americas, 1750–1870* (Durham, NC, 2016), 72–80; Antonio Feros, *Speaking of Spain*, 277.

71. Hamnett, *End of Iberian Rule*, 176–77.

72. McFarlane, *War and Independence in Spanish America*, 145–75. On the rivalry between Buenos Aires and Montevideo, see Fabricio Prado, *Edge of Empire: Atlantic Networks and Revolution in Bourbon Rio de la Plata* (Berkeley, CA, 2015); Lynch, *Spanish American Revolutions*, 58–71.

73. Eduardo Posado-Carbo, "The American Revolution and the Independence of Colombia" (talk at the Pontifical University of Chile, 5 December 2018); Eduardo Posado-Carbo, "Spanish America and US Constitutionalism in the Age of Revolution," in Gabriel Paquette and Gonzalo Quintero Saravia, eds., *Spain and the American Revolution: New Approaches and Perspectives* (New York, 2020), 212–18; Josep Fradera, *The Imperial Nation: Citizens and Subjects in the British, French, Spanish, and American Empires* (Princeton, 2018), 65; Breña, "The Cadiz Liberal Revolution and Spanish American Independence," 83; Anthony McFarlane, "The American Revolution and Spanish America, 1776–1814," in Paquette and Quintero, eds., *Spain and the American Revolution*, 46–48.

74. Karen Racine, " 'This England and This Now': British Cultural and Intellectual Influence in the Spanish American Independence Era," *Hispanic American Historical Review*, 90 (2010), 423, 425; Racine, "Proxy Pasts: The Use of British Historical References in Spanish American Independence Rhetoric, 1808–1828," *English Historical Review*, 132 (2017), 864.

75. Cristina Soriano, *Tides of Revolution: Information, Insurgencies, and the Crisis of Colonial Rule in Venezuela* (Albuquerque, NM, 2018).

76. Eric Van Young, *The Other Rebellion: Popular Violence, Ideology, and the Mexican Struggle for Independence, 1810–1821* (Stanford, 2001), 496–503; Williamson, *Penguin History of Latin America*, 214–20; Lynch, *Bolívar*, 44.

77. Scott Eastman, " 'America Has Escaped from Our Hands': Rethinking Empire, Identity and Independence during the *Trienio Liberal* in Spain, 1820–1823," *European Historical Quarterly*, 41 (2011), 428–43; Anthony McFarlane, "Spanish American Colonial Wars in Comparative Perspective" (talk at the Pontifical University of Chile, 4 December 2018).

78. For this, see especially Peter Blanchard, *Fearful Vassals: Urban Elite Loyalty in the Viceroyalty of Rio de la Plata, 1776–1810* (Pittsburgh, 2020), 165–66,

206–7. My thanks to Professor Blanchard for showing me a draft when the book was in production.

79. On this, see Adelman, *Sovereignty and Revolution*, ch. 5.

80. Williamson, *Penguin History of Latin America*, 166; Langley, *Americas in the Age of Revolution*, 167.

81. Eliga Gould, "Entangled Histories, Entangled Worlds: The English-Speaking Atlantic as a Spanish Periphery," *American Historical Review*, (2007), 768.

82. For these insights, I am indebted to Anthony McFarlane, "Spanish American Colonial Wars in Comparative Perspective"; and Peter Blanchard, "Elites, Slaves, and Changing Loyalties in Pre-Independence Rio de la Plata" (talk at the Pontifical University of Chile, 5 December 2018).

83. On this, see Brian Hamnett, *Roots of Insurgency: Mexican Regions, 1750–1824* (Cambridge, 1986), 12–13, 21; Marichal, *Bankruptcy of Empire*, 260.

84. Peter Blanchard, "Elites, Slaves, and Changing Loyalties"; Lynch, *Spanish American Revolutions*, 51, 56.

85. Lynch, *Spanish American Revolutions*, 68–69, 96, 105; Robin Blackburn, *The Overthrow of Colonial Slavery, 1776–1848* (London, 1988), 409.

86. Anne Eller, " 'All Would Be Equal in the Effort': Santo Domingo's 'Italian Revolution,' Independence, and Haiti, 1809–1822," *Journal of Early American History*, 1 (2011), 105–41.

87. Jorge Miguel Viana Pedreira, "From Growth to Collapse: Portugal, Brazil, and the Breakdown of the Old Colonial System (1750–1830)," *Hispanic American Historical Review*, 80 (2000), 846, 850.

88. For Brazil and Portugal in these years, and for what follows, see Gabriel Paquette, *Imperial Portugal in the Age of Atlantic Revolutions: The Luso-Brazilian World, c. 1770–1850* (Cambridge, 2013), 84–103; Adelman, *Sovereignty and Revolution*, 220–57.

89. For how war precipitated this move, see Paquette, *Imperial Portugal in the Age of Atlantic Revolutions*, 85–91.

90. Kirsten Schultz, *Tropical Versailles: Empire, Monarchy, and the Portuguese Royal Court in Rio de Janeiro, 1808–1821* (New York, 2001), 67–87. The quotes come from Paquette, *Imperial Portugal in the Age of Atlantic Revolutions*, 96–97.

91. Williamson, *Penguin History of Latin America*, 213.

92. On this, see John Tutino, "The Americas in the Rise of Industrial Capitalism," and David Sartorius, "Cuban Counterpoint: Colonialism and Continuity in the Atlantic World," in Tutino, ed., *New Countries: Capitalism, Revolutions, and Nations in the Americas, 1750–1870* (Durham, NC, 2016), 40–49, 184.

93. Toby Green, *A Fistful of Shells: West Africa from the Rise of the Slave Trade to the Age of Revolution* (Chicago, 2019), 394, 396, 402, 431, 446–41.

94. Green, *A Fistful of Shells*, 451, 462.

95. Paul Lovejoy, *Jihad and West Africa during the Age of Revolutions* (Athens, OH, 2016); Manuel Barcia, *West African Warfare in Bahia and Cuba: Soldier Slaves in the Atlantic World, 1807–1844* (New York, 2014); James Searing, *West African Slavery and Atlantic Commerce* (Cambridge, 1993), 156. On Napoleon's war making in global context, including Louisiana, see Mikaberidze, *Napoleonic Wars.*

96. Sara Johnson, *The Fear of French Negroes: Transcolonial Collaboration in the Revolutionary Americas* (Berkeley, 2012), 157–58; Ada Ferrer, *Freedom's Mirror: Cuba and Haiti in the Age of Revolution* (New York, 2014), 271–85; Elena Schneider, *The Occupation of Havana: War, Trade, and Slavery in the Atlantic World* (Chapel Hill, 2018), 266–70.

97. Stuart Schwartz, "Cantos and Quilombos: A Hausa Rebellion in Bahia, 1814," in Jane Landers and Barry Robinson, eds., *Slaves, Subjects, and Subversives: Blacks in Colonial Latin America* (Albuquerque, 2006), 247–54.

98. João José Reis, *Slave Rebellion in Brazil: The Muslim Uprising of 1835 in Bahia* (Baltimore, 1993), 93–111; Manuel Barcia, *Seeds of Insurrection: Domination and Resistance on Western Cuban Plantations, 1808–1848* (Baton Rouge, 2008), 13–16; Manuel Barcia, " 'Weapons from Their Land': Arming Strategies and Practices among West African–Born Soldiers in Nineteenth-Century Bahia and Cuba," *Slavery and Abolition*, 39 (2018), 479–95.

99. Jones, *Great Nation*, 518; Gueniffey, *Bonaparte*, 377–82; Bell, *Total War*, 211; Edward Said, "Orientalism: The Cultural Consequences of the French Preoccupations with Egypt," in Robert Tignor, ed., *Napoleon in Egypt: Al-Jabarti's Chronicle of the French Occupation, 1798* (Princeton, 2004), 167–80; Robert Tignor, "Introduction," in Tignor, ed., *Napoleon in Egypt*, 6–15. Christopher Bayly introduces the idea of conjunctural revolution in *The Birth of the Modern World, 1780–1914* (London, 2003), 117.

100. For the ambiguities of Napoleon's aims in reenslaving the island's population, see Scott, "Paper Thin: Freedom and Re-enslavement in the Diaspora of the Haitian Revolution," 1066.

101. Dubois, *Avengers of the New World*. On how disease defeated the French, see J. R. McNeill, *Mosquito Empires: Ecology and War in the Greater Caribbean, 1620–1914* (Cambridge, 2012), 255–58.

102. Rafe Blaufarb, "The Western Question: The Geopolitics of Latin American Independence," *American Historical Review* 112, (2007), 742–63.

103. Sujit Sivasundaram, *Waves across the South: A New History of Revolution and Empire* (Chicago, 2020), 81, 122, 133, 181.

104. Gueniffey, *Bonaparte*, 702; Mikaberidze, *Napoleonic Wars*, 136–37; Popkin, *A New World Begins*, 538.

105. DuVal, *Native Ground*, 244.

106. Peter Kastor, *The Nation's Crucible: The Louisiana Purchase and the Creation of America* (New Haven, 2004).

107. Hämäläinen, *The Comanche Empire* and *Lakota America*.

108. On this, see Benedict Anderson, *Imagined Communities: Reflections on the Origin and Spread of Nationalism* (London, 1983), 97; and especially Edward Andrew, *Imperial Republics: Revolution, War, and Territorial Expansion from the English Civil War to the French Revolution* (Toronto, 2011); Thierry Lentz, "Imperial France in 1808 and Beyond," and Howard Brown, "The Origins of the Napoleonic System of Repression," in Michael Broers, Peter Hicks, and Augustin Guimerá, eds., *The Napoleonic Empire and the New European Political Culture* (Basingstoke, 2012), 35, 38.

109. Sanjay Subrahmanyam, "Stumbling across Revolutions: An Eighteenth-Century Franco-Irish Experience," *French History and Civilization*, 9 (2020), 18–43; Dziennik, "Peasants, Soldiers, and Revolutionaries," 105; José Shane Brownrigg-Gleeson Martínez, "Irlanda, los Irlandeses en los Estados Unidos y las independencías iberoamericanas: Una interpretación transatlántica (1808–1820)" (Ph.D diss., University of Salamanca, July 2017), 152–58. On global boundary crossers, especially in imperial foreign service, see Nicholas Canny, "How the Local Can Be Global and the Global Local: Ireland, Irish Catholics, and European Overseas Empires, 1500–1900," in Griffin and Cogliano, eds., *Ireland and America*, 33–34.

110. Vanessa Mongey, *Rogue Revolutionaries: The Fight for Legitimacy in the Greater Caribbean* (Philadelphia, 2020).

## Chapter Six. Singeing the Fray

1. For international views and activities of O'Connell, see Maurice Bric and William Mulligan, eds., *A Global History of Anti-Slavery Politics in the Nineteenth Century* (London, 2013). On rechanneling or funneling the social and economic into the political, see James Donnelly, *Captain Rock: The Irish Agrarian Rebellion of 1821–1824* (Madison, WI, 2009), 145.

2. *Freeman's Journal*, 8 September 1845; Frederick Douglass, "Thoughts and Recollections of a Tour in Ireland," Library of Congress, Washington, D.C., Frederick Douglass Papers [1886], accessed 18 April 2019, https://www.loc.gov/item/mfd.24015/; Fionnghuala Sweeney, " 'The Republic of Letters': Frederick Douglass, Ireland, and the Irish Narratives," *Éire-Ireland* 36, (2001), 58n22; David Blight, *Frederick Douglass: Apostle of Freedom* (New York, 2020), 180; Tom Chaffin, *Giant's Causeway: Frederick Douglass's Irish Odyssey and the Making of an American Visionary* (Charlottesville, VA, 2014), 3, 188–89. For the relationship, see Christine Kinealy, *Daniel O'Connell and the Anti-Slavery Movement: "The Saddest People the Sun Sees"* (London, 2011); and Bruce Nelson, " 'Come Out of Such a Land, You Irishmen': Daniel O'Connell, American Slavery, and the Making of the 'Irish Race,' " *Éire-Ireland* 42, (2007): 58–81.

3. *Saunder's News-Letter*, 17 December 1824; O'Connell to General Bolívar, 18 April 1820, in Maurice R. O'Connell, ed., *The Correspondence of Daniel O'Connell*, 8 vols. (Dublin, 1972–1980), vol. 2, 257–58; Roberto Breña, *El*

*primer liberalismo español y los processos de emancipación de América, 1808–1824* (Mexico City, 2006), 61. Also see José Shane Brownrigg-Gleeson Martínez, "Irlanda, los Irlandeses en los Estados Unidos y las independencías iberoamericanas: una interpretación transatlántica (1808–1820)" (Ph.D. diss., University of Salamanca, July 2017), 3; and Patrick Geoghegan, *King Dan: The Rise of Daniel O'Connell, 1775–1829* (Dublin, 2008), 206–7. The son was not the only one. More than six thousand Irishmen and Britons would fight for South America's liberation. See Tim Fanning, *Don Juan O'Brien: An Irish Adventurer in Nineteenth-Century South America* (Cork, 2020), 49; John Lynch, *Simón Bolívar: A Life* (New Haven, 2006), 122.

4. James Crimmins, "Jeremy Bentham and Daniel O'Connell: Their Correspondence and Radical Alliance, 1828–1831," *Historical Journal*, 40 (1997): 359–87. For this view of O'Connell, see Geoghegan, *King Dan*, 23; and Patrick Geoghegan, *Liberator: The Life and Death of Daniel O'Connell, 1830–1847* (Dublin, 2010), 161–64.

5. John Lynch, *The Spanish American Revolutions, 1808–1826* (New York, 1986), 294. On this interpretation of Bolívar, see Lynch, *Simón Bolívar*, xi.

6. For notions of disequilibrium and equilibrium in this period, see Jeremy Adelman, "Empires, Nations, and Revolutions," *Journal of the History of Ideas*, 79, (2018), 73–88. For O'Connell the reformer, see Roy Foster, *Modern Ireland, 1600–1972* (London, 1988), 289–317.

7. On this, see Charles Maier, *Leviathan 2.0: Inventing Modern Statehood* (Cambridge, MA, 2014), 5.

8. Josep Fradera, *The Imperial Nation: Citizens and Subjects in the British, French, Spanish, and American Empires* (Princeton, 2019), 1, 12, 235–36.

9. For a suggestive look at national settlement and continuing porousness after the age, this one dealing with Haiti and the United States, see Julia Gaffield, "Race and Nation during the Age of Revolution," *Reviews in American History*, 45 (2017), 404–9. On this moment as a time when space was fundamentally reorganized, see Matthias Middell and Katja Naumann, "Global History and the Spatial Turn: From the Impact of Area Studies to the Study of Critical Junctures of Globalization," *Journal of Global History*, 5 (2010), 150, 160.

10. See James Oakes, *The Radical and the Republican: Frederick Douglass, Abraham Lincoln, and the Triumph of Antislavery Politics* (New York, 2007), xx, 15.

11. Brian Balogh, *A Government out of Sight: The Mystery of National Authority in Nineteenth-Century America* (New York, 2009); Max Edling, *A Revolution in Favor of Government: Origins of the U.S. Constitution and the Making of the American State* (New York, 2003). For a counterbalance to this interpretation, one that brings the states back into the picture, see Gary Gerstle, *Liberty and Coercion: The Paradox of American Government from the Founding to the Present* (Princeton, 2015).

12. Little wonder, because, as a rule, constitutions of this period throughout the Atlantic were drawn up to end the state of war. Framers were preoccupied

with the threat of disorder—from without and, most important, from within. In fact, soldiers featured in much of the drafting of such instruments. The United States established the trend. Washington did what others, such as Louverture, Napoleon, and Bolívar, would do. See Linda Colley, *The Gun, the Ship, and the Pen: Warfare, Constitutions, and the Making of the Modern World* (New York, 2021). On relative weakness, see Gary Gerstle, "A State Both Strong and Weak," *American Historical Review*, 115 (2010), 779–85; and R. M. Bates, "Government by Improvisation? Towards a New History of the Nineteenth-Century American State," *Journal of Policy History*, 33 (2021), 287–306.

13. Seth Cotlar, *Tom Paine's America: The Rise and Fall of Transatlantic Radicalism in the Early Republic* (Charlottesville, VA, 2011), 211.

14. Armin Mattes, *Citizens of the Common Intellectual Homeland: The Transatlantic Origins of American Democracy and Nationhood* (Charlottesville, VA, 2015), 141–84.

15. On popular sovereignty, see Edmund Morgan, *Inventing the People: The Rise of Popular Sovereignty in England and America* (New York, 1988). For participation in the military and how this changed the calculation of political order, see Charles Royster, *A Revolutionary People at War: The Continental Army and American Character, 1775–1783* (Chapel Hill, 1980), 295–370.

16. Patrick Griffin, *America's Revolution* (New York, 2012), 255–76; T. H. Breen, *The Will of the People: The Revolutionary Birth of America* (Cambridge, MA, 2019); Alan Taylor, *Liberty Men and Great Proprietors: The Revolutionary Settlement on the Maine Frontier, 1760–1820* (Chapel Hill, 1990), 229–44; Colley, *The Gun, the Ship, and the Pen*; Annette Gordon-Reed, "The Contract for America," in Patrick Griffin and Francis D. Cogliano, eds., *Ireland and America: Empire, Revolution, and Sovereignty* (Charlottesville, VA, 2021), 278.

17. David Waldstreicher, *In the Midst of Perpetual Fetes: The Making of American Nationalism, 1776–1820* (Chapel Hill, 1997), 62–86. On the nature of institutional power, see Max Edling, *A Hercules in the Cradle: War, Money, and the American State, 1783–1867* (Chicago, 2014).

18. Peter Onuf, "Preface," in Onuf, *Statehood and Union A History of the Northwest Ordnance* (Notre Dame, 2019), xiii; Onuf, *Jefferson's Empire: The Language of American Nationhood* (Charlottesville, VA, 2000), 53–57; Francis Cogliano, *Emperor of Liberty: Thomas Jefferson's Foreign Policy* (New Haven, 2014), 172–203. For an argument that suggests the United States did not have an empire in this period but remained an economic dependency of Britain, see Anthony Hopkins, *American Empire: A Global History* (Princeton, 2018).

19. Pekka Hämäläinen, *The Comanche Empire* (New Haven, 2008); Kate Fullagar and Michael McDonnell, "Introduction: Empire, Indigeneity, and Revolution," in Kate Fullagar and Michael McDonnell, eds., *Facing Empire: Indigenous Experiences in a Revolutionary Age* (Baltimore, 2018), 12–13; Gerstle, *Liberty and Coercion*.

20. For this idea, I rely on Onuf, *Statehood and Union*; and Gerstle, *Liberty and Coercion*.
21. On fears of Haiti, see James Dun, *Dangerous Neighbors: Making the Haitian Revolution in Early America* (Philadelphia, 2016); Ashli White, *Encountering Revolution: Haiti and the Making of the Early Republic* (Baltimore, 2010).
22. Aaron Fogleman, "From Slaves, Convicts, and Servants to Free Passengers: The Transformation of Immigration in the Era of the American Revolution," *Journal of American History*, 85 (1998), 43–76; David Brion Davis, *The Problem of Slavery in the Age of Revolution, 1770–1823* (New York, 1999). On slavery and its tangled relationship with the Enlightenment, see Robin Blackburn, *The Overthrow of Colonial Slavery, 1776–1848* (New York, 1988).
23. George Van Cleve, *Slaveholders' Union: Slavery, Politics, and the Constitution in the Early American Republic* (Chicago, 2010).
24. For the ties between slavery and abolition in the three places, see Seymour Drescher, *Abolition: A History of Slavery and Antislavery* (New York, 2009). On how empire lived on past the age, see Jeremy Adelman, "An Age of Imperial Revolutions," *American Historical Review*, 113 (2008), 319–40. Revolution had not ended the institution, but it did force slaveowners to change their rationale for enslaving. In the United States, something called "amelioration" represented one attempt to try to square slavery with the changes to the world. On amelioration, see Christa Dierkesheide, *Amelioration and Empire: Progress and Slavery in the Plantation Americas* (Charlottesville, VA, 2014); Justin Roberts, *Slavery and Enlightenment in the British Atlantic, 1750–1807* (New York, 2013); and Sarah Thomas, "Envisaging a Future for Slavery: Agostino Brunias and the Imperial Politics of Labour and Reproduction," *Eighteenth-Century Studies*, 52 (Fall 2018), 115–33.
25. This oppression, it should be added, was by no means limited to the South in the United States. It animated the whole. Racism affected the lives of African Americans throughout the nation, even if some would be among the first to fight for the promise of its foundational documents and ideals to be realized. See Kate Masur, *Until Justice Be Done: America's First Civil Rights Movement, from the Revolution to Reconstruction* (New York, 2021); Manisha Sinha, *The Slave's Cause: A History of Abolition* (New Haven, 2017).
26. Alan Taylor, *The Civil War of 1812: American Citizens, British Subjects, Irish Rebels, and Indian Allies* (New York, 2010), 7, 43; Maya Jasanoff, *Liberty's Exiles: American Loyalists in the Revolutionary World* (New York, 2011).
27. Alexander Mikaberidze, *Napoleonic Wars: A Global History* (New York, 2020), 541–44.
28. Lawrence Hatter, *Citizens of Convenience: The Imperial Origins of American Nationhood on the U.S.-Canadian Border* (Charlottesville, VA, 2017); Michel Ducharme, *The Idea of Liberty in Canada during the Age of Atlantic Revolutions, 1776–1838* (Montreal, 2014).
29. John Waters, "An Irish Republican Constitution for the American Colonies of Spain" (lecture, Ireland and Latin America Conference, Pontifical

University of Chile, 11 December 2018); Tim Fanning, "A Plot to Invade Mexico," *Irish Times*, 29 August 2021. On anxiety and the Burr episode, and Workman's tangled relationship to it, see James Lewis, *The Burr Conspiracy: Uncovering the Story of an Early American Crisis* (Princeton, 2017), 12, 220–21, 238.

30. Caitlin Fitz, *Our Sister Republics: The United States in an Age of American Revolutions* (New York, 2016), 7, 56, 119.

31. For these insights, I am indebted to Peter Onuf, "The Age of Revolutions" (lecture, Pontifical University of Chile, 10 December 2018). For just one example of how Latin America somehow lagged behind the others, see Jürgen Osterhammel, *The Transformation of the World: A Global History of the Nineteenth Century* (Princeton, 2014), 407. James Sanders argues that Latin America should be seen as the rule, not the exception for the age. See *The Vanguard of the Atlantic World: Creating Modernity, Nation, and Democracy in Nineteenth-Century Latin America* (Durham, 2014), 9–13.

32. Carol Berkin, *Revolutionary Mothers: Women in the Struggle for America's Independence* (New York, 2006), 149–56; Linda Kerber, *Women of the Republic: Intellect and Ideology in Revolutionary America* (Chapel Hill, 1997), 265–88.

33. Katie Jarvis, *Politics in the Marketplace: Work, Gender, and Citizenship in Revolutionary France* (New York, 2019), 10; Suzanne Desan, "Recent Historiography on the French Revolution and Gender," *Journal of Social History*, 52 (2019), 567.

34. Jennifer Ngaire Heuer, "Did Everything Change? Rethinking Revolutionary Legacies," in David Andress, ed., *The Oxford Handbook of the French Revolution* (New York, 2015), 632.

35. Colin Jones, *The Great Nation: France from Louis XV to Napoleon* (New York, 2003), 507–17, 570; Patrice Gueniffey, *Bonaparte: 1769–1802* (Cambridge, MA, 2015), 782–85. On fatigue, see François Furet, *Revolutionary France, 1770–1880* (Oxford, 1988), 265.

36. Michael Broers, "Introduction: Napoleon, His Empire, Our Europe and the 'New Napoleonic History,'" in Michael Broers, Peter Hicks, and Agustín Guimerá Ravina, eds., *The Napoleonic Empire and the New European Political Culture* (Basingstoke, 2012), 1–2; Howard Brown, *Ending the French Revolution: Violence, Justice, and Repression from the Terror to Napoleon* (Charlottesville, VA, 2006), 4, 316, 325, 353–54; Richard Evans, *Pursuit of Power: Europe, 1815–1914* (New York, 2016), 12; Furet, *Revolutionary France*, 248.

37. Brown, *Ending the French Revolution*, 4.

38. Philip Dwyer, "Napoleon, the Revolution, and the Empire," in David Andress, ed., *The Oxford Handbook of the French Revolution* (New York, 2015), 577–78; Guillame Mazeau and Clyde Plumauzille, "Penser avec le genre: Trouble dans la citoyennete révoltionnaire," *La Revolution française*, 9 (2015), 1–28; Jeremy Popkin, *A New World Begins: The History of the French Revolution* (New York, 2019), 554–55.

39. David Bell, *The First Total War: Napoleon's Europe and the Birth of Warfare as We Know It* (Boston, 2007), 189–90; Jones, *Great Nation*, 520; Tim Blanning, *Pursuit of Glory: Europe, 1648–1815* (New York, 2007), 347–49. On the uses of nation to bind a fractured society, see David Bell, *The Cult of the Nation in France: Inventing Nationalism, 1680–1800* (Cambridge, MA, 2001).

40. Arno Mayer, *The Furies: Violence and Terror in the French and Russian Revolutions* (Princeton, 2002), 539; Gueniffey, *Napoleon*. 782.

41. Andrew Roberts, *Napoleon: A Life* (New York, 2014), 272; Ambrogio Caiani, *To Kidnap a Pope: Napoleon and Pius VII* (New Haven, 2021).

42. Blanning, *Pursuit of Glory*, 347, 349, 350.

43. Paul Cheney, *Revolutionary Commerce: Globalization and the French Monarchy* (Cambridge, 2010), 228; Blanning, *Pursuit of Glory*; Evans, *Pursuit of Power*, 14.

44. Maier, *Leviathan 2.0*, 49; Brian Vick, *The Congress of Vienna: Power and Politics after Napoleon* (Cambridge, MA, 2014), 233–77; Evans, *Pursuit of Power*, 20, 27. On the conservatism, and oppression of the new system, see Mike Rapport, *1848: Year of Revolution* (New York, 2009), 2–14.

45. Popkin, *New World*, 557; Blanning, *Pursuit of Glory*, 351. On the problems of demobilization, see Leighton James, "The Experience of Demobilization: War Veterans in the Central European Armies and Societies after 1815," in Alan Forrest, Karen Hagemann, and Michael Rowe, eds., *War, Demobilization and Memory: The Legacy of War in the Era of Atlantic Revolutions* (Basingstoke, 2016), 68–83.

46. Blanning, *Pursuit of Glory*, 673.

47. Jones, *Great Nation*, 549–50; Sophus Reinert, *Translating Empire: Emulation and the Origins of Political Economy* (Cambridge, MA, 2011), 7; Joyce Appleby, *The Relentless Revolution: A History of Capitalism* (New York, 2010), 157–160; C. A. Bayly, *The Birth of the Modern World, 1780–1914* (London, 2003), 243; Emma Rothschild, *Economic Sentiments: Adam Smith, Condorcet, and the Enlightenment* (Cambridge, MA, 2001), 226–47.

48. On this theme, see Peter Onuf, "Epilogue: Imperial Peoples: America, Ireland, and the Making of the Modern World," in Patrick Griffin and Francis Cogliano, eds., *Ireland and America: Empire, Revolution, and Sovereignty* (Charlottesville, VA, 2021), 301–21.

49. Osterhammel, *Transformation of the World*, 525. For a good recent statement on how Britain survived and then thrived, see David Cannadine, *Victorious Century: The United Kingdom, 1800–1906* (London, 2017). On the imperial nation it would become, see Fradera, *The Imperial Nation*, 89–110.

50. This is Cannadine's take in *Victorious Century*; John Bew, "The Challenges of Peace: The High Politics of Postwar Reconstruction in Britain, 1815–1830," in Alan Forrest, Karen Hagemann, and Michael Rowe, eds., *War, Demobilization and Memory: The Legacy of War in the Era of Atlantic Revolutions* (New York, 2016), 166–181.

51. For an interpretation that suggests the industrial revolution represented Britain's experience of revolutionary change in this period, see Eric Hobsbawm's classic account, *The Age of Revolution, 1789–1848* (New York, 1962).

52. Cannadine, *Victorious Century*, 163.

53. Blackburn, *Overthrow of Colonial Slavery*, 157, 340; J. R. Oldfield, *Transatlantic Abolitionism in the Age of Revolution: An International History of Anti-Slavery, c. 1787–1820* (Cambridge, 2013), 173. On the many complexities of this story, see Christopher Brown, *Moral Capital: Foundations of British Abolitionism* (Chapel Hill, 2006).

54. Blackburn, *Overthrow of Colonial Slavery*, 436; Padraic Scanlan, *Freedom's Debtors: British Antislavery in Sierra Leone in the Age of Revolution* (New Haven, 2017), 14. On the transatlantic networks that went into ending the slave trade, see Brown, *Moral Capital*, 105–14; Oldfield, *Transatlantic Abolitionism*, 13–14.

55. Katherine Paugh, "The Politics of Childbearing in the British Caribbean and the Atlantic World during the Age of Abolition, 1776–1838," *Past and Present*, 221 (2013), 120.

56. Karen Racine, " 'This England and This Now': British Cultural and Intellectual Influence in the Spanish American Independence Era," *Hispanic American Historical Review*, 90 (2010), 423–54.

57. Sujit Sivasundaram, *Waves across the South: A New History of Revolution and Empire* (Chicago, 2020); John Shovlin, *Trading with the Enemy: Britain, France, and the Eighteenth-Century Quest for a Peaceful World Order* (New Haven, 2021), xxxiv–xxxv.

58. For this discussion, see Cheney, *Revolutionary Commerce*, 17–18; Cannadine, *Victorious Century*, 122. On informal empire and its grip on the United States, see Hopkins, *American Empire*, 36, 160–61. Also see Rafe Blaufarb, "The Western Question: The Geopolitics of Latin American Independence," *American Historical Review*, 112 (2007), 762.

59. Hopkins, *American Empire*, 158–66, 192–96. For a different take, one positing that the American tail wagged the British free trade dog, see James Fichter, *So Great a Profit: How the East Indies Trade Transformed Anglo-American Capitalism* (Cambridge, MA, 2010).

60. I am obliged to Eliga Gould and Anthony Hopkins on this point. It will feature in Gould's forthcoming book provisionally entitled *Crucible of Peace: The Turbulent History of America's Founding Treaty* (Oxford University Press). And it does in *American Empire*. For a longer elaboration, refer to Patrick Griffin, "Imperial Confusion: America's Post-Colonial and Post-Revolutionary Empire," *Journal of Imperial and Commonwealth History*, 49 (2021), 414–30.

61. Gregory Evans Dowd, "Indigenous Peoples without the Republic," *Journal of American History*, 104 (2017), 19–41; James Belich, *Replenishing the Earth: The Settler Revolution and the Rise of the Angloworld* (Oxford, 2009); Peter Way, "Militarizing the Atlantic World: Army Discipline, Coerced Labor, and Britain's Commercial Empire," in *Rethinking the Age of Revolution*, ed. Michael

McDonnell, 45–69. On British strongarm tactics in colonies throughout the world during and just after the age, see Lisa Ford, *The King's Peace: Law and Order in the British Empire* (Cambridge, MA, 2021).

62. On this broad theme but from the perspective of Indigenous peoples, see Kate Fullagar and Michael McDonnell, "Introduction: Empire, Indigeneity, and Revolution," in Fullagar and McDonnell, eds., *Facing Empire: Indigenous Experiences in a Revolutionary Age*, 1–13. On Greater Britain, see David Armitage, "Greater Britain: A Useful Category of Historical Analysis?" *American Historical Review*, 104 (1999), 427–45.

63. On the Union and its implications, see Alvin Jackson, *The Two Unions: Ireland, Scotland, and the Survival of the United Kingdom, 1707–2007* (Oxford, 2011), 104–14.

64. Cannadine, *Victorious Century*, 44; Seamus Deane, "Down on the Plantation," *Dublin Review of Books* (February 2019). On the tension created by union without emancipation, see Alvin Jackson, *Ireland, 1798–1998: War, Peace, and Beyond* (London, 2010), 27–36. For the increased tension within cities, see David Dickson, *The First Irish Cities: An Eighteenth-Century Transformation* (New Haven, 2021), 258–61. For this interpretation of modernity, I rely on Enda Delaney's forthcoming book with Oxford University Press, provisionally entitled *Making Ireland Modern: The Transformation of Society and Culture*.

65. Anthony McFarlane, *War and Independence in Spanish America* (New York, 2014), 69; Cannadine, *Victorious Century*, 66, 114, 123. That tumult started here when it did has challenged historians, who would want to tie all together into one broad revolutionary moment for the age. Why did things start so "late" here as opposed to other places? This problem is articulated nicely by Clement Thibaud in a roundtable entitled "Les indépendances dans l'espace atlantique, v. 1763-v. 1829," *Annales historiques de la Révolution française*, 384 (2016), 167–98.

66. Blaufarb, "The Western Question."

67. Lynch, *Simón Bolívar*, 65.

68. Marixa Lasso, "Anti-Colonialism and Race in the Age of Revolution: Colombia, Haiti, and the United States" (talk at the Pontifical University of Chile, 4 December 2018); Edwin Williamson, *Penguin History of Latin America* (London, 1992), 213.

69. See Rebecca Earle, "From Colony to Nation," and in particular her treatment of Roberto Breña's book *El primer liberalismo español y los processos de emancipación de América, 1808–1824* (Mexico City, 2006), *Latin American Research Review*, 43 (2008), 247; Breña, *El primer liberalismo español*, 180; Lynch, *The Spanish American Revolutions*, 353; Brian Hamnett, *The End of Iberian Rule, 1770–1830* (Cambridge, 2017), 147.

70. Wim Klooster, *Revolutions in the Atlantic World: A Comparative History* (New York, 2018), 134–41; Hamnett, *The End of Iberian Rule*, 145–75; Marcela Echeverri, "Popular Royalists, Empire, and Politics in Southwestern

New Granada, 1809–1819," *Hispanic American Historical Review*, 91 (2011), 237–69. Also see Marcela Echeverri, *Indian and Slave Royalists in the Age of Revolution: Reform, Revolution, and Royalism in the Northern Andes, 1780–1825* (New York, 2017), 1–3, 14.

71. Hamnett, *The End of Iberian Rule*, 148. For the fragmentation based on mass mobilization, see McFarlane, *War and Independence in Spanish America*, 5, 77–78. Also refer to Francisco Ortega, "The Conceptual History of Independence and the Colonial Question in Spanish America," *Journal of the History of Ideas*, 79 (2018), 89–103; Blackburn, *The Overthrow of Colonial Slavery*, 340. The best study of how the collapse of sovereignty led to existential crisis and war throughout the continent is McFarlane, *War and Independence in Spanish America*.

72. Klooster, *Revolutions in the Atlantic World*, 134–41; McFarlane, *War and Independence in Spanish America*, 417.

73. For a full treatment of this, see Charles Walker, *Smoldering Ashes: Cuzco and the Creation of Republican Peru, 1780–1840* (Durham, 1999).

74. McFarlane, *War and Independence in Spanish America*, 66; Klooster, *Revolutions in the Atlantic World*, 138–39; Lynch, *The Spanish American Revolutions*, 253; Lynch, *Simón Bolívar*, 104–106.

75. McFarlane, *War and Independence in Spanish America*, 85–86, 111; Hamnett, *The End of Iberian Rule*, 157–59; Anthony McFarlane, *War and Independence in Spanish America*, 111–12; Lynch, *The Spanish American Revolutions*, 256; Lynch, *Simón Bolívar*, 90.

76. On these dynamics in Chile, see Juan Luis Ossa, *Armies, Politics, and Revolution: Chile, 1808–1826* (Liverpool, 2015); and Hamnett, *The End of Iberian Rule*, 138–41.

77. McFarlane, *War and Independence in Spanish America*, 182; Lynch, *The Spanish American Revolutions*, 172; Lynch, *Simón Bolívar*, 167–75, 184; Cecilia Mendez, *The Plebeian Republic: The Huanta Rebellion and the Making of the Peruvian State, 1820–1850* (Durham, NC, 2008), 52–60; Ossa, *Armies, Politics, and Revolution*; Lynch, *The Spanish American Revolutions*, 154.

78. Williamson, *Penguin History of Latin America*, 222–35; McFarlane, *War and Independence in Spanish America*, 286, 307, 367, 409.

79. Klooster, *Revolutions in the Atlantic World*, 150–51; Lynch, *The Spanish American Revolutions*, 341–56; Mendez, *The Plebeian Republic*.

80. Klooster, *Revolutions in the Atlantic World*, 154–55, 163; Lynch, *Simón Bolívar*, 146–51; Laurent Dubois and John Garrigus, *Slave Revolution in the Caribbean, 1789–1804* (New York, 2006), 39.

81. Peter Blanchard, *Under the Flags of Freedom: Slave Soldiers and the Wars of Independence in Spanish South America* (Pittsburgh, 2008), 160–66; Lester Langley, *The Americas in the Age of Revolution, 1750–1850* (New Haven, 1996), 194; Blackburn, *The Overthrow of Colonial Slavery*, 360–68; Karen Racine, " 'This England and This Now': British Cultural and Intellectual Influence in the Spanish American Independence Era," *Hispanic American Historical Review*, 90 (2010), 437.

82. Hamnett, *The End of Iberian Rule*, 9; Klooster, *Revolutions in the Atlantic World*, 168–69; Marixa Lasso, *Myths of Harmony: Race and Republicanism during the Age of Revolution, Colombia, 1795–1831* (Pittsburgh, 2007), 151–59.

83. For a study of Mexico that places Spain's troubles at the heart of the crisis in Mexico and the ways that most wanted only autonomy early on, not independence, see Jaime Rodriguez O., *"We Are Now the True Spaniards": Sovereignty, Revolution, Independence, and the Emergence of the Federal Republic of Mexico, 1808–1824* (Stanford, 2012). Also see Gabriel Paquette, "The Dissolution of the Spanish Atlantic Monarchy," *Historical Journal*, 52 (2009), 199.

84. Hamnett, *The End of Iberian Rule*, 150–56; McFarlane, *War and Independence in Spanish America*, 219; Lester Langley, *The Americas in the Age of Revolution*, 179–83; Lynch, *The Spanish American Revolutions*, 296–301, 306–19.

85. Williamson, *Penguin History of Latin America*, 225–26; McFarlane, *War and Independence in Spanish America*, 387. On the struggle between creole elites and peasants, largely indigenous, as the critical issue in Mexico, see Eric Van Young, " 'To Throw Off a Tyrannical Government': Atlantic Revolutionary Traditions and Popular Insurgency in Mexico, 1800–1821," in Michael Morrison and Melinda Cook, eds., *Revolutionary Currents: Nation Building in the Transatlantic World* (New York, 2004), 128–29. On the ways Iturbide, O'Higgins, and San Martín saw Britain as a model for governance, see Karen Racine, " 'This England and This Now,' " *Hispanic American Historical Review*, 90 (2010), 429.

86. Eric Van Young, *The Other Rebellion: Popular Violence, Ideology, and the Mexican Struggle for Independence, 1810–1821* (Stanford, 2001), 2–4, 523; Lynch, *The Spanish American Revolutions*, 319–326.

87. Hamnett, *The End of Iberian Rule*, 152; Lynch, *The Spanish American Revolutions*, 333–40; Alfredo Avila and John Tutino, "Becoming Mexico: The Conflictive Search for a North American Nation," in John Tutino, ed., *New Countries: Capitalism, Revolutions, and Nations in the Americas, 1750–1870* (Durham, NC, 2016), 234.

88. Brian Hamnett, *Roots of Insurgency: Mexican Regions, 1750–1824* (Cambridge, 1986), 208–13.

89. Hamnett, *The End of Iberian Rule*, 288–303; Lynch, *Simón Bolívar*, 189. On Peru, see Monica Ricketts, *Who Should Rule? Men of Arms, the Republic of Letters, and the Fall of the Spanish Empire* (New York, 2017), 197–202; Paquette, "The Dissolution of the Spanish Atlantic Monarchy," 205; Paul Gootenberg, *Between Silver and Guano: Commercial Policy and the State in Post-Independence Peru* (Princeton, 1989); Walker, *Smoldering Ashes*, 207–21.

90. Ada Ferrer, *Freedom's Mirror: Cuba and Haiti in the Age of Revolution* (New York, 2014), 12–15, 336–39; Jane Landers, *Atlantic Creoles in the Age of Revolutions* (Cambridge, MA, 2010), 205–25; Blackburn, *The Overthrow of Colonial Slavery*, 383, 391. For a study of Cuban exceptionalism, see David

Sartorius, "Cuban Counterpoint: Colonialism and Continuity in the Atlantic World," in Tutino, ed., *New Countries*, 175–200.

91. Lynch, *Simón Bolívar*, 250, 276. Roberto Breña calls his plans great and accomplishments rather meager. These stem from how he could not manage his varied dilemmas. See *El primer liberalismo español*, 93–94.

92. Fradera, *The Imperial Nation*, 127–53. For a discussion of how it remained globally entangled, see Jorge Luengo and Pol Dalmau, "Writing Spanish History in the Global Age: Connections and Entanglements in the Nineteenth Century," *Journal of Global History*, 13 (2018), 425–45.

93. Roderick Barman, *Brazil: The Forging of a Nation, 1798–1852* (Stanford, 1988), 5–6.

94. Jeremy Adelman, *Sovereignty and Revolution in the Iberian Atlantic* (Princeton, 2006), 247–57, 325–26; Barman, *Brazil*, 31–39.

95. Kirsten Schultz, *Tropical Versailles: Empire, Monarchy, and the Portuguese Royal Court in Rio de Janeiro, 1808–1821* (New York, 2001), 190–97.

96. Emilia Viotti da Costa, *The Brazilian Empire: Myths and Histories* (Chicago, 1985), xix, 8; Gabriel Paquette, *Imperial Portugal in the Age of Atlantic Revolutions: The Luso-Brazilian World, c. 1770–1850* (Cambridge, 2013). See especially pp. 142–49.

97. Paquette, *Imperial Portugal in the Age of Atlantic Revolutions*, 140–55.

98. Adelman, *Sovereignty and Revolution*, 332–43; Paquette, *Imperial Portugal in the Age of Atlantic Revolutions*, 142.

99. Hamnett, *The End of Iberian Rule*, 274–76; Barman, *Brazil*, 227–28.

100. Kirsten Schultz, "Atlantic Transformations and Brazil's Imperial Independence," in Tutino, ed., *New Countries*, 219–24.

101. Emilia Viotti da Costa, *The Brazilian Empire: Myths and Histories* (Chapel Hill, 2000), 131–32, 145–46.

102. Adelman, *Sovereignty and Revolution*, ch. 8. Also see Kirsten Schultz, "Slavery, Empire and Civilization: A Luso-Brazilian Defense of the Slave Trade in the Age of Revolutions," *Slavery and Abolition*, 34 (2012), 103; Blackburn, *The Overthrow of Colonial Slavery*, 384, 391.

103. Maier, *Leviathan 2.0*, 61.

104. Fradera, *The Imperial Nation*, 233, 70–72; Jorge Miguel Viana Pedreira, "From Growth to Collapse: Portugal, Brazil, and the Breakdown of the Old Colonial System (1750–1830)," *Hispanic American Historical Review*, 80 (2000), 839, 852; Roquinaldo Ferreira, "Waves of Sedition across the Atlantic: Angola in the Wake of Brazilian Independence," in Wim Klooster, ed., *Cambridge History of the Age of Revolution* (forthcoming). My thanks to Professor Ferreira for sharing a copy of this essay.

105. For the continuing entangled nature of Brazil's relationship to Angola, and how it affected Portugal, I rely on Roquinaldo Ferreira, "Atlantic Entanglements between Angola and Brazil" (talk at the "Empires and Atlantics" forum, University of Chicago, 12 March 2021).

106. Laurent Dubois, *Avengers of the New World: The Story of the Haitian Revolution* (Cambridge, MA, 2004), 280–81.

107. On this point, I am indebted to Peter Thompson, "Exporting and Importing the Democratic Revolution in the Western Hemisphere" ("Revolutionizing the Age of Revolution" conference, Rome, 18 December 2018). On the gap between creole and African, and how it was bridged in revolution, see Deborah Jenson, "Jean-Jacques Dessalines and the African Character of the Haitian Revolution," *William and Mary Quarterly*, 3rd ser., 69 (2012), 615–28. On the Declaration, see Julia Gaffield, *Haitian Connections in the Atlantic World: Recognition after Revolution* (Chapel Hill, 2015), 1–12.

108. Blackburn, *The Overthrow of Colonial Slavery*, 540–41; Dubois, *Avengers of the New World*, 3.

109. On this, see the original work done by Gaffield, *Haitian Connections in the Atlantic World*, especially 182–83. The double-debt idea and the jaw-dropping amount of the ransom is covered in Catherine Porter, Constant Méheut, Matt Apuzzo, and Salem Gebrekidan, "The Ransom: The Roots of Haiti's Misery: Reparations to Enslavers," *New York Times*, 20 May 2022.

110. Gaffield, *Haitian Connections in the Atlantic World*, 195; Marlene Daut, *Tropics of Haiti: Race and the Literary History of the Haitian Revolution in the Atlantic World, 1789–1865* (Liverpool, 2016).

111. Julius Scott, *The Common Wind: Afro-American Currents in the Age of the Haitian Revolution* (New York, 2018), 203–211.

112. For what a state could, should, and had to do at this moment, see Osterhammel, *The Transformation of the World*, 572–629.

113. Osterhammel, *The Transformation of the World*, xv.

114. Hamnett, *The End of Iberian Rule*, 304–13; Paquette, "The Dissolution of the Spanish Atlantic Monarchy," 187, 198, 202. On war and identity, Paquette relies on the fine work of Clement Thibaud. See *Repúblicas en armas: Los ejércitos bolivarianos en la guerra de indepdencia en Colombia y Venezuela* (Bogota, 2003). For the North American case, see Waldstreicher, *In the Midst of Perpetual Fetes*; and Nathan Perl-Rosenthal, *Citizen Sailors: Becoming American in the Age of Revolution* (Cambridge, MA, 2015).

# Chapter Seven. Reknitting the Fabric

1. As Daniel Carey suggests, "The novel's basic mythos of shipwreck, survival, and self-sufficiency had been embedded at the deepest level of cultural imagination." See "Reading Contrapuntally: Robinson Crusoe, Slavery, and Postcolonial Theory," in Daniel Carey and Lynn Festa, eds., *Postcolonial Enlightenment: Eighteenth-Century Colonialism and Postcolonial Theory* (Oxford, 2008), 107; *Illustrated London News*, 24 September 1870; Katherine Frank, *Crusoe: Daniel Defoe, Robert Knox and the Creation of a Myth* (London, 2012), 287–92.

2. Robert Mahony, "Swift and George Faulkner: Cultivating Irish Memory," in *Jonathan Swift: The Irish Identity* (New Haven, 1995), 20–24.

3. Guy Beiner, *Remembering the Year of the French: Irish Folk History and Social Memory* (Madison, WI, 2006), 243; Edward Vallance, "Introduction: Revolution, Time, and Memory," in *Remembering Early Modern Revolutions: England, North American, France, and Haiti* (London, 2018), 7–8; Pascal Dupuy, "The Revolution in History, Commemoration and Memory," in Peter McPhee, ed., *A Companion to the French Revolution* (London, 2012), 486–501.

4. See Eric Weeks, "Forging an Identity in Bronze: Nation-Building through Ottawa's Memorial Landscape," *Études Canadiennes/Canadian Studies*, 78 (2015), 50, which explores the work of Eric Hobsbawm and Terence Ranger in this regard. Memorials do many things. They can impress or intimidate. They also remind us who we are. They can sustain community, or they can become foci of hostility. For the varied work statues do, see Peter Hughes, *A History of Love and Hate in 21 Statues* (London, 2021), 2–3, 191. The best statement on memorialization in this period, one that focuses on how they sustained elite rule in varied contexts, is Eveline Bouwers, *Public Pantheons in Revolutionary Europe: Comparing Cultures of Remembrance, c. 1750–1850* (London, 2011). On the importance of forgetting, see Guy Beiner, *Forgetful Remembrance: Social Forgetting and Vernacular Historiography of a Rebellion in Ulster* (New York, 2018).

5. On the ubiquity of Rome in the eighteenth century, see J. G. A. Pocock's five-volume work *Barbarism and Religion* (New York, 2001–11); and Edward Andrew, *Imperial Republics: Revolution, War, and Territorial Expansion from the English Civil War to the French Revolution* (Toronto, 2011).

6. Matthijs M. Lok, "Un oubli total du passé? The Political and Social Construction of Silence in Restoration Europe (1813–1830)," *History and Memory*, 26 (2014), 40–75.

7. On revolutions and exceptionalism, see Annie Jourdan, *La Révolution, une exception française* (Normandie, 2003). For the case from the American perspective, see Philipp Ziesche, *Cosmopolitan Patriots: Americans in Paris in the Age of Revolution* (Charlottesville, VA, 2010), 167.

8. On national narratives, see Paul Ronceur, *Time and Narrative*, book 1 (Chicago, 1990). I noted this when I was doing work on the Famine. See John Crowley, "Sites of Memory," in John Crowley, William Smyth, and Mike Murphy, eds., *Historical Atlas of the Great Irish Famine* (Cork, 2012), 619n11. On the different paths to national ideals, see Helke Rausch, "The Nation as a Community Born of War? Reception of Public Statues in Late Nineteenth-Century Western European Capitals," *European Review of History*, 14 (2007), 73–101.

9. Josep Fradera, *The Imperial Nation: Citizens and Subjects in the British, French, Spanish, and American Empires* (Princeton, 2018), 240. For an interesting take on monuments, and how they sanitize and create myths that yoke the state to certain aspects of the past, see Michel-Rolph Trouillot, *Silencing the Past:*

*Power and the Production of History* (New York, 2015), 116. Some argue that memorials became in a new guise what they had been before the age: political weapons. See Alan Forest, Karen Hagemann, and Michael Rowe, "Introduction: War, Demobilization and Memory in the Era of Atlantic Revolution," in *War Demobilization and Memory: The Legacy of War in the Era of Atlantic Revolutions* (London, 2016), 4.

10. François Furstenberg, *In the Name of the Father: Washington's Legacy, Slavery, and the Making of a Nation* (New York, 2006); Patrick Griffin, *America's Revolution* (New York, 2012), 276–85.

11. Paul Staiti, *Of Arms and Artists: The American Revolution through Painters' Eyes* (New York, 2016), 282–84, 207–13.

12. On vanishing points and history, see H. W. Smith, *The Continuities of German History: Nation, Religion, and Race across the Long Nineteenth Century* (Cambridge, 2008), 13–38.

13. On this idea, see Annette Gordon-Reed and Peter Onuf, *Most Blessed of the Patriarchs: Thomas Jefferson and the Empire of the Imagination* (New York, 2016), xv–xxi.

14. For this ideal of how liberty would be won with time, see Gordon Wood, *The Radicalism of the American Revolution* (New York, 1992). On forgetting Loyalists, see Rebecca Brannon, *From Revolution to Reunion: The Reintegration of the South Carolina Loyalists* (Charleston, 2016).

15. Benjamin Park, *American Nationalisms: Imagining Union in the Age of Revolutions* (New York, 2018).

16. On the image of Washington, see Edward Lengel, *Inventing George Washington: America's Founder in Myth and Memory* (New York, 2011); and Matthew Costello, *The Property of the Nation: George Washington's Tomb* (Lawrence, KS, 201). On Washington and his city, see Adam Costanzo, *George Washington's Washington: Visions for the National Capital in the Early American Republic* (Athens, GA, 2018); and Furstenberg, *In the Name of the Father.* For the early plans, see Robert Kapsch, *Building Washington: Engineering and Construction of the Federal City, 1790–1840* (Baltimore, 2018), 1–30.

17. Andrew, *Imperial Republics,* 94–97; Gordon Wood, "Prologue: The Legacy of Rome in the American Revolution," in Peter Onuf and Nicholas Cole, eds., *Thomas Jefferson, the Classical World, and Early America* (Charlottesville, VA, 2011), 26–27; Isabelle Gournay, "The French Connection in Washington, D.C.: Context and Issues," in Cynthia Field, Isabelle Gournay, and Thomas Somma, eds., *Paris on the Potomac: The French Influence on the Architecture and Art of Washington, D.C* (Athens, OH, 2007), 1–35. Also take the case of perhaps the most famous arch in the United States, the one memorializing Washington in Greenwich Village in New York City. See Elizabeth Macauley-Lewis, "Triumphal Washington: New York's First 'Roman' Arch," in Anastasia Bakogianni and Valerie Hope, eds., *War as Spectacle: Ancient and Modern Perspectives on the Display of Armed Conflict* (London, 2015), 222–38.

18. On memorialization and vanishing, see Andrew Denson, *Monuments to Absence: Cherokee Removal and the Contest over Southern Memory* (Chapel Hill, 2017).

19. Theodore Juste, *Memoirs of Leopold I, King of the Belgians*, vol. I (London, 1868), 335–36; Jo Tollebeek, "An Era of Grandeur: The Middle Ages in Belgian National Historiography, 1830–1914," in Robert Evans and Guy Marchal, eds., *The Uses of the Middle Ages in Modern European States: History, Nationhood, and the Search for Origins* (London, 2010), 113–35; Gevert Nortemann, "Memories and Identities in Conflict: The Myth Concerning the Battle of Courtrai (1302) in Nineteenth-Century Belgium," in Jane Fenoulhet and Lesley Gilbert, eds., *Narratives of Low Countries History and Culture: Reframing the Past* (London, 2016), 63–72.

20. Brigitte D'Hainaut-Zveny, "Place Saint-Michel, Place Verte, Place des Martyrs (1774–2017)," *Cahiers Bruxellois*, 49 (2017), 131–42.

21. Canadian Heritage, "War of 1812 Monument, Triumph Through Diversity," 2014. Accessed on 28 March 2019, http://www.pch.gc.ca/eng/141519954605 3/1415199883351; Weeks, "Forging an Identity in Bronze," 49–75.

22. Alan Gordon, *Making Public Pasts: The Contested Terrain of Montreal's Public Memories* (Ottawa, 2001), xi–xvi, 76–80, 118; Art Public Montreal website. On the pug and poodle, which I missed when I visited Montreal, I am indebted to Guy Beiner.

23. National Battlefields Commission Plains of Abraham website; Joan Coutu and John McAleer, " 'The Immortal Wolfe'? Monuments, Memory, and the Battle of Quebec," in Phillip Buckner and John Reid, eds., *Remembering 1759: The Conquest of Canada in Historical Memory* (Toronto, 2012), 45–49.

24. Tim Blanning, *Pursuit of Glory: Europe, 1648–1815* (New York, 2007), 675; Peter Onuf, "Epilogue: Imperial Peoples: America, Ireland, and the Making of the Modern World," in Patrick Griffin and Francis Cogliano, eds., *Ireland and America: Empire, Nation, and Sovereignty* (Charlottesville, VA, 2021), 302; Rogers Brubaker and Frederick Cooper, "Beyond 'Identity,' " *Theory and Society*, 29 (2000), 15, 20. Also see Nathan Perl-Rosenthal, *Citizen Sailors: Becoming American in the Age of Revolution* (Cambridge, MA, 2015). For the idea that secularization was critical for nationalism, see Benedict Anderson, *Imagined Communities: Reflections on the Origin and Spread of Nationalism* (New York, 2016).

25. Thomas Bender, *The Unfinished City: New York and the Metropolitan Idea* (New York, 2002), 240. For the quote, see Anne-Marie Thiesse, *La création des identités nationales: Europe, XVIIIe–XXe siècle* (Paris, 2014), 11, 284. For the idea of nations similarly trying to look dissimilar, see Philipp Ziesche, *Cosmopolitan Patriots: Americans in Paris in the Age of Revolution* (Charlottesville, VA, 2010), 5. On the idea of Latin America leading the way, see Anderson, *Imagined Communities*, 67. For the counterargument, see William Sewell, "The French Revolution and the Emergence of the Nation Form," in Michael Morrison and Melinda Zook, eds., *Revolutionary Currents: Nation*

*Building in the Transatlantic World* (New York, 2004), 91–94, 117. Also see
Sinisa M ⸱⸱⸱⸱ic, *Nation-States and Nationalisms: Organization, Ideology, and
Solidarity* (Cambridge, 2014), 8–16. For the rise of nationalism through mass
mobilization, see Andreas Wimmer, *Waves of War: Nationalism, State Formation and Ethnic Exclusion in the Modern World* (Cambridge, 2013). On empires
as nations, see John Breuilly, "Modern Empires and Nation-States," *Thesis
Eleven*, 139 (2017), 11–29.

26. On the power of the past, see Stefan Berger, *The Past as History: National
Identity and Historical Consciousness in Modern Europe* (London, 2014), 4; and
John Coakley, "Mobilizing the Past: Nationalist Images of History," *Nation-
alism and Ethnic Politics*, 10 (2004), 531–60.

27. Peter Onuf, "Epilogue," in Griffin and Cogliano, eds., *Ireland and America*.
On bonds of dependence, see Claudio Lomnitz, "Nationalism as a Practical
System: Benedict Anderson's Theory of Nationalism from the Vantage Point
of Spanish America," cited in Nicola Miller, "The Historiography of Nationalism and National Identity in Latin America," *Nations and Nationalism*, 12
(2006), 207–8. On encouraging and containing, see Michael Rowe, "The
French Revolution, Napoleon, and Nationalism in Europe," in John Breuilly,
ed., *The Oxford Handbook of the History of Nationalism* (Oxford, 2013), 144.

28. Eric Storm, "A New Dawn in Nationalism Studies? Some Fresh Incentives
to Overcome Historiographical Nationalism," *European History Quarterly*, 48
(2017), 115. Also see Malesevic, *Nation-States and Nationalisms*, for the ways
in which nation can only be conceived of in the modern era and how revolution played a critical role. The idea that the nation begins with the "modern" world has been called the modernist perspective. For a view of this
literature, see Eric Storm, "A New Dawn in Nationalism Studies?" 113–29.

29. Pierre Nora was director of a seven-volume study of memory entitled *Les lieux
de mémoire*, which has been condensed into three volumes in English and entitled *The Realms of Memory: The Construction of the French Past* (New York, 1996).

30. Nicola Miller, "The Historiography of Nationalism and National Identity in
Latin America," *Nations and Nationalism*, 12 (2006), 201–21; Hilda Sabato,
"On Political Citizenship in Nineteenth-Century Latin America," *American
Historical Review*, 106 (2001), 1311. For the complexity—and precocity—
of Spanish American nationalism and modernity, see James Sanders, *The
Vanguard of the Atlantic World: Creating Modernity, Nation and Democracy in
Nineteenth-Century Latin America* (Durham, 2014).

31. Rebecca Earle, " 'Sobre héroes y tumbas': National Symbols in Nineteenth-
Century Spanish America," *Hispanic American Historical Review*, 85 (2005),
415–16; Thomas Benjamin, *La Revolución: Mexico's Great Revolution as Memory, Myth, and History* (Austin, TX, 2000), 101; Christopher Archer, "Death's
Patriots—Celebration, Denunciation, and Memories of Mexico's Independence Heroes: Miguel Hidalgo, José Maria Morelos, and Agustín de Iturbide," in Lyman Johnson, ed., *Death, Dismemberment, and Memory: Body
Politics in Latin America* (Albuquerque, NM, 2004), 92–93.

32. Thomas Benjamin, *La Revolución*, 101–2, 121–23; Archer, "Death's Patriots," 93–95; Jaime Pensado, *Rebel Mexico: Student Unrest and Authoritarian Political Culture during the Long Sixties* (Stanford, 2013), especially chaps. 6 and 8. On different visions of the idea of revolution, see Pensado, " 'To Assault with the Truth': The Revitalization of Conservative Militancy in Mexico during the Global Sixties," *Americas*, 70 (2014), 518.

33. Malesevic, *Nation-States and Nationalisms*, 12. On bifurcations of interests in the revolutionary years, see John Lynch, *The Spanish American Revolutions, 1808–1826* (New York, 1986), 345–50. For bifurcation in Russia in these years, see Alexander Martin, "Moscow after Napoleon: Reconciliation, Rebuilding, and Contested Memories," in Alan Forrest, Karen Hagemann, and Michael Rowe, eds., *War, Demobilization and Memory: The Legacy of War in the Era of Atlantic Revolutions* (London, 2016), 287–88.

34. On the challenges of creating ideals of nation from this moment in Latin America, see Miguel Angel Centeno, "War and Memories: Symbols of State Nationalism in Latin America," *European Review of Latin American and Caribbean Studies*, 66 (1999), 78, 83, 90. Echoing the United States, the issue memorialists struggled with early on was how or if to include all the immigrants streaming in from Europe into a national story and how to incorporate so many fractious regions into that national story. The national, local, and immigrant vied with one another. On this, see Lilia Ana Bertoni, *Patriotas, cosmopolitas y nacionalistas: La construcción de la nacionalidad Argentina a fines del siglo XIX* (Mexico, City, 2001), 10–12. The San Martín quote comes from Rebecca Earle, " 'Sobre héroes y tumbas,' " 375.

35. On the fracturing of memory in Argentina, in particular bifurcation, see Michael Goebel, *Argentina's Partisan Past: Nationalism and the Politics of History* (Liverpool, 2011), 25–32. For memory struggles, see Emilio Crenzel and Eugenia Allier-Montano, "Introduction," in *The Struggle for Memory in Latin America: Recent History and Political Violence* (London, 2015), 1.

36. Maureen Shanahan and Ana Maria Reyes, "Bolívar Unhinged," in *Simón Bolívar: Travels and Transformations of a Cultural Icon* (Gainesville, 2016), 1–2, 9–10; John Lynch, *Simón Bolívar: A Life* (New Haven, 2006), 299–304. One of the states he created, Colombia, was sustained by myths that tried to whitewash a struggle defined by racialized rancor, a chapter that he featured in. See Marixa Lasso, *Myths of Harmony: Race and Republicanism during the Age of Revolution, Colombia, 1795–1831* (Pittsburgh, 2007). For the role of Bolívar in the United States, see Caitlin Fitz, *Our Sister Republics: The United States in the Age of American Revolutions* (New York, 2016), 116–55.

37. For the long afterlife of O'Higgins, see Tim Fanning, *Paisanos: The Forgotten Irish Who Changed the Face of Latin America* (Dublin, 2016), 219–23.

38. Francisco Ortega, "The Conceptual History of Independence and the Colonial Question in Spanish America," *Journal of the History of Ideas*, 79 (2018), 89–103; Gabriel Paquette, "The Dissolution of the Spanish Atlantic Monarchy," *Historical Journal*, 52 (2009), 208; Earle, " 'Sobre héroes y tumbas,' "

416. In the immediate wake of independence, new national leaders created such "historias patrias" to create a myth of national emancipation from Spanish "despotism." All Latin American nations struggled to create a sense of distinctiveness from the same tropes, even as they suggested that it was here, in Latin America, where the New World's republican promise would be borne out, even if by the time this statue went up such hopes were fading. Most did not have the confidence to employ symbols other than founding fathers and foundational moments from the age. See Anthony McFarlane, *War and Independence in Spanish America* (New York, 2014), 2. On the 1840s to 1870s and the belief in Latin American leading the way in realizing democracy, see Sanders, *The Vanguard of the Atlantic World*.

39. Fanning, *Paisanos*, 222–23; Larry Rohter, "O'Higgins the Liberator Is Reclaimed from the Military," *New York Times*, 10 March 2006. For the focus on military men, and the centrality of O'Higgins, see Alfonso Salgado, "Escultura publica e identidad nacional: Chile, 1891–1932," in Gabriel Cid and Alejandro San Francisco, eds., *Nacionalismos e identidad nacional en Chile, siglo XX* (Santiago, 2000), 162–63.

40. However much this may have been the case, images abounded throughout Brazil of this memorial. It appeared on everything from textiles to plates. Some of these are included in the 2019–20 exhibition on the history of São Paulo in the Meseu Afro Brasil in Ibirapuera Park, São Paulo, entitled "An Iconographic City."

41. http://napoleonmonuments.eu/Napoleon1er/Gerone.htm; http://www.sitiohis toricolosarapiles.com/CiudadRodrigo_eng.pdf; Francisca Vives Casas, "El Monumento a la Batalla de Vitoria (1917): Génesis, Concurso y Ejecución," *Sancho El Sabio*, 39 (2016), 205.

42. Javier Moreno-Luzon, "Fighting for National Memory: The Commemoration of the Spanish 'War of Independence' in 1908–1912," *History and Memory*, 19 (2007), 68–94. For the centrality of these events to Spanish historical memory, see Mark Lawrence, "Peninsularity and Patriotism: Spanish and British Approaches to the Peninsular War, 1808–14," *Historical Research*, 85 (2012), 453–68.

43. Maria Cristina Moreira and Sergio Veludo, "Evolution of Portuguese Military Uniformology in the Nineteenth Century: Examples from Sculptural Monuments in Public Spaces, Portugal," *Portuguese Studies Review*, 16 (2008), 94–96; "Alminhas da Ponte," Patrimonio Cultural, Repùblica Portugesa, http://www. patrimoniocultural.gov.pt/pt/patrimonio/patrimonio-imovel/pesquisa-do-patrimonio/classificado-ou-em-vias-de-classificacao/geral/view/71533.

44. Filipe Ribeiro de Meneses, "The Portuguese Expeditionary Corps in France (1917–18) and the Long Shadow of the Peninsular War against Napoleon," *Journal of Portuguese History*, 16 (2018), 1–23.

45. For instance, during the Revolution itself, a collector scurried around Paris to take in those pieces that had been abandoned or nearly destroyed in fits of iconoclasm. The Musée Révolutionnaire would use the fragments of the

ancien régime as a counterexample of the enlightened neoclassicism of the age. See Geneviève Bresc-Bautier and Beatrice de Chancel-Bardelot, eds., *Un musée révolutionnnaire: Le Musée des monuments français d'Alexandre Lenoir* (Paris, 2016).

46. Colin Jones, *The Great Nation: France from Louis XV to Napoleon* (New York, 2003), 522; Neni Panourgia, "Colonizing the Ideal: Neoclassical Articulations and European Modernities," *Angelaki: Journal of Theoretical Humanities*, 9 (2004), 172; Albert Boime, *Art in the Age of Revolution, 1750–1800* (Chicago, 1987); Andrew, *Imperial Republics*. Also see Garry Wills, *Mr. Jefferson's University* (Washington, DC, 2002). On the ways the grand tour stimulated interest in the classical, see Boime, *Art in the Age of Revolution*, 60–62.

47. Jones, *Great Nation*, 531.

48. For just one example, focused on property, see Rafe Blaufarb, *The Great Demarcation: The French Revolution and the Invention of Modern Property* (New York, 2016).

49. Priscilla Parkhurst Ferguson, *Paris as Revolution: Writing the Nineteenth-Century City* (Berkeley, 1994), 12.

50. Bouwers, *Public Pantheons in Revolutionary Europe*, 92–93, 122; Blanning, *Pursuit of Glory*, 511–12; Colin Jones, *Paris: The Biography of a City* (New York, 2005), 296–98.

51. For the importance of Rome to Napoleon's plans, see Diana Rowell, *Paris: The "New Rome" of Napoleon I* (London, 2014).

52. Avner Ben-Amos, "Monuments and Memory in French Nationalism," *History and Memory*, 5 (1993), 65; Richard Clay, *Iconoclasm in Revolutionary Paris: The Transformation of Signs* (Oxford, 2012); Annie Jourdan, *Les monuments de la Révolution française, 1770–1804: Une histoire de representation* (Paris, 1997); Pierre Nora, "Preface," in Nora, ed., *Realms of Memory*, vol. 1, xix–xx.

53. The sacred center of power is that of Avner Ben-Amos, cited in Eveline Bouwers, *Public Pantheons in Revolutionary Europe*, 125. James Leith explores the way a new order was created in *Space and Revolution: Projects for Monuments, Squares, and Public Buildings in France, 1789–1799* (Montreal, 1991).

54. C. A. Bayly, *The Birth of the Modern World, 1780–1914* (London, 2003), 88; Ben-Amos, "Monuments and Memory in French Nationalism," 50, 62–65, 81; Richard Burton, *Blood in the City: Violence and Revelation in Paris, 1789–1945* (Ithaca, 2001), 62; Hughes, *A History of Love and Hate in 21 Statues*, 101–4.

55. Jonathan Ribner, *Broken Tablets: The Cult of the Law in French Art from David to Delacroix* (Berkeley, 1993), 82–88; Jones, *Paris*, 401–4, 431–34; Burton, *Blood in the City*, 174–75, 181–91.

56. Claude Langlois, "Catholics and Seculars," in Nora, ed., *Realms of Memory*, vol. 1, 116; Christian Amalvi, "Bastille Day," in Nora, ed., *Realms of Memory*, vol. 3, 132–33.

57. On this in South America, see Catherine Davies, Clare Brewster, Hilary Owen, *South American Independence: Gender, Politics, Text* (Liverpool, 2006), 15–33, 45–48.

58. Jones, *Paris*, 348–57.
59. On this, see Laurence Cole, *Military Culture and Popular Patriotism in Late Imperial Austria* (Oxford, 2014), 19–62. I owe this to John Deak's "After War Made the State: The Hapsburg Empire" (talk at "The New History of the State" conference, University of Notre Dame, 23 February 2018).
60. Christopher Clark, *The Iron Kingdom: The Rise and Downfall of Prussia, 1600–1947* (Cambridge, MA, 2006), 375; Daniel Moran, "Introduction: The Legend of the Levée en Masse," in Daniel Moran and Arthur Waldron, eds., *The People in Arms: Military Myth and National Mobilization since the French Revolution* (New York, 2002), 4–5. For a fuller treatment, see Karen Hagemann, *Revisiting Prussia's Wars against Napoleon: History, Culture, and Memory* (New York, 2015).
61. Clark, *Iron Kingdom*, 378–85.
62. On the history and iconic status of the gate, see Sarah Pogoda and Rudiger Traxler, "Branding the New Germany: The Brandenburg Gate and a New Kind of German Historical Amnesia," in Karin Bauer and Jennifer Ruth Hosek, eds., *Cultural Topographies of the New Berlin* (New York, 2017), 162–67; Neil MacGregor, *Germany: Memories of a Nation* (New York, 2015), 3–8; Paal Stangl, "Restoring Berlin's Unter der Linden: Ideology, World View, Place and Space," *Journal of Historical Geography*, 32 (2006), 368; Sean Forner, "War Commemoration and the Republic in Crisis: Weimer Germany and the Neue Wache," *Central European History*, 35 (2002), 518; Brian Ladd, *The Ghosts of Berlin: Confronting German History in the Urban Landscape* (Chicago, 1997), 74–75.
63. For the ways it was rechristened by the Soviets, see Stangl, "Restoring Berlin's Unter der Linden," 352–76. Stangl calls it "layering" (p. 356).
64. Stangl, "Restoring Berlin's Unter der Linden," 360–63; MacGregor, *Germany*, 397–417; Forner, "War Commemoration and the Republic in Crisis," 513–49; Ladd, *Ghosts of Berlin*, 220–21.
65. Bouwers, *Public Pantheons in Revolutionary Europe*, 45, 54.
66. On these themes, see Holger Hoock, *Empires of the Imagination: Politics, War, and Arts in the British World, 1750–1850* (New York, 2010), 172–79, 184–87, 361–72.
67. For details of this painting, see Patrick Griffin, *The Townshend Moment: The Making of Empire and Revolution in the Eighteenth Century* (New Haven, 2017), 244–46.
68. I owe these insights to Morna O'Neill, who gave a workshop entitled "Daniel Maclise and the Canon of Irish Art" at the University of Notre Dame, 8 February 2019. On Maclise, I am indebted to the Royal Academy's podcast "An Introduction to 'Daniel Maclise: The Waterloo Cartoon,'" by Annette Wickham, 2016.
69. Bouwers, *Public Pantheons in Revolutionary Europe*, 65, 50; David Cannadine, *Victorious Century: The United Kingdom, 1800–1906* (London, 2017), 88, 194; Hoock, *Empires of the Imagination*, 361–72.
70. Cannadine, *Victorious Century*, 1–2.
71. Kirsten Carter McKee, *Calton Hill and the Plans for Edinburgh's Third New Town* (Edinburgh, 2018).

72. It is even referred to by James Joyce in *Ulysses*, tongue in cheek of course, as Ireland's Mount Pisgah, the point from which the promised land could be glimpsed. See John Banville, *Time Pieces: A Dublin Memoir* (New York, 2018), 115–20; Yvonne Whelan, *Reinventing Modern Dublin: Streetscape, Iconography, and the Politics of Identity* (Dublin, 2019), 1–2, 43–50.

73. Whelan, *Reinventing Modern Dublin*, 50–51; Paula Murphy, "Deification in the Early Century," in *Nineteenth-Century Irish Sculpture: Native Genius Reaffirmed* (New Haven, 2010), 7–9. I learned of the bridge by viewing Jack B. Yeats's *Crossing the Metal Bridge* (1928). See the National Gallery of Ireland, *Images in Yeats* (Dublin, 1990), 38–39.

74. Hoock, *Empires of the Imagination*, 367–69; Roger Bowdler and Steven Brindle, *Wellington Arch, Marble Arch and Six Great War Memorials: English Heritage Red Guides*; Julius Bryant, *Apsley House: The Wellington Collection: English Heritage Guidebooks* (2007).

75. Cannadine, *Victorious Century*, 23–24, 79. On the totemic moments for the Union, see Alvin Jackson, *The Two Unions: Ireland, Scotland, and the Survival of the United Kingdom, 1707–2007* (Oxford, 2011), 153–63.

76. Frederick Douglass, "Thoughts and Recollections of a Tour in Ireland," Library of Congress, Washington, DC, Frederick Douglass Papers [1886]. Accessed April 18, 2019, https://www.loc.gov/item/mfd.24015/.

77. Whelan, *Reinventing Modern Dublin*, 53–64; Nuala Johnson, "Cast in Stone: Monuments, Geography, and Nationalism," *Environment and Planning*, 13 (1995), 58–59; Bouwers, *Public Pantheons in Revolutionary Europe*, 82, 214.

78. Roy Foster quoted in Colm Toibin, *Mad, Bad, Dangerous to Know: The Fathers of Wilde, Yeats, and Joyce* (New York, 2018), 29.

79. On this memorial, see *Dictionary of Irish Architects, 1720–1940* (www.dia.ie); Whelan, *Reinventing Modern Dublin*, 86–87.

80. Banville, *Time Pieces*, 123.

81. Paula Murphy, "Deification in the Early Century," 20. For the 1953 monument and the 1876 pyramid structure, and how 1798 would generally be remembered, see Beiner, *Remembering the Year of the French*, 269–74.

82. Beiner, *Remembering the Year of the French*, 243–75.

83. On the exile motif of migration, see Kerby Miller, *Emigrants and Exiles: Ireland and the Irish Exodus to North America* (New York, 1985). For Barry, see Eisenhower to President Sean O'Kelly, 16 September 1956, *Public Papers of the Presidents of the United States: Dwight D. Eisenhower* (2012), 776.

84. Beiner, *Forgetful Remembrance*, ch. 7.

85. On exile, statelessness, and citizenship, see Lucy Salyer, *Under the Starry Flag: How a Band of Irish Americans Joined the Fenian Revolt and Sparked a Crisis over Citizenship* (Cambridge, MA, 2018). On the creation of the idea of the Fenian discursively and how it was set against the state, see James Adams, "The Negotiated Hibernian: Discourse on the Fenian in England and America," *American Nineteenth Century History*, 11 (2010), 47–77. For how transatlantic radicalism was at the heart of fears of the image of the

Fenian, see Michael de Nie, " 'A Medley Mob of Irish-American Plotters and Irish Dupes': The British Press and Transatlantic Fenianism," *Journal of British Studies*, 40 (2001), 213–40.

86. Richard Bourke, "Political Theory and the Philosophy of History" (talk at the University of Notre Dame's Department of Political Science, 10 April 2018).

87. See, for instance, Linda Colley, *Britons: Forging the Nation, 1707–1837* (New Haven, 2009).

88. Peter Onuf, "Preface to the 2019 Edition," in Peter Onuf, *Statehood and Union: A History of the Northwest Ordnance* (Notre Dame, 2019), xiii–xx; Gary Gerstle, *Liberty and Coercion: The Paradox of American Government from the Founding to the Present* (Princeton, 2015), 21–27.

89. Laurent Dubois, *Haiti: The Aftershocks of History* (New York, 2012).

90. Carlo Celius, "Neoclassicism and the Haitian Revolution," in David Patrick Geggus and Norman Fiering, eds., *The World of the Haitian Revolution* (Bloomington, 2009), 352–89; Laurent Dubois, *Avengers of the New World: The Story of the Haitian Revolution* (Cambridge, MA, 2004), 212.

91. Charles Forsdick, "The Pantheon's Empty Plinth: Commemorating Slavery in Contemporary France," *Atlantic Studies*, 9 (2012), 279–97.

92. For an enlightening interpretation of this monument, on which this interpretation is based, see Trouillot, *Silencing the Past*, 31–69. For a reconsideration of Christophe and all that he did, I am indebted to Marlene Daut, "The Kingdom of Haiti and the Age of Revolution," the Fennell Lecture, University of Edinburgh, 12 May 2022.

93. Christopher Clark, *Time and Power: Visions of History in German Politics, from the Thirty Years' War to the Third Reich* (Princeton, 2019), 75.

94. Gert Oostindie, "Stony Regrets and Pledges for the Future"; Achille Mbembe, "The Subject of the World," in Gert Oostindie, ed., *Facing up to the Past: Perspectives on the Commemoration of Slavery from Africa, the Americas and Europe* (London, 2002), 11, 21–25. On how racism clouds memory, see Ana Lucia Araujo, *Slavery in the Age of Memory: Engaging the Past* (London, 2020). For a broad discussion of slavery and memory, see Ana Lucia Araujo, Mariana Candido, and Paul Lovejoy, *Crossing Memories: Slavery and African Diaspora* (Trenton, NJ, 2011).

95. Manuel Barcia, " 'Weapons from Their Land': Arming Strategies and Practices among West African–Born Soldiers in Nineteenth-Century Bahia and Cuba," *Slavery and Abolition*, 39 (2018), 479–80; Jane Landers, *Atlantic Creoles in the Age of Revolution* (Cambridge, MA, 2010), 224. Myra Ann Houser, "Avenging Carlota in Africa: Angola and the Memory of Cuban Slavery," *Atlantic Studies*, 12 (2015), 49–52.

96. Ana Lucia Araujo, "Welcome the Diaspora: Slave Trade Heritage Tourism and the Public Memory of Slavery," *Ethnologies*, 32 (2010), 145–78; Ama Ata Aidoo, "Of Forts, Castles, and Silences," in Oostindie, ed., *Facing up to the Past*, 30.

97. Araujo, "Welcome the Diaspora," 145–50.
98. Entry for Ghana Museums and Monuments, "Slavery and Remembrance," Colonial Williamsburg Foundation, http://slaveryandremembrance.org/partners/partner/?id=P0039; "International Slave Route Monument," Le Morne Heritage Trust Fund, http://www.lemorneheritage.org/slave-route.html; Marley Brown, "Ouidah, Benin," *Archaeology* (September/October 2018), https://www.archaeology.org/issues/310–1809/trenches/6881-trenches-benin-ouidah; Kebba Jeffang, "Juffureh after Slavery: A Tale of Forgiveness and Identity," *Chronicle* (13 February 2020).
99. Madge Dresser, "Set in Stone? Statues and Slavery in London," *History Workshop Journal*, 64 (2007), 162–99. See, for instance, these pieces and the responses in an English newspaper: https://www.theguardian.com/artanddesign/2010/may/27/yinka-shonibare-fourth-plinth; https://www.theguardian.com/world/2017/aug/24/we-wouldnt-put-up-a-statue-to-nelson-or-robert-e-lee-today.
100. For the ceremony, see https://www.westminster-abbey.org/abbey-news/olaudah-equiano-black-abolitionist.
101. Joy Mead, *Words and Wonderings: Conversations with Present-Day Prophets* (London, 2011).
102. Vincent Carretta, "Olaudah Equiano or Gustavus Vassa? New Light on an Eighteenth-Century Question of Identity," *Slavery and Abolition*, 20 (1999), 96–105. For a thoughtful response, see Paul E. Lovejoy "Autobiography and Memory: Gustavus Vassa, alias Olaudah Equiano, the African," *Slavery and Abolition*, 27 (2006), 317–47.

# Epilogue

1. This is what Wim Klooster sees as the end point in *Revolutions in the Atlantic World: A Comparative History* (New York, 2018), 1.
2. Gabriel Paquette, *Imperial Portugal in the Age of Atlantic Revolutions: The Luso-Brazilian World, c. 1770–1850* (Cambridge, 2013); Kenneth J. Andrien and Lyman L. Johnson, *The Political Economy of Spanish America in the Age of Revolution, 1750–1850* (Albuquerque, NM, 1994); Jaime E. Rodríguez O., *Mexico in the Age of Democratic Revolutions, 1750–1850* (Boulder, 1994).
3. See, for instance, R. R. Palmer, *The Age of Democratic Revolution* (Princeton, 1964); Janet Polasky, *Revolutions without Borders: The Call to Liberty in the Atlantic World* (New Haven, 2015), 15; Malick W. Ghachem, "Law, Atlantic Revolutionary Exceptionalism, and the Haitian Declaration of Independence" in Julia Gaffield, ed., *The Haitian Declaration of Independence: Creation, Context, and Legacy* (Charlottesville, VA, 2016), 95–114.
4. Rafe Blaufarb, *The Revolutionary Atlantic: Republican Visions, 1760–1830* (New York, 2018), 506–7. On the difficulties of establishing end dates, particularly when it comes to the formation of republics, see Clement Thibaud, "Pour une histoire polycentrique des républicanismes atlantiques (Années

1770–Années 1880)," *Revue d'histoire du XIXe siècle*, 56 (2018), 155. It is even more difficult if we reject the notion of a revolutionary wave or sequence. See Roberto Breña, "The Cadiz Liberal Revolution and Spanish American Independence," in John Tutino, ed., *New Countries: Capitalism, Revolutions, and Nations in the Americas, 1750–1870* (Durham, NC, 2016), 71–72. This simple question conjures many answers. See, for instance, Sarah Knott, "Narrating the Age of Revolution," *William and Mary Quarterly*, 3rd ser., 73 (2016), 3–36; Keith M. Baker and Dan Edelstein, "Introduction," in *Scripting Revolution: A Historical Approach to the Comparative Study of Revolutions* (Stanford, 2015), 7–10; C. A. Baily, "The Age of Revolutions in Global Context: An Afterword," in David Armitage and Sanjay Subrahmanyam, eds., *The Age of Revolutions in Global Context, c. 1760–1840* (Basingstoke, 2010), 209–17.

5. Caitlin Fitz, *Our Sister Republics: The United States in the Age of American Revolutions* (New York, 2017), 241; David Waldstreicher, *In the Midst of Perpetual Fetes: The Making of American Nationalism, 1776–1820* (Chapel Hill, 2012).

6. Charles Royster, *The Destructive War: William Tecumseh Sherman, Stonewall Jackson, and the Americans* (New York, 1991). Afterward, North and South, which had mobilized their societies by tying their respective causes to the same founding, would create an uneasy peace but would never really reconcile. From this point forward, memory in America would be divided, even if it was made of the same ideological materials from the American Revolution. See Caroline Janney, *Remembering the Civil War: Reunion and the Limits of Reconciliation* (Chapel Hill, 2013). On the fraying, see Joanne Freeman, *The Field of Blood: Violence in Congress and the Road to the Civil War* (New York, 2018), 151.

7. James M. McPherson, *Abraham Lincoln and the Second American Revolution* (Oxford, 1990), 3–22; Gordon Wood, *The Radicalism of the American Revolution* (New York, 1992), 186; Jack P. Greene, *Peripheries and Center: Constitutional Development in the Extended Polities of the British Empire and the United States, 1607–1788* (New York, 1990), 216; A. G. Hopkins, *American Empire: A Global History* (Princeton, 2018), 238.

8. Seymour Drescher, *Abolition: A History of Slavery and Antislavery* (New York, 2009). For an interpretation that characterizes the "Age" as responsible for the end of slavery, see Robin Blackburn, *The Overthrow of Colonial Slavery: 1776–1848* (New York, 2011).

9. Mark Mazower, "Revolutionary Reckonings: Greek Independence, 1821 and the Historians," *Times Literary Supplement*, 26 March 2021, 12–13. On the mixing of emotions, the sordid search for sovereignty, and how well it fits the Atlantic paradigm, see Mazower, *The Greek Revolution: 1821 and the Making of Modern Europe* (London, 2021).

10. This is the date favored by Jonathan I. Israel, *The Expanding Blaze: How the American Revolution Ignited the World, 1775–1848* (Princeton, 2017); and Michael Levin, *Political Thought in the Age of Revolution 1776–1848: Burke to*

*Marx* (London, 2011). On the revolutions themselves, as well as the notion of aftershocks, see Richard Evans, *The Pursuit of Power: Europe, 1815–1914* (New York, 2016), 82, 188–228; and Mike Rapport, *1848: Year of Revolution* (New York, 2008). Lincoln is quoted in Hopkins, *American Empire*, 217. For 1848 as reaction to what he regards as a dual revolution creating a bourgeois Atlantic, see Eric Hobsbawm, *The Age of Revolution, 1789–1848* (New York, 1962).

11. Christopher Clark, *Time and Power: Visions of History in German Politics, from the Thirty Years' War to the Third Reich* (Princeton, 2019), 135.

12. Andre M. Fleche, *Revolution of 1861: The American Civil War in the Age of Nationalist Conflict* (Chapel Hill, 2012).

13. Fitz, *Our Sister Republics*, 246–47; Mark Power Smith, *Young America: The Transformation of Nationalism before the Civil War* (Charlottesville, VA, 2022); Gregory Downs, *The Second American Revolution: The Civil War–Era Struggle over Cuba and the Rebirth of the American Republic* (Chapel Hill, 2019); Guy Thompson, ed., *The European Revolutions of 1848 and the Americas* (London, 2002). This was the age of varied "Young" movements, all tied to rising nationalism, according to Hobsbawm. See *The Age of Revolutions*, 132–33. It should be noted that despite the movement on the slave trade, the Brazilian economy, like that of the South in the United States, would still rely on slave labor to buoy its export economy. See Roderick Barman, *Brazil: The Forging of a Nation, 1798–1852* (Stanford, 1989), 227–35; Emilia Viotti da Costa, *The Brazilian Empire: Myths and Histories* (Chapel Hill, 2000), 132.

14. Levin, *Political Thought in the Age of Revolution*, 10, 159, 177–81; Dan Edelstein, *The Terror of Natural Right: Republicanism, the Cult of Nature, and the French Revolution* (Chicago, 2009), 265–66; Evans, *The Pursuit of Power*, 269–70. On 1848 as an echo of the French Revolution, see Jonathan Sperber, *The European Revolutions, 1848–1851* (Cambridge, 1994), 239–59; and Rapport, *1848*, 14, 211–12. One prominent scholar has argued that this should mark the end of the age, that by now the world "was out of balance," with industrial development galloping at a breakneck speed, along with a political movement to contest it, but institutional channels not able to address it. See Hobsbawm, *The Age of Revolution*, 4, 303.

15. Roy Foster, *Modern Ireland, 1600–1972* (London, 1988), 316; Miles Taylor, "The 1848 Revolutions and the British Empire," *Past and Present*, 166 (2000), 146–80. On the story of Meagher, see Timothy Egan, *The Immortal Irishman: The Irish Revolutionary Who Became an American Hero* (New York, 2016).

16. See Jaime Rodriguez O., *The Independence of Spanish America* (New York, 1998), xi.

17. Edward James Kolla, *Sovereignty, International Law, and the French Revolution* (New York, 2017), 277–82.

18. Neil MacGregor, *Germany: Memories of a Nation* (New York, 2015), 3–16; Paal Stangl, "Restoring Berlin's Unter der Linden: Ideology, World View, Place and Space," *Journal of Historical Geography*, 32 (2006), 368–70.

19. Ernesto de la Torre Villar, *Hidalgo entre escultores y pintores* (Morelia, MI, 1990).

20. James Sanders, *The Vanguard of the Atlantic World: Creating Modernity, Nation, and Democracy in Nineteenth-Century Latin America* (Durham, NC, 2014), 4.

21. On this point, I am indebted to the sociologist John Brewer. See "Memory, Truth and Victimhood in Post-Trauma Societies," in Gerald Delanty and Krishan Kumar, eds., *The SAGE Handbook of Nations and Nationalism* (London, 2006), 214–24. The best study of forgetting and its many costs is Guy Beiner, *Forgetful Remembrance: Social Forgetting and Vernacular Historiography of a Rebellion in Ulster* (New York, 2018).

22. The famous historian François Furet argued that only in 1880 "the French Revolution was coming into port." See *Revolutionary France, 1770–1880* (Oxford, 1988), 537. He had also argued that the Revolution lived on as an unresolved force well into the twentieth century, only to finally peter out. See François Furet, *Interpreting the French Revolution* (Cambridge, 1981), 4–6.

23. Roger Cohen, "France Battles over Whether to Cancel or Celebrate Napoleon," *New York Times*, 5 May 2021; Marlene Daut, "Napoleon Isn't a Hero to Celebrate," *New York Times*, 18 March 2021.

24. Brandon Byrd, *The Black Republic: African Americans and the Fate of Haiti* (Philadelphia, 2019).

25. James Oakes, *The Radical and the Republican: Frederick Douglass, Abraham Lincoln, and the Triumph of Antislavery Politics* (New York, 2007), 91, 223.

26. Ashley Southall, "Statue Unveiled, Douglass Is hailed for Equality Fight," *New York Times*, 19 June 2013; Frederick Douglass Memorial," NYC Parks, https://www.nycgovparks.org/parks/central-park/monuments/2098; John W. Thompson, *An Authentic History of the Douglass Monument: Biographical Facts and Incidents in the Life of Frederick Douglass* (Rochester, 1903), 125; Benjamin Quarles, "Frederick Douglass in Bronze," *Negro History Bulletin*, 20 (1957), 75. On the tearing down of Douglass's statue in Rochester in 2020, see Peter Hughes, *A History of Love and Hate in 21 Statues* (London, 2021), 248–49.

27. On this and the erection of the statue in 2013, see David Blight, *Frederick Douglass: Apostle of Freedom* (New York, 2020), 13–14.

28. Laurent Dubois, *Avengers of the New World: The Story of the Haitian Revolution* (Cambridge, MA, 2009), 305; Christine Kinealy, *Frederick Douglass in Ireland: In His Own Words* (New York, 2018).

29. "Mary Wollstonecraft Blue Plaque Unveiled," *London SE1*, 4 July 2004, https://www.london-se1.co.uk/news/view/1084; Maryonthegreen.org; Rhiannon Lucy Cosslett, "Why I Hate the Mary Wollstonecraft Statue: Would a Man Be 'Honored' with His Schlong Out?" *Guardian*, 11 November 2020; Eleanor Nairne, "A Naked Statue for a Feminist Hero?" *New York Times*, 12 November 2020.

30. For an interesting suggestion that Charlottesville should erect a statue to Queen Charlotte—an abolitionist sympathizer and perhaps part African

herself—in the place of Robert E. Lee or Stonewall Jackson, see Krishan Kumar, "Queen of Hearts: Why Charlottesville Should Memorialize the Wife of George III," *Times Literary Supplement*, 20 August 2021.

31. Olivier Zunz, *The Man Who Understood Democracy: The Life of Alexis de Tocqueville* (Princeton, 2022), 1–2, 299–300.

32. Eveline Bouwers, *Public Pantheons in Revolutionary Europe: Comparing Cultures of Remembrance, c. 1790–1840* (London, 2011), 57; Marie F. Busco, "The 'Achilles' in Hyde Park," *Burlington Magazine*, 130 (1988), 920–24; "Fine Arts. Achilles. A Statue Erected in Hyde Park to the Duke of Wellington," *European Magazine*, 82 (1822), 161–63. On the conundrum of what to do with weapons, and how those used in Europe found new homes in places like Latin America, see Rafe Blaufarb, "Arms of Revolutions: Military Demobilization after Napoleonic Wars and Latin American Independence," in Alan Forest, Karen Hagemann, and Michael Rowe, eds., *War, Demobilization and Memory: The Legacy of War in the Era of Atlantic Revolutions* (London, 2016), 100–113.

33. For a point along these lines, see James Hall, "At the Mercy of the Public: Is it Necessary to Kill Some Statues, or Could We Add to Them?" *Times Literary Supplement*, 9 April 2021.

# Acknowledgments

I finished up this book while the Harmsworth Professor at the Rothermere American Institute and the Queen's College at the University of Oxford. I wrote a great deal of it as Honorary Professor of the University of Edinburgh. I conceived of it and drafted most of it at the University of Notre Dame, where I teach. I did so with a great deal of help from the Keough-Naughton Institute, which I directed while I was working on the book. I also received a fellowship from the Notre Dame Institute for Advanced Study, when the project was in its early stages. I owe a debt to all of these institutions and the good people who people them.

As is evident in chapter 7, I roved the Atlantic world in search of monuments to the age of revolution. And I had some experiences doing so. Years ago, my family and I traipsed up Vinegar Hill on a sunny day. I spent a memorable day with the late Joe Buttigieg in Buenos Aires. I revisited the monuments I had seen so many times in my youth in New York with my daughter Maggie. I escorted her on a school trip to New York, and I slowed her and the group down as I insisted on lecturing them on the arch in Washington Square Park. I was joined by my graduate adviser, Tim Breen, as we met archaeologist Michael Gibbons to do a tour in pissing rain of monuments in the West of Ireland. I did a nocturnal run with my son Michael in the streets of Berlin to see what we would find of Prussia and the age. We hit pay dirt. I had a run-in with the late Queen Elizabeth as I was studying the iconography on Wellington Arch in London. As luck would have it, she was escorted by the horse guards as I happened to be at the arch. She looked out of the window of her Land Rover, saw me, looked down, and wagged her head in seeming disgust. My late Irish republican father would have been so proud. I discussed monuments over drinks with John Banville in Dublin as he recounted his own adventure to find the head of Nelson. Later, I found the head myself. I dragged graduate students to the heights above Edinburgh in the rain to search for memorials. I had my daughter Annie pace out steps near Place de la Concorde in Paris to see if La Madelaine was farther from the obelisk than the National Assembly. We laughed as we counted with scooters whirring around us. I had a leisurely walk with my wife, Mary Hope, through the hills above the Vatican to get a sense of how Romans memorialized the age. I braved one of the coldest days I could remember with my son Liam as we walked to a monument to Wolfe on the far edge of the Plains of Abraham in Quebec. We froze our asses off that Christmas morning. Between bars serving Belgian beers, three of my friends and I stopped to discuss statues we came across in Bruges and Ghent. I hopped fences—and was almost arrested—in successive visits with my friend Frank Cogliano to get close to the O'Higgins monument in Santiago de Chile. My wife and I dodged skateboards as we walked to a great memorial in São Paulo. I could go on and on. But you, dear reader, get the point. I have seen nearly all of the places I discuss. I have dragged so many good people on my own scavenger hunts. And I have a great many people to thank.

In ways big and small, in little chats and in big conferences, in sit-downs and in passing, usually over a drink, the following people helped me come to terms with so much complex stuff. They might not remember the conversations. But I do. I wish to recognize, in no particular order, Brad Gregory, Will Hay, Chris Hodson, Katlyn Carter, Guy Beiner, Walter Hawthorne, Annette Gordon-Reed, Enda Delaney, Steve Pincus, Bill Doyle, Sam Fisher, Colin Jones, Katie Jarvis, Bertrand Van Ruymbeke, Tom Bartlett, Peter Blanchard, Christa Dierksheide, Pekka Hämäläinen, Ian McBride, Tim Breen, Nicholas Canny, Jon Coleman, Joanna Innes, Chuck Walker, Peter Onuf, Toby Green, Ciaran O'Neill, Jan Stievermann, John Deak, Robert Ingram, Peter Thompson, Elliot Visconsi, Brendan O'Leary, José Brownrigg-Gleeson, David Armitage, Jorge Cañizares-Esguerra, Trevor Burnard, Juan Luis Ossa, Dan Carey, Michael Brown, Diarmuid Ó Giolláin, Roquinaldo Ferreira, Brian Ó Conchubhair, Colin Barr, Simon Fennell, Gordon Wood, Tom Kselman, Tony Hopkins, Wim Klooster, Paul Buser, Cole Jones, Morna O'Neill, Jay McAllister, Jim Smyth, Ted Beatty, Jaime Pensado, Jessica Roney, Patrick Geoghegan, Eric Pullin, Julia Gaffield, Johann Neem, and Brendan McConville. I am grateful to all of them for their generosity.

I also gave talks and received helpful feedback on this project over the years from colleagues at the following institutions, most person-to-person but a number online (again, in no particular order): University of Oxford; University of Edinburgh; University of Cambridge; Osaka University; University of Chicago; Purdue University; University of São Paulo; University of Montana; Boston College; Pontifical University, Chile; University of Melbourne; Princess Grace Library, Monaco; University Sorbonne Nouvelle, Paris Trois; American Philosophical Society; Notre Dame's Irish Seminars in Dublin, Rome, and Buenos Aires; Heidelberg University; Colonial Society of Massachusetts; Notre Dame's Institute for Advanced Studies; Brigham Young University; Newberry Library;

University of Liverpool; University of Notre Dame Law School; University of Hong Kong; Huntington Library; Carthage College; Yale University; and Mississippi State University.

A few people deserve some special thanks. One new friend, Fidel Tavarez, helped immensely with Latin America and read a good chunk of the manuscript. One old friend, Frank Cogliano, labored through the whole thing. Two other dear friends, along with Frank, were constant sources of ideas and inspiration. These would be Lige Gould and Andrew O'Shaughnessy.

The following provided first-rate research help: Anna Vincenzi, David Carlson, John Nelson, and Emily DeFazio. Jarek Jankowski and Tianyi Tan did research for me while I was a fellow at NDIAS. All their work was organized by Don Stelluto. Logistical support came from Beth Bland and Mary Hendriksen. Help along the way for a number of conferences on the topics this book covers at Kylemore Abbey, the best place in the world for a scholarly get-together, was offered by Lisa Caulfield and Catherine Wilsdon. I appreciate all they did.

I am grateful to Adina Berk and Ash Lago for shepherding the book through Yale University Press. Erin Greb produced the lovely maps. The two anonymous readers who worked through two drafts, and the three who read the proposal, gave me a great deal of thoughtful guidance.

I was first introduced to the age of Atlantic revolution long ago at Saint Peter's Prep. One of my history teachers, Carl DeLorenzo, presented us with a good many questions this book tussles with. My British literature teacher, Rich Kennedy, opened a door to the world of the transatlantic. I owe so much to the Prep.

Last but certainly not least are my family. My mother, Johanna Griffin, passed away while I was writing this book. She was and is a model for me of what a person can and should be. I miss her every day. My father-in-law, Joseph Doran, passed away as this book neared completion. He was a good man. My sister Joan and my nieces Reagan and Cailin ensured I did not take myself too seriously. My immediate family—Mary Hope, Michael, Liam, Maggie, and Annie—were there for every trip and every word of this. They are the finest people I know.

This book is theirs—the living and the dead of my family—as much as it is mine.

# Index

204–5, 209–10; Board of Trade, 67–68; Caribbean colonies, 74; creole elites in, 65–66, 68, 70–73, 75–76, 78, 80, 201, 204–5; East India Company, 76; and free trade, 42, 174, 197–99, 200–201; vs. French Empire, 95, 96, 97, 98–99, 100, 101; George III, 97; George IV, 255; industrial revolution, 197, 286n6; and liberty, 66, 71, 159, 196, 199; memorials in, 220, 221–23, 231–32, 253–56, 253–59, 261, 268, 282–83, 352n72; military, 68–69; patriotism in, 159–60, 161; Proclamation Line, 69, 74–75; reform of, 50–51, 60, 64, 65–81, 83, 85, 95, 96, 99, 106–7, 109–10, 168–69, 196–97, 199–200; relations with Brazil, 211; relations with India, 176, 198, 199; relations with Indigenous peoples, 18, 45, 47, 69, 74–75, 78, 136, 177, 199, 204–5; relations with Portugal, 58, 163, 172, 173, 174, 210, 244, 327n57; relations with United States, 136, 188, 198–99, 211; and Saint-Domingue, 162; and settler colonialism, 199, 200; and Seven Years' War, 42, 43–44, 45–46, 47, 50–51, 69, 95; slave trade abolished, 176, 197–98, 205, 211, 268; smuggling in, 29, 67, 68, 75; source of troops in Ireland and Scotland, 68–69, 87–88, 106, 147, 157, 159–60, 180; sovereignty of, 31, 65–68, 76, 77, 78, 80, 85, 96, 97, 100, 101, 110, 131, 133; vs. Spanish Empire, 69, 110; taxation in, 50, 66, 67, 72. *See also* American Revolution; Ireland; Jamaica; Parliament
Brown, William, 260
Buenos Aires, 46, 62, 165, 204, 206; creole elites in, 29, 166–67, 168, 170, 171, 202; May Pyramid, 238; memorials in, 236–38, 239; San Martín memorial in Metropolitan Cathedral, 236–38
Burke, Edmund, 67, 84, 110, 119, 131, 143; vs. Paine, 6–7, 77, 123, 280–82,

283; on salutary neglect, 76, 77, 80; on violence, 118
Burr, Aaron, 189

Cadiz, 24, 26–27, 29, 30, 165, 167
Calonne, Charles-Alexandre de, 95–96
Canada: Catholics in, 231–32; *The Fight for Canada* memorial, 230–31; memorialization in, 230–32, 233; nationhood of, 230–32, 234; relations with United States, 187–88, 230–31
Canary Islands, 23
capitalism, 43; and the Atlantic, 21–22; as global, 42
Caracas, 165, 168, 169
Carey, Mathew, 108
Carrera, José Miguel, 203–4
Carrier-Belleuse, Albert, 239
Cartagena, 166, 168, 202
Carvalho e Melo, Sebastião José de, 58, 59, 61
Castro, Fidel, 266
Catholicism, 27–28, 33, 34, 83; Catholic Church in France, 119, 121, 159, 160, 193–94, 231; Catholics in Canada, 231–32; Catholics in Ireland, 73, 88–89, 106, 107–8, 113, 131, 157, 158, 160, 179–80, 181, 182, 189, 199–200, 256, 259–60, 261, 311n24; Jesuits, 33, 58; Napoleon's concordat with Church, 193–94
Charleston, 134
Chile, 205, 207; La Moneda, 239, 241–42; memorials in, 239–41; Pinochet regime, 241–42; violence in, 203–4
Christophe, Henri, 264–65
class, 24, 89, 107, 120, 159, 170–71, 197
cocoa beans, 28
coffee, 21, 28, 48, 211, 213
Colombia, 168, 202, 205, 207, 348n36
Company of Grão Para and Maranhão, 58–59
Comunero Revolt, 64, 70
Condorcet, Marquis de, 84, 85, 102, 118, 247
Confederation of the Rhine, 155, 177